Titles in this series

POLYTECHNICAL EDUCATION IN THE U.S.S.R.

edited by S. G. SHAPOVALENKO

Corresponding member of the
R.S.F.S.R. Academy of Pedagogical Sciences

UNESCO

Published in 1963 by the United Nations
Educational, Scientific and Cultural Organization
Place de Fontenoy, Paris-7ᵉ
Printed by Drukkerij Holland N.V., Amsterdam

PREFACE

Following the 1958 reform of education in the U.S.S.R., several important changes were introduced into the school system. Some of the developments included the extension of the ten-year secondary school by one year, the introduction of vocational training into the last three grades of secondary schooling and the broadening of the scope of general and polytechnical education.

The details of this reform, the reasoning behind it and the steps taken to implement it have all been described in detail by staff-members and members of the Academy of Pedagogical Sciences of the Russian Soviet Federative Socialist Republic. The editing of the studies has been done by S. G. Shapovalenko, also of the Academy.

To him and to all the contributors, Unesco wishes to express its appreciation for the preparation of a comprehensive work.

It is hoped that this publication will fill a gap which has existed in material available in English and French on education in the U.S.S.R. The opinions expressed in this book are naturally those of the authors and do not necessarily reflect the views of Unesco.

CONTENTS

7

PART TWO

POLYTECHNICAL EDUCATION AS ILLUSTRATED IN THE
TEACHING OF INDIVIDUAL SUBJECTS

FOREWORD

General secondary schools in the U.S.S.R. are at present being reorganized in accordance with the Law 'On the strengthening of the ties of the school with life and on the further development of the public education system in the U.S.S.R.', adopted at a session of the Supreme Soviet of the Union of Soviet Socialist Republics on 24 December 1958.[1]

The problem of providing polytechnical education for school-children, and the further improvement of the standard of that education, occupies an important place among the tasks which this Law sets the schools. This book has been written in order to satisfy the interest in that problem among teachers and others active in the field of education outside the U.S.S.R.

Polytechnical education, giving the younger generation a knowledge of the most important branches and general principles of the techniques, technology and organization of socialist production, and equipping the young with habits of work and experience of socially productive work, is one of the means used in the U.S.S.R. for the all-round development and moral education of young people and their preparation for work in building a communist society; for training an ability to assimilate the changes wrought in labour techniques as a result of technical progress; for raising the productivity of work done on behalf of society, achieving an abundance of products, gradually overcoming the substantial differences between physical and intellectual work, and gradually removing the existing division of labour. In other words, the polytechnical education of the rising generation is regarded in the U.S.S.R. as an important constituent of the programme of the Soviet people's effort to build a communist society. Great importance is therefore attached in the U.S.S.R. to polytechnical education, which is given by the schools with the participation

1. See Appendix I, p. 375.

11

and day-to-day assistance of factories and other industrial establishments, collective and State farms, building and other undertakings, trade unions, party and Soviet organizations, engineers, agronomists, industrial workers, collective farmers and employees: it is being made a reality by the entire Soviet people.

This book discusses the history of the origins and development of the idea and theory of polytechnical education, experience of its practice in Soviet schools before their reform (up to 1958), the reform of general secondary schools on the basis of the Law referred to above and, in connexion with that reform, questions concerning the reorganization of polytechnical education. It takes up the question of giving the polytechnical education of workers a greater part to play in connexion with the creation of the material and technical basis for communism in the U.S.S.R. and the achievement of technical progress in production; consideration is also given to the question of the need for developing as rapidly as possible the polytechnical system in the schools. This book devotes considerable attention to setting forth the objects, principles, content, organization and methods of polytechnical education, the role of general education subjects (physics, chemistry, biology, mathematics, art, geography and history) and general technical subjects (mechanical and electrical engineering), manual and technical training and socially productive work in polytechnical education and its significance in the education of schoolchildren. Information is given concerning the training and further training of teaching staff, their working experience in putting polytechnical education into effect, and the material facilities for the extension of polytechnical education in Soviet schools.

Questions of polytechnical training are discussed in close connexion with the further raising of the standards of general education and the introduction of vocational training for young people in the senior school grades. Polytechnical training is based on general education and at the same time helps to improve it by reinforcing its links with life, helping pupils to a more concrete, more intelligent and firmer grasp of knowledge, and forming practical working habits. General and polytechnical education serve as a basis for industrial training by means of which pupils in the senior grades receive training for the occupation or trade they have chosen and are familiarized with socially useful work in the sphere of material production or in the fields of culture and everyday life. Training in special branches of industry is, at the same time, an important means of polytechnical education, since by this means polytechnical training is carried to its logical conclusion, that is to say, the introduction of the pupils to productive work, which they are required to perform with the degree of efficiency attained in Soviet society. Industrial training also has a favourable effect on general education in the same way as polytechnical training.

This book also deals in detail with the question of establishing a close link between training and education on the one hand and socially productive work on the other, and with the significance of that link in the upbringing of school children.

Soviet general polytechnical secondary schools give their pupils a complete secondary education (up to school-leaving certificate standard) which opens the way to higher educational establishments, as well as specialized skills which fit them to take part in socially useful work and to achieve material security in their lives. On completing the secondary school course, young people either enter higher educational establishments or obtain work. Even today, one-third of all workers in industry have had a secondary or incomplete secondary education; in ten years' time, the entire working class of the U.S.S.R. is expected to hold a secondary-school-leaving certificate and a certificate of training in a technical trade at some kind of school.

The content, organization and methods of polytechnical education described in this book should not, of course, be regarded as unalterable. Polytechnical education will develop in step with the development of the country's national economy, science, technology and culture; questions of polytechnical education are therefore discussed with reference to the present stage of development of Soviet general secondary schools.

This book has been written by members of the academic staff of the Scientific Research Institute for General and Polytechnical Education of the R.S.F.S.R. Academy of Pedagogical Sciences, under the direction of S. G. Shapovalenko, corresponding member of the Academy. I. M. Rumyantsev, a member of the institute's staff, assisted in preparing the manuscript for publication and compiling the bibliography.

The question of the reorganization of general secondary schools is discussed by I. A. Kairov, president of the Academy of Pedagogical Sciences, to whom thanks are due for his contribution,

PART ONE

GENERAL ASPECTS
OF POLYTECHNICAL EDUCATION

CHAPTER I

MARXIST-LENINIST IDEAS ON POLYTECHNICAL EDUCATION

by M. N. Skatkin

POLYTECHNICAL EDUCATION AS A COMPONENT OF A
COMMUNIST UPBRINGING

The Soviet secondary school is intended to give the rising generation a communist upbringing. The aim of this is to achieve all-round development of the pupil's personality, to inculcate in him the materialist outlook and communist morality and to prepare him to play an active part in building a society striving for world peace and friendship among all nations.

The most important aspects of a communist upbringing are intellectual training and productive, polytechnical, aesthetic, physical and moral education. All these aspects are indissolubly bound up with one another, interpenetrating and complementing one another, and together ensure a well-balanced development of the child's physical and mental capabilities.

In providing this education, a distinction is made, according to the purpose desired, between general, polytechnical and vocational education.

General education

The purpose of general education is to provide the basic knowledge of nature, human society and thought, together with the intellectual accomplishments and practical skills relevant to these branches of knowledge, which are essential to every individual irrespective of his future occupation. The mastery of these subjects forms the basis for a scientific outlook on life and helps to develop the individual's cognitive powers and capabilities. The general education provided by Soviet secondary schools has a broad and all-embracing character. It comprises the humanities, science and mathematics.

Under the heading of the humanities, a pupil receives theoretical and practical instruction in his mother tongue, in Russian, and in a non-Soviet language, as well as in literature, in ancient, mediaeval, modern and contemporary history (including the history of the U.S.S.R. and its constituent Republics), the Constitution of the U.S.S.R., the economic geography of the U.S.S.R. and other countries, music, singing and the fine arts. Under science and mathematics, a pupil receives a thorough theoretical and practical grounding in mathematics (arithmetic, algebra, geometry, trigonometry and the rudiments of advanced mathematics), technical drawing, physics, chemistry (organic and inorganic), biology (botany, zoology, anatomy and physiology, general biology and the fundamentals of Darwinism) and the physical geography of the U.S.S.R. and the various parts of the world. The rudiments of an aesthetic education are acquired in classes on literature, drawing and singing.

General education, which forms the groundwork for polytechnical and vocational education, also includes theoretical and practical training in health and hygiene, gymnastics and sport.

Polytechnical education

Polytechnical education gives the pupil a knowledge of the main branches of production and the scientific principles on which these depend, and accustoms him to handling common tools and instruments of labour. This training helps to develop creative technical abilities and to inculcate a love and respect for physical labour and work. By providing a wide general technical background, polytechnical education gives the student an opportunity to choose freely his future trade, to master a variety of the jobs to be done in production and to play an active part in technical progress. This education, however, is not sufficient preparation for any of the comparatively complicated jobs in production; to obtain this, at the level of efficiency required in a given branch of production, vocational education is also necessary.

Vocational education

This provides the specialized theoretical and practical knowledge essential to a worker in a particular trade or profession, at a level sufficient to enable him to follow his profession successfully and contribute towards raising the standard of efficiency in it.

Vocational education is not the same as polytechnical education nor is it a substitute for it. It is based on and related to general and polytechnical education, which give the student the breadth of outlook and the general scientific and technical knowledge he needs for a rapid and thorough mastery of the theory and practice of his trade.

Before the recent reform, the Soviet ten-year secondary school provided general and polytechnical education. The December 1958 Law 'On the strengthening of the ties of the school with life and on the further development of the public education system in the U.S.S.R.' widened the scope of the general secondary school. As a result, the pupils in the senior classes (grades IX, X and XI) are now given vocational training side by side with their general and polytechnical education. In order not to place too heavy a strain on the pupils and thus lower the level of general and polytechnical education, the Law extended the period of secondary schooling by one year, from ten to eleven years.

COMBINING INSTRUCTION WITH PRODUCTIVE WORK—THE MOST IMPORTANT PRINCIPLE IN SOVIET EDUCATION

The most important principle in education as a whole, including polytechnical education, is that of combining instruction with productive work. Research by Soviet physiologists, psychologists and educationists has shown that an intelligent combination of mental occupations with physical work has a beneficial effect on both the physical and the mental development of the pupil.

Modern physiology offers a scientific explanation of this. The psychic activity of a human being is in origin and function a reflex activity of the cerebral cortex. Knowledge, intellectual accomplishments and skills are all systems of conditioned reflexes formed under the influence of an external stimulus.

The physiological theory originated by the eminent Russian scientist Pavlov notes that the higher nervous activity proceeds in the form of two contrary processes, excitation and inhibition, which possess the properties of irradiation and concentration. When identical stimuli are acting on the cerebral cortex all the time, protective inhibition sets in, with the result that reflexes already developed become diminished, and the formation of new reflexes becomes difficult. This often happens when pupils are kept busy day after day only with mental work or with the same school subjects. They quickly tire, become inattentive and start to lose the facility for understanding and assimilating the subject matter. This does not happen if different types of activity—mental work, gymnastics and sport and physical work—are intelligently alternated. Physical effort causes excitation of different parts of the cerebral cortex from those affected by study and, as a result, those parts of the cortex which are used to master a school subject are inhibited, and consequently rested. When the pupil is engaged in mental work, those parts of the cortex used to bring about labour processes are inhibited while the parts used in the activity of learning arrive at a condition of optimum excitation, thus ensuring a high degree of efficiency in both types of work.

Moreover, physical labour leads to the formation of new nervous connexions and associations and to the training of accomplishments and skills useful in production. This has a beneficial effect in widening the pupil's general experience. The knowledge acquired in class is applied in work and in this process this knowledge is concretized and deepened. In working, schoolchildren often feel the need for new knowledge which is essential to the fulfilment of some technical task. This heightens their interest in learning and stimulates them to seek for themselves the answers to questions that arise.

Manual work also plays a large part in the moral upbringing of the pupils. As they enter into a variety of relationships with their fellow-students and with adults on the job, the children become accustomed to working as part of a team and uniting their personal interests with the interests of the community.

The Marxist-Leninist idea of combining instruction with socially useful work, including productive work, is basic to the recent school reform.

Socially useful work is classified under two headings: (a) productive work which is work in a branch of material production—industry, agriculture, building, transport and communications serving material production and trade; and (b) work in non-productive fields such as education, public health, housing and communal services, passenger transport, public administration, co-operative and social organizations, banking and insurance and communications serving the general public and the non-productive branches of the economy.

As the present inquiry is concerned with polytechnical instruction, the connexion between instruction and productive work is discussed below.

Productive work is either socially useful work in material production or work which creates material values indispensable for the satisfaction of man's needs.

The school must devote itself principally to the preparation of children for work in material production (industry, agriculture, construction, transport, communications) for it is such work which is regarded as the base of human existence.

While still in the first eight grades, children are encouraged to do things for themselves which are within their powers. They plant and grow flowers, vegetables and trees, run a pets' corner and take care of rabbits and birds, look after the school yards, playing-fields and the streets and squares adjacent to the school; in the school workshops they make and repair school supplies, rebind library books and make simple articles needed by the school, kindergarten, collective farm or patronal enterprise.

In grades IX to XI instruction is combined with work in factories and plants, on collective and State farms, on building sites and in various communal and trading establishments.

Since the combination of instruction with socially useful work is a guiding principle throughout the Soviet schools, it applies fully to polytechnical instruction too. The scientific basis of production is not only expounded by the teacher in class but is also grasped in practice by the pupils in the process of working in the school workshops, on experimental farms and in factories, plants, collective and State farms. The Soviet general secondary school is therefore not only polytechnical but also a school of productive work, contributing to the all-round physical, intellectual and aesthetic development and moral training of the pupils.

IDEAS ON LABOUR EDUCATION IN THE PRE-MARXIST PERIOD

The idea that the main purpose of education is to prepare a young person to take his part in working life, and that to this end instruction must be combined with manual work, dates back to the Renaissance. Its origin was connected with the radical changes taking place in production methods and the development of science at that time.

The mediaeval system of schooling did not meet the new requirements of social development, industry, science and technology. It was very difficult and even impossible in those days to bring the school into closer touch with life. Eminent thinkers of the time, men such as Thomas More, Tommaso Campanella and others, worked out in theory the idea of combining science with life and regarded the participation of everyone in productive work as a typical feature of the ideal society of the future.

In his description of the ideal society based on universal equality, More devotes considerable space to the problems of organizing labour education. As work is absolutely obligatory for all members of society, the schools pay great attention to it. All children study agriculture and become familiar with it in practice. Again, every child learns some trade, not in school but in a family, according to mediaeval apprenticeship.

Campanella, in his *Civitas Solis*, pictures, like More, an ideal state in which all the citizens take part in productive work. All children learn various production processes in the course of their upbringing and are then drawn into productive work, which they alternate with intellectual pursuits.

More's and Campanella's ideas on education were Utopian, yet they undoubtedly contained a kernel of rationality.

In the seventeenth century, John Bellers, who had been concerned with economic problems, arrived at the idea that labour instruction was essential. In his proposal for a 'college of industry' —an original form of labour association which would get rid of poverty—he broached educational questions as well. Bellers recognized the importance of combining intellectual education with physical, productive work. To him, the college of industry was not merely a labour association of adults but also a model educational institution where children would learn all the useful sciences, develop physically and, above all, master different trades, at the same time acquiring a love and respect for manual work. He believed that his colleges could be established by voluntary donations on the part of the rich.

The eighteenth century, the century of enlightenment, gave the world a great many outstanding thinkers, who prepared the way ideologically for the major historic event of the century, the French Revolution. The great leader of eighteenth-century thought was Jean-Jacques Rousseau, whose ideas on education had an exceptionally powerful influence on the development of educational theory. Subjecting to devastating criticism the class education which handicapped children mentally, morally and physically, Rousseau advanced the idea of labour instruction. His premiss was that man, living in society with his fellow-men, inevitably enjoyed the fruits of their labour. That being so, every human being should himself take part in work. In order to do so, he must know how. Rousseau suggested that everyone should be familiar with the fundamentals of agriculture and with the main methods of work used in different trades. He therefore thought of labour instruction not as a training for any particular trade but rather as a general training for work, a process of developing skills and accomplishments enabling their possessor to master any trade as required. Rousseau offered no concrete embodiment of these ideas; his merit lies primarily in having posed the problem. Ways of solving it in practical terms were outlined in the schemes for popular education drawn up during the French Revolution, but these schemes remained unfulfilled.

At the end of the eighteenth and the beginning of the nineteenth centuries Pestalozzi was carrying on his educational work. This famous teacher believed that education, properly organized, could make the poor independent of the favours of the rich. To this end he proposed combining elementary intellectual education with craft pursuits. Pestalozzi was perhaps the first educator to try to put into practice the idea of combining instruction with labour. His theories on organizing manual instruction are expounded in his novel on social and educational themes, *Leonard and Gertrude*, in which he advocates that, while still at school, peasant children should acquire practical skills in agriculture and the crafts they are likely to practise later in life. The children's work should be productive and pay for the upkeep of the school.

Pestalozzi attempted to run a school on these lines on his own estate at Neuhof. Orphans and children of very poor parents received an elementary education, with instruction in reading, writing and arithmetic, and at the same time worked on the farm in summer and in the spinning and weaving shop in winter. His idea was that the children could pay for their keep by their work.

Under the production methods of the day, however, it was impossible to make the school self-supporting on child labour without exploiting the children. Pestalozzi therefore had to cover the cost of maintaining them out of his own pocket; in the end, this ruined him financially and the first experiment in running a labour school ended in failure.

Robert Owen, the most distinguished of the Utopian socialists, lived in England at a time when his country was faced with unemployment, exploitation of wage labour, and child labour. He observed the sufferings of the people and became convinced that the worker's life must be improved. In 1800 he had become manager of a big cotton-mill in New Lanark, Scotland. There, he carried through a series of measures to improve the conditions of life and work for the mill-hands and to educate the young. He shortened the working day, which at that time lasted from fourteen to sixteen hours, reducing it to ten and a half hours; he raised wages, built new houses for the workers, took steps to enlighten the adults and provide public education for the children. He opened an infant school for children between the ages of one and six, an elementary school for children from six to ten years of age and an evening school for adolescents working in the mills.

Owen devoted a great deal of attention to the manual training of the children at the elementary school. The girls learned dressmaking, how to prepare appetizing food and how to keep themselves and their homes clean and tidy. The boys were taught simple types of manual work.

23

Owen's idea was that special training should be given to the middle and senior age-groups on the basis of industrial labour. This was an innovation compared with Rousseau's and Pestalozzi's theory of labour education, for they had relied on craft work. Adolescents working in the mills attended evening classes at the school, where they learned mechanics and chemistry, and studied general and special subjects connected with their work.

Marx thought well of Owen's experiments to combine instruction with productive work on the basis of high technical standards: 'From the factory system budded, as Robert Owen has shown us in detail, the germ of the education of the future, an education that will, in the case of every child over a given age, combine productive labour with instruction and gymnastics, not only as one of the methods of adding to the efficiency of production, but as the only method of producing fully developed human beings.[1]

Disappointed, however, in his efforts to convince the manufacturers and others of the need to reorganize the world on rational socialist principles, Owen modified his philosophy and arrived at a Utopian communist set of ideas. He tried to put these ideas into practice in a colony, called New Harmony, which he founded in America, after moving from England with a number of sympathizers. This new experiment swallowed up a large part of his resources and after first ruining him, failed.

In Russia, ideas on labour education were worked out and propagated by the revolutionary democrats Chernyshevsky (1836–61) and Dobrolyubov (1828–89). Regarding labour as the basic form of human activity, they pointed out the necessity of using it for the purpose of educating the young. The urge to be active was the human organism's most vital demand. This demand should not be stifled but, on the contrary, developed in every possible way. If a child's powers were left unexercised, the child would get used to being lazy. The child's upbringing should so direct the development of his need for activity as to permit him to grow up into an adult capable of work useful to himself and to society.

Chernyshevsky and Dobrolyubov regarded manual work as the most important means of training willpower and character. Strength of character is developed by systematically overcoming difficulties and obstacles. By working, a human being makes efforts and gets to know the measure of his own powers. Once he has learned to overcome difficulties and obstacles, he can work well, and the consciousness that the effort he has expended has been of use to others gives him moral satisfaction. In the process of manual

---

1. Karl Marx, *Kapital*, Moscow, Gospolitizdat, 1949, Vol. I, p. 489.

labour man becomes conscious of his own inalienable rights and acquires the self-respect that comes from being useful to others; in the same way, the character traits of a citizen, those of a fighter and toiler, are formed: love of work, firmness of character, honesty, truthfulness, love and respect for labouring folk.

Chernyshevsky and Dobrolyubov rightly believed that the capacity for all-round development was ingrained in man's very nature, the spiritual and material origins of which could not be regarded as separate. 'Only recently', wrote Debrolyubov, 'has science repudiated the schoolmen's dualistic view of man and begun to examine him in his complete make-up of inseparable body and soul without trying to split one from the other.'[1]

Dobrolyubov stressed that in one-sided occupations involving only physical labour the muscles work strenuously while the development of the brain is stultified. If, on the other hand, one engages solely in mental labour, the muscles do not develop as they should, physiological processes in the organism take place in the wrong way and the result is a morbid condition. If the human organism is to develop normally, it needs 'human health, where the development of the body does not interfere with the development of the soul but assists it'.[2]

Labour of one kind alone results in one-sided development. Labour that takes various forms is not monotonous and fosters all-round development.

'Everyone knows from day-to-day experience', wrote Chernyshevsky, 'that a change of occupation often provides relaxation when relaxation could otherwise be achieved only by total inactivity; that if a person does different jobs turn and turn about he can work without fatigue for several hours longer than if he keeps on at the same job. Different muscles or different mental capacities are brought into play for different jobs, so that some relax and refresh themselves while the others are working.'[3]

Chernyshevsky believed that in the future society every individual would do a variety of jobs, both industrial and agricultural. Labour in different branches of production—in the field and at the bench, on the building site and at various crafts—would offer abundant material for intellectual growth. Skills in different kinds of physical labour are based on a number of general principles; mastery of these skills helps to build up experience in labour and develops intellectual capacities. A variety of physical tasks which

1. N. A. Dobrolyubov, *Collected Works*, Moscow, State Belles-Lettres Press (GIKHL), Gospolitizdat, 1934–41, Vol. II, p. 95.
2. ibid., p. 96.
3. N. G. Chernyshevsky, *Collected Works*, Moscow, Gospolitizdat, 1939–51. Vol. IX, p. 183.

are within a person's powers and are performed voluntarily and with eagerness make him healthy and strong. A well-balanced development of the healthy body helps the formation of aesthetic concepts, and the nurturing of healthy tastes, habits and interests.

The ideas of Chernyshevsky and Dobrolyubov were shared by other progressive teachers and public figures in Russia in the second half of the nineteenth century: for instance, Pisarev, Shelgunov, Ushinsky. Pisarev and Shelgunov proposed making physical labour an integral part of social upbringing, in order to 'combine in the same persons scientific development and physical labour'. The eminent Russian educator K. D. Ushinsky wrote: ' . . . work satisfies man, not merely by fulfilling his demands and extending their scope, but also by acting on him with its own natural, inner strength, a strength inherent in work alone, independent of the material values it provides. *The tangible fruits of work constitute human property; but the only source of human dignity, and at the same time of morality and happiness, is the inner, spiritual, life-giving power of work itself.*

'*Without physical work man cannot advance; he cannot stay in the same place, but must go backwards.* The body, heart and mind of man demand manual work, and this demand is so insistent that if for some reason a man does not find his own personal work in life, he loses his way.'[1]

The idea of combining instruction with productive work, which had caught the imagination of progressive teachers and public figures in the seventeenth, eighteenth and nineteenth centuries, was later forgotten. Factories had greatly simplified the worker's labour, turning him into an appendage of the machine, performing monotonous, simple operations. The machines themselves were not yet sufficiently complicated to demand high intelligence from those who operated them.

Yet, while the idea of a labour school obtained neither its due scientific rationale nor practical embodiment in the period under consideration, the thoughts expressed by progressive teachers and public men on labour education were of great importance in the subsequent history of education.

THE SCIENTIFIC RATIONALE PROVIDED BY MARX AND ENGELS FOR THE IDEAS OF POLYTECHNICAL EDUCATION AND FOR COMBINING INSTRUCTION WITH PRODUCTIVE WORK

The problems of polytechnical education and of combining instruction with productive work were posed scientifically by Marx

1. K. D. Ushinsky, *Collected Works*, Moscow, R.S.F.S.R. Academy of Pedagogical Sciences, 1948, Vol. II, p. 337–40.

and Engels. They established the necessity for polytechnical education and for such a combination, by analysing the nature of large-scale industry, connecting it with the division of labour and the all-round development of the human being, and showing the role and significance of polytechnical education in the future communist society.

The nature of a human being's activity exercises a decisive influence on his development. When craft work prevailed, the craftsman made all his products from beginning to end, performing a variety of work operations in turn, all different in content, using different mental and physical exercises.

In the transition from craft work to manufacture, a radical change occurred. The entire process of making goods was broken up into a series of separate, partial operations. As Engels notes, 'Manufacture splits up each trade into its separate fractional operations, allots each of these to an individual labourer as his life calling, and thus chains him for life to a particular detailed function and a particular tool.'[1]

With the fragmentation of labour goes the fragmentation of man himself. The knowledge, foresight and will manifest in the work of the individual craftsman performing an entire production process from beginning to end, gradually pass from the individual worker, as the division of labour increases, to the workshop as a whole; the individual worker is left with the mechanical performance of a single operation day after day, month after month, year after year. The result, as Marx points out, is that: 'Manufacture converts the worker into a freak, artificially cultivating in him just one narrow skill and suppressing his whole world of productive propensities and talents.'[2]

The growth of large-scale industry brings further changes in the division of labour. 'Modern industry never looks upon and treats the existing form of a process as final. The technical basis of that industry is therefore revolutionary, while all earlier modes of production were essentially conservative. By means of machinery, chemical processes and other methods, it is continually causing changes not only in the technical basis of production, but also in the functions of the labourer and in the social combinations of the labour process. At the same time it thereby also revolutionizes the division of labour within the society and incessantly launches masses of capital and of workpeople from one branch of production to another. . . . Modern industry, by its very nature, therefore

---

1. F. Engels, *Anti-Dühring*, Moscow, Gospolitizdat, 1948, p. 276.
2. Karl Marx, *Kapital*, op. cit., p. 368.

necessitates variation of labour, fluency of function, universal mobility of the labourer. . . .'[1]

By nature, then, large-scale industry calls for variation of labour and great mobility of function on the part of the worker. 'But if variation of work is at present preparing its way simply after the manner of an irresistible natural law and with the blindly destructive force of a natural law meeting resistance at every point, large-scale industry itself, on the other hand, through the catastrophes it causes, makes it a life-and-death question that variation of work, and consequently the maximum possible versatility on the part of the workers, be recognized as a universal law of social production, a law to which relations must be so adapted that it may function normally.'[2]

Marx, on the basis of his analysis of the nature of large-scale industry, formulated one of the laws of social production—the law of variation of labour and versatility on the part of the workers, or the absolute adaptability of the human being to changing requirements in labour.

This law produces new phenomena in the sphere of education of the young as well. Polytechnical and agricultural schools begin to appear spontaneously, along with vocational schools in which workers' children gain some acquaintance with technology and the practical use of various instruments of production.

Marx and Engels called on the working class to fight for legislation shortening the working day for children and for the combination of productive work with instruction and for polytechnical education, 'which would acquaint the pupil with the basic principles of all production processes and at the same time give a child or adolescent skill in handling the simplest instruments used in every kind of production'.[3]

Stressing the importance of fighting for such legislation, Marx and Engels pointed out that 'the most enlightened sections of the working class are well aware that the future of their class, and consequently of mankind, depends entirely on the upbringing of the younger generation of workers', and that 'the combination of paid productive work, mental training, physical exercise and polytechnical instruction raises the working class far above the level of the upper and middle classes'.[4]

About a century ago, when a law was passed in England obliging factory owners to provide elementary education for

1. ibid., p. 492.
2. ibid., p. 492-3.
3. Karl Marx and F. Engels, *Collected Works*, Moscow, Gospolitizdat, 1936, Vol. XIII, Pt. 1, p. 199.
4. ibid.

children working in production, the inspectors noted that although the factory children received instruction for only half as long as ordinary schoolchildren, they learnt just as much and sometimes even more. This is explained by Marx when he cites the *Report of the Inspectors of Factories*, dated 31 October 1865: 'This can be accounted for by the simple fact that, with only being at school for one-half of the day, they are always fresh and nearly always ready and willing to receive instruction. The system on which they work, half manual work and half school, renders each employment a rest and a relief to the other; consequently, both are far more congenial to the child than would be the case were he kept constantly at one.'[1]

Quoting from Senior's speech at the Social Science Congress in Edinburgh in 1863, Marx agrees with him that in ordinary schools the monotonous, unproductive and long school hours of upper- and middle-class children add unnecessarily to the labour of the teacher, while not only fruitlessly but absolutely injuriously wasting the time, health and energy of the children. From this Marx concludes that to combine instruction with productive labour is useful and desirable both for production and for the development of the young.

Looking to the future, after the coming to political power of the working class, Marx and Engels predicted that to raise social production to an unprecedented level, '... mechanical and chemical auxiliary resources alone would not suffice. A corresponding development of the abilities of the people mobilizing these resources would also be needed.... The social management of production cannot be effected by people as they are today, when each individual is subordinated to some branch of production, chained to it, exploited by it, developing only one side of his capacities at the expense of all the others, knowing only one branch or part of some branch of his own production. Even today, industry is becoming less and less able to use such people. But industry run socially and according to plan by the whole of society all the more presupposes people with all their capabilities developed, able to find their bearings anywhere in the productive system.'[2]

For this, the first essentials are to abolish the old division of labour and to institute a corresponding system for the upbringing of young people which must result in their all-round development and give them a good general idea of the whole process of production. Such an upbringing 'consequently liberates them from the

---

1. Karl Marx, *Kapital*, op. cit., p. 488.
2. Karl Marx and F. Engels, *Collected Works*, op. cit., Vol. IV, p. 335.

monotony which the modern division of labour imposes on every single individual. In this way, society, organized on communist principles, will provide all its members with a chance to use their own many-sided aptitudes developed to the full.'[1]

'LABOUR SCHOOLING' IN THE SECOND HALF OF THE NINETEENTH AND THE BEGINNING OF THE TWENTIETH CENTURIES

In the second half of the nineteenth century the idea that instruction for work was essential gained currency, more widely than ever before.

The idea of a 'labour school', or rather the notion of introducing manual work into a course of instruction at school, was supported by financial and industrial circles and also by those concerned with handicrafts and interested in improving what is known as domestic industry. Large-scale mechanized industry was showing a demand for intelligent, adroit, physically fit workmen with a certain amount of elementary knowledge of the fundamentals of science to enable them to look after increasingly complicated machinery. Government circles also supported the idea of labour schooling.

For this reason manual work was introduced into the curricula of some schools in the Scandinavian countries, Germany, France, Russia, Italy, the United States of America, Japan and elsewhere during the 1880s and 1890s and at the beginning of the twentieth century. In the same period a great many different teachers' associations were formed, rallying those who supported the use of manual labour in the schools.

The most typical late nineteenth- and early twentieth-century views on the role and aims of manual instruction were perhaps those expressed in Germany by Kerschensteiner and in the U.S.A. by John Dewey.

Georg Kerschensteiner was one of the influential educationists in Germany during this period. To him, the aim of education was to train useful citizens who would be devoted subjects of the State. He believed the main way to achieve this sort of 'citizen's upbringing' was by turning the public elementary schools into labour schools. The elementary labour school would have to prepare its pupils to choose a trade while inculcating the conviction that it was essential, in their future jobs, to assist Germany to become stronger and mightier.

As the children attending the elementary schools would come

---

1. ibid., p. 336.

from a wide section of the population, and as their lot would be physical labour (to which they were on the whole predisposed), Kerschensteiner thought that various types of employment in this category ought to be included in the school curriculum. Here it must be noted that he regarded labour as an independent, self-contained branch of teaching, unconnected with general education. The aim of manual instruction in the school workshop was to develop certain occupational skills and reflexes.

Since the prime object of the public elementary school was to train adolescents from workers' families for a trade, the educational aims of the school were relegated to second place and the level of general education reduced to a minimum.

The aims of 'citizen's upbringing' were also to be pursued by further educational schools established by Kerschensteiner for adolescents who had completed their elementary schooling and were already working at some trade, since at the moment when their characters were being formed, young workers needed to be protected against the social-democratic and revolutionary ideas current in society.

As to the organization of these further educational establishments and the content of the education they would dispense, Kerschensteiner required obligatory attendance twice a week for two years by all young workers who had completed the course at the ordinary elementary school; but any extension of general education for these adolescents was scarcely contemplated at all, since the subjects studied at these schools were to be adapted to the pupils' trades. Attention was devoted mainly to improving the pupils in their trades, but at the same time much emphasis was laid on the development of such qualities as diligence, persistence, self-control, sense of duty and loyalty to the State, in other words all the qualities essential in an obedient, and at the same time highly qualified worker.

As can be seen, Kerschensteiner's labour school was not a school for general education, common to the whole of the younger generation, but a school for the labouring masses, which provided no polytechnical education but developed only certain accomplishments and skills needed in labour and instilled obedience and a sense of loyalty to the Kaiser's State.

The theory of the activity school originated in the U.S.A. by John Dewey at the end of the nineteenth century was developed by his disciples and successors during the twentieth century. The basic postulate was that upbringing should proceed from the interests and experience of the child ('pedocentrism'), its end purpose being to adapt the child to life. Dewey regarded his school

31

as an activity school, but he treated the concept in an essentially different way from the Europeans.

Dewey's model schools had attached to them a series of craft workshops for joinery, metal-working, weaving, sewing, shoe-making and cooking. The teaching in school was geared to the 'practical' needs of the children, with the inevitable consequence that systematic instruction was ruined, the pupils' knowledge was scrappy and the general educational level of the young people was lowered. The activity school did not aim at giving the young a polytechnical training answering the requirements of modern production with its up-to-date technical equipment. The children learned mainly craft work and became acquainted with the tools of manual activity; the picture they got of industrial production was far from adequate. Thus the idea of combining work with study was not realized in Dewey's schools.

At the end of the nineteenth century, 'new schools' began to appear in many European countries. These were boarding-schools for the children of the privileged, usually situated a good way from the towns in the heart of the countryside. The high fees paid at these schools made them inaccessible to the children of workers. Conditions in the schools were thoroughly comfortable: a separate room for each pupil, showers, baths and bathing were provided, there was plenty of physical exercise, sports, games, good food, sensible clothing, long hours of undisturbed sleep—everything to make the children strong. Physical exercise included labour in the workshop and in the open air, market-gardening, horticulture, hay-making, building summer-houses, dovecots, boat-houses and so forth.

Analysing the experience of these schools, N. K. Krupskaya commented that in comparison with conventional secondary schools the 'new schools' possessed a number of educational advantages. They were not at all, however, the labour-polytechnical schools the working class needed.

Their purpose was to meet the need for an educated, intelligent section of the population possessing the initiative required in senior officials and able industrial leaders. But the atmosphere of the comfortable living-quarters isolated the pupils from the life of the ordinary people. The role of physical labour was narrowed down mainly to that of an aid to health and the development of physical agility, quick-wittedness and curiosity.

The pupils, Krupskaya noted, were trained for the 'higher intellectual professions'; they were not going to earn their living by physical labour. As both teachers and pupils knew this, their attitude to labour was to treat it as merely a diversion, a sport. The schools did not set themselves the task of giving their pupils a polytechnical education or acquainting them with the main branches and scientific principles of social production.

Isolation from life prevented the pupils from really learning about social relations. Rousseau had proposed to teach children not only the joiner's craft, but the joiner's life as well. The 'new schools' did not do this; it could only be done through productive work in factories and other establishments.

Krupskaya, writing in 1915, drew the following conclusion: 'Educationally, the country boarding-schools are in many respects run on intelligent lines; but in purpose and spirit they are designed to meet the special requirements of certain sections of the bourgeoisie. Working-class democracy will make use of their educational experience but will build its own schools differently.'[1]

LENIN'S DEVELOPMENT OF THE IDEA OF POLYTECHNICAL EDUCATION AND THE COMBINATION OF INSTRUCTION WITH PRODUCTIVE WORK

The idea of polytechnical education and of combining instruction with productive work was further developed in the works of Lenin. Like his predecessors Marx and Engels, Lenin considered all questions concerning culture and popular education in relation to the material conditions of social life, to the class struggle, and to the policy of the revolutionary workers' party. This applies equally to the problems of polytechnical education and of combining instruction with productive labour.

The development of capitalism in Russia, after the abolition of serfdom, led to the widespread involvement of women and children in production. In Lenin's classic *Development of Capitalism in Russia*, a great deal of factual information is adduced to show this process. The question arose, how to regard this extensive involvement of women and children in production, how to assess the phenomenon from the standpoint of working-class interests.

Lenin regarded it as a progressive phenomenon. 'Particularly in speaking of the way the people's lives have been transformed by the factory', he wrote, 'it is essential to note that the involvement of women and adolescents in production is a fundamentally progressive phenomenon.'[2]

While condemning the conditions under which women and children were at the time employed, Lenin thought it reactionary and Utopian to try to stop them altogether from doing industrial

---

1. N. K. Krupskaya, *Works on Education*, Moscow, R.S.F.S.R. Academy of Pedagogical Sciences, 1957, Vol. I, p. 348.
2. V. I. Lenin, *Works*, Vol. III, p. 480.

work or to support the patriarchal way of life which excluded such work. Large-scale mechanized industry, by drawing women and adolescents into the process of social production, gave impetus to their development and made them more independent.

The productive work of children and adolescents, on the other hand, must be combined with their instruction in order to ensure the rising generation's all-round development. Lenin pointed out that it was 'impossible to picture the future society without combining productive labour with the instruction of the young; without productive work, instruction and education could not reach the level required by the technical standards of today and the state of scientific knowledge, nor could productive labour without parallel instruction and education'.[1]

While attaching importance to the combination of instruction with productive labour, Lenin was merciless in his criticism of the *narodnik* Yuzhakov, who had debased this Marxist idea with his plan to set up farm-secondary schools (*gimnazii*) which would support themselves on the summer labour of their pupils. Lenin, criticizing this, pointed out that in order to combine universal productive labour with general instruction it was essential to impose on *everyone* the obligation to take part in productive labour. Yuzhakov made participation in physical labour obligatory not on everyone, but only on the indigent. 'Compulsory productive labour, therefore, according to our *narodnik*, is not a condition for general all-round development, but simply a way of paying the instruction fees at the *gimnazija*. . . . The whole basis of Yuzhakov's plan is that the indigent pupil should work off his fees', Lenin concluded.[2]

Lenin's wife, Krupskaya, gave a detailed exposition of Marxist ideas on the combination of productive labour with instruction and on polytechnical education, in her book (*Popular Education and Democracy*), which introduced these views to educational literature. Lenin rated the book high. Sending the manuscript to Gorky in Petrograd in 1916, he wrote, 'The pamphlet brings together personal observations and information about the new schools in Europe and America. As you will see from the table of contents, the first half also contains an outline history of democratic views. . . . You would do me a great favour if you would lend a hand, directly or indirectly, in getting this pamphlet published. I imagine there is now a greatly increased demand for literature in this field in Russia.'[3]

In April-May 1917 the Party Central Committee was engaged

---

1. ibid., Vol. II, p. 440.
2. ibid., Vol. II, p. 441, 442.
3. ibid., Vol. XXIX, p. 331.

in revising the Party programme. It instructed Lenin to make available documentary material for general discussion. The pamphlet he brought out contained draft amendments to those items in the Party programme relating to education. These amendments were drawn up by his wife, Krupskaya. The Draft Constitution of the democratic Russian republic must guarantee 'free, compulsory general and polytechnical education (theoretical and practical familiarization with all the main branches of production) to all children, of either sex, up to 16 years of age; instruction must be closely linked with socially productive labour on the part of the children'.[1]

The old programme had referred to free compulsory general and vocational education for all children of either sex up to the age of 16 and there was no demand for combining instruction with productive labour. In the pamphlet *Material on the Revision of the Party Programme* the word 'polytechnical' is substituted for 'vocational' on the grounds that the aim of schooling is to train not specialists, but people capable of doing any type of work. A further point is made, in the comments, that Marx constantly insisted on the necessity of polytechnical education, which had immense general educational importance, while practical knowledge of various branches of production helped all-round physical development and promoted the acquisition of general labour skills.

The draft Party programme required that employers be forbidden to use the labour of children under sixteen years of age. On the other hand, if children were to be completely isolated from production, this would mean cutting them off from the working class. To obviate this serious danger, the draft programme required the schools, instead of the employers, to introduce children and adolescents to productive labour.

The requirements in connexion with polytechnical education and the close link-up of instruction with socially productive work were incorporated, with slight changes in formulation, in the programme of the Communist Party adopted at the Eighth Party Congress in 1919.

The question of accustoming young people to socially useful labour was posed by Lenin in practical terms. The country, devastated by war and foreign intervention, lacked food supplies. In addition to the fight against hunger, disease and illiteracy, it faced wider and more complicated problems—the revival of industry and agriculture on the basis of electrification. Lenin called on the young people to devote their energies to these national

---

1. ibid., Vol. XXIV, p. 435.

problems, and called for an arrangement of their studies in such a way that no day would pass in any town or village without the young people tackling some job of public importance, however small or simple. He pointed out, however, that not all kinds of labour could serve this purpose. As examples of work in the common cause Lenin cited the anti-illiteracy campaign, the development of suburban market-gardens, participation in *subbotnik* work (i.e., work done for the community in free time) and work in connexion with the country's economic revival.

Lenin's ideas on education in communist morality in the process of socially useful labour and on socialist competition underlie the present educational reforms. In order to raise the productivity of labour, Lenin believed that the first essential was to develop heavy industries: fuel and iron production, engineering, the chemical industry and the electrification of the country. A second condition for raising labour productivity, he believed, was to raise the educational and cultural standard of the mass of the people and improve the workers' discipline, skill at work, speed and intensity of labour and organization of their work.

'Learn how to work! This is the task the Soviet regime must set the people, in all its aspects', wrote Lenin in his article 'The next tasks of the Soviet regime'.[1]

Lenin also examined the question of polytechnical education for the young in close connexion with the problem of productive labour. He pointed out that communist society could not be built unless industry and agriculture were revived on a modern technical basis, the electrification of the country. In appealing to the young to join in collective labour to revive industry and agriculture, he pointed at the same time to the necessity of mastering technical subjects so as to perform this task successfully: 'You know very well that illiterates will never manage electrification—and mere literacy does not count for much here. Here it is not enough to understand what electricity is. You need to know how to apply it to industry, agriculture and the different branches of industry and agriculture. This has to be learnt; the entire younger generation of workers must be taught it.'[2]

On Lenin's initiative, a plan for the electrification of Russia was worked out. The draft resolution governing this plan, written by Lenin, stated that the study of the plan must be introduced into all educational establishments, without exception, throughout the republic. Every power-station, every tolerably well-supplied plant

---

1. ibid., Vol. XXVIII, p. 229.
2. ibid., Vol. XXXI, p. 264.

and State farm was to become a centre of propaganda and systematic teaching of the electrification plan. Every single person with the necessary scientific or practical training was to be mobilized as a propagandist for the plan and to teach the subjects required in order to understand it.

In 1922, I. I. Stepanov's book (*The Electrification of the R.S.F.S.R. in Relation to the Transition Phase of World Economy*) was published. Lenin wrote a preface in which he put forward a series of practical proposals in connexion with the propaganda campaign for the plan: it was essential to get several copies of this 'textbook' into every district (*uezd*), and every rural district (*volost*) library; every power station in Russia must not only have the book, but must make arrangements for public readings, open to everyone, on electricity, the electrification of the U.S.S.R. and engineering in general; every teacher in every school must read and master the book—to help in this, a team or group of engineers and physics teachers must be formed in each district—but also be able to reproduce its content in simple, intelligible terms for his pupils and the young peasants in general.

Krupskaya recounts that Lenin closely followed the development of education, familiarized himself with new ideas in Soviet pedagogics and with the workers in this field, and read their works. He kept a copy of P. P. Blonsky's *Labour School*, annotated by himself, in his library. Lenin's attention was attracted by this author's idea that the industrial and labour school should bring mankind's impressive technical culture within the reach of the pupils, teach them to be strong and to bring the forces of nature under their control and teach them to work with the maximum of success.

But in order to raise the technological level of the nation, extensive propaganda about production and work on polytechnical education was essential. In his theses on propaganda about production, Lenin recommends organizing the publication of a mass popular newspaper giving pride of place to the national economic plan, the labour front and so forth. The material printed in the newspaper and received by the newspaper, as well as other matter, should be regularly reprinted in pamphlet and leaflet form and compulsorily issued to libraries, and then to all factories and enterprises. Along with textbooks and reviews of foreign technology, this material should be used to spread vocational-technical and, in particular, polytechnical education.

Krupskaya recalls how from the very first days of the Soviet regime, Lenin insisted that the People's Commissariat for Education should undertake the introduction of polytechnical education into the schools. They succeeded in doing this, without any previous experience, under conditions of severe economic dislocation. In those days, polytechnical education took the form mainly of the pupils' doing things for themselves in the joinery, sewing or book-binding shops, with wretched equipment. Lenin, however, wanted every educational establishment to provide instruction on electrification, so as to acquaint the pupils with the scientific principles of modern production, its main branches and the fundamentals of industry in general.

Lenin insisted that a Party conference on popular education be held. The report to this conference was entrusted to Krupskaya. Lenin was shown the preliminary summary of the report, on which he made a number of comments which are of great fundamental significance for an understanding of his ideas on the essence of polytechnical education, its aims and the ways of achieving it. First and foremost, Lenin wanted the summary to mention the fundamental importance of polytechnical education in Marx's thought and in the Party programme. 'Ilich (Lenin) himself', writes Krupskaya, 'attached immense importance to it. He believed that polytechnical schooling would help create the basis for building a classless society, and he wanted this emphasized in my summary.'[1]

In the circumstances existing at the time, however, it was impossible even to think of any full-scale establishment of polytechnical education. Even without taking into account the sad reality of the country's economic situation at the time, notions of polytechnical education could appear in the abstract as belonging to the distant future. To avoid this, Lenin suggested that it be clearly stated in the preliminary summary that 'we cannot in the slightest degree repudiate either the principle or the immediate implementation, *insofar as it is possible*, of an education which is, precisely, polytechnical'.[2]

By emphasizing the words 'insofar as it is possible', Lenin avoided postponing the settlement of this question and instead proposed that action on it be taken without delay but with sober allowance for the actual conditions of life in the country and the real possibilities within the schools.

As a result of war and military intervention, the young Soviet Republic was at that time in a very serious economic plight. To restore its war-ravaged economy, the country desperately needed skilled workers (joiners, carpenters, metal-workers and so forth). In these conditions, Lenin believed it possible and essential to

---

1. N. K. Krupskaya, *Works on Education*, 4, Moscow, R.S.F.S.R. Academy of Pedagogical Sciences, 1959, p. 536-7.
2. V. I. Lenin, *Works*, Vol. XXXVI, p. 490.

merge the senior classes of the general education schools (children from 13 to 14 years of age), according to the recommendations and decision of the teachers, with the technical trade schools. At the same time, to avoid the danger of mediocre standards, Lenin laid down the following rules: (a) early specialization was to be avoided; (b) general educational subjects were to be given more time in all technical trade schools, with new syllabuses being drawn up for each year.

Lenin saw the aim of the senior secondary school classes as the training of a joiner, carpenter, or a metal-worker who would really know his job and be fully capable of becoming a master craftsman, except that this 'craftsman' would have a wide general education, would be a communist, would have a polytechnical outlook and the rudiments of a polytechnical education. In particular he must acquire the fundamental principles of electricity, the application of electricity to chemical and mechanical industry, the plan for the electrification of the country and the basis of agricultural science.

He pointed out that the polytechnical principle did not call for instruction on everything, but did demand study of the fundamentals of industry in general, and theoretical and practical study of the main branches of production. Minimum standards of knowledge must be laid down precisely and in detail for all these branches of instruction.

Lenin's concern for a high level of general education and breadth of polytechnical outlook in the young was the natural response to the problems of rebuilding the country's economy, which had to be solved on the basis of modern science and technology.

Having set the speedy transition to polytechnical education as an unconditional task, Lenin indicated the following steps towards its fulfilment: visits to the nearest electric power station and a series of lectures, accompanied by experiments, at the station; a series of practical exercises, as far as possible connected with electricity; excursions to any reasonably well-equipped factories and State farms; mobilization of all engineers, agronomists and university graduates in physics and mathematics to carry these measures into effect; the establishment of small museums of polytechnical education, railway trains, steamers and so forth.

Lenin's plan for achieving universal labour and polytechnical instruction for the young was based on consideration of the actual historical conditions of the period and was intended to draw young people into socially productive labour, into the work of building up socialism, as well as to ensure their all-round development. His plan was further developed and made specific in the directives and decisions of the Communist Party of the Soviet Union.

CHAPTER II

SOVIET EXPERIENCE IN POLYTECHNICAL EDUCATION BEFORE THE REFORM (1917–58)

by M. N. Skatkin

THE FIRST STEPS

The building of the Soviet school system has been a complicated and difficult task. The story is one of a battle between old and new ideas on questions of schooling, a battle to establish a unified socialist system of polytechnical education.

The Soviet regime faced great practical difficulties in its early attempts to build this unified system. The outward conditions were unfavourable: the essential material basis for polytechnical instruction was lacking during the years of civil war and foreign intervention; the teachers were without the training and experience necessary to build a new school system, and every question had to be dealt with on pioneering lines. Yet even in those years a massive effort was made throughout the country to give the schoolchildren a labour upbringing and a polytechnical education. The October Revolution had awakened new powers in the working people, and the most advanced and revolutionary-minded section of the teaching community was guided by the aims and purposes of communist education as proclaimed by the Communist Party and the Soviet Government, which made for the full development of the pupil's personality. They enthusiastically rallied to the task of building a new system of schooling, and succeeded even in those early days in making a valuable contribution, especially in linking the school with life and with the revolution.

Various methods of making use of the labour of children and adolescents for educational purposes were tried out in the process of building the new school system. In some schools, teachers took the idea of combining instruction with labour to employ more active teaching methods, to make extensive use of visual aids and organize manual occupations in which the pupils could participate. Other schools introduced jobs unconnected with school work where the pupils made useful objects, the aim being to instil a love of labour and at the same time meet day-to-day needs. Still others combined general educational subjects with labour processes in the school workshops (inevitably, at that period, equipment was primitive) and on the school grounds. These labour processes were combined, in many schools, with the 'self-service' type of job.

Useful experiments in combining instruction with productive work by schoolchildren in industry and agriculture were conducted by the pilot schools and adult education centres which were set up by the People's Commissariat for Education in 1919–20, and which were the pioneers of polytechnical education.

In certain places school communes sprang up—labour colonies where the basic educational principle was to link up the instruction and education of the pupils with productive work in workshops, plants and factories and on State and school farms. 'Summer schools' were also opened at this time where studies, classes and games were conducted out of doors.

The years of economic reconstruction brought the need to create a type of labour school which would fit the requirements of the time while still being able to evolve into a genuine poly-technical school combining the elements of general polytechnical education and vocational training.

In the period 1920–22, two types of labour school offering a three-year course for young workers and peasants came into being and took definite shape during the course of the next few years. These were (a) the factory apprenticeship schools, and (b) the schools for rural youth.

The former were attached to large industrial establishments. The basis for admission was completion of the four-year primary school course, and the school turned out skilled tradesmen for the branch of industry with which the parent plant or factory was concerned.

The schools for rural youth (renamed 'collective farm schools' after 1930) were set up in rural areas. Here, again, admission was based on the four-year primary course, with the young people being trained for the new kind of rural life while being familiarized with agricultural theory and practice.

The curricula of these types of labour school included not only special subjects but also a set minimum of general and poly-technical subjects. Great attention was paid to the study of work in industry and agriculture and to socially useful work among the people. These schools won public esteem and quickly spread throughout the country.

In 1925, the basic type of polytechnical school for general education, the seven-year factory school, became consolidated as an incomplete secondary school giving the children a general and polytechnical education and involving them in socially productive work in school workshops and plant and factory shops designed to instil in them the habits of socialist labour conduct—social purposefulness, team spirit on the job, sense of organization and conscious work discipline. In addition, instruction was given in the fundamentals of agricultural production. Pupils completing the course qualified for admission to the factory apprenticeship and technical schools (*tehnikum*).

The organization of these schools—the factory apprenticeship, rural youth and seven-year factory schools—adapted as they were to the requirements of large-scale industry and agriculture and to the needs of young workers and peasants anxious to combine labour with education, marked an important step forward in school education and in the implementation of the principles of poly-technical schooling coupled with preparation for life and work.

The general secondary schools of that time were nine-year schools which prepared the pupils for admission to higher education. This type of school, which offered no labour training for practical work, aroused great dissatisfaction among public bodies and the general public, and in the school year of 1924/25 an attempt was made to reorganize the senior classes so as to provide a general education combined with polytechnical and vocational training. They were given a vocational bias (co-operative trading, economic adminis-tration, cultural and educational work, medicine, industrial and technical work and so forth), with the main object of meeting the growing demand in the municipal labour field and the conditions peculiar to a small-town environment with a relatively low level of production. The idea was that the school-leavers would have sufficient knowledge of some particular branch of labour to qualify as skilled workers during their probationary period on the job. They could also go on to higher studies if necessary, on completing the nine-year course.

This reorganization failed to achieve the desired effect and in 1930 a decision was taken to convert the senior classes at secondary schools into technical schools where general, polytechnical and vocational education could be combined, with productive work in actual production and the pupils' participation in social and political life.

All the above-mentioned types of school were given the task of linking instruction more closely with actual life and giving the pupils an all-round insight into actual labour activities. The curricula issued by the State Academic Council of the R.S.F.S.R. People's Commissariat for Education treated this all-round study of labour activities and performance of socially useful work by the pupils as the basis of labour and polytechnical instruction and as the interconnexion between the various subjects bearing on natural and social phenomena.

The distinctive features of Soviet education during this period were the linking of educational work in general with the social realities of the time, the activities of the working people, and the provision of training in the skills and habits needed for collective life, study and work. By the mid-twenties, the schools had already become a lively social body, solidly linked to other social bodies and to the people's fight for a new life. The teacher had become an active social worker capable of setting and fulfilling social tasks along with his pupils, and of taking an active part in helping to transform society on socialist lines. The extensive organization of socially useful work performed by the schools with the object of getting the pupils to join in socialist construction was one of the hallmarks of the polytechnical school of the U.S.S.R.

The State Academic Council's 1927 curricula for general education reflected to some extent the polytechnical principle regarding the teaching of the fundamentals of science. In teaching nature study, physics and chemistry theoretical work had to be linked with practical work and active participation by the pupils in the life around them (for example, the conscientious performance of a number of labour tasks to improve agriculture, health and living conditions, and so on), with organized visits to large industrial plants and farms to participate in the production process.

The labour curricula for grades I–IV at primary schools and grades V–IX at secondary schools were aimed primarily at teaching the basic scientific principles of labour of all kinds, familiarizing the pupils with the materials and instruments used in the most important and commonest fields of production, and instilling a conscientious attitude to work within the context of the industrialization of the national economy. The labour instructors had to teach their pupils to think the job out, applying the knowledge and skills they had acquired as the prerequisites for the performance of any labour process; inculcate the knowledge and skills necessary for further self-education in labour and technique; familiarize their pupils with the production aspects of their environment; and help to develop their vocational sense and widen their polytechnical outlook.

The curriculum provided for the following types of manual labour in classes V–VII: metalwork and woodwork; electrical installation; work with textiles, paper and cardboard; domestic science; and doing 'self-service' jobs. True, the wide range of manual work to be covered in a very limited time, the inadequate formulation of labour instruction methods, the lack of proper equipment in school workshops and other factors often resulted in superficial teaching; nevertheless, the leading schools set an example by their persistent struggle for the inclusion of systematic labour instruction, and achieved good results thanks to the creative work of their teaching staffs.

During the period of socialist economic reconstruction, when the foundations of a socialist economy were being laid in the U.S.S.R., the acute problem arose of training skilled workers and creating a Soviet cadre of production specialists. The establishment of a well-developed system of labour and polytechnical instruction now became an important and urgent politico-economic and educational task. In order to train the future skilled workers, engineers and technicians, it was imperative that general educational, poly-technical and specialized subjects be organically and correctly combined at every level of the school system. A great deal of work was done in this connexion and the content of the entire teaching programme in every type of educational establishment was clearly defined, together with the place and role of polytechnical in-struction.

Proceeding from the Marxist-Leninist teachings on polytechnical education, a definition was worked out of the proper content of labour and polytechnical education in Soviet schools. 'Poly-technism' is a complete system based on the study of technology in its various forms, considered from the standpoint of its development and all its relations. It covers the study of 'natural technology', as Marx called living nature, and the technology of materials; the study of the implements of production and their mechanisms; and the study of energy. It also covers the study of the geographical basis of economic relations, the influence of extractive and process-ing methods on the social forms of labour, and the influence of the latter on social life in general.

'Polytechnism is not a separate teaching subject but should permeate every discipline, be reflected in the choice of subject matter whether in physics, chemistry, natural science or social science. These disciplines must be linked with each other, with practical activity and especially with labour instruction. Only thus can labour instruction be given a polytechnical character.'[1]

Extensive propaganda work was done to promote polytechnical education and to mobilize broad sections of the working population and social and economic bodies in its favour. Schools were attached

---

1. N. K. Krupskaya, *Works on Education*, Moscow, R.S.F.S.R. Academy of Pedagogical Sciences, 1957, Vol. IV, p. 195.

to industry on a large scale, and the fact of bringing the schools close to production and introducing the system of productive work performed by the senior pupils was of extreme importance in transforming the general-education school into a polytechnical school. The manual instruction received by primary school-children in the school workrooms and by pupils in grades V–VII at secondary school workshops forming part of the system of social production and seeking to produce articles needed by the parent industrial undertakings or other bodies constituted the preparatory stage for production at the undertakings themselves.

During these years the Soviet school made substantial progress in combining school instruction with productive and social work. The link between school and life, the link with socialist construction, became stronger, and the school made a turn towards production. Productive labour in industry, on State farms, at machine and tractor stations and on collective farms provided schoolchildren with training in labour, collectivism and working-class solidarity and aroused their interest in technology and technical creativeness. The school broke with the old traditions of theoretical book-learning isolated from practice and became a new force in socialist construction.

POLYTECHNICAL EDUCATION FROM 1931 TO 1945

But along with the achievements in educational practice described above, the door had been left open to distortions and mistakes, to which attention was drawn in a resolution adopted by the Central Committee of the Communist Party on 5 September 1931 on the subject of primary and secondary education.

In a number of schools, polytechnical instruction had taken on a formal character, due to its divorce from a solid and systematic study of the fundamentals of science, while the work in the individual undertakings was given no educational objectives but was geared solely to the economic ends of helping the undertakings to fulfil their industrial and financial plans.

A radical defect in many of the schools was that they lowered the standard of general education and failed to equip pupils with a systematic knowledge of the elements of science necessary for work in production and for admission to technical schools and higher educational establishments. The labour and polytechnical instruction imparted along formalistic lines did nothing to help raise the quality of the theoretical instruction or assist pupils to master scientific principles more conscientiously and successfully.

45

On the basis of the resolution in question, and of other resolutions and decisions of the Communist Party and the Soviet Government, a new educational system was created, consisting of the primary school (grades I–IV), the seven-year 'incomplete' secondary school (grades I–VII) and the complete ten-year secondary school (grades I–X). Curricula and syllabuses were worked out anew, and great attention was paid to giving pupils a solid and systematic grounding in the mother tongue, history, literature, mathematics, physics, chemistry, biology, geography and other subjects. For purposes of polytechnical instruction, special attention was given to providing a good basis in mathematics, physics, chemistry and biology and to linking up these subjects with the study of production. The schools were given the job of teaching labour skills and polytechnical subjects both in work lessons in the school workshops and during practical work in production. For purposes of polytechnical instruction, they were required to make use of plants, factories, State and collective farms —that is, the socialist undertakings, which had rapidly increased in number and were steadily improving their technical standard. The work done in the school workshops, on the school experimental farms, in the factories and on the farms was subordinated to the school's academic and educational aims.

During the period between 1931 and 1933, model schools were set up in every district, with the aim of providing the academic and educational experience from which teachers, workers, collective farmers and pupils could learn how to build up a polytechnical school. The model-school competitions held in 1933–34 showed that they were doing good work in developing labour and polytechnical education not merely within their own walls but also in neighbouring schools. They made intelligent use of the industrial or agricultural undertakings to which they were attached, both to improve the material basis and teaching equipment of the school workshops and study rooms and also to enlist the help of the workers and the engineering and technical staffs in arranging for their pupils to have production practice. In the better of the labour schools, the combination of teaching and socially productive work by the pupils yielded valuable results. The competitions drew public attention to the schools and showed the particular achievements not only of the model schools but also of other leading ones.

The way in which labour instruction had been tackled in the general education schools was in sharp contrast to the steadily rising level of instruction in general subjects. Lack of qualified labour teachers and poor technical equipment in the workshops had led to a situation in which labour instruction bore a craft character, was divorced from scientific principles and modern production and was not serving the purpose of polytechnical instruction. In these circumstances, it had failed to yield positive educational results, and in 1937 it was cut out of the curriculum.

The schools had reached a stage where they gave their pupils an excellent preparation for continuing their education at technical and higher schools but had weakened the link between instruction and life, between theory and practice. As a result, general education had become formalistic, giving rise to formalism in classwork and in the pupils' knowledge of subjects. The one-sided turn given to education and development was aggravated by the use of bookish methods of classroom instruction and the lack of a carefully devised system of independent practical pursuits and socially useful labour.

The situation that had come about conflicted with the doctrine that the younger generation must receive a communist upbringing and with the needs of the U.S.S.R.'s expanding national economy. This made it difficult for young people to find their proper vocation and choose a lifetime career. By the end of the thirties, it had become necessary to reform the academic and educational work of the schools in the sense of further strengthening their link with life. The reform was dictated also by the fact that the number of secondary school leavers exceeded the admission quotas for the higher educational establishments.

After discussion in the press and at conferences, the following proposals were made for educational reform with a view to improving the preparation of urban schoolchildren for their future occupations: (a) the pupils should be familiarized with the real application of the knowledge they acquired; (b) the syllabus material for each discipline should be linked with the acquisition of a set of proficiencies and skills; (c) active methods should be used in teaching general subjects (laboratory experiments, practical work, visits, self-study and so on); (d) out-of-class work with the pupils should be further intensified.

The reorganization of teaching given in the rural schools (just before the 1941–45 war) followed a different course. With the extension of collective farming, the prerequisites had been created for improving the academic and educational quality of the schools and reorganizing the children's agricultural work so as to prepare them for their future work in farming. However, collective farmers were rightly complaining that the rural schools were not meeting the needs of farming; the teaching of biology fell short of the required level, and the schools were failing to take advantage of the achievements of front-rank farmers and innovators or to familiarize

47

their pupils with the problems of introducing mechanization and with the use of chemicals in farming. In 1940, under a decision of the People's Commissariat for Education, the following directives were issued for rural schools: (a) practical work and visits to farms were to be introduced in grades V–X in connexion with biology, physics, chemistry, mathematics and drawing lessons; (b) various types of out-of-class activities were to be introduced in connexion with agriculture. Allotments were to be set aside for all schools for experimental work, and agronomists and farm mechanization experts enlisted to advise pupils and teachers on agricultural matters.

'The new type of man', wrote the newspaper *Pravda*, outlining the tasks of the schools for the academic year 1940/41, 'is unthinkable without such qualities as discipline, industry and conscientiousness in the line of duty. These qualities cannot be taught without imbuing the pupils with respect for labour or without drawing them into direct labour activity. The school must prepare its pupils for serious and sometimes arduous work. Only then will it produce people truly fitted for life. In the coming school year, the work of the schools must undergo a radical change and their links with real life, with practical socialist construction, must be strengthened.'[1]

This was a momentous challenge. The experience of the leading rural schools had shown that theoretical instruction in scientific principles could be combined with practical studies and farm visits and the preparation of school-leavers for their future work in agriculture without disrupting the structure of the secondary rural school or lowering the level of general education. The leading schools had succeeded in becoming transmitters of agricultural biology to the general body of collective farmers and in correctly organizing the productive labour of their pupils—the collective-farm children—during out-of-school periods and holidays.

Another of their valuable achievements was the development of young naturalists' and young technicians' groups, which functioned in out-of-school periods and were a useful supplement to basic classwork on the elements of science. Simultaneously, group-courses began to be formed to train senior pupils as tractor drivers, automobile drivers, electrical engineering assistants, laboratory assistants, meteorologists and the like.

The demand for the rapid training of skilled agricultural workers increased enormously during the war period. In accordance with syllabuses specially worked out by the R.S.F.S.R. People's Commissariat for Education, senior pupils at secondary

1. *Pravda*, 1 September 1940.

schools were given special training in agricultural techniques which included theoretical and practical work on plant-growing, livestock-raising and technical agronomy. The teachers were also given agro-technical training and placed in charge of school brigades which went to work on collective and State farms during the summer holidays.

Year after year, millions of Soviet schoolchildren patriotically and enthusiastically served their country at that time, and this widely developed, socially useful work which they performed in conjunction with school work and political education to assist the front-line fighters, collective and State farms and servicemen's families, heightened their political consciousness and activity and helped to foster their sense of discipline and organization. Setting an example of labour discipline, organization and teamwork, they played a great part in raising production indices, and many were the regional or district Soviet executive committees which expressed their gratitude to the children and teachers for their self-sacrificing and devoted work. The names of many of them were inscribed on rolls of honour.

After the war, the work of schoolchildren in production ceased and the schools' main efforts concentrated as before on preparing them for higher and specialized secondary education, without adequate attention being paid to polytechnical instruction.

RECOVERY AND FURTHER EXPANSION OF THE NATIONAL ECONOMY DURING THE POST-WAR PERIOD, AND IMPLEMENTATION OF POLYTECHNICAL EDUCATION

During the years of the first post-war Five-Year Plan, the Soviet people not only healed their war-inflicted wounds but raised the national production figures beyond pre-war levels. The prospect of advancing rapidly from socialism to communism opened up before Soviet society, which meant that the question of achieving a rapid rate of technical progress and raising the cultural and technical level of the nation had become particularly urgent. And one of the major means of helping to solve these problems was polytechnical education.

To meet the urgent demands imposed by the realities of the time, the Nineteenth Congress of the Communist Party, held in 1952, issued directives for the development of polytechnical instruction at the general education schools.

In implementation of the Congress decisions, the Ministries of Education of the Union Republics and the R.S.F.S.R. Academy of

Pedagogical Sciences, with substantial help from teachers, scientists and production experts, did a certain amount of work in defining the aims and content of polytechnical education and the measures to put it into effect, at the new stage of development of socialist society.

In the school syllabuses for physics, chemistry and biology, provision was made for familiarizing the pupils with the main branches of production, and more time was set aside for visits and practical studies. In the drawing syllabus, more emphasis was placed on the rudiments of technical drawing.

But in the general subjects it was impossible to impart all the essential information on the scientific principles of production, let alone inculcate labour skills, without upsetting the logical sequence of the subject matter. New subjects were therefore introduced into the curriculum: work periods in grades I–VII and practical work on mechanical engineering, electrical engineering and agriculture in grades VIII–X.

However, many important questions connected with training for life and productive labour were left unsettled during this period.

At the Twentieth Congress of the Communist Party in 1956, the academic and educational work of the schools came in for serious criticism. The Congress noted a certain divorce of instruction from real life and inadequacy in the training of school-leavers for work; it defined the aims and future lines of development of polytechnical instruction in Soviet schools and stressed the necessity of familiarizing the pupils with the main branches of modern production, of ensuring a close link between instruction and socially useful labour, and of educating the young in a communist attitude to labour.

'In order to strengthen the link between school and life', said N. S. Krushchev at the Congress, 'the schools must not only introduce new subjects which teach the pupils the fundamentals of technology and production but also accustom them systematically to working in factories, on collective and State farms, on experimental allotments and in school workshops. The secondary school curriculum must be revised in the direction of greater specialization from the standpoint of production, so that young boys and girls leaving the ten-year school will have a good general education opening the way to higher education and at the same time be trained for practical activity, since the majority of school-leavers will immediately be absorbed into work in the various branches of the national economy.'[1]

---

1. N. S. Khrushchev, *Report of the Central Committee of the CPSU to the Twentieth Party Congress*, Moscow, Pravda Press, 1956, p. 77.

In pursuance of the directives of the Twentieth Congress, the Ministry of Education and the Academy of Pedagogical Sciences made further changes in the content and structure of polytechnical education. The new school syllabus included a larger number of periods on labour instruction in grades I–VII, while a new subject, 'principles of production', covering the following headings, was introduced for grades VIII–X.

TABLE 1

Grade	Urban schools	Rural schools
VIII	Mechanical engineering.	Cultivation. Agricultural machinery.
IX	Principles of industrial production, as exemplified at the production point.	Livestock-raising. One branch of agriculture typical of the area where the school is located.
X	Motor vehicles. Electrical engineering.	Tractors or motor vehicles. Electrical engineering.

This arrangement of the course, while providing a common basis of fundamental knowledge on production questions, permitted a certain degree of specialization by urban and rural schoolchildren. The study of production principles also included practical work at the production point, for which four hours a week were set aside in grade IX.

To give students the possibility of broader and more intensive training in any given branch of productive work, special periods were set aside in grades VIII–X for optional practical courses. To meet the demands of local undertakings for trained workers, optional courses were arranged in fitting, turning, milling, electrical engineering, radio engineering, motor mechanics, agricultural machinery, horticulture, industrial crops, seed production, greenhouse cultivation, dairy farming, poultry farming and so on.

At the same time, the education authorities and schools took various steps to create the essential material basis, select instructors in labour and production principles, and equip general-subject teachers with a scientific knowledge of production and practical skills so that these reforms could be carried into effect and school work placed on a polytechnical basis. Factories and plants were given government permission to make available equipment suitable for polytechnical instruction to the schools free of charge, and it was not long before many of the schools, with the help of

51

the public, had their own workshops for teaching metalwork and woodwork, mechanical and electrical engineering, and a considerable number of additional physics, chemistry and biology laboratories and experimental school allotments.

To equip teachers with the necessary knowledge and skills, extensive changes were made in the system of teacher-training and advanced training. New curricula and syllabuses were introduced in the training colleges in the academic year 1954/55, and courses, seminars and practical classes for general-subject teachers and labour instructors were organized.

A considerable amount of literature on polytechnical instruction was issued by the educational publishing houses and the Academy of Pedagogical Sciences, while the output of children's literature on technical and labour subjects for out-of-class reading was stepped up.

The new system of polytechnical education took shape and was introduced into the schools step by step. It was first tried out at a few experimental schools run by the Academy, and then introduced into another 580 schools in the academic year 1956/57 before being finally extended to all schools throughout the country.

The measures taken had helped to improve the provision of polytechnical instruction at schools but had still not eliminated the main shortcomings pointed out by the Twentieth Congress—the divorce of instruction from real life and the poor preparation of pupils for work.

In other words, one of the major questions originally raised by Lenin and the Communist Party programme, that of combining instruction with productive work, had not yet been adequately solved. In many schools, the involvement of the children in productive work remained restricted and sporadic. Notable exceptions were the rural schools in the Stavropol and Krasnodar regions and the Ryazan district, which had succeeded in systematically accustoming their pupils to adult labour and had demonstrated its beneficial effect on the mental, physical, moral and labour upbringing of the rising generation.

In view of this situation, the Ministry of Education, in conjunction with the Academy, took steps to ensure a further improvement in the work of the schools. In the school year 1957/58, a combination experiment was conducted at fifty schools in the R.S.F.S.R., with the senior pupils spending 50–70 per cent of their time on school work and the remaining 30–50 per cent on productive work. It was found impossible to combine the two in this way within the framework of the ten-year course, as it would have led either to a gross overburdening of the pupils or a drastic reduction of the scope of the general subjects learnt. The course was therefore extended to eleven years in these pilot schools.

The production training included theory and practice, and was conducted in such a way as to get the pupils to perform competent productive work in their chosen trade as soon as possible. As they progressively mastered their trade, they were required to take periodical examinations on the job in order to obtain a higher rating. The length of their working day was fixed in accordance with the current legislation on working hours, taking their age into account. Their labour was paid for out of the funds of the undertaking concerned, payment being calculated on the basis of the volume and quality of their output (or on a workday basis on collective farms, with due regard to the fulfilment of production norms).

While working in factories, on building sites or on collective or State farms, the children were drawn into the social life of the undertaking and took an active part in socialist competition.

The total amount of general-subject and polytechnical teaching given in the experimental classes was the same as in all other general education schools but was spread over three years instead of two.

The timetable arrangement for teaching and work periods was decided locally in the light of the special features of the type of production on which the children would be working. In the urban schools, where the work was in plants and factories, the two were alternated every other day or every three days; in the rural schools, the winter season was devoted mainly to class lessons, and in the spring, summer and autumn more time was spent on farm work.

The results of the 1957/58 experiment were favourable.

A special investigation was conducted by the Academy's Institute for General and Polytechnical Education on the pedagogical efficiency of combining instruction with productive work. This showed that participation in the latter did in fact have a good effect on the former: the children's interest in their studies was heightened, the studies themselves became more concrete and lively; the children's polytechnical outlook was broadened and they acquired a wide range of labour skills in the course of their production work. In addition, anthropometric measurements made by doctors and health experts showed that participation in productive labour helped to improve the children's physical development and health.

In all the experimental classes, where instruction was combined with productive work, the pupils became more adult, serious and disciplined. They developed a more responsible attitude towards

53

the work entrusted to them, took a greater interest in sports and out-of-school reading, and were more active in social work. By participating in socialist competition, they shared in the workers' and collective farmers' struggle for increased production, and they learned to respect labour as the creator of material values.

'At the factory', wrote a girl in grade X at Chelyabinsk Secondary School No. 91, 'I have come to know the joy of work. . . . I now realize how honourable is the worker's labour, how necessary and important his work. But I have also realized how essential it is to keep on improving and widening one's knowledge of production.'

The parents themselves remarked on how work in the factory had noticeably improved their children's behaviour. The children began to study diligently and developed an interest in many aspects of technology and a desire to stay in the factory or collective farm on leaving school.

Workers in one of the shops at the Stalingrad tractor works had the following to say about the grade X children from Secondary School No. 1: 'By working in harmony with us, they have come to feel themselves members of the shop team. Working at the bench, they have mastered production principles and at the same time been a great help to the shop in fulfilling the production plan. They have also worked on their own at the bench, and in the last months of the school year we entrusted them with such responsible jobs as looking after the piston line. . . . We shop leaders and foremen welcome this method of teaching our young people so that they learn production principles while at secondary school.'

CHAPTER III

THE REORGANIZATION OF GENERAL SECONDARY EDUCATION

by I. A. Kairov

N. S. KHRUSHCHEV'S PROPOSALS FOR SCHOOL REFORM

In the previous chapter reference was made to the Twentieth Congress of the CPSU, which focused the attention of Party organizations and educationists on the tasks of raising the general educational level of schooling and training for practical activity, and noted that certain steps were taken after this Congress to improve labour and polytechnical instruction, with an experiment in combining instruction with productive work at fifty schools in the R.S.F.S.R. Following the example of the Stavropol region and the Ryazan district, a number of other areas organized student brigades and experimental farms. In the towns and industrial centres of the Kuibyshev and the Kemerovo districts, training workshops were established and building brigades formed.

In the Ukrainian S.S.R., 50 per cent of the secondary schools introduced production-training classes leading to a trade rating along with the school-leaving certificate, and similar classes were started by individual schools in other Union Republics: Kishinev No. 34 (Moldavia), Orsha No. 1 (Byelorussia), Riga No. 1 (Latvia), Baku No. 208 (Azerbaijan), Kobuleti No. 1 (Georgia) and others. All these new educational shoots heralded practical ways of forging the required link. However, most schools were still working along the old lines. The amount of production practice given to accustom the pupils to factory or farm labour was negligible, which meant that no close link was possible.

In the summer of 1958, N. S. Khrushchev submitted a memorandum to the Presidium of the Central Committee of the C.P.S.U. on 'Strengthening the ties of the school with life and further developing the public education system'. In it he noted the value of all that was being done to make polytechnical instruction a reality and give schoolchildren a labour education, but he regarded what was being done as totally inadequate. The schools remained divorced from life; production and labour had still not become the basis for the education of the young.

In his memorandum, as in earlier statements, N. S. Khrushchev pointed out that labour alone had created and was creating material and spiritual values and that it alone could lead to the full and final triumph of communism. On the basis of the socialist transformations already achieved, the country, led by the Communist Party, had now gone over to the extensive construction of a communist society. The time had come to think about training the man of the future and in these circumstances, the important role of Soviet schools was becoming immeasurably greater. In order to train future citizens, education and upbringing must be closely linked with life, labour, production and the practical aspects of building communism. The secondary schools must make it their chief aim to train young people for the socially useful labour whereby material and spiritual values were created. Participation in the work of building communism was the basis of the moral upbringing of schoolchildren, and the education system had to be reformed so that all boys and girls would be drawn into socially useful labour from the age of fifteen or sixteen and receive a complete secondary education closely bound up with it.

The Presidium of the Central Committee of the CPSU adopted N. S. Khrushchev's memorandum, which then became the basis for the theses drawn up on this subject by the Central Committee and the U.S.S.R. Council of Ministers. After being ratified by the November 1958 Plenum of the Central Committee, the theses were thrown open to nation-wide discussion.

Developing Lenin's ideas on the younger generation, the memorandum and the theses were tremendously important documents for charting the way to the reorganization of the secondary, vocational and higher schools to meet the needs and prospects of the new stage of communist construction. They also testified, once again, to the Party's parental concern for education and its further improvement.

SUMMARY OF THE DISCUSSION ON THE THESES OF
THE CENTRAL COMMITTEE OF THE CPSU AND THE
U.S.S.R. COUNCIL OF MINISTERS

The discussion on the theses was nation-wide. The preliminary returns listed around 199,000 meetings in the R.S.F.S.R. attended by over thirteen million people and addressed by over 800,000 speakers. In the Ukrainian S.S.R., there were over 90,000 meetings and conferences attended by ten million people and addressed by over 500,000 speakers. The corresponding figures were about 17,000, 1,300,000 and 100,000 for the Kazakh S.S.R. and 6,200, 400,000 and 18,000 for Lithuania. The discussion was on the same scale in all the other Union Republics. Everywhere, even in the remotest corners of the vast territory of the Soviet Union, controversy raged about the best way to reorganize the schools.

The Soviet people were enthusiastic in their support and approval of the theses, and particularly welcomed the basic idea of the reform—the implementation of the principle of combining instruction with productive work, linking the school with life and associating together general, polytechnical and vocational education at the secondary level.

A fine example of the people's profound understanding of the demands of the new stage of Soviet construction was the rapid spread of the idea started by members of the Party and the Young Communists working at the Moscow marshalling yards in forming the first communist labour brigades. It was these same marshalling yards, incidentally, which in 1919 started the celebrated communist *subbotniks* referred to by Lenin as the 'great beginning'.

At the Kemerovo coking plant, the chemists came forward with an interesting set of about a hundred suggestions for improving the organization of workers' instruction. Specially noteworthy was a proposal by the Party committee at the plant for a seven-year plan to provide tuition of all types for 5,000 workers.

The collective farmers were as enthusiastic as the workers, and the theses also met with a lively and favourable response from parents, as could be expected in a matter concerning the future of their children.

Running through all the proposals put forward was the idea that young people must study and work, work and study, combining labour with healthy recreation.

The December 1958 session of the Supreme Soviet of the U.S.S.R. and the sessions of the Supreme Soviets of the Union Republics, which followed in November 1959, examined the theses, adopted them in accordance with the public's wishes and passed appropriate laws[1] which would ensure the successful implementation of the Leninist principles on the education of the young people of the Soviet Union as active builders of communism.

---

1. The full text of the Law 'On the strengthening of the ties of the school with life and on the further development of the public education system in the U.S.S.R.' will be found in Appendix I, p. 375.

The Soviet school played a leading part in the growth of socialism in the U.S.S.R. Developing along the lines mapped out by Lenin and the Party programme, it made a major contribution to the communist education of the working people and the consolidation of socialist ideology in Soviet society. Before the October Revolution, three-quarters of the population of Russia was illiterate and about four-fifths of all children and adolescents received no schooling whatever. Now, the number of pupils in the senior grades at secondary schools is nearly forty times greater than before the Revolution.

The Soviet school has helped to raise the cultural level of all the peoples of the multinational Union, who now all have schools teaching in their own languages and free access to further study and culture. Under the Soviet regime, the number of pupils at educational establishments has increased fifty-fold in Kirghizia, eighty-four-fold in Uzbekistan and ninety-eight-fold in Tadjikistan. Before the Revolution, barely 2 per cent of the indigenous Kazakh population were literate; only one school-age child in fifty went to school; while girls, in general, received no education at all. Today, Kazakhstan has 9,915 schools attended by 1,425,280 children, including 670,000 girls.

It may be asked why, if Soviet national education had been so successful, it needed reforming. The reply is that the reform was staged not because the school system was bad but because life was marching on and the schools had to be able to cope with the tasks imposed by the new period in Soviet history—the period of all-out effort to build a communist society. Marxist-Leninist teachings consider that a necessary condition for this is the progressive elimination of the major differences between intellectual and physical work which prevent people from acquiring an all-round development.

The prospects for technical and economic growth in the U.S.S.R. are such that increasingly higher demands are being made on all workers in Soviet society, and the need for an all-round education becomes paramount.

Could the schools, in their existing form, provide such an education? Not entirely. The fact had to be recognized that at a certain stage of socialist construction there were shortcomings in the school system which under the new conditions were becoming intolerable. Prominent amongst these was the divorce of instruction from life. In the 1930s, when the educational system was taking shape, the schools were faced with the task of preparing a well-educated people with a good grounding in science for higher education. By and large, they succeeded in this, but the tasks of polytechnical and labour training, the imparting of the practical knowledge and skills essential for life and labour, were relegated to second place.

Young people who are not required to take part in socially useful physical labour suffer seriously not merely in their physical and moral upbringing but also in terms of their mental development. The thread running through the theses was that of labour training and the combination of instruction with productive work; the successful implementation of this is closely linked with the development and improvement of general education.

THE PROBLEMS INVOLVED IN THE REFORM

The main problems involved in the reform were described in the theses. The first essential was to modify the aims of the school and require it, as its main task, to train people with an all-round education, a good knowledge of the fundamentals of science and a capacity for systematic labour, and to instil in young people the aspiration to be socially useful and play an active part in work essential for society.

The new type of secondary schooling was based on the systematic application of the principle of combining instruction with productive work, as the universal imperative in bringing up young people in Soviet society. The implementation of this principle in the secondary school opened this level of education to workers and collective farmers.

The idea was to start preparing children psychologically, right from grade I, for their future participation in socially useful activities and the creation of the values essential for the development of a socialist society. The object was not to use child labour for some economic end, but to organize it solely in the interests of the child's own upbringing.

Such manual work could take various forms: for the younger age-group, it would mean work in workrooms, in class, in school workshops or on training-and-experimental allotments—work of value for everyday purposes in the school and at home. For the lower secondary school age-group socially useful work would be gradually increased in step with the progress of the child's studies and his mastery of the fundamentals of science. A strict system was to be laid down to ensure that work and recreation were properly balanced: the duration of the child's manual work would have to be fixed and the type of labour defined in terms of its suitability to the child's powers and understanding; the work would have to have educational value and not overburden the child, and care would have to be taken to fortify his health and ensure that the intellectual, labour, moral, physical and aesthetic aspects of his development were properly balanced.

As the child moves up into the senior grades, his participation in socially useful productive work needs to become more complex and systematic. In preparing children for modern labour, they have to be given a fundamental knowledge of the natural and social sciences, a grounding in the technical sciences, and the skills and aptitudes essential for work. Labour education had to be provided in conjunction with general and polytechnical education. But for the purposes of highly productive labour this was still not sufficient: general and polytechnical education had to be supplemented by vocational education so as to provide training for specific types of modern labour.

THE GENERAL EDUCATIONAL SYSTEM: TYPES OF SCHOOLS

In order to put the labour education provided by schools on a better footing and allow for age differences, school education had to be divided into two stages.

The first stage was to be the compulsory eight-year school, which replaced the existing seven-year school. The change was designed to give the schools a chance to impart a wider range of knowledge in all subjects and at the same time eliminate the overloading that occurred in the seven-year school, to deal more effectively with the task of giving the children a communist upbringing and a labour and polytechnical education, and to turn out physically stronger adolescents prepared psychologically and practically for their part in socially useful activities.

The eight-year school was to be a general labour and polytechnical school. Compared with the seven-year school, it marked a considerable advance in general schooling. On the other hand, it was not a complete secondary school but only the first link in the education system.

The proposal to divide school education into two stages and go over from seven to eight years of compulsory schooling met with unanimous public approval.

To give the whole of the younger generation an equal and genuine opportunity of receiving secondary education, the second stage was to be provided for in a number of different ways, the most important of which were the following.

Young persons going into industry or agriculture on completing the eight-year school would either receive initial training at a vocational school or through brigade apprenticeship or a training course, and would then attend schools for young workers or rural youth while working in production—this would be the main method; or, alternatively, on completing the eight-year school, they would enter a secondary labour polytechnical school providing general education together with production training; or they would enter a technical school providing a general secondary education (*tehnikum*, college, etc.).

The main method would be applied in general secondary schools with classes held in the evening or on a shift basis; studies would be arranged to fit in with the conditions of work at the place of employment. These schools could be either urban or rural, with tuition given in class or by correspondence. They would not only give young workers a complete secondary education but also improve and deepen their vocational knowledge and turn them into skilled and educated men and women for industry or the collective farms. The course was to cover three years, with hours of instruction not exceeding eighteen a week for each pupil. Given a good tutorial system and the necessary textbooks, it was considered that the pupils would be able to work on their own for the rest of the time.

In view of the fact that a number of young and adult workers had not had a seven-year schooling, the evening or shift schools would continue for some time to have all classes beginning with a syllabus of a level equal to that of grade III, as well as special classes for adults.

The idea was to provide the same amount of general and polytechnical education at secondary evening schools as at other types of secondary school, but according to different curricula and syllabuses. The students would improve their qualifications and deepen their vocational training through specialized courses in electrical engineering, technical drawing and so forth, or by completing a course of theoretical and practical studies necessary for receiving higher trade ratings.

As these schools would have to become the main means whereby young men and girls working in production acquired a secondary education as well as an important means of training industrial workers and collective farmers for admission to higher educational establishments and technical colleges, provision was made to create conditions favourable to their work.

Student workers showing particular interest and desire for knowledge and making successful progress would receive material assistance from the State and would be released from work for one day a week and possibly altogether in the final stage of their studies.

Industrial undertakings, State farms and institutions would be required, in drawing up their plans for supplementary youth labour, to allow for a fixed percentage of the young people to be drawn into education; collective farms were recommended to give full encouragement to their young workers to attend evening school while continuing at work, and to release them partially from work where necessary.

The second type of school was to be a secondary polytechnical school providing a general education together with production training, to be set up in towns and rural areas. In addition to a complete secondary education, the pupils would receive vocational training for work in a branch of the national economy or cultural life. The course would last three years, and the curriculum would provide for one-third of the school time to be spent on theoretical and practical training in production and on productive work, and the other two-thirds on general-education subjects.

The relative amount of time devoted to production theory and practice and the timetable arrangement of labour instruction would be based on the type of specialized training required, which would determine whether instruction was to be given in the training and production shops of nearby factories, or in student brigades on collective and State farms, or on training-and-experimental farms, or in the training-and-production workshops of a school.

In step with their acquisition of labour skills and proficiency, the secondary schoolchildren in the towns would be drawn into productive work, first as apprentices and then, after receiving a trade rating, as workers, and would be paid at the current rates according to their output. Secondary school children working on State farms would be paid agricultural workers' rates, while those working on collective farms would be paid on a workday basis.

On completing their studies, the pupils would receive a certificate of secondary education and a diploma giving them a rating in their chosen trade, and would be entitled to enter a higher educational establishment.

In undertakings where labour instruction was combined with work, the labour plan would provide for a corresponding quota for adolescents.

This type of secondary school could be set up either separately from an eight-year school or together with it.

Meanwhile, a new type of educational establishment was to be developed—the boarding-school, where the State would have the opportunity of making better and more systematic provision for the education of young people. The vast possibilities for the further growth of these schools can be judged from the fact that the Seven-Year Plan control figures provided for a fourteen-fold increase in the number of boarding-school pupils: from 180,000 in 1958 to 2,500,000 in 1965. It was specified that the schools could be set up as either eight-year or eleven-year schools, and that they would follow the curricula of the eight-year and secondary schools giving production training.

Some misgivings were expressed at the time as to whether the volume of general education would not be reduced as a result of this reform. The figures show that there is no such danger. According to the Soviet planners' calculations, the number of pupils at eight-year general schools will have risen to 36 million by the end of the seven-year period, as compared with 26 million in grades I–VII in 1958. By 1965, the number of pupils at schools for young workers and rural youth would be more than double—4.8 million, as against 2.2 million in 1958. The number of school-leavers from grade XI at secondary schools providing production training and from the schools for young workers and rural youth will have increased by 28 per cent. The total number of pupils at the general schools, including adults, is expected to amount to 45.3 million by 1965, as against 31.6 in 1958, an increase of 43 per cent. In other words, the plans provide for a vast expansion, not a decrease.

The sole objective was, in fact, to change secondary education methods and procedures and run the entire system of training and educating young people in a way that meets the demands of the times.

It was stressed in the theses that the level of general and poly-technical education laid down for the ten-year schools had to be raised in all secondary schools under the new system, and that a proper balance had to be struck between general, polytechnical and vocational education in compiling the new curricula and syllabuses.

The reform also called for improvements in teaching methods and organization. Formalism and abstract ways of teaching the fundamentals of science had to be firmly rejected. The reform would require pupils to do more work on their own with textbooks, reference books and other material, become accustomed to working with measuring instruments and laboratory equipment and do extensive practice in calculation, mensuration and graph work. Class lessons would be the basic but not the sole form of organizing studies: other methods would have to be extensively used, such as prolonged observation of nature, experiments on school or student brigade allotments, excursions and so on.

The radical improvement in the content, organization and methods of instruction would make it possible to avoid the present overloading of schoolchildren, it was contended; but however high the level of school education, it could not teach the child everything, and it was therefore important for the schools to inculcate a desire for self-education and sound habits of independent study.

THE TASK OF CHILDREN'S UPBRINGING AT SCHOOL

In order to help raise the general cultural level of the pupils, develop their capabilities and satisfy their demands and interests, it was proposed that there should be an extensive range of out-of-class and out-of-school activities, for which time should be set aside in the curricula.

The approach to school education had to be such that the schools would have an active influence in raising the cultural level of the nation. Their task, in educating the young, would not only be to meet the demands and requirements of society but also to influence the inner world of the individual. For the school in communist society will have to be the cultural centre of the region in which it is situated.

Decisive steps had to be taken to improve the ideological and political upbringing of the children and to inculcate in them a love of socially useful labour and respect for working people. Here the participation of young people in productive labour side-by-side with adult workers would play an important part: they would come to share the interests of the working community, with its productive and social traditions.

It was also necessary to draw parents and public bodies into playing a greater part in bringing up the children and inculcating in them habits of good behaviour at school, at home, in the streets and in other public places. The moral character of young Soviet people had to become the concern of the whole nation, in fact, in line with Lenin's not-to-be-forgotten dictum, 'Education is a long and arduous business'.

It was further stipulated that the education and health authorities would be under the obligation to take constant care of the young people's health and keep a strict watch over the correct sequence of work and recreation so that the pupils were not overburdened.

The school reform posed in a new way the question of the work of the Young Pioneer and Young Communist League organizations in the schools. The eight-year schools would be attended by children of Young Pioneer age, which meant that the organizing role of the Pioneer brigades would become immeasurably greater. In the evening or shift schools and secondary schools providing production training, the students would be of Young Communist age, and the permanent link with production and life would open up vast opportunities for raising the ideological level of Young Communist work at schools.

THE TEACHER AND PEDAGOGICAL SCIENCE

The educational reform would have been unthinkable without also re-equipping the teachers, for the teacher has to be thoroughly alive to the immense importance of the tasks facing him. For decades, Soviet teachers had been trained mainly to teach young people the fundamentals of science and prepare them for admission to higher educational establishments; but now they had to teach not only those fundamentals but also the ability to apply this knowledge in practice; they would also be preparing their pupils for admission not only to higher education but also to factory and farm. In other words, they had to have a profound personal knowledge of life and labour and be able to show their pupils what to do and how to do it. This applied with particular force to teachers of natural science, physics and mathematics. In addition, teacher trainees and practising teachers had to be taught the principles of technology and agriculture, while steps had to be taken to improve teachers' working and living conditions and raise their ideological and theoretical level and professional qualifications.

To ensure the successful fulfilment of the tasks facing the schools, the pedagogical efficiency of the entire educational process needed to be greatly increased. Pedagogical practice had to be based on scientific findings which, however, had 'failed up to the present to tackle many fundamental problems of upbringing and education posed by life itself', as the theses put it.

To help the school to cope with its new and vital tasks, pedagogical science had to develop theoretical research on a wider scale, make bolder experiments and a more thorough study of the experience of leading schools and teachers from every angle, and apply it resolutely in educational practice. As Lenin saw it, the task of the new pedagogy was to link teaching work with the problems of the socialist organization of society. In other words, pedagogical science must be inseparably linked with the work of the schools and teachers; once this is done, it will have developed in the way Lenin referred to when he spoke of the problem of

65

mastering scientific knowledge in general: 'science', he said, 'would cease to be a dead letter or catchword and become flesh and blood, an integral part of life.'

ORGANIZATIONAL QUESTIONS CONCERNING THE REFORM

The reform had to be carried out according to carefully devised plans. In each Republic, specific measures had to be worked out for changing over to universal and compulsory eight-year schooling, strengthening the teaching and material basis of the schools and organizing boarding facilities for senior pupils at rural schools.

Parents and guardians, as well as local Soviets, were made strictly responsible for seeing that all children received instruction. Particular attention was paid to girls belonging to the various nationalities in the Union and in the autonomous Republics in the eastern parts of the U.S.S.R., seeing that they attended the full eight-year school course and continued their education in the senior grades.

The reform came into operation on 1 September 1959 and will be completed in 1962. The evening or shift schools providing general education are already developing at a rapid rate. About 4,000 polytechnical schools providing production instruction were organized in 1959–60 and the rest are to be converted over a period of three to four years under the plans in each Union Republic, although this period may be shortened where local conditions and possibilities permit.

Pupils in grades VIII–X at ten-year schools at the time of the reform were to be allowed to complete their secondary school studies under the existing curricula and syllabuses, which would, however, make greater provision for labour training.

The number of 'after-school-hours' groups for children whose parents are working is being considerably increased, arrangements are being made for hot lunches, and a compulsory education fund is being created, from budget resources and from the resources of collective farms, co-operatives, organizations and factories, to provide material assistance to needy children (free meals, footwear, textbooks, etc.).

The Ministries of Education of the Union Republics and their local offices, in conjunction with the R.S.F.S.R. Academy of Pedagogical Sciences and other scientific research institutions in the Republics were given the task of producing new curricula, syllabuses and textbooks and carrying out the necessary re-training and upgrading of teachers in good time.

The necessary capital investments have been made and building materials allotted to collective farms constructing schools and pupils' hostels through their own efforts.

Production of up-to-date teaching and polytechnical equipment by factories coming under the National Economic Councils is being increased and a number of new specialized factories are being erected for this purpose.

As stated, many suggestions on ways of reorganizing the schools were put forward during the theses discussion.

A number of them concerned the admission of children to grade I at the age of eight. The Supreme Soviet decided against this. Practice had shown the advisability of preparing children for school while they were still in the older groups of the kindergarten. Schooling from the age of seven had stood the test of practice, and all that was necessary was to review various questions relating to methods of work with children in grade I so as to avoid a sharp break between kindergarten and school.

One suggestion concerned the teaching of languages. In Soviet schools, the consistent application of Leninist national policy had resulted in the use of the mother tongue as the language of instruction. During the nation-wide discussion, the representatives of the Union and autonomous Republics pointed out that in their schools the study of Russian was taken seriously, as an important means of communication between the different nationalities and of strengthening the friendship between the people of the U.S.S.R. and making the treasures of Russian and world culture generally available.

The participants in the discussion were in complete agreement with the view expressed in the theses on the subject of the over-burdening of schoolchildren in the Union and autonomous Republics, with three languages being studied simultaneously— the mother tongue, Russian and a foreign language. The main concern with foreign languages, it was argued, should be to provide schools with teachers possessing a colloquial mastery of the foreign language, and improve the quality of instruction. The Soviet schools spent a great deal of effort in studying foreign grammar but with poor results. That situation had to be changed: the main object of study should be the living language, and grammar made to subserve it, Meanwhile, schools which lacked the proper facilities should remove foreign languages from the list of compulsory subjects. The Supreme Soviet approved this suggestion.

The line taken in the theses that parents should have the right to decide to which school (as regards language of instruction) they would send their children was also approved. As stated in the theses, children in schools where instruction was given in one of the languages of one of the Union or autonomous Republics should be allowed to study Russian as an optional subject. In schools where instruction was given in Russian, they should be allowed to study the language of one of the Union or autonomous Republics as an optional subject. This would, of course, be done only where there were enough children to make up a class. This, it was considered, was the most democratic solution, eliminating any sort of bureaucratic approach to the matter and making it possible to avoid overburdening children with language teaching.

A number of people expressed themselves strongly in favour of the principle of continuity between the instruction given to children and that given to adolescents. Here, the combining of instruction with productive work offered wide opportunities. If an adolescent only works or only studies, he develops one-sidedly. Every young worker—and the older ones too for that matter—needs to study, and every student from the age of fifteen or sixteen needs to work.

Finally, the Supreme Soviet noted that the school reform could not be carried into effect by the efforts of Ministries of Education of the Union Republics and of the local education authorities alone, but necessitated a great deal of work by the Supreme Soviets and Councils of Ministers of the Union Republics, the Soviets of workers' deputies and the party, trade union and Young Communist organizations. It was stressed that the further improvement of education among all the peoples of the U.S.S.R. was one of the most vital tasks for the immediate future, and was the guarantee for a general advance in all branches of the country's economy, science and culture.

THE TWENTY-FIRST EXTRAORDINARY CONGRESS OF THE CPSU ON SCHOOL REFORM

In January 1959, the Twenty-first Congress of the CPSU endorsed the theses and the Education Reform Law and issued directives for the reorganization of the schools. It directed that the transition from seven-year to eight-year universal compulsory education should be covered by the control figures for the development of the national economy over the period 1959–65, in conjunction with labour and polytechnical instruction and the large-scale involvement of schoolchildren in interesting types of socially useful labour suitable to their age. The Congress also issued directives for the reorganization of the senior grades at ten-year schools into various types of urban and rural secondary labour schools where the pupils, by combining study with work in factories, on collective farms or in special workshops, would obtain both a complete general secondary and polytechnical education and a specialized training for a trade, depending on local labour requirements.

'The educational reform', said N. S. Khrushchev at the Congress, 'is fully in the spirit of Marxist-Leninist teachings on the education and upbringing of the young, and opens the way to the further expansion of polytechnical education in the schools.'

After the Congress, work on the school reform developed on a wide front, with the emphasis on raising still higher the level of polytechnical education in the schools.

•

CHAPTER IV

CREATION OF THE MATERIAL AND TECHNICAL BASIS FOR COMMUNISM

by S. G. Shapovalenko

SCIENTIFIC AND TECHNICAL PROGRESS FOR BUILDING THE MATERIAL AND TECHNICAL BASIS FOR COMMUNISM

Addressing the All-Russian Teachers' Congress (in 1960), N. S. Khrushchev declared: 'We are now fulfilling two historical tasks —the creation of the material and technical basis for communism and the education of a new type of man.' These two tasks are intimately connected, and the polytechnical education of the rising generation and of all workers is extremely important for both of them.

The demands involved in creating the material basis for communism and ensuring technical progress make it necessary, as far as the education of the rising generation and its training in production are concerned, to provide polytechnical instruction as quickly as possible and to raise its standard.

Examining this question more closely, one finds that the material and technical basis for a communist society will be large-scale, fully mechanized production based on total electrification, the automation and chemicalization of industrial processes and the widespread use of atomic energy and other scientific and technical advances. Automation will progressively cover the whole of industry, and this implies the extensive concentration, specialization and co-ordination of production and the application of effective methods of organization to production processes and labour. This material and technical basis has to exist in order to ensure a high level of labour productivity and is now being created in order to reach an abundance of material and cultural wealth to satisfy the needs of the Soviet people so that they can enjoy a full and happy life, a life of prosperity and culture and the all-round development of the individual.

But communism is built by people. Only by highly skilled and devoted labour performed to its fullest capacity can the Soviet people build the necessary basis and develop the communist mode of production. This means that the men of the future must be educated now, taking full account of the characteristics of labour under conditions of highly mechanized and automated production.

The decisive step in building this material and technical basis will be the successful completion of the current Seven-Year Plan, for which the aim of overtaking the productivity of the most advanced capitalist countries has been set, while the decisive factor in fulfilling the Plan and creating the general material and technical basis is scientific and technical progress.

The main feature of the Plan, as decided on at the Twenty-first Congress of the CPSU in 1959, is technical progress in all branches of production, to be achieved by the rapid development of electrification, the replacement and modernization of obsolete equipment, the introduction of new high-output machines, machine tools and technological processes, the elimination of heavy labour by mechanizing production processes, the automation and further specialization of production, and the widespread use of scientific and technical achievements and discoveries, particularly in the field of electronics, radio-isotopes, semiconductors and nuclear energy. The rapid development of the chemical industry, ensuring the production of new materials and the development of new processes, must also play an important part in speeding technical progress.

The work of economic and Party organizations and scientific research institutes in bringing about the desired progress was examined by the July 1959 Plenum of the Central Committee of the CPSU, which outlined important measures to ensure quicker results. The July 1960 Plenum took note of the successful application of these measures and gave new directives with a view to increasing labour productivity and the rate of development of production. Scientific and technical progress has assumed the following forms in the U.S.S.R.

Electrification

It was Lenin who taught that the electrification of the country was the highroad to technical progress and the creation of the material and technical basis for communism. His is the short and graphic formula explaining the significance of the electrification of the country carried out on the basis of the Soviet system: 'Communism = Soviet power + electrification of the whole country'.

The reason why electric power plays the leading role in technical progress is that it constitutes the bedrock for advanced technology.

71

In fulfilment of Lenin's behests on electrification, the U.S.S.R. has already become the largest electricity producer in Europe and the second largest in the world. In 1958—the year before the adoption of the Seven-Year Plan—it produced 233,000 million kWh, or 123 times the amount produced in Tsarist Russia in 1913 and five times the figure for the pre-war year of 1940.

The Seven-Year Plan, covering the period 1959–65, includes the large-scale construction of power stations to produce 520,000 million kWh. by 1965 and 800,000–900,000 million kWh. by 1972. The Plan concentrates mainly on building large thermal stations working on low-cost coal, natural gas and fuel oil, as the faster and cheaper method of solving the power problem. This does not mean, however, that no more hydro-electric stations will be built. They will, indeed, but will be of the type that requires a comparatively low capital expenditure. Once the urgent task of rapid power development has been solved by thermal plants, the Soviet Union will be in a position to exploit its abundant hydro-electric resources to the full in order to electrify the entire country. The Plan also provides for the construction of atomic power stations to supply electricity to the national economy.

The U.S.S.R. is also solving the problem of the long-distance transmission of electric power, and already has transmission lines operating at tensions of up to 500,000 volts. This makes it possible to link power plants to the general network and to interconnect all power systems in order to achieve total electrification.

Total electrification of the country likewise involves the development of turbine construction, electrical engineering and automation, and the Seven-Year Plan makes provision for this. Steam turbines of 300,000–500,000 kW. are being built and others of 600,000 kW. and over are projected, while hydraulic turbines of 200,000 kW. and over and high-efficiency gas turbines are also under construction. By 1965, the Soviet power system will be producing turbines of all types with a capacity of 18.7 to 20.4 million kW., and generators for the turbines with a total capacity of 17.5 to 18.4 million kW., or three times more than in 1958.

The operation of the large and complicated power plants is being based on the principle of extensive use of automation and remote control. The main power systems and large sub-stations are to be converted to automatic and remote control over the next two years while all new thermal plants will also be automatically controlled.

All-round mechanization and automation of production processes

Electrification provides the basis for the all-round mechanization and automation of production. All-round mechanization covers both the technological and the auxiliary processes of production, such as loading, unloading, transport and packing. Its success can be judged from the fact that output in the mechanical engineering and metal-processing industries in the U.S.S.R. in 1958 was 240 times higher than in 1913. The technological processes are now almost entirely mechanized, while the auxiliary processes will be mechanized in the course of the seven-year period. In this way all-round mechanization will be virtually completed by 1965 and heavy manual labour eliminated in all branches of production.

In turn, electrification and all-round mechanization provide the basis for a massive extension of the automation of production, covering not only the process of converting raw material into semi- and fully-manufactured articles but also the control, regulation, adjustment and direction of production.

Modern automation was foretold by Marx. 'As soon as the working machine can perform without human aid all the movements requisite for the elaboration of raw material so that nothing more than supervision is needed,' he wrote, 'we have an automatic system of machinery.'[1]

During the eighteen months following the adoption by the Twenty-first Congress of the control figures for the development of the national economy during 1959–65, more than 2,300 important new types of machinery and equipment were built, a great number of instruments and materials were developed, more than 2,000 automatic and semi-automatic conveyor belts and production lines were introduced, and over 1,000 types of obsolete machines and instruments were scrapped to make way for more modern equipment.

The main attention in automation is focused on advancing from the automation of individual production operations to the creation of fully automatic processes, workshops and undertakings, particularly in branches of production where automation has the maximum economic effect.

In a socialist society, the all-round mechanization and automation of production is in the vital interests of the workers, since it lightens their work, increases productivity, and creates the conditions permitting a shortening of the working day and the

---

1. Karl Marx, *Kapital*, Moscow, Gospolitizdat, 1949, Vol. I, p. 387.

liquidation of the existing distinctions between intellectual and physical labour.

The development of the chemical industry

Another important means of achieving technical progress is the development of the chemical industry and the introduction of chemical processes in all branches of production.

Before the October Revolution, there was virtually no chemical industry in the U.S.S.R., while now a powerful industry exists. The May 1958 Plenum of the Central Committee of the CPSU adopted a large-scale programme for the further and accelerated expansion of the chemical industry, and especially the production of polymers (plastics, rubbers, artificial and synthetic fibres) and their by-products, in order to meet national needs. The Twenty-first Congress approved this programme and confirmed the control figures for this industry under the Seven-Year Plan.

At present, there are over 50,000 inorganic and approximately 3,000,000 organic substances known to chemists. The Soviet chemical industry is to produce over 20,000 of them. During the seven-year period, the output of the chemical industry is to increase threefold, as compared with an increase in gross production of 80 per cent for Soviet industry as a whole. To that end, 140 large chemical plants are to be constructed and over 130 reconstructed, while it is planned to build more than fourteen new factories and rebuild forty-two existing ones in order to supply the chemical industry with the necessary equipment.

The use of semiconductors and atomic energy

The remarkable properties of semiconductors likewise have an important part to play in technological progress. In his report on the future development of Soviet science, A. N. Nesmeyanov, speaking as the then President of the U.S.S.R. Academy of Sciences, had this to say on the matter.

'There is every reason to believe that semiconductors will become of the utmost importance to the national economy within the next few years. Powerful current rectifiers will be widely used and miniature wireless and television sets built. Electronic computers, which at the moment depend mainly on fragile and rather cumbersome electron-lamps will be converted to small transistor elements, with great advantage from the point of view of size, transportability and sturdiness.

'Powerful thermo-electric generators and transistor refrigerators will be manufactured; solar batteries will be built to feed special installations, at first on artificial earth satellites, and later on, we hope, thermal batteries and photo-elements will make direct use of the sun's energy to provide electricity.'

It is not long since these words were spoken, and already semi-conductors have gone into everyday use and—in the words of the leading transistor expert, Academician A. F. Ioffe—are producing advances in technology matching the prospects held out by nuclear physics.

Nuclear energy is the latest and most progressive form of power, for small quantities of atomic fuel contain enormous amounts of energy. At present, the peaceful uses of atomic energy have followed two directions: (a) conversion into electrical power, for which atomic power stations and other installations are being built, and (b) the use of radio-isotopes in various branches of industry.

One of the first atomic power stations was opened in the U.S.S.R. Other large power stations are now under construction in the Urals at Ulyanovsk, and in the Voronezh and other provinces. In September 1958, the Soviet Union started up the first unit of the atomic power station with a capacity of 100,000 kW. Its total capacity is 600,000 kW.

But even more exciting vistas are opened up by the future use of controlled thermonuclear reactions, on which intensive work is now being done.

'The first half of the twentieth century', stated Academician I. V. Kurchatov, 'concluded with a tremendous scientific break-through—the solution of the problem of using the vast power stored within the heavy atomic nuclei of uranium and thorium. This type of fuel, which is consumed in atomic furnaces, is not to be found in the earth's crust in very large quantities. If the world's entire energy were to depend on uranium and thorium, the supplies would last for only 100 to 200 years at the present rate of increase in power consumption. The coal and oil reserves would also be exhausted over the same period.

'The second half of the twentieth century will be the age of thermonuclear energy. In thermonuclear reactions, energy is released during the conversion of hydrogen into helium. Fast thermonuclear reactions have been achieved in the U.S.S.R., the U.S.A. and the United Kingdom in hydrogen bombs, and science and technology is now faced with the task of producing thermo-nuclear reactions not as explosions but in the form of a slow and controlled process. Once this problem is solved, it will be possible to use the earth's vast hydrogen resources as nuclear fuel.'

As regards radio-isotopes, they are already being widely used in production to control technological processes and the quality of products; in automatic equipment, to control and regulate the various processes; in chemistry, to stimulate chemical and technical processes; in agriculture, to produce new and useful forms of plants and micro-organisms and to protect plants from pests and diseases; in medicine, to treat malignant tumours; in experimental research, as radioactive tracers, and so on. The demand for radio-isotopes is increasing year by year.

These are the basic trends in technological progress.

The improvement of production techniques, in its turn, has a direct bearing on the improvement of technology and production organization, while the emergence of new technological processes and new principles of production organization in turn have repercussions on techniques.

In accordance with a decision of the June 1959 Plenum, technological processes and improvements will be widely applied during the years ahead in the following industries and fields: ferrous metallurgy, non-ferrous metallurgy, chemical industry, oil and gas, coal, mining, mechanical engineering, construction and building materials and transport.

Technical progress is also manifested in a number of ways in the field of production organization. All-round mechanization and automation create favourable conditions for specialization and co-operation between enterprises, and the introduction of continuous flow methods and a switch to mass production. Automation itself leads to the standardization of products and technological processes. The structure of undertakings undergoes a transformation: functional workshops are replaced by item shops where various processes involved in the manufacture of a particular item are carried out (in mechanical engineering, for example, hot and cold processing, assembling, finishing and packing). Production is speeded up, the interval between the movements of the raw material and semi-manufactured product is narrowed and delays in intermediate and secondary processing are reduced.

With the advent of automation and closer production contacts between undertakings and economic areas, it becomes particularly important to ensure precise and rhythmic work in all sections and shops and the proper arrangement, briefing and training of the staff.

Future scientific development

As science develops to meet production requirements, it exerts considerable influence in its turn on the methods, technology and organization of production, gives birth to new production branches and helps to bring about a massive increase in productive forces. Technical progress is thus intimately linked with scientific progress, and bases itself on the wide application of advances made in mathematics, physics, chemistry, power production, hydraulics, radio engineering, electronics, semiconductors, computers and telemechanics (i.e., the remote control and supervision of machinery), thus necessitating the further intensive development of research work in the various branches of science and technology. The level of Soviet scientific achievement can be judged from the single fact of the perfection reached in the automatic remote control of spaceships, which for the first time in history were put into orbit and brought back to earth with animals and men aboard.

Soviet scientists are now collaborating with industrial workers in the colossal task of carrying out the instructions of the Twenty-first Congress on the development of science.

'At the present stage in the construction of a communist society, science is becoming of ever-increasing importance', a resolution adopted by the Twenty-first Congress stated. Charting the future development of Soviet science, the resolutions adopted by the Congress stressed the fact that 'the leading role in the natural sciences is held by physics, the successful development of which governs the progress of other sciences and the national economy. At the present time, the prospects of further technological progress depend primarily on achievements in the main branches of physics. The efforts of Soviet physicists will be concentrated on studying the problems connected with cosmic rays, nuclear reactions and semiconductors.'

The Soviet Union has more than 4,000 scientific research institutes and higher educational establishments in which over 300,000 scientists are engaged in intensive research. The State releases funds on a lavish scale for the further development of these institutions, the training of staff and the acquisition of the latest equipment.

EFFECT OF TECHNICAL PROGRESS ON THE NATURE OF THE WORK PERFORMED IN PRODUCTION

Technical progress—the introduction of new machines, equipment and technological processes—greatly affects the labour performed by workers in production. Certain trades and specialities disappear, new ones arise and the nature of the work in old trades which remain is changed.

To consider first the effect of all-round mechanization in this respect, the use of machinery in production processes eliminates heavy manual and often unskilled labour and creates new trades and specialities corresponding to the new technical equipment and processes involved. The machines and machine tools call for higher professional qualifications and skills which are impossible to acquire from production experience only: they will have to be obtained through instruction and training. The worker has to understand the construction and principles of the new machinery, be familiar with the scientific principles governing the processes involved, and be skilled in operating, controlling, adjusting and repairing the equipment in use. Workers will have to be conversant with the processing stages preceding and following their own so that they can perform their part of the work in accordance with the technical requirements. All this will act as a stimulus to the development of the production training of workers.

It is interesting to note that the mechanization of production processes, though changing the nature of the work performed, does not have the effect of intensifying the social division of labour. The reasons for this are, firstly, that many old trades die out; secondly, that the remaining specialities merge as a result of the broadening of functions which the new technology requires of the worker; and thirdly, that new types of work which were classified as new specialities and even trades when they first appeared have proved in practice to be similar or even identical. This reduction in the number of trades also reflects the fact that despite the variety of technical processes, they have more and more in common on account of the standardization of machinery and equipment. This leads to a demand for workers possessing similar knowledge and skills, and hence to a unification of specialities and trades that are different in name but similar in nature.

The change produced by automation is more radical still, as can be seen from the example of automatic lines in engineering production, or automated workshops in chemical production. Automatic production lines which carry out a complete manufacturing process from beginning to end do many different types of processing, from preparation of the basic materials, fabrication by pressure and cutting, and thermal processing, to the assembly, finishing and packing of the finished product. Automation leads to the concentration in a small area of a variety of technical equipment which, being interconnected, often performs multifarious operations and movements of the materials and semi-manufactured products simultaneously. This type of technique embraces dozens of machine tools and working heads, hundreds of electric motors, terminal and travelling switches, as well as instruments for measuring various parameters, while the electric wiring is often dozens of kilometres in length. The operation of these automatic machines is based on electronics, telemechanics and programme control—a technique which gives birth to new technical processes and performance methods.

All this means a sharp change in the composition of the workers required on automatic lines and their labour functions. Although automatic lines in an engineering works still apply the processes of turning, threading, milling, drilling, grinding, boring and thermal processing, the services of turners, drillers, milling-machine operators, grinders and so on are no longer required, for these operations are now included in the work of the 'adjuster'. The latter, who sees to the mechanical part of the automatic line, is responsible for the functioning of its component mechanisms and for setting, adjusting and lubricating them. In order to carry out this work, he has to be well acquainted with the technical requirements of the product, the technological process, the characteristics of the materials processed, the construction and working principle of all the machinery and equipment in his part of the line, the procedure for servicing them, the layout of the whole line, the interrelation of each piece of machinery and equipment, the instruments and devices ensuring continuous and automatic operation, the nature of defects in their work, the possible causes of failure and ways of eliminating them, and safety regulations.

It is obvious that an adjuster's most important qualification is the broad technical knowledge he must have in order to control an automatic system, for without it he will be unable to acquire the necessary skill. Skill in production work is essential, of course, but is no longer of the kind possessed by the old-style turner, milling-machine operator or grinder but a new all-round one comprising various elements of those possessed by the turner, milling-machine operator, driller, fitter, electrician and old-style tooler—united, cemented and illuminated by a wide scientific and technological education. Without becoming simple, however, the adjuster's work is becoming less arduous than that of the workers he has replaced; he is under less physical strain, the proportion of intellectual effort has increased, and the work is becoming more varied. He moves from one job to another, carrying out the universal function of organizer, manager, director and supervisor of a production process. His work is becoming more creative, approaching that of a technician or engineer.

Similarly, the most important figure in automated chemical undertakings is the 'operator', who sits at the control desk, follows the readings of the control and measuring instruments, rapidly evaluates them and judges how the process is progressing. If it deviates from the routine laid down, he makes rapid decisions and actions or instructs the adjuster or repair-man to eliminate the fault. To control the system, he must be very well acquainted with the scientific principles and parameters of the technological process, measuring techniques, the construction and working principles of the apparatus and the measuring and control instruments, the methods of correcting the system, and possible causes of failure and ways of repairing them. He must have good powers of observation and memorization of the many data observed, and the ability to make a quick analysis and take rapid decisions. He must also have a highly developed sense of responsibility. His work combines elements of the work of the various operatives formerly engaged in non-automated production, but it is an entirely different type of work in which scientific and technical knowledge and mental effort preponderate, although some of the elements of physical labour are, of course, retained. In this case, also, the work approaches that of the engineer or technician. Both on the automatic production lines in engineering works and in the automated workshops of chemical factories, the adjuster and operator respectively are greatly assisted by the repair-man. He, too, is performing entirely new functions; not those of the former fitter, assembler, electrician or machine attendant. He is a worker whose many-sided duties combine features of all those trades. He must be capable of performing the work of a fitter or electrician, doing soldering and welding, grinding tools and lubricating the lathes. And although he must master many different skills, they will have to be applied on the basis of broad scientific and technical knowledge. His work, too, covers many different specialities and is akin to that of an engineer or technician.

Thus the tendency towards the elimination of the old division of labour and a reduction in the number of specialities and trades, with their unification in the many-sided function of supervising the new techniques and controlling, regulating and adjusting their operation is becoming increasingly marked in the case of all-round automation, as a higher form of production mechanization.

As production reaches an even higher level of automation, with the application of self-controlling, self-regulating, self-tuning and self-operating systems based on the wide use of radio-isotopes, radio-electronics, telemechanics and control equipment, the work will become even more highly skilled and varied, and narrow and restricted specialization will no longer serve. Production workers will have to have an even more thorough technical and general education, including detailed knowledge of electronics and control equipment. This will go even further towards combining specialities and overcoming the present distinction between physical and intellectual work, and giving the worker's job the variety of that of the engineer or technician. The likelihood is that there will still be a division of functions, and a broad specialization as in the case of engineers, but no longer within the framework of the formerly closed trades. In the future, the worker will perform various jobs at different times.

Technical progress will also gradually reduce the working day to four to six hours and the free time gained will be mainly devoted to occupations connected with science, technology, invention, the rationalization of production, art and sport, and all this will result in further all-round development. It is difficult to conceive of the increase in the size of the contribution the workers will make to the expansion of production and the liberation of mankind from toil. To fulfil these various functions workers will need to receive the necessary training, instruction and education to ensure their all-round development.

Marx and Engels pointed out that the development of production under communism would not be brought about by people belonging to narrow and restricted trades, and that production developing on the basis of higher technology and fully satisfying the needs of the people required an all-round development and general orientation of the workers in all branches of production, training for changes in the nature of work and the possibility of passing from one kind of job to another. This would be achieved when the various social functions become 'alternative modes of activity'.[1] This will also lead to the elimination of the old system of division of labour, which confines man for the whole of his life within the framework of a restricted trade.

TRAINING YOUNG PEOPLE FOR WORK IN THE FIELD OF MATERIAL PRODUCTION

As explained above, the U.S.S.R., while creating the material and technical basis of communism, is at the same time training a new type of person capable of taking part in the creation of that basis and of living and working in a communist society. This new type of person should combine the following characteristics: love and respect for work; knowledge and skills necessary to work in

---

1. Karl Marx, *Kapital*, op. cit., Vol. I, p. 493.

mechanized and automated production so as to guarantee high-quality, low-cost products; interest in scientific and technological developments; all-round intellectual, physical, technical, aesthetic and manual development; high cultural and moral standards based on an understanding of his obligations to society; a communist outlook and a devotion to his country.

Inasmuch as certain trades and specialities exist and will continue to exist for many years to come, the training of the young generation is bound, as indicated by the Law 'On strengthening the ties of the school with life . . .'. Young people are being trained for trades and specialities with full account being taken of the lines along which the latter are developing. As stated, the tendency is towards an extension in the range of functions of production workers and to a combination of various specialities, thus reducing the number of main trades. This trend is particularly accentuated by the all-round automation of production. Accordingly, young people will continue to be trained in the main trades and specialities but the training will ensure that production workers have a comprehensive and thorough technical knowledge and a wide range of labour skills.

Again, technical progress is constantly introducing changes into work, the training must be such as to enable the young people to adapt themselves to these changes and take part in technical progress. They must, therefore, be familiar with the whole of the production system, the structure and functioning of modern machines and mechanism, the principles of the all-round mechanization and automation of production, modern methods for the treatment of materials, and the elements of production organization and economy, while they must also have a general technical training and be taught how to handle modern tools. In other words, they must receive a good polytechnical education.

The growing demands of the Soviet people and Soviet national economy for more and more new products are bringing more and more new branches of production into existence. Meanwhile, the specialization of production processes, stimulated by automation is leading to wider differentiation of production, with the result that over 300 branches of industrial production already exist in the Soviet Union, apart from many branches of agriculture and sub-divisions of transport, building and communications.

It is obviously impossible to teach the future workers, now at school, about all these branches of production. How then is the problem to be tackled?

It is stated in the Party programme and the Twentieth Congress resolutions that pupils must be taught about the main and most important branches of production so as to give them a poly-technical outlook and a grasp of the production system as a whole.

Which are the most important branches of present-day production about which children must be taught?

The five main branches of production are: industry, agriculture, building, transport, and communications. Each of these contains various sub-divisions, the number of which is constantly changing as a result of technical progress. In other words, the production system comprises a large variety of branches, the most important of which must be selected for study at secondary schools.

For purposes of selection, the following closely interlinked criteria were laid down. The branches selected must be:

1. The most important ones from the standpoint of the national economy as a whole, i.e., those forming the basis for the development of all other branches, supplying the national economy with the main means of production and providing people with the necessities of life.

2. Those most suitable as a basis for teaching children about the general principles of production, the special technological methods for obtaining various products and the most important technical achievements.

3. Those which children can understand at their stage of scientific training and general development.

4. Those whose study will serve as a basis for an understanding of all the other branches of the national economy.

Proceeding from these criteria, the main branches of modern production will be the following: power production, metallurgy, mechanical engineering, chemical industry, building, plant-growing, stock-breeding, transport and communications.

The most important of these is power production, since no enterprise can function without power, and a knowledge of this subject is essential for the understanding of any section of the national economy. The main factor in power production is electrification; and Lenin's theories on the matter, the importance of the electrification of the country and the use of electricity in the various branches of production provide the guiding lines for the study of this subject.

Metallurgy (providing the national economy with metals), mechanical engineering (supplying machines), the chemical industry (providing chemicals and various materials for the manufacture of machinery and equipment) and the building industry (supplying production with premises and the workers with dwellings) are undoubtedly most important branches of production both from the standpoint of the national economy (in that they provide the basis for the development, mechanization, automation and chemicalization of the national economy) and from the pedagogical standpoint (in that they illustrate the basic principles of all branches of modern industry). All the main achievements of scientific and technical progress are concentrated in and can easily be studied in these sectors, which thus constitute an important basis for an understanding of the multifarious branches of modern industry.

For agriculture, the most important sectors from both standpoints are plant-growing and stock-breeding. Experience of school work shows that children easily grasp these subjects, which form a good basis for the study of other sectors of agriculture.

The transport system is important for the movement of raw and other materials and semi-finished products between the various stages and branches of production; while the communications system provides information on production and a means of controlling it. Between them, transport and communications share in many of the scientific and technical achievements of our age (jet propulsion, radio, television and so on) which interest children immensely and are of great polytechnical and educational importance.

Numerous though the branches of production are, the methods of production are limited to three, applied in various combinations: physico-mechanical, physico-chemical and biological. The first are used for changing the structure, form and interrelations of the materials processed, for driving the working parts of machines, and for passing materials on from one production stage to the next or arranging them in accordance with an architectural plan. The second are used for changing the composition and structure of materials in order to obtain products to satisfy man's needs, and the third for obtaining products through making use of biological phenomena.

It is the first which are most widely used and which are applied in all branches of production without exception, and above all in mechanical engineering. The second are used in the traditional form in the chemical industry and are also used extensively in all other branches of industry (process of chemicalization).

In other words, selected sectors of production provide good material for teaching children about the methods of modern technology and their various combinations.

Instruction in the main branches of production must be given in such a way that children acquire a general practical idea of each branch and its specific features, as well as a grasp of the common element linking all of them and revealing the unity within their multiplicity and illustrating the scientific principles of socialist production in general.

What are these principles about which children must be taught as part of a polytechnical education?

Firstly, there are the general *socio-economic* principles of socialist production, namely:

Public ownership of the means of production.

Maximum satisfaction of the steadily increasing material and cultural needs of society through constant expansion and improvement of production due to technical progress.

Planned development and direction of production, with the participation of all workers under the leadership of the Communist Party and the Soviet Government.

Continuous increase in labour productivity and the quality of production, and systematic reduction of production costs.

Continuous lightening of the labour of production workers, and all-round measures for labour protection.

Communist attitude to labour on the part of production workers, expressed in readiness to work for the common good, socialist competition on a national scale, constant rise in the labour productivity and the quality of production, reduction of production costs, enthusiastic participation in technical progress and the combination of labour with study and cultural recreation.

In the view of Soviet educators there is a very close connexion between polytechnical education and these socio-economic factors. The aim is not to produce more executants but creative workers, who understand the production system and are ideologically equipped to contribute to the quick and effective creation of a communist society. To divorce polytechnical education from ideological and political training is a serious mistake.

The second group of general principles of socialist production are of a *technical and economic* character. They are:

Use of top-grade raw materials, their improvement and all-round exploitation.

Widest possible application of the achievements of natural sciences and mathematics in devising techniques and methods for transforming raw materials into finished products.

Systematic application of all the various modern technological processes (physico-mechanical, physico-chemical and biological) for transforming raw materials into finished products in every branch of production.

All-round mechanization, automation, chemicalization and electrification of production processes.

Application in production, on an economically sound footing, of the latest technical equipment and technological processes.

The third category of general principles relates to *organization and economy*. They are:

Standardization of manufactured articles.

Large-scale standardization of technical equipment and technological processes.

Change-over from individual to serial and mass production.

Adoption of the continuous flow method.

Organization of shops for the production of specific items rather than the performance of a variety of functions.

Reduction of the movements of raw materials and semi-finished products, and delays between manufacturing stages.

Reduction of auxiliary tasks.

Socialist organization of labour.

Combination of production processes with a view to better utilization of raw materials and fuel, and reduction of transport costs.

Specialization of production, concentrating on a specific type of product so as to increase labour productivity and reduce production costs.

Co-operative production, i.e., organization of permanent links between individual enterprises and branches of production engaged in the manufacture of a particular product.

Planned geographical distribution of production throughout the country with a view to developing the economy of formerly backward national regions as rapidly as possible, distributing labour properly between the various economic regions, and bringing production machinery, by all possible means, closer both to the raw materials sources and consumption areas.

The points of particular importance, in acquiring a knowledge of these general principles, are the study of machines, electrical engineering, all-round mechanization and automation of production, the main problems of the chemicalization of production, and the organizational and economic basis of production.

The July 1959 Plenum stressed how important it was for workers, at the present juncture, to receive a basic engineering and technical training.

But real technical training is possible only if the provisions of the Education Law of 1958 are observed and children receive psychological and practical preparation for work in material production from a very early age and, at a given stage laid down by law, are drawn under the system of production training. This would enable them to participate in socially productive work on the job and receive their further training in close connexion with that work. It is essential also, in order to teach young people general technical work skills, to include practical work of all kinds, in the natural sciences, mathematics and technical courses. In this way, work training provides the basis for moral education.

Since technical progress is based on advances in the natural sciences and mathematics, whereas new organizational forms of labour and production stem from the social sciences, it is essential that young people be given a sound and systematic grounding in these subjects, with special emphasis on those aspects which throw light on the main trends of technical progress. The electrification of production involves the study of electricity, heat, liquids, gases, light, mechanics, i.e., of all branches of physics. Future production workers must, therefore, have a sound basic knowledge of physics. All-round mechanization, and in particular the automation of production, involves the use of machines and electrical equipment and of modern materials, semiconductors, radio-electronics, telemechanics and control machines. Hence young people must have a sound grasp of these subjects, entailing a thorough study of the corresponding branches of physics, chemistry, mathematics and technical drawing. Again, since the chemicalization of production processes is based on the application of physics and chemistry, a knowledge of these subjects is necessary for understanding this field of technical progress also; while a sound knowledge of biology, including human anatomy and physiology, is essential as a basis for learning about scientifically organized agriculture and about labour protection and hygiene in whatever sphere.

The standard of general education in Soviet schools had reached a high level but needed to be raised still higher in face of the increased demands made on young people as a result of technical progress. Divorced to some extent from everyday life and production, the teaching—as stated earlier—had been mainly verbal and conveyed almost entirely by means of formal lessons; in short, neither the content nor the methods used were adequate for preparing young people for their future lives and work, nor were they taught how to apply what they knew in practice or in production work. Hence the immediate importance of the demand put forward in the Education Law for raising the level of general education by extending its content so as to cover the new scientific discoveries and achievements, and for the improvement of teaching methods so as to link education more closely with real life and production, with the children being taught work skills and becoming accustomed to doing independent creative work.

Polytechnical training and general education thus have a vital part to play in preparing young people for work in material production; and their importance will increase and their standard will need to be higher as the automation of production extends.

By teaching future production workers about the main sectors and the general foundations of the production system and imparting work skills, polytechnical training will gradually help to bridge the gap between manual and intellectual work and eliminate the present division of labour.

To sum up, the schools, in order to prepare young people for work in material production and adjust themselves to the constant changes in the nature of work, are required to provide:

An up-to-date general education, including mathematics, physics, chemistry, biology, technical drawing, history, the pupil's mother tongue, a foreign language, and literature.

A sound grasp of the whole system of socialist production, acquired through the study of its main branches.

A knowledge of the general technical bases of modern production and a wide range of general technical skills.

A thorough knowledge of the pupil's chosen profession or broad speciality, together with the corresponding work skills.

Experience of socially productive work, serving to help young people to acquire a communist attitude to work and a grounding in modern culture.

Linked with all the above forms of training and education, experience of socially useful work.

The reorganization of the schools is now proceeding in accordance with the Twenty-first Congress decisions and the 1958 Education Law.

The first stage in this reorganization was to draw up new curricula and syllabuses designed, among other things, to raise the standard of polytechnical education.

CHAPTER V

THE NEW CURRICULA AND SYLLABUSES AS THE BASIS FOR POLYTECHNICAL EDUCATION

by S. G. Shapovalenko

Polytechnical training is not a separate school subject but is conveyed through instruction in general and technical education and various optional subjects; through production training and productive work; and through out-of-class and out-of-school work. For the reader to have a clear idea of the place occupied by polytechnical training in the general education provided in Soviet schools, he has to know at least something about the new curricula for eight-year and secondary schools which were drafted after the promulgation of the 1958 Education Law.

Each of the Union Republics has its own curricula and syllabuses designed to prepare the children for life, and for socially useful work, to raise the level of general and polytechnical education, to produce educated people with a good knowledge of the fundamentals of science, and to instil a spirit of profound respect for socialist principles and communist ideas. The main emphasis, both in teaching the elements of science and in training the young generation in the principles of communist ethics, is on linking education more closely with life, with industry and with the practical work of building communism. The education system ensures unimpeded passage from eight-year schools to secondary schools, and from secondary schools to higher education establishments.

The curricula and syllabuses of the different Union Republics have much in common, since the aims of general educational schools are identical everywhere; at the same time, the schools in each of them have many individual features, for their aim, apart from providing a general education, is to give their pupils a sound knowledge of their mother tongue and of the history, geography, economic production and literature of their own country. But the ground covered in the various subjects is basically the same in all types of school, thus ensuring that children can continue their education without a hitch in the event of their parents transferring to another Republic, and also that children completing the course in a school in one Republic have no trouble in pursuing their studies in another.

Soviet education is completely secular: the teaching of any religious doctrine is forbidden, and pupils receive a consistently scientific education and are trained in the spirit of scientific dialectical materialism.

The aim of education being to develop all sides of the personality, the school curricula combine general and polytechnical education and moral, aesthetic and physical training and try to strike a proper balance between the humanities and the natural sciences.

Since the schools cannot impart the entire stock of knowledge about the world which mankind has amassed and systematized into a multitude of sciences, they select the basic elements without which it is impossible to conceive of an educated modern man, whatever his occupation.

PROCEDURE FOR THE PREPARATION OF THE NEW CURRICULA
AND SYLLABUSES

Each Union Republic has a pedagogical research institute coming under the Ministry of Education, whilst the R.S.F.S.R. has an Academy of Pedagogical Sciences comprising ten research institutes and attached to the R.S.F.S.R. Ministry of Education. These institutes, acting on instructions from the Ministries of Education, do the main work in drawing up new curricula and syllabuses, the drafts of which they prepare on the basis of the Education Law after careful study of the demands imposed on education by the development of science and technology, and taking due account of the experience acquired in educating and training the young generation at earlier stages in the work of Soviet schools. Scientists, teachers, industrial and collective-farm workers, building workers, office workers and others helped in preparing the draft texts, which after preliminary consideration by the respective Ministries of Education, were printed and submitted to universities, institutes, scientific establishments and teachers for general discussion. In the R.S.F.S.R., for example, the draft texts covering all types of schools were discussed in all of its regions, provinces, territories and autonomous republics. Some 75,000 comments and suggestions were received on the drafts for grades I–IV and over 125,500 on those for grades V–XI and were then analysed by the pedagogical research institutes. The drafts, after being revised on the basis of that analysis, were submitted for confirmation to the Board of the Ministry of Education, which took account, in the process, of the views expressed by wide circles of the teachers and scientists.

THE CURRICULA AND SYLLABUSES FOR EIGHT-YEAR SCHOOLS

As stated earlier, eight-year schools are incomplete general and polytechnical secondary schools catering for children aged from seven to fifteen or sixteen. This type of school fulfils the aims of communist education by giving a grounding in general and polytechnical knowledge, inculcating a love of work and a readiness to engage in socially useful activity, and providing moral, physical and aesthetic education, and the curricula and syllabuses for these schools in all the Union Republics are designed accordingly. Those for the eight-year schools in the R.S.F.S.R. may be taken as an example.

The eight-year school timetable (see Table 2) shows the subjects covered divided into three groups. Group 1 comprises Russian language, literature, mathematics, history, Constitution of the U.S.S.R., natural science, geography, biology, physics, chemistry, technical drawing, foreign language. Group 2 consists of subjects providing artistic and physical training: drawing, music and singing, physical culture. Group 3 consists of manual and technical training, socially useful work and production practice (for grades V–VII).

These subjects obviously cover everything necessary for an all-round education: the elements of science, the rudiments of art, physical culture and manual and technical training combined with work of a socially useful nature.

Children in grades I–IV (the primary course) are taught the Russian language, arithmetic, natural science, history, handicrafts, singing, drawing, physical culture, and the teaching in these grades aims mainly at developing their powers of speech and thought, giving them their first notions of the world of nature, the structure of society and man's working activities, initiating them into habits of work, and giving them the necessary physical and artistic training.

Russian-language teaching in these grades comprises reading and writing, reading with explanations, spelling, and practice in

TABLE 2. Timetable for eight-year schools

Subjects taught	I	II	III	IV	V	VI	VII	VIII	Per week	Per year
	Number of periods [1] per week for each grade								Total number of periods	
Russian language . .	12	12	12	10	6	5	3	2	62	2184
Literature	—	—	—	—	2	3	2	3	10	357
Mathematics . .	6	6	6	6	6	6	6	5	47	1663
History: U.S.S.R. Constitution . .	—	—	—	2	2	2	2	3	11	391
Natural science . .	—	—	—	3	—	—	—	—	3	105
Geography . . .	—	—	—	—	2	2	2	2	8	286
Biology	—	—	—	—	2	2	2	2	8	249
Physics	—	—	—	—	—	2	2	3	7	142
Chemistry . . .	—	—	—	—	—	—	2	2	4	142
Technical drawing .	—	—	—	—	—	—	1	1	2	71
Foreign language .	—	—	—	—	4	3	3	3	13	465
Total . . .	18	18	18	21	24	25	25	26	175	6055
Drawing. . . .	1	1	1	1	1	1	1	—	7	248
Music and singing .	1	1	1	1	1	1	1	1	8	283
Physical culture .	2	2	2	2	2	2	2	2	16	566
Total . . .	4	4	4	4	4	4	4	3	31	1097
Manual and technical training . . .	2	2	2	2	3	3	3	3	20	708
Socially useful work .	—	—	2	2	2	2	2	2	12	426
Production practice in grades V–VIII . .	—	—	—	—	—	—	—	—		180
Total . . .	2	2	4	4	5	5	5	5	32	1314
GENERAL TOTAL .	24	24	26	29	33	34	34	34	238	8466

1. A period normally lasts 45 minutes.

speaking and writing, and takes first place both in importance and as regards the time allotted to it. This subject is an essential factor for the development of children's powers of thought and cognition, and it constitutes the main groundwork for a general education.

During the periods devoted to reading with explanations, the children in grades I–III read articles about history and natural history, have object lessons and go on excursions, thus acquiring their first notions about nature, society and the work people do.

In grade IV the history lessons consist of stories about the past and present of the U.S.S.R.; while in natural-science lessons the children are given an elementary idea of the properties of water, air, certain rocks and minerals, as well as the structure and functions of the human body. They also receive their first instruction in geography on the basis of a study of their own part of the country.

Arithmetic plays an important part in primary education, the aim here being to teach children to calculate systematically, quickly and correctly, both mentally and on paper; and to solve arithmetical problems appropriate to their age. The primary course consists mainly of learning to perform the four arithmetical operations with whole numbers. Arithmetic develops children's conception of space and makes them proficient in measuring and calculating. The rudiments of visual practical geometry have been included in this course with that object in mind.

Considerable attention is paid in grades I–IV to manual training. The children have lessons in handicrafts where they acquire initial labour skills in making objects out of paper, cardboard and cloth, and growing flowers and vegetables. They also study domestic science and do such socially useful work, both in school and out, as is appropriate to their age. During the lessons, the children learn the correct ways of carrying out various operations, study the properties of the materials handled, the use of the simplest tools, methods of planning and calculation, the use of technical drawings in making things, and the basic principles of the organization of collective labour.

Now that the number of hours spent on manual training has been increased, the teachers have more opportunities for linking these lessons with others (e.g., speech development, or calculation and measurement).

Singing in the primary classes is taught with a view to arousing an interest in and love of music, training the children to sing intelligently, correctly and expressively, and developing their ear for music and sense of rhythm. The children in grades I and II accompany their singing with simple movements in the form of games and round dances.

Instruction in drawing in grades I–IV includes drawing from nature, design, drawing to illustrate a theme, and talks on graphic art.

Physical culture in the primary grades consists mainly of basic gymnastics, including exercises for all-round development, walking and running, throwing small balls, jumping, balancing, climbing and performing rhythmical and dance movements.

From grade III onwards, basic gymnastics include simple acrobatics and surmounting obstacles of various kinds; and from grade IV onwards, vaulting, and exercises with standard gymnastic equipment. Considerable time is also spent on active games, and from grade III onwards a special period is devoted to preliminary training for ski-ing, light athletics and basketball.

The instruction given in grades I–IV prepares pupils for the work of grades V–VIII, where they make a systematic although elementary study of Russian language and literature, mathematics, history, geography, biology, physics, chemistry and foreign languages.

The systematic course on the elements of science taught in the senior grade is designed to give pupils completing the eight-year school a fairly comprehensive range of knowledge sufficient to enable them, after the requisite vocational training, to take up practical work in industry, agriculture or other establishments, or else to continue their secondary studies. With a view to preparing pupils for work, the curriculum for these senior grades provides for three periods a week in manual and technical training, two hours a week for socially useful work, and a total of two weeks of production practice.

Meanwhile, it has proved possible, thanks to the slight increase in the amount of time devoted to school study as compared with the seven-year schools, to rearrange the school subjects better and to regularize the pupil's study-load.

An important place in grades V–VIII is occupied by the study of the humanities.

In the Russian-language classes, the pupils receive instruction in spelling, punctuation and style. At the cost of compressing the theoretical side somewhat, considerable time is devoted to practical instruction. In addition, arrangements are made in schools catering for the different nationalities for the study of the mother tongue.

The literature course is designed to provide pupils with a sound ideological, aesthetic, moral and patriotic training through reading and studying Russian classics and works of Soviet literature appropriate to their stage of development, as well as works on folklore. It also aims to teach the elements of literary theory and to develop powers of speech. In general the course has a much greater effect in raising the pupil's cultural level than that previously given on literary reading. In schools in the Union Republics, the syllabus also includes a study of the literature of the mother tongue.

History teaching is also radically reorganized. Previously, pupils not proceeding beyond the seven-year school received a very inadequate grounding in history, and left school knowing nothing beyond the history of the ancient world and the Middle Ages, plus such limited knowledge of national history as they acquired in grade IV.

The new history course is designed to give the eight-year pupils an elementary but fairly comprehensive grasp of the subject. Grade V is given an elementary course in the history of the ancient world; grade VI takes mediaeval history; and grades VII and VIII take an elementary course on the history of the U.S.S.R., including the most important events in modern and recent history, and make a cursory study of the social and State structure of the U.S.S.R. At the same time, they learn about the part played by socially productive work in the development of human society, about forced and free labour, socialist and communist labour, and the communist attitude towards work, all of which studies play an important part in preparing pupils for embarking on useful work once they leave school.

In grades V–VIII, the pupils study English, French, German or some other foreign language. The modern-language teaching has a practical aim—to enable the pupils to carry on a simple conversation in a foreign language and to read, understand and translate original foreign texts. In order to acquire this knowledge and proficiency, the children have to master a compulsory minimum of linguistic material.

The curriculum for grades V–VIII also devotes a considerable amount of time to the study of natural sciences and mathematics which, together with manual and technical training, provides the means of fulfilling the primary tasks of polytechnical education, namely, to familiarize the pupils with the main branches of modern production and to teach them how to handle the basic implements of labour. Since the amount of time spent on natural sciences and mathematics is longer than it was in the seven-year schools, the eight-year schools are able to organize more thorough teaching of such subjects as mathematics, physics, chemistry and biology, an arrangement which will certainly facilitate the development of polytechnical knowledge and skills.

As regards mathematics, the pupils in grades V–VIII take a complete course in arithmetic; in their second half-year in grade VI, they begin an algebra course which continues right up to the end of the eighth year and ends up with quadratic equations. Grades VI–VIII take geometry, including a simplified but systematic course in plane geometry, and acquire some idea of solid geometry, though their study of the latter is not systematic and is confined to the minimum necessary for calculating the volume of solids. The grade VIII geometry course includes the study of the trigonometry of acute angles, which is important from the practical

95

point of view and essential as a basis for the study of physics and the acquisition of a polytechnical education. Considerable stress is laid in these lessons on teaching pupils to make practical measurements, calculations and computations, including the measurement of surfaces and volumes.

Since a knowledge of physics is regarded as the basis for training the pupils for work of all kinds, the curricula and syllabus cover the elements of all the main branches of physics such as mechanics, sound, heat, electricity and light. The pupils also acquire practical skills and work habits and the ability to carry out observations and experiments, measure different physical quantities and apply their knowledge for the solution of various technical problems in physics. More than any other subject in this course, the study of physics helps to give pupils a broader polytechnical outlook and familiarize them with power engineering, machines and engines and the uses of electricity in production. With the time now allotted to physics in the curriculum, the pupils are able to spend more time on demonstration and laboratory experiments, solving problems and visiting production plants.

Grades V–VIII also take an elementary course in chemistry in close connexion with the physics course. The time allotted to this subject is slightly longer than in the seven-year schools. The course covers the rudiments of chemical elements, simple substances and compounds, and their molecular and atomic structure, and the main types of chemical transformations and the laws which govern them. Pupils study the properties and practical applications of such substances as oxygen, hydrogen, the oxides, acids, alkalis, salts and organic substances, and also learn about fuel and its uses, iron and steel production, and mineral fertilizers and their use in agriculture. Through studying the production of certain salts, they acquire a preliminary insight into the chemical industry.

Through laboratory work, finally, the students gain practical experience of handling substances, assembling apparatus, and carrying out chemical changes.

In the biology course, they study botany, zoology, human anatomy and physiology, hygiene and sanitation; and they also make a fairly detailed study of the biological principles involved in agricultural and livestock production and the suppression of agricultural pests and diseases.

In addition they take an elementary course in geography comprising the physical geography of the various continents and the geography of the U.S.S.R. They also learn to read and prepare maps.

The mathematics, physics, chemistry, biology and geography

syllabuses allow time for visiting undertakings engaged in various branches of production, seeing films dealing with production, and engaging in various practical occupations designed to link class instruction with everyday life and production and give the children a polytechnical outlook, to teach them practical skills and to show them how to apply scientific knowledge in practice.

Great emphasis is laid in the eight-year schools on aesthetic training, in the form of lessons in drawing, singing, music, litera- ture, etc., during which the children, besides reading literary works and learning singing and drawing, become acquainted with outstanding works of art, music and literature, and learn about the lives of famous artists, sculptors, composers and musicians, and writers. In grades V–VIII, a certain amount of time is devoted in the drawing lessons to technical drawing, with its close bearing on labour. From grade VII onwards there is a course in draughtsmanship which carries straight on from the earlier drawing lessons, and is an important feature in polytechnical education and labour training.

The physical culture periods for grades V–VIII cover general gymnastics and various types of sport. The school programme includes a daily drill lesson taken at many schools by all the children together, to the accompaniment of the radio.

The distinguishing feature of the instruction for grades V–VIII is the emphasis on education for work, which takes the form of manual training, participation in socially useful work, production practice and also, as stated earlier, the acquisition of a poly- technical outlook and technical skills through lessons in general education.

The pupils in those grades also learn to do simple metalwork (fitting and assembling) and electrical work, and study crop cultivation, and raise and care for small farm animals. In addition, the boys do woodwork and the girls are taught home economics (sewing, cooking, housework). It is in these classes that children receive their first training in operating machines and machine tools (drilling machines, lathes, sewing machines, etc.), and learn to make and read sketches and simple blueprints, study the technology of materials, and visit production plants in order to learn about machine operation and compare it with manual work.

In the process of their manual training, the children produce useful objects; the time allocated for socially useful work and production practice is spent entirely on producing things they need, making educational equipment and teaching aids for the school, improving the amenities of the school building and grounds, planting trees and shrubs in nearby streets and squares, looking after public gardens, parks and boulevards, executing simple orders from nursery schools, industrial and other enterprises, collective and State farms in the school workshops, doing agricultural jobs on experimental school plots and on collective and State farms, and so on.

Thanks to their manual training, the socially useful work they perform and their visits to various plants, the children become acquainted with different types of work, gather information giving them a basis on which to choose their careers, prepare themselves psychologically for taking up work on leaving school; and learn how to combine intellectual and physical work.

All the boys and girls attending school follow the same programme and take all the subjects included in the curriculum. In order to cater for children with a special bent or talent, or a special interest in a particular branch of science or technology or in a particular activity, Soviet schools have a well-developed system of out-of-class courses, 'circles' or clubs, evening events and lectures. Participation in out-of-class work is voluntary, and is based on activity by the children themselves.

The school year begins on 1 September and ends on the following dates: for grades I–IV on 31 May; for grades V–VII on 19 June; for grade VIII on 25 June (children in this grade take the school-leaving examination). The school year is divided into four terms, with a holiday between each. The duration of the school year is: 35 weeks for grades I–IV; 38 weeks for grades V–VII (including two weeks of production practice); and 39 weeks for grade VIII (including two weeks of production practice and two weeks for preparing for and taking the school-leaving examinations).

THE CURRICULA AND SYLLABUSES FOR SECONDARY SCHOOLS

The curriculum and syllabuses for secondary polytechnical schools (see Tables 3 and 4), providing general education together with production training, are designed to provide pupils who have completed the eight-year school course with a complete secondary education qualifying them for entering a higher education establishment as well as with vocational training for work in one of the branches of the national economy or cultural life. Two-thirds of the teaching time is spent on general educational and polytechnical subjects and one-third on production training and productive work. The principle of combining academic education with socially productive work is carried into effect by sending

TABLE 3. Timetable for an urban secondary school providing production training

Subjects taught	Number of periods per week for each grade			Total number of periods	
	IX	X	XI	Per week	Per year
Literature	3	3	3	9	339
Mathematics . . .	4	4	4	12	452
History	2	3	4	9	335
Principles of political knowledge . . .	—	—	2	2	70
Economic geography .	—	2	2	4	148
Physics	4	4	2	10	382
Astronomy	—	1	—	1	39
Chemistry	2	3	2	7	265
Biology	3	—	—	3	117
Technical drawing .	2	—	—	2	78
Foreign language . .	2	2	3	7	261
Physical culture . .	2	2	2	6	226
Total	24	24	24	72	2712
General technical subjects, production training (theoretical and practical), and productive work .	12	12	12	36	1356
GENERAL TOTAL .	36	36	36	108	4068
Optional subjects . .	2	2	2	6	226

pupils to work in industrial undertakings on collective and State farms, on building projects and in cultural institutions.

The purpose is to give boys and girls advanced scientific training fitting them to continue their studies at higher education establishments and to accustom them to work as a necessary preparation for their post-school careers. Practical work in these schools is an important feature of education and upbringing and constitutes the main basis of the pupils' moral training.

The evening secondary schools (see Table 5) cater for boys and girls who have completed the eight-year school course and are either employed in industry or doing cultural or social work. These schools provide them with a complete secondary education and improve their professional competence.

TABLE 4. Timetable for a rural secondary school providing production training

Subjects taught	Number of periods per week for each grade			Total number of periods	
	IX	X	XI	Per week	Per year
Literature	4	3	4	11	338
Mathematics . . .	5	4/5	5	14.5	445
History	3	4	4	11	338
Principles of political knowledge . . .	—	—	2	2	64
Economic geography .	—	3/2	2/3	5	155
Physics	5	5	3/2	12.5	380
Astronomy	—	1	—	1	30
Chemistry	2/3	3	3	8.5	261
Biology	4	—	—	4	120
Technical drawing .	3/2	—	—	2.5	75
Foreign language . .	3	3	3	9	276
Physical culture . .	2	2	3	7	216
Total	31	28	29	88	2698
Principles of agricultural production and production training (theoretical and practical) . . .	5	8	7	20	614
Total	36	36	36	108	3312
Production work according to season:					
number of days .	54	54	18	—	126
number of hours .	324	324	108	—	756
GENERAL TOTAL .	—	—	—	—	4068
Optional subjects . .	2	2	2	6	184

The curricula and syllabuses for secondary schools are designed to raise the standard of general and polytechnical education above that reached by the ten-year schools. The eight-year schools provide the necessary basis for this and prepare children more effectively than seven-year schools for the second stage of polytechnical and vocational education.

A great deal of attention is paid in the two above-mentioned types of secondary school to giving young people a better education

TABLE 5. Timetable for evening (shift, seasonal) secondary general-education schools

Subjects taught	Number of periods per week for each grade			Total number of periods per week
	IX	X	XI	
Literature	2	2	2	6
Mathematics . . .	3	3	3	9
History	1	2/1	2	4.5
Principles of political knowledge . . .	—	—	1	1
Economic geography .	—	2/1	1/2	3
Physics	3	3	2	8
Astronomy	—	0/1	—	0.5
Chemistry . . .	1/2	2	2/1	5
Biology	2/1	—	—	1.5
Technical drawing .	1/2	—	—	1.5
Foreign language . .	2/1	1/2	2	5
Total	15	15	15	45
Optional subjects for improving the student's trade rating .	2	2	2	6
Tutorials	3	3	3	9
GENERAL TOTAL .	20	20	20	60

in the humanities. Grades IX–XI take a course in the history of pre-revolutionary and Soviet literature in which they study the outstanding works of the peoples of the U.S.S.R. and foreign classics. The study of history has also become more thorough and covers more ground. Pupils take a course on the history of the U.S.S.R., modern and recent, and a course is to be arranged from the 1961/62 school year onwards on the principles of political knowledge. On the basis of the physical geography taught in eight-year schools, the pupils make a serious study of the economic geography of foreign countries and the economic geography of the U.S.S.R., while they also continue their study of a foreign language, with the main emphasis, here again, on developing fluency of speech and on reading, understanding and translating simple foreign texts.

The level of instruction in natural sciences and mathematics in these grades is also being raised. In mathematics, the pupils take a systematic course in elementary algebra, geometry and trigonometry, functions and their analysis, and derived functions. Great

101

importance is also attached to teaching the pupils how to use slide-rules and made approximate calculations and measurements of distances, areas and the volume of solids.

In the technical-drawing lessons the pupils are taught how to execute and interpret technical drawings.

In addition, there is a full course in elementary physics, including such subjects as atomic physics, supersonics and the physical properties of plastics. The pupils learn about the artificial satellites of the earth and sun, and study the physical principles of modern power engineering, the use of electric power in production, the physical principles governing the all-round mechanization and automation of production, and the technical mechanism of transport and communications.

In chemistry, they study the main groups of Mendeleev's periodic system of elements and the main classes of organic compounds, including the properties, structure, classification and methods of synthesis of polymers, as well as the general scientific principles governing the chemical and metallurgical industries, and the application of chemicals in industry, agriculture, building, transport and everyday life.

There is also a course in general biology which includes the principles of Darwinism formerly taught in the ten-year schools and which provides a good grounding for study of the principles of agriculture in that it gives students a scientific and innovating approach to the subject.

The astronomy course acquaints students with the main problems of the universe, and serves, in combination with the other natural-science subjects, to develop their materialist outlook.

Under the section 'General technical subjects and production training', the curriculum for urban and rural secondary schools provides for instruction on the rudiments of machine operation and electrical engineering, these being of great importance in raising the level of polytechnical education. The pupils are familiarized with machine parts, handle various mechanisms, machine tools, electrical measuring instruments, transformers, d.c. and a.c. generators, and are taught the elementary principles governing the all-round mechanization and automation of production.

In production training, they are given theoretical and practical instruction and acquire various technical skills in preparation for mastering the trade or speciality of their choice. The practical instruction is given on the job in training sections and workshops, in training shops at factories and plants, on experimental training plots and in training brigades attached to collective and State farms. The production training programme is so designed that the pupils are put to work as soon as possible in the undertaking themselves, after which their independent work is coupled with further improvements in their trade qualifications.

The object of the evening-shift secondary schools is to enable young workers to improve their qualifications by studying general technical and technological subjects, including questions relating to the all-round mechanization and automation of industrial production, the all-round mechanization of agriculture and scientific methods of modern farming.

All the subjects covered by the curriculum as well as all the syllabus matter are compulsory for boys and girls alike. The optional subjects, which they choose themselves, are intended to develop a special interest in a particular branch of science, technique, production or culture, and to cater for their particular talents or inclinations.

The autonomous Republics are entitled to introduce such changes into such curricula and syllabuses for eight-year and secondary schools as are necessary in order to provide for the teaching of the mother tongue and its literature, and to enable pupils to make a more detailed study of the history and geography of their own Republic.

The school year for secondary schools providing industrial training is from 1 September to 25 June (including, for grade XI, four weeks spent preparing for and taking examinations). It is divided into two terms, from 1 September to 29 December, and from 11 January to the end of the class work. The length of the autumn, winter and spring holiday periods is the same as for the eight-year schools, and the average length of the school year for all grades is thirty-nine weeks.

For the evening secondary schools, the length of the school year is thirty-six weeks for urban establishments and twenty-six weeks for rural ones, plus an extra three weeks for grade XI for the final examinations.

Boarding-schools follow either the eight-year school curricula and syllabuses or those of the secondary school providing production training.

COMPARISON BETWEEN THE NEW AND PRE-REFORM CURRICULA

During the period of reconstruction of the national economy and the first five-year plans the Soviet Union solved the problem of training senior and intermediate personnel for all branches of the economy and cultural life by having the secondary schools

103

concentrate on raising the general educational level and preparing students for admission to the *tehnikums*[1] and higher education establishments and by giving them a thorough general education and a good grounding in the fundamentals of science. The curriculum for general-education secondary schools at that period devoted a substantially larger proportion of time to general subjects. Subsequently, the emphasis was shifted slightly in favour of polytechnical subjects. Thus in the curriculum adopted in 1955 for ten-year schools the proportion of time allotted to the various subjects was as follows: general subjects (humanities group), 4,653 periods (47 per cent); general subjects (natural sciences and mathematics group), 3,671 periods (37.2 per cent); technical and practical work, production practice, excursions, 716 periods (7.3 per cent); artistic training and physical culture, 856 periods (8.5 per cent).

It is true that this curriculum did indeed promote all-round education; but the fact that over 80 per cent of the total teaching time was spent on the elements of science and only 7.3 per cent on manual, technical and practical work and excursions shows that education of young people under the conditions imposed by it was somewhat one-sided.

In the new curricula and syllabuses for eleven-year polytechnical schools providing general education combined with production training, the proportion of time devoted to the different groups of subjects has changed, as the following figures show: general subjects (humanities group), 4,550 periods (36 per cent); general subjects (natural sciences and mathematics group), 4,135 periods (32.5 per cent); manual and trade training, production practice, production training and general technical subjects, 2,671 periods (21 per cent); artistic training and physical culture 1,323 periods (10.5 per cent).

A simple comparison of these two sets of figures shows that the new curricula achieve a better balance between general and polytechnical education, labour training, artistic education and physical culture.

The advantages of the new curriculum become more apparent when they are considered in relation to the education of children of different age-groups.

The eight-year school curriculum ensures a higher standard of general and polytechnical education than the former seven-year school; 7,300 periods are devoted to general and polytechnical subjects as against 6,256 periods in the seven-year school. Again, it allocates seventy-two periods weekly in all grades for Russian

---

1. Specialized vocational secondary school.

language and literature, as against seventy-one periods in the seven-year school; eleven periods instead of eight for history (which now includes lessons on the social and State structure of the Soviet Union); seven periods instead of five for physics; thirteen periods for a foreign language as against eleven; and twice as much time for technical drawing.

The increase in the amount of time spent on teaching general-education subjects makes it possible in some cases to extend the ground covered in varying degrees, to give more scope and practicality to the subjects taught, and—particularly important— gives the pupils a firmer and more conscious grasp of the knowledge they acquire. In Russian language, for example, the material formerly covered in three years (seventy-one periods weekly in all grades) is now covered in four years, with the result that it can be studied more systematically and effectively, eliminating the overloading which the syllabus formerly entailed. Another factor in raising the standard in this subject is that the new draft syllabus included practice in reading, speaking and writing the language, in addition to learning the grammar, with a special section being prepared for each class covering 'Sample methods and subjects for work on coherent speech development'.

The new curriculum for eight-year schools also permits a more thorough study of arithmetic, geometry and algebra by paying more attention in the mathematics syllabus to the practical aspects of the subject without, however, neglecting the theoretical side (particularly in the senior grades). A great deal of attention is devoted to the study of decimals in view of their importance in everyday life; and to the calculation of area and volume, the use of simple tables and the slide-rule, and the making of approximate calculations.

The physics course, again, deals more fully with mechanics and electricity, and also includes a study of sound and light and the structure of the atom, which seven-year schools did not touch.

The chemistry course has similarly been extended and includes a study of carbon and its combinations, fuel, fertilizers and iron metallurgy.

The children also take a complete course in geography, biology and history, whereas this was not so at the seven-year school.

But the basic distinction between the seven-year and eight-year school is that the latter provides for systematic education for productive work so as to prepare children, both psychologically and practically, for socially useful work.

In the secondary schools (grades IX–XI) the teaching of general and polytechnical subjects is planned at a higher level than that in the ten-year schools, thanks to the higher standard that children will have attained before entering grade IX, as a result of the increased number of periods a week devoted to certain subjects and the better selection and arrangement of the teaching material and the inclusion in it of new scientific questions. Another factor making for a higher standard of general education is that it is further developed in the course of general technical training, production training and production work. Thanks to production training, polytechnical education achieves its logical culmination in actual work in the modern production system.

CREATIVE ROLE OF TEACHERS IN IMPLEMENTING THE SYLLABUSES

The curricula and syllabuses only stipulate, in a general way, the subjects to be taught in each class and the manual and technical skills to be acquired; for the rest, the individual schools and teachers are left free to use their own initiative. Every school and every teacher has the possibility of making changes in the selection of scientific and technical teaching material and altering teaching methods accordingly. In teaching their subject, they are encouraged to take every opportunity of bringing in material from everyday life and the practical construction of communism, and they are free to tell their pupils about the latest achievements of science and engineering not included in the syllabus. In addition, every teacher 'localizes' the State syllabus so as to take account of the special features of the district in which his school is located. For instance, biology teachers adapt the syllabus to make room for instruction about local flora and fauna; geography teachers include data on their area; physics and chemistry teachers include data on local production; literature teachers tell the children about the works of regional writers and poets, history teachers devote special attention to the history of their particular province, region or Republic; and so on. Teachers are also allowed to rearrange the time devoted to the various items of the syllabus as they think fit. All this enables them to adapt their teaching of a subject to their own inclinations and the interests of their pupils.

The only stipulation is that by the end of the school year the children will have acquired all the knowledge and skills required under the State syllabuses and be ready to move up into the next grade.

The teachers also examine the syllabus in the light of practical experience and propose any improvements they consider necessary, and the Ministry of Education takes careful note of all proposals of this kind.

In implementing the syllabus teachers can count on any help and advice they may need either in or out of school. Each school has its teachers' groups to deal with teaching methods for each subject or set of subjects, while every district has its methodological group for each subject. The district methodological groups and 'method rooms', and the regional, provincial and Republic institutes for the further training of teachers, give regular assistance to teachers, discuss their experience and take steps to make it known to other teachers. Before the beginning of the school year and during the winter holidays, district conferences of teachers and methodological group meetings are held in order to acquaint teachers with the latest achievements of science and technology and successful experiences in implementing the syllabuses and to advise and instruct them about their work; while every year or every other year 'pedagogical readings' are organized in all regions, provinces and autonomous Republics to enable teachers to exchange experiences. Those methods which proved most successful are subsequently introduced into the schools.

As regards the syllabuses for manual, technical and production training, these are worked out by the Ministry of Education and the Academy of Pedagogical Sciences but as guiding lines only. Taking them as a basis, the schools draw up their own detailed syllabuses for socially useful work and for production training in the trades for which they cater.

In the Soviet Union the individual work done by teachers in implementing the curricula and syllabuses is held in high esteem and the results achieved are publicized in local and national newspapers and periodicals. In addition to general pedagogical reviews, there are specialized journals dealing with individual subjects; while every year the pedagogical publishing houses of the Ministries of Education and the Academy of Pedagogical Sciences Publishing House produce a large number of books describing the results achieved and the initiative shown by Soviet teachers in carrying out their job.

CHAPTER VI

THE TASKS, PRINCIPLES AND SCOPE OF POLYTECHNICAL EDUCATION IN SOVIET SCHOOLS

by S. G. Shapovalenko

THE TASKS AND PRINCIPLES OF POLYTECHNICAL EDUCATION

The tasks and content of polytechnical education during the period of communist construction are determined by the training requirements in respect of production personnel as dictated by scientific and technical progress and by the need to create the material and technical basis for communism.

Polytechnical education, in preparing pupils for life and work, has to carry out the following tasks:

Familiarize them with the main branches of modern production—their techniques, technology and organization.

Acquaint them with the general scientific principles of socialist production.

Impart general technical and vocational skills.

Involve them in the socially productive work of the Soviet people.

Promote a further improvement in the communist education of the rising generations and the increased efficiency of production in general.

The main principle of polytechnical education is its subordination to the aims of communist upbringing which require pupils to be active and energetic members of a communist society capable of living and working in communist style.

'Education is only part of the work of the schools and the teachers, although a very important and vital part. But education by itself does not amount to much.' This was how N. S. Khrushchev put it at the All-Russian Conference of Teachers in 1960. 'But the work of the pupils', he went on, 'is important not merely for its own sake and not so much for what it produces. The main thing is to use their productive work correctly and in every possible way to inculcate in the young people a love of work for the common good. The schools must teach their pupils how to work as a team: that is, in the last analysis, how to live and work as communists.

Remember what Vladimir Ilych Lenin said about communist labour in 1920: "It is willing labour," he said, "labour beyond the norm, labour carried out without thought of reward, as a result of having the habit of working for the common good, labour which is a necessity for every healthy organism. It is for such labour that we must prepare our children and our young people." "[1]

It is these tasks of ensuring the communist upbringing of the rising generation and moulding their behaviour in the spirit of communist ethics that polytechnical education in Soviet schools subserves.

Another vital principle of polytechnical education, as indeed of all education and training in Soviet schools, is the close link between instruction and life, work and the practical construction of communism.

Where polytechnical education is divorced from productive labour, it becomes unrealistic, one-sided and depreciated. The participation of pupils in actual work enables theoretical knowledge of production to take concrete shape and teaches them how to apply their knowledge. In the course of productive labour, work skills are formed, developed and perfected.

Pedagogical scientists and teachers are required to study the present situation and development trends in the main sectors of socialist production in order to derive the available present and future material from this study and include it in the polytechnical education process. Up-to-date and forward-looking polytechnical education is an important principle flowing from the broader principle of linking education and upbringing with life.

In the process of polytechnical education, the pupils become acquainted with the basic measures being taken to develop the main branches of the national economy in their own part of the country, and through their work take a personal part, according to their capabilities, in bringing about this development in local undertakings (particularly those which are patrons of their schools). The local undertakings assist in the instruction and upbringing of the children by supplying key personnel and material resources, arranging excursions and organizing the children's work in their workshops and brigades.

The supporting undertakings play an important part in keeping the training on a practical footing and ensure the progressive familiarization of the pupils with local production processes and industrial principles in general.

---

1. N. S. Khrushchev, *A Plea for Lasting Peace in the Name of the Happiness and Bright Future of the Peoples*, Moscow, 1960, p. 26–8.

In oil-producing regions, the supporting enterprises will generally be the oilwells and refineries; in coal- and steel-producing areas, the mines and steelworks; in textile areas, the mills; in the Far North regions, the reindeer-breeding, fur and fishing industries, and so on.

The supporting undertakings provide opportunities for developing a concrete acquaintance with a variety of questions relating to power, for example, for every type of production has its own power basis; while its machine park can serve to give a graphic idea of the principles of machine construction, machine operation and electrical engineering. They all, at one point or other, apply physical, mechanical or chemical processes in the treatment of their materials, and these processes can be demonstrated to the pupils. Finally, they all provide an excellent presentation of the characteristics common to the whole range of production branches. The fact remains, however, despite their importance in this respect, that no single factory is sufficient, on its own, to give pupils the information they need on the main production branches or on those of particular importance in their own region. This drawback can be overcome by staging a series of excursions to undertakings in the region, and arrangements of this kind have been made and carried out by a number of schools in co-operation with the National Economic Councils, agricultural administrations and other economic organizations.

The next important principle in polytechnical education is that of linking it with the general education and vocational training of the pupils.

General education gives pupils a basic scientific knowledge of nature, human society and thought, and the corresponding essential ability and skills. This general scientific knowledge provides the foundation for a scientific outlook, greatly facilitates the development of the pupils' cognitive powers and capacity, and is the basis of specialized professional knowledge and skills.

However, it can only play its part if it is linked with life, production and the practical construction of communism. Soviet teachers give both theoretical and practical instruction on how to apply scientific knowledge in the building of communism—in the national economy as in the fields of culture, health, public welfare and labour.

Based on general education (on the study of mathematics, physics, chemistry, biology, geography, drawing, history, the principles of political science, and other subjects), polytechnical education makes the widest use of this material for its own specific ends as a foundation for the accumulation of knowledge and skills in the techniques, technology, organization and economics of modern production, and as a vital component thereof.

Conversely, polytechnical education based on general education has an extremely beneficial influence on the teaching of general-education subjects, since it helps to eliminate the random element in determining the questions of production technology, organization and economics in which the study of the elements of natural and social sciences must be linked with life and work in order to prevent it from becoming formal and bookish. When general-education knowledge and skills are applied to the study of these subjects they become alive and significant, and they are more firmly implanted in the mind of the pupil.

Furthermore, polytechnical education helps to raise the level of general education by giving expression to the demands of life and work, by stimulating the inclusion among general-education subjects of new aspects of science which have found application in modern production. A close link between general and poly-technical education is thus essential for both of them in order to avoid formalism and abstractness, and in order to raise their level at schools.

Based on general and polytechnical education alike, vocational training provides the knowledge and skills necessary in order to carry out a given type of work at the level of productivity normally achieved in society; and the knowledge and skills developed by the former are a fundamental and integral part of those of the latter. Technical progress imposes very high standards on the vocational and technical training of workers in socialist industry and that training, in turn, imposes higher standards on general and polytechnical education. This explains the present task of raising the level of general and polytechnical education and making full use of them for vocational training, arranging the curriculum accordingly so as to establish a series of links between general-education subjects (physics, chemistry, biology, etc.), general technical subjects (machine operation, electrical engineering) and specialized subjects.

Founded on general and polytechnical education, vocational training in its turn exerts a retroactive influence on them, determining their scope to some extent, increasing the interest, concreteness and applicability of the knowledge imparted by them and creating the right conditions for the formation of a communist world outlook and code of behaviour.

Experience of well-planned production training closely linked with socially useful labour and with general and polytechnical education has shown that pupils in grades IX to XI can successfully master trades and acquire work skills in production while making a substantial contribution towards increasing the material good of society and developing respect and love for work and the habit of working for the common weal so that they leave school fully prepared for life and work. Polytechnical and production training are successfully serving the main aims for which the schools were reorganized. 'The main thing in reorganizing the schools', said N. S. Khrushchev at the All-Russian Conference of Teachers, 'is to combine instruction with socially useful work and intensify the educational efforts of the schools. The struggle for the triumph of communism requires an all-round balanced development of Soviet man. This means not only that he must master the sum total of knowledge of nature, technology and society but must also learn how to make practical use of this knowledge in order to take a direct part in the work of communist construction. We must not only acquire knowledge, but must convert it into profound ideological convictions, such as to give rise to powerful feelings expressing themselves in action and in deeds for the good of the nation.'[1]

The significance of the two principles of polytechnical education referred to above—the linking of instruction with labour, and the linking of polytechnical education with general education and vocational training—in preparing the rising generation for work and in developing social production was explained by N. S. Khrushchev at the above Conference. 'There are some people', he said, 'who reason as follows: "What is the use of trigonometry to a dairymaid, or of biology to a fitter or electrician?" In their opinion, physical labour does not demand much education, and hence it is not worth bothering children with the sciences unless they are assured of a place at a university. This is quite wrong. . . . Knowledge is also essential for the dairymaid or the shepherd. The worker, too, whatever his work, needs knowledge, for knowledge makes life easier and gayer. Take the example of the Ryazan region. The most valuable and vital achievement of the Ryazan region schools is their success in inculcating in young people a love of labour and an interest in agriculture. Thousands of boys and girls with secondary education have flocked into the collective and State farms of the region during the past three years. And it has turned out to be true, in fact, that a knowledge of physics, chemistry and trigonometry is of very great use to dairymaids. The high educational level of the new generation has been a vital factor in the successes of this region and in increasing labour productivity.

---

1. ibid., p. 26.

Other regions and districts should ponder well this example—and not merely ponder but make apt use of the experience of their Ryazan comrades.'[1]

Finally, there is a further principle to be noted: that every individual production object or process, when carefully studied, is seen to be representative of a specific class of production phenomena. In an individual machine, for example, there are constructional elements (parts, units, mechanisms) which often recur in the most varied types of machines. Or, again, in analysing the processing of parts on a lathe, the same general principles governing the machine-cutting of the most varied materials recur.

Taking this principle as a guide, the schools are able, in the process of polytechnical instruction, to familiarize their pupils with the principles of industry in general by studying a relatively small number of typical production objects and processes.

The method of disclosing the general in the particular is based on comparison; and the comparison of machines, lathes, technical processes, properties of materials and so on should run all through polytechnical instruction.

It is the above-mentioned principles which are followed in choosing teaching material, preparing syllabuses, selecting types of work and determining the methods to be used in polytechnical education, i.e., in organizing all aspects of polytechnical education and carrying them through.

ANALYSIS OF THE MAIN BRANCHES OF PRODUCTION WITH
A VIEW TO SELECTING TEACHING MATERIAL FOR POLYTECHNICAL
EDUCATION

In the first volume of *Kapital*, Karl Marx notes that the production process has three main factors: material, which is subjected to processing; processing tools, whereby the material is converted into finished products; and labour, which consists of converting the material into finished products by means of processing tools. A production process arises and exists only when these three factors are found in interaction.

It follows from this that a concrete knowledge of each of the main branches of production can only be obtained if the pupils are familiarized with: (a) the output of production (pattern, composition, properties and field of utilization); (b) the raw material and other materials used; (c) the scientific principles

---

1. ibid., p. 29–30.

governing the conversion of the raw materials into the finished product; (d) the technology of production; (e) the technique of production (construction and operation of machines, machine tools and equipment); (f) the organization of production (planning, supply of energy and raw materials, technical organization of the production process, organization of labour). The question is, how much knowledge of each branch of production should the pupil be expected to acquire?

In answer to this question, an analysis was made of the main branches of production to determine the amount of information on each branch which pupils needed to be given in order to satisfy the requirements of polytechnical education. A brief examination of the analysis for power production, chemical production and agriculture will serve as an example.

Power production

Modern industry, agriculture and transport use various forms of power: mechanical, chemical, internal combustion, thermal electric and light. All these forms of power have the property of being able to change. When one form changes into another, an amount of energy is conserved. This special characteristic is revealed by the fundamental law of modern science—that of the conservation and transformation of energy.

The sources of power are as follows: moving water (rivers) and air (wind); fuel (coal, oil, peat, wood, shales and natural gases) which releases energy during combustion; and various chemical elements which release atomic energy in nuclear reactors.

To make use of the energy of moving water, dams are built and the water level is raised, after which the water is released through special sluices and the energy of the falling water is used to drive hydraulic turbines coupled to electric generators, thus producing electric power.

The operation of hydro-electric stations is based on the laws of mechanics (hydraulics) and electricity. For an all-round polytechnical knowledge and a solidly based modern polytechnical education it is absolutely essential to study these laws and understand how they are used by man to obtain vast quantities of power, how hydraulic turbines and electric generators are constructed and operate, and how the electricity thus obtained is transmitted over long distances.

Energy is obtained by burning different kinds of fuels. The thermal power thus obtained is used in production processes, but more often it is used for obtaining steam or gas, the energy of which is then used for technological purposes such as drying, evaporating, heating and so on, or for obtaining mechanical power by means of steam engines and turbines, internal combustion engines and jet engines. The mechanical power of steam engines and internal combustion engines is easily turned into electric power. Steam engines, steam turbines, internal combustion engines and jet engines are widely used, both separately and in conjunction with electric generators and electric motors, in transport (diesel-engined ships and diesel locomotives, motor vehicles, aircraft, etc.) and in industry and agriculture (steam power in factories, tractors in agriculture, and so on).

The utilization of fuel, its conversion into thermal energy, and the means of increasing its efficiency are based on the laws of combustion, which are studied in chemistry, and on the laws of thermodynamics, which are dealt with in physics. The production of steam and gas, and their utilization for producing mechanical and electric power, are based on the laws of thermodynamics, electricity and mechanics. In view of the enormous significance of thermal energy in the Soviet national economy, secondary school children are required to learn about the various types of fuel, how they should be burnt, and the construction and principles of operation of thermal equipment.

As to wind power, a large variety of wind motors have been developed in order to make use of it. The mechanical energy thus obtained is used for driving water pumps and other equipment, or for generating electricity. The construction and operation of wind motors is based on the application of the laws of aerodynamics.

Electric power has the following notable features: (a) it can be converted into other forms of energy; (b) it can be stored, and hence used when required; (c) it can be used in exactly the amounts required; (d) it can be transmitted over long distances; (e) it can be easily fed to the machines running on it; (f) it can readily be converted into mechanical power which is economical and practical; and (g) it is readily convertible into light, thermal or chemical energy.

These features of electric power have led, as already noted, to its widespread use in all branches of production and technique.

From all the above material, the following items have been included in the subject matter of polytechnical education so as to familiarize the pupils with the production and utilization of power:
1. Types of energy. Law of the conservation and transformation of energy.
2. Moving water and air as power sources. Natural and artificial fuels (solid, liquid and gaseous). Composition and properties

of the various types of fuel. Combustion of fuel. Ways of obtaining artificial types of fuel. Phenomena responsible for the formation of these sources of energy in the earth. Geographical location of the power resources of the Soviet Union. Nuclear reaction as a source of atomic energy.

3. Laws of hydraulics, aerodynamics, thermodynamics, electricity and chemistry as the scientific basis of the production of power.
4. Construction and principles of operation of hydraulic, thermal and electrical machines used for power production.
5. Characteristics of electric power. Electric power as a universal form of energy. Transformation of electric power and its long-distance transmission. Electric generators. Accumulators. Electric motors. Electric propulsion. Use of electricity for technological purposes. Use of electricity for lighting. Use of electricity for the automation of production.
6. Electrification as the main line of technical progress. Lenin's theses on the electrification of the country. Achievements in the electrification of the Soviet Union during the years of Soviet power. Electrification of the country under the national economic development plan.

The techniques of power production are varied and complex, and it is impossible, of course, to familiarize the pupils in sufficient detail with every type of prime mover. Obviously, the pupils will be instructed in greater detail on electric motors and internal combustion engines, as these are the most widespread in modern production and will have to be dealt with most often in after-school life. It is essential to teach the children how to handle electric motors in practice, and how to drive a car or tractor. As regards the remaining details of power technology, all that is necessary is to make them familiar with its physical principles.

Chemical production

The special feature of chemical production consists of the processing of natural and artificial materials, resulting in a change in their chemical composition or structure, thus giving rise to substances (materials) possessing new qualities.

Chemical production provides other branches of production with the most varied products: metals and alloys, artificial types of fuel, rubber, artificial and synthetic fibres, plastics, building materials, fertilizers, chemicals for combating plant pests and diseases, and so on. The natural materials used for chemical processing are: minerals, coal, oil, natural and manufactured gases, wood, etc.

116

Chemical production covers a very wide range. First of all, there is metallurgical production, which may be chemical (production and refining of metals) or physico-mechanical (rolling, wire-drawing etc.) in character. Then there is the preparation of various types of artificial fuel, lubricating oils, and materials for organic and inorganic industrial chemistry (gasification of fuel, refining and cracking of oil, coking of coal, conversion of solid fuel into liquid fuel, and so on). Chemical production also covers the production of glass, cement, ceramics and other building materials. The chemical industry produces chemical fertilizers, insecticides and fungicides for agriculture, artificial fibres for the textile industry, plastics and rubber for the machine-construction industry, and so on.

It takes the waste material from other industries and converts them into valuable products. For example, sulphur dioxide, which is a by-product of copper and zinc smelting, is turned into sulphuric acid. Chemistry enables natural materials to be improved and given properties and qualities rendering them more valuable to man. Thus sawdust is turned into alcohol, rubber, methylated spirits, acetic acid, artificial silk and other useful products.

In order to turn natural materials and waste products into materials suitable for use in other branches of production or for satisfying human needs, various chemical reagents are necessary: acids, alkalis, salts, etc. Without these, it would obviously be impossible to carry out a single chemical reaction. The branch of the chemical industry which produces them is known as the basic (or heavy) chemical industry, and it covers the production of hydrochloric, nitric and sulphuric acids, the electrolytic production of alkalis and chlorine, etc. Heavy organic chemistry, as a further subdivision, covers the production of methylated spirits, formaldehyde, acetic acid, ethyl alcohol and other substances from which various organic compounds are synthesized. High-molecular organic compounds (rubber, plastics, artificial fibres) play an increasingly important part in modern industry, and their synthesis is carried out on the basis of methane, acetylene, ethylene and other simple products of the gasification and chemical treatment of coal and oil.

It is clearly impossible to teach pupils all about every branch of chemical production, and a study of its main branches is sufficient to familiarize them with the general principles. The main branches are those which supply the national economy with the most important types of materials and chemicals, and which thus play a decisive part in the chemicalization of the country as well as concentrate within themselves the most advanced scientific

117

principles applicable to the chemical industry as a whole. They are: (a) the heavy chemical industry[1] dealing with inorganic and organic substances, and the fertilizer industry; (b) the chemical processing of wood, coal and oil; (c) metallurgy; and (d) the building materials industry.

These branches of chemical production are most intimately connected with one another, and a good knowledge of them makes it easy to understand the other branches of chemical production, and the latter in general.

Every single branch of it, in fact, is based on carrying out chemical reactions, the main indices in respect of which (together with the increase in labour productivity and the reduction of production costs) are the speed of the reaction and the completeness of the degree of utilization of the reagents. The principles applied in order to speed up reactions and increase the degree of utilization are as follows: enrichment of the raw material, optimum development of the surface areas or reactants, use of optimum concentrations, temperatures and pressures, use of active catalysts, and use of counter-current and circulating processes. These principles govern the design of apparatus and the selection of the parameters for production processes in the chemical industry.

From a study of these main branches, the pupils can be taught, in a graphic and comprehensible manner, about the general principles of chemical production as a whole.

To understand those principles, it is essential, of course, to have some knowledge of general chemistry and not just a knowledge of the individual chemical reactions used in production: pupils have to be familiar with the laws governing the course of chemical reactions, including the effect of concentrations of the reactants, temperature, particle size and catalysts on the speed of reaction, and the disturbance of chemical equilibrium resulting from changes in concentration, temperature and pressure. Nor is a knowledge of chemistry sufficient on its own for mastering the principles of chemical production. A chemical process takes place by means of mechanical, thermal, electrical and other action on a particular substance, and a knowledge of physics and mathematics and their extensive application in elucidating chemical-production processes is essential for an understanding of the latter.

To sum up, the knowledge of chemical production which should be imparted to pupils as part of their polytechnical education is as follows:

---

1. The chemical industry is a component part of chemical production. The latter term is broader than the former.

1. Characteristics of chemical production as compared with the other main branches of production. Different types of chemical production.
2. Methods of speeding up chemical reactions and achieving complete utilization of the reactants: enrichment of the raw material, optimum development of the surface areas of the reactants, use of optimum concentrations, temperatures and pressures, and use of catalysts, counter-current and circulation processes.
3. Basic (heavy) inorganic chemical industry (production of hydrochloric acid by synthesis, production of sulphuric acid by the contact process, industrial synthesis of ammonia, production of nitrate fertilizers, electrolytic production of alkalis and chlorine); production of synthetic acetic acid as an example of heavy organic synthesis. Construction and principles of operation of typical equipment of the heavy chemical industry (kilns and furnaces, scrubbing and absorption towers, contact apparatus, refrigerators, heat exchangers, electrolytic vats, etc.).
4. Chemical processing of fuel. Gasification of coal and use of combustible gases as fuel and as raw material for the chemical industry. Coking of coal. Distillation and cracking of oil. Construction and principles of operation of gas generators, coke-oven batteries, pipe stills and cracking installations.
5. Metallurgy. Production of pig-iron and steel. Production of alloy steels. Production of aluminium from bauxite.
6. Production of building materials—glass, cement and ceramics.
7. Mechanization, automation and electrification of chemical production. Continuous flow in chemical production. Links with other branches of production; combined operation. Chemicalization of the national economy of the U.S.S.R. as one of the lines of technical progress. Achievements in chemicalizing the national economy. Geographical distribution of chemical production. Chemicalization targets under the national economic development plan.

In the course of their studies of chemistry, the pupils will need to learn about the properties of different materials processed in chemical production and ways of using the various chemical products (e.g., acids, alkalis, fertilizers, and insecticides) in the national economy.

Agricultural production

The characteristic feature of the agricultural production is the growing of plants and raising of livestock in order to provide food (grain, vegetables, meat, fats, dairy products, etc.) and commercial raw materials for the manufacture of clothing, footwear, food products and so on (leather, fibres, etc.).

The Communist Party has laid down the task of producing a sharp improvement in agriculture: increase in the yield of all crops, further increase in head of livestock together with an increase in the productivity of livestock, and in total commodity production from arable and stock farming by further consolidating and developing the social economy of collective farms and improving the work of State farms and technical repair stations (RTS) by introducing the latest techniques of running agricultural production.

The tasks facing agriculture are being solved on the basis of all-round mechanization, chemicalization, electrification and the application of the latest developments in agricultural economy and animal husbandry. An enormous part will be played in achieving these aims by soil improvement, the controlled selection and raising of agricultural plants and livestock, the correct combination of cultivation and stock-raising in a single farming unit and the rational organization of labour on collective and State farms.

In arable farming, it is possible to single out scientific agronomical knowledge which applies equally to the cultivation of field, orchard, industrial and food crops, perennial leys, etc. This basic knowledge covers general knowledge of the soil, conditions of growth and development of agricultural crops, soil working and fertilization, seed preparation, sowing, tending of plants, harvesting and the basis of crop rotation.

Apart from an explanation of the scientific bases of farming techniques, the pupils have to be given an understanding of the methods of soil preparation and plant cultivation which result in the creation of new heavy cropping varieties and increased fertility of the soil. Maize-growing has to be given particular attention.

Since all the basic farming operations are carried out in socialist agriculture by means of machinery and equipment, the pupils have to be familiarized with the agricultural machinery used for tilling the soil and for preparing and sowing the seeds and spreading fertilizers (seed-pickling machines, seed cleaners, seed drills, maize drills, and so on), for tending agricultural crops (extirpators, cultivators), and for harvesting (mowers, binders, threshers, combines).

In animal husbandry, similarly, attention has to be drawn to a number of essential aspects whose scientific basis must be understood by the pupils from the example of at least one or two types of livestock. Chief among these are the development of highly productive breeds of livestock, the feeding, maintenance and care of livestock and the rearing of young animals. Attention should be drawn at this point to the technical equipment for animal husbandry: automatic drinking troughs, feed cutters, mixers, milking machines, etc.

Account also has to be taken of the power basis of collective and State farms: tractors, power plants and electric and other motors.

The characteristic scientific basis of agriculture in general is, of course, biology. The provision of a sound and systematic knowledge of the fundamentals of plant and animal morphology, anatomy and physiology and the principles of Darwinism is therefore an essential task of general and polytechnical education. At the same time, agricultural production also rests on physics (inasmuch as it explains the scientific basis of mechanization and electrification) and on chemistry (inasmuch as it explains the scientific basis of the use of fertilizers, chemical means for combating plant pests and diseases, protection of machines from corrosion, and so on).

Hence polytechnical education should provide instruction on the following aspects of agricultural production:

1. Characteristics of agricultural production as compared with other branches of production. Branches of agriculture. Agricultural and veterinary science as the science of agricultural production. The tasks facing socialist agriculture.

2. Fundamentals of the morphology, anatomy and physiology of plants and livestock. Michurin's teachings as the scientific basis of agriculture.

3. General principles of the science of agriculture. Elements of soil science. Conditions of growth and development of agricultural plants (light, water, nutritive substances, heat, air, micro-organisms). Problems and methods of tilling the soil (ploughing, cultivating, harrowing). Nitrate, phosphate and potash fertilizers. Liming and chalking. Soil-dressing with mineral fertilizers. Local fertilizers: dung, compost, peat, soot and green manure. Cleaning and sorting of seeds. Seed pickling. Methods of sowing. Tending of crops. Scientific bases of crop rotation. Cultivation of maize, wheat (or rye) and other crops. Methods of controlled selection.

4. General principles of veterinary science. Conditions for the growth and development of livestock. Amount and preparation of fodder. General care of livestock and their young. Improving

the breed of livestock. Introduction of new breeds of highly productive livestock.

5. General construction and principles of operation of the main agricultural machines and prime movers. Tractors, electric tractors, ploughs, cultivators, harrows, seed drills, sorting machines, winnowers and threshers. The combine harvester as a combination of farm machines performing separate functions.

6. General principles for increasing crop yields. All-round mechanization, electrification and chemicalization. Soil improvement. Correct combination of arable and stock farming on a single farm.

7. Decisions of the Communist Party calling for a sharp improvement in agriculture and steps to implement them.

PROCEDURE FOR FAMILIARIZING PUPILS WITH THE MAIN BRANCHES OF PRODUCTION AND ITS GENERAL SCIENTIFIC PRINCIPLES

The task of familiarizing pupils with the main branches of production and imparting technical skills is carried out in the process of teaching the general-education and general technical subjects of manual and technical instruction and production training. Apart from systematic polytechnical instruction, the syllabuses for these subjects include excursions to factories and other undertakings, practical work in offices, on school experimental plots and in the factories themselves and the showing of films, slides and other visual teaching aids which deal with production and help to develop the pupils' polytechnical outlook.

In addition, they are taught the social and economic principles of socialist production during their history lessons, and the principles of political science both during those lessons and on their excursions in connexion with other subjects, during which production questions are studied.

During the natural-science lessons (especially physics), they learn about the all-round mechanization, automation and electrification of production; but in order to avoid drawing teachers of all subjects too deeply into the technical heart of these questions, and also to take account of the particularly great significance for mastering certain types of work and knowledge, their study has been singled out as a separate topic in grade VIII, and as separate courses (machine operation and electrical engineering) in grades IX–XI.

With a view to the further improvement of polytechnical education in grade XI at all types of schools, it is proposed to introduce, side-by-side with the work of the pupils in production, a finishing course on production principles, consisting of three main sections: mechanization and automation of production, methods of modern technology, and fundamentals of production organization and economics. This course will summarize and systematize all the polytechnical knowledge required by the pupils in studying the fundamentals of science and during manual and technical instruction and production training, and will supplement, deepen and develop this knowledge by explaining the nature of automatic systems of machines, the way in which they control, regulate and adjust themselves automatically and the effect of automation on production technology and organization. The idea is to give this instruction by using examples from various branches of production, with particular emphasis on the one in which the pupils are working. This will not only serve to broaden their polytechnical outlook but will also raise the level of their vocational training to the level required by modern needs. The course on the principles of production would be supplemented by excursions to undertakings, the showing of specially produced films, and practical work which will bring out the technical essentials of the study subjects and develop the pupils' constructive ideas and creativeness.

SCOPE OF THE KNOWLEDGE CONCERNING THE MAIN BRANCHES AND GENERAL SCIENTIFIC PRINCIPLES OF MODERN PRODUCTION ACQUIRED BY PUPILS AT EIGHT-YEAR AND SECONDARY SCHOOLS

Under the new curriculum, the pupils at eight-year and secondary schools will acquire a wide knowledge of the main branches and main scientific principles of modern production from the teachers of all the subjects concerned.

In the eight-year schools, the pupils' knowledge of natural sciences and mathematics will still be limited, and the instruction given about production will therefore be very elementary, covering:

Power production

Explanatory reading, nature study and other subjects in grades I–IV. Elementary idea of the construction of the simplest wind motors and hydraulic plants.
Introductory study of fuels: coal, peat, oil.

Physics (grades VII–VIII). Forms of energy. Law of the conservation and transformation of energy.
Generation of energy (from chemical fuels, water resources or air

flows) in steam installations, internal combustion engines, steam turbines and hydraulic or wind motors.

Electric power. Electrical measuring instruments—voltmeter, ammeter.

Generation of electricity, its transmission and utilization in industry, agriculture and communications.

Electric motors, generators and transformers.

Principles of atomic energy.

Chemistry (grade VIII). Forms of natural and artificial fuel. Solid, liquid and miscellaneous fuels. Gas production. Proper conditions and methods for fuel combustion.

Manual and technical instruction (grades VII and VIII). Elementary instruction about electrically-driven and electrified instruments (spiral drills, vibro-shears, planes, etc.).

Elementary instruction on the use of electricity for operating lathes.

Elementary instruction on three- and four-phase a.c. systems.

Instruction on the construction of a commutator motor, an asynchronous motor and an electric drive.

Elementary instruction on the installation and operation of domestic lighting systems.

Measurement of current, voltage and wattage by means of technical electrical measuring instruments.

Geography (grade VII–VIII). Use of water power in hydro-electric plants. Hydro-electric plants in the U.S.S.R. Distribution of energy resources (oil, gas, coal) in the U.S.S.R.

Metallurgy

Explanatory reading and nature study in grades I–IV. Introductory study of iron and copper ores and pig-iron production.

Physics (grade VII). Physical principles of metal-casting. Alloys and their uses.

Chemistry (grade VIII). Raw materials for pig-iron production. Physico-chemical basis of blast-furnace operation. Construction and principles of operation of blast furnaces. Technical process of pig-iron production. Types of pig-iron and its uses.

Technical and manual instruction (grades V–VIII). Elementary practical study of the physical and technical properties of metals (steel, aluminium, copper) and alloys (brass).

Different forms of ferrous and non-ferrous metals: sheets, bars, strip, wire.

Geography (grades VI–VIII). Heavy industry, Iron, copper and gold ores. Distribution of ferrous and non-ferrous ores and their use in the national economy.

Machine construction

Explanatory reading, nature study and other subjects in grades I–IV. Familiarization with the fitters' shop, blacksmith's shop and a machine-building factory. Familiarization with a sewing machine and with the external appearance of agricultural machines.

Physics (grades VI–VIII). Physical properties of bodies: elasticity. plasticity, heat conductivity. Melting and evaporation. Electrical conductivity.
Hydraulic press. Water and air pumps.
Mechanisms: lever, block and tackle, inclined plane, belt and gear transmissions. Efficiency of mechanisms. Ball and roller bearings.

Chemistry (grade VIII). Oxy-acetylene welding and cutting of metals. Physical properties and uses of aluminium, copper, tungsten, chromium, tin, lead. Iron and steel. Rusting of steel and its protection by coating and lacquering.

Technical and manual training (grades V–VIII). Technology of fitting and assembly.
Mensuration. Transfer of measurements from the drawing to the material; checking of the completed work.
Technical documentation: drawings, technical charts, etc.
Introductory study of parts, basic mechanisms and machines. Construction and operation of a sewing machine. Construction and principles of operation of domestic appliances (washing machine, floor-polisher, vacuum cleaner).
Technology of metal-cutting on universal machines (lathes, milling machines, drilling machines).
General acquaintance with the techniques and technology of a metalwork shop.
Elementary instruction on the mechanization, electrification and automation of production processes.

Geography. Distribution of machine-construction plants in the Union Republics.

Chemical industry

Chemistry (grades VII–VIII). Scientific principles governing the industrial production of oxygen. Water purification, and means of purifying water in industry. Production of quicklime. Construction of a kiln.

Building construction

Explanatory reading, nature study and other subjects in grades I–IV. Introductory study of building materials: wood, stone, sand, clay. Manufacture of bricks and cement mixtures. Method of house-building (excursions).

Labour-saving building machinery: their outward appearance and mode of operation.

Physics (grades VI–VII). Domestic water system. Domestic central heating system.

Chemistry (grade VIII). Use of lime in building.

Geography. Types of natural building materials (wood, stone) and their distribution in the pupils' own region and in the Union Republics.

Manual and technical instruction. Basic building units and methods of assembling them.

Construction and equipment of school recreation, PT and sports grounds, model topographical sites and holiday camps.

Transport

Explanatory reading, nature study and other subjects in grades I–IV. Introductory study of the operation of urban transport (tramcars, trolleybuses, buses and underground) rail, water and air transport.

Physics. Physical principles governing water transport (construction and operation of a steamship and a diesel-engined ship).

Physical principles governing the construction and operation of a diesel locomotive.

Geography (grades VI–VIII). Basic types of transport.

Communications

Explanatory reading, nature study and other subjects in grades I–IV. Introductory study of the working of the postal and telegraph systems. Radio and television.

Physics. Principles of operation of the telephone and telegraph.

Arable farming

Explanatory reading, nature study and other subjects in grades I–IV. Elementary instruction on the soil, its composition and properties. Study of the most important field, orchard and garden plants and their cultivation, together with details of the most common weeds and certain pests.

Cultivation of various farm and room plants.

Elementary instruction on the typical crops of various regions: maize, wheat, cotton, rice, tea, sugar beet, flax.

Biology (grades V–VI). Biological principles governing the production of high yields of agricultural products—seeds, their germination and conditions of growth, times and depths of planting, depending on the biological characteristics of the plant; the soil, its composition, properties and significance in the life of the plant; organic and mineral fertilization; plant-feeding and the formation of organic matter (photosynthesis).

Propagation of plants by sowing, cutting or grafting.

Biology of wheat, maize, potatoes, cabbages, beans and fruit.

Biology of insects—agricultural pests and how to combat them.

Elements of hygiene and health precautions in socialist agriculture and on the school experimental plot.

Chemistry (grade VIII). Mineral fertilizers and their use in agriculture.

Geography (grades V–VIII). Soil and climatic conditions of the various zones, and their rational exploitation for agricultural development.

Natural wealth: apatites, phosphorites, potash salts and peat. Their distribution and use for enriching the soil.

Manual and technical instruction (grades V–VIII). Study of the main vegetable crops of the region and the features of their cultivation. Growing of fruit trees from seedlings and berry-bearing bushes from cuttings.

Problems of growing vegetables locally. Conducting of experiments to determine the best way to grow vegetables under local conditions, taking account of the biological characteristics of the plants.

Study of the mechanization of vegetable-growing. Excursion.

Study of the main locally-produced fruit or berry crops and the mode of cultivation (planting. tending, harvesting).

Laying-out of a fruit nursery, transplanting of stock, grafting, care of stock.

Techniques of growing wheat, maize, potatoes and seeds of biennial vegetables.

Methods of combating local insect pests.

Recent local experience with fruit, berry and field crops, biennial vegetables, and fruit-tree stocks.

Study of the mechanization of market gardening (excursion).

Principles governing the production of high yields of maize, sugar beet, potatoes, flax, sunflower seeds, etc., on collective and State farms. Organization and carrying-out of experiments.

Technique and mechanization of grain and industrial crop production. Main types of weeds, and how to combat them.

General acquaintance with the construction of equipment for tilling the soil, and equipment for cleaning and sowing seeds.

General acquaintance with the economy of a local collective or State farm, organization and payment of farm labour, and achievements of the leading workers.

Animal husbandry

Explanatory reading, nature study and other subjects in grades I–IV. Familiarization with domestic animals and their care (cows, horses, pigs, sheep, rabbits, hens, ducks, geese, camels, reindeer).

Familiarization with stock and poultry farms, and the work carried out on them.

Biology (grades VI–VII). Biological principles governing the keeping, feeding and breeding of livestock (poultry and mammals).

Biological principles governing bee-keeping, silkworm-breeding, fish-breeding, and care of wild animals.

Livestock breeding locally.

Manual and technical instruction (grade VII). Principles of rabbit and poultry keeping. Mechanization of labour-consuming work and animal husbandry (excursion). Raising of young cattle. Organization and payment of stock-farm labour, and achievements of leading farm workers.

Geography (grades VII–VIII). Development of stock farming in the different zones of the U.S.S.R.

The pupils, during the lessons on the history and Constitution of the U.S.S.R., will also learn about the social side of production —labour and its significance to society; forced labour, and free labour, socialist and communist labour; the communist attitude to labour, and its forms of expression (socialist), emulation and invention, workers' participation in technical progress, work and life of communist labour brigades and collective communities; main differences between socialist and capitalist production; importance of socialist production in raising the level of prosperity, education and culture of the workers; problems of developing socialist production, and the successes achieved; construction of the material and technical basis of communism during the next fifteen to twenty years and the significance of this for the whole of mankind; obligation of every citizen of the U.S.S.R. to work for the common good, enthusiastically, creatively, by force of habit, and to the limit of his capabilities.

An important place in the instruction given on the main branches of production is occupied by visits to production points, during which the pupils gain an elementary knowledge of the corresponding techniques, technology and organization of labour. An acquaintance with the various types of work is an important contribution towards the vocational guidance of the pupils and helps those completing courses at eight-year schools to choose their future occupation with a knowledge of the facts.

At the secondary school (grades IX–XI) the pupils' knowledge of the main branches and basic scientific principles of production is widened and deepened, for those grades mark a big step forward in studying physics, chemistry, biology, mathematics and other sciences which constitute the basis for acquiring a sound knowledge of production. In addition, the subjects of machine operation and electrical engineering and the principles of mechanization and automation of production are further developed.

Under the new syllabuses, pupils completing their studies in the secondary school will have been equipped with the following knowledge of production:

Power production

Physics. Types of energy used in modern industry (mechanical, internal combustion or thermal, and electric power); law of the conservation of energy and its transformation from one form into another; scientific principles governing the production and utilization of these forms of power; principles of atomic energy.

Physical principles governing the construction and operation of prime movers; water turbines, wind motors, steam engines, steam turbines, internal combustion engines, electric motors. Properties of the operating media; steam, gas, water. Physical principles governing the construction and operation of electrical generators of various kinds.

Chemistry. Main forms of solid, liquid and gaseous fuel, their composition and properties. Chemical principles governing the proper combustion of fuel; extraction, processing and use of oil, coal and natural gas. Gasification of solid fuel.

Machine operation and electrical engineering. Construction and operation of internal combustion engines (car or tractor). Construction and operation of a.c. and d.c. generators. Transformers. Construction and operation of electric motors, and of various types of electric drive.

Metallurgy

Chemistry. Main ores, and methods of preparing them for smelting. Main methods of producing metals on an industrial scale: pig-iron, steel; aluminium and various other light metals.

Physics. Physical principles governing metal-rolling at metallurgical plants.

129

Machine construction

Physics. The machine as an-assembly of very simple mechanisms; various forms of power transmissions. Ball and roller bearings. Relays, photoelectric cells, transmitting elements, magnetic releases and electronic regulators, as used in the mechanization and automation of production. Use of semiconductors in production.

Basic physical properties of solids and various forms of deformation (a knowledge of which is essential for understanding the technology of metalwork and machine construction); physical principles governing casting, forging and stamping; principles of operation of cutting tools.

Chemistry. Physical and chemical properties of the main metals and alloys. Elements of metal corrosion, and methods of protecting metals from damage by it. Electrochemical methods of giving metals a protective coating.

Technical drawing. Elements of machine drawing. Execution of geometrical constructions used in drawing machine parts. Regular conventional symbols used in machine drawing.

Practical work. Manual working of metal and wood. Construction of fitters' and carpenters' tools, including electrical equipment; manual assembly and finishing of metal and wooden articles.

Machine operation and electrical engineering. Metal-cutting and pressing. Metal-cutting machines: their construction and operation. Assembly and finishing of machines and lathes. System with return signals. Automatic machines, groups, production lines and workshops. Technical apparatus and equipment used in the automation of production. Self-checking electric drive.

Chemical industry

Chemistry. Production of hydrochloric, sulphuric and nitric acid, ammonia, alkalis and fertilizers; chemical processing of oil and coal; production of synthetic acetic acid. Natural, by-product and oil-refinery gases: their utilization in industry. Production of artificial acetate fibre, phenol-formaldehyde plastics and butadiene rubber. General principles of chemical production.

Arable farming

Biology. Structure, life and development of plants, and the application of this knowledge in arable farming. Plant pests and how to combat them. Importance of technology for cultivating crops and achieving high yields.

Chemistry. Properties of the main fertilizers; methods of determining the type of fertilizer needed. Chemical means of combating plant pests and diseases.

Manual and technical instruction. Tilling the soil, preparing seeds and seedlings, sowing and planting, tending of growing plants, harvesting.

Machine operation. Agricultural machinery and equipment used for carrying out the above processes.

Animal husbandry

Biology. Structure, life and development of animals, and the utilization of this knowledge in the various branches of animal husbandry. Stimulators and vectors of animal diseases and how to combat them. Breeds of domestic animals, and ways of developing new breeds. Biological principles governing the keeping and care of livestock.

Manual and technical instruction. Breeds of livestock, their feeding and care. Machinery and equipment used in feeding and tending livestock. Methods of obtaining high productivity from livestock.

Building construction

Chemistry. Properties and use in building construction of lime, cement, concrete, glass and other materials. Production of certain of these (lime, cement).

Physics. Calculation of loads and stresses. Strength and resistance of materials. Coefficients of elasticity of the main building materials; safety factors in buildings. Installation of central heating, ventilation and electric lighting in dwellings. Use of simple mechanisms on building sites.

Technical drawing. Reading of plans and sections of buildings. Most common conventional symbols for basic building elements and items of sanitary or technical equipment. Drawing of simple plans and sections.

Transport

Chemistry. Properties of the main types of fuel used in transport; conditions for the proper combustion of these fuels in transport equipment. Methods of purifying water for use in machines. Lubricants used in transport.

Physics. Physical principles governing the construction and operation of diesel and steam locomotives, aircraft (propellor and turbojet), motor vehicles, steamships and diesel-engined ships.

Machine construction and operation. Construction of motor vehicles, and how to drive, maintain and operate them.

Communications

Physics. Physical principles of the telephone, telegraph and radio. Principles governing the construction and operation of telephone, telegraph and radio receiving equipment.

In the lessons on economic geography, the pupils learn about the importance of all these branches of production to the national economy; their geographical distribution and sources of raw material; combination, specialization and co-operation in production; the structure and interlinking of the various branches of production; the electrification of the country and the creation of grids; and the successes achieved in developing the various branches of production under the national economic plan.

In the lessons on history and the principles of political science, the pupils learn about the social aspect of production as indicated in the tabulation of the factors common to all branches of socialist production and about Communist Party and Soviet Government policy on labour and production and its implementation in everyday life.

In addition the pupils at urban schools learn about the branch of production covering the plant where they have their production practice, while those at rural schools are given a more thorough training in agriculture.

Familiarization on these lines with the main branches of modern production gives the pupils a broad polytechnical outlook and equips them with the knowledge and skills enabling them, on the basis of production as a whole, to master the more detailed knowledge and understand the latest technical achievements.

RANGE OF POLYTECHNICAL WORK SKILLS DEVELOPED IN THE PUPILS

As stated above, technical progress produces radical changes in the nature of the skills which the present-day worker or collective farmer must possess if he is to work and participate in that progress successfully. Nowadays, it is not enough for a worker to put forward certain physical efforts and be able to carry out certain manual operations, the number of which is constantly decreasing with the increased mechanization of production. In addition to his physical powers, he must now possess solid powers of observation, be able to make various measurements, calculate and execute graphical and geometrical constructions, read complicated technical drawings, have the skills of a fitter and an electrician, know how to operate machines and equipment and carry out minor adjustments, and have some knowledge of technical organization. In addition, for successful work in agriculture, the worker must have some knowledge of agricultural science; while for experimental and rationalization work in production he must have experimental skills also. The more modern the speciality becomes in the technical sense, the more these skills are demanded of the worker. In the school itself, there is insufficient time for practice to develop all the necessary skills, and only a limited number of them can be taught. But the school can and must give its pupils the necessary practical knowledge and working ability which can then develop into trade skills with subsequent practice under production conditions.

The syllabuses of the eight-year and secondary schools for mathematics, physics, chemistry, biology, drawing, machine operation and electrical engineering, manual and technical instruction and production training provide the basis for the further acquisition by the pupils, in the process of practical and productive work, of a considerable range of practical polytechnical knowledge which in many cases brings them to the required standard of proficiency and skill.

The pupils at the eight-year school acquire the following polytechnical work skills:

Mensuration

Mathematics. Measurement of distances (by pacing out distances, using a rule, tape-measure or field compass). Measurement of angles and segments on paper and field work. Measuring-glasses. Measurement of the areas of polygons and right-angled triangles and the volume of cubes.

Physics. Measurement of length, volume, weight, force, speed and coefficients of friction and efficiency; use of rulers, beam compasses, tape-measures, measuring-glasses, balances, dynamometers, stop-watches and speedometers. Measurement of temperature, quantity of heat and pressure, and use of thermometers, calorimeters and barometers. Measurement of electric current and voltage; use of ammeters and voltmeters.

Chemistry. Measurement with measuring-cylinders and balances.

Technical drawing. Measurement of rectangular objects with rulers, calipers and beam compasses.

Manual and technical instruction. Taking of measurements in preparing and marking out materials. Measurement with rulers, beam compasses and micrometers when working on materials.

Calculation, geometrical and graphical construction

Mathematics. Calculations with whole numbers and fractions, percentage calculations and proportional division; calculations with the aid of abbreviated multiplication formulae; solution of equations with one unknown, and calculation of square roots.

Solution of problems involving right-angled triangles. Finding of the area of polygons; circumferences and area of circles. Finding the area and volume of cubes and rectangular solids. Plotting of points according to their co-ordinates (and vice versa). Construction of geometrical figures.

Physics. Calculation of various physical values; use of tables and graphs.

Chemistry. Calculations based on formulae and equations for reactions. Calculations using the gram-molecule and gram-atom principles. Calculations involved in the preparation of percentage solutions.

Technical drawing. Constructions of lines, angles and figures in making sketches, technical drawings and plans of objects.

Manual and technical instruction. Miscellaneous calculations involved in determining the dimensions of semi-finished goods and in processing them. Construction of plane geometric figures in marking out objects from sketches and drawings.

Practical knowledge, skill and experience in technical drawing and design

Technical drawing. Practice in the use of drawing-instruments and the execution of geometrical constructions in marking out and drawing objects; work in pencil and Indian ink, using the T-square, set squares, ruler, compasses and dividers. Drawing of straight lines and curves, marking out and tracing shapes of parts containing straight lines and curves.

Practice in reading sketches and drawings of everyday objects and machine parts of rectangular, cylindrical and prismatic shape, using the conventional method of representing screw threads.

Manual and technical instruction. Execution of simple sketches, blueprints, and technical drawings in connexion with the manufacture of parts, assembly and finishing of articles, and assembly and dismantling of machines. Reading of sketches, blueprints, technical drawings and diagrams essential for the execution of practical work.

Practice in designing elementary parts and assemblies of ready-made parts. Practice in designing for a given drawing project.

Initial practical knowledge and experience in processing and fitting

Physics. Installation of various instruments and their utilization (particularly electrical instruments).

134

Chemistry. Assembly of simple apparatus for obtaining materials and studying their properties.

Manual and technical instruction. Practice in working with paper and cardboard—marking out, cutting, bending and folding, gluing together, binding, external finishing, etc.

Practice in working with cloth—marking out, folding, cutting, sewing, knitting and mending.

Woodwork—marking out, sawing (with and against the grain), planing, drilling, chiselling, nailing, screwing, gluing, dowelling, finishing and painting.

Metalwork—marking out, cutting, drilling, bending, cutting internal and external screw threads, and assembling with rivets, nuts and bolts.

Joining, branching and terminal connexion of wires. Wiring up domestic lighting equipment. Installation of a lighting system from a single lighting point and socket. Elementary repair of domestic electrical fittings.

Operation of machines and equipment

Manual and technical instruction. Simple setting of drilling machines and lathes, and their utilization for simple work.

Practical knowledge and experience in agricultural technology

Plant growing. Determining the mechanical composition and other properties of local soils; tilling the soil with a spade, rake and hand cultivator. Determining the quality of the seed material. Calculating the amounts and methods of application of fertilizers. Sowing and planting by hand. Weeding, thinning, feeding, irrigation and harvesting. Methods of combating weeds and pests.

Animal husbandry. Determining, from external signs, the quality of various feeding-stuffs. Composition of daily rations. Manual preparation of feeding-stuffs. Observance of diets. Measurement and distribution of feed. Care of young cattle and poultry. Execution of simple veterinary and prophylactic measures.

Practical knowledge and experience of technical organization

Manual and technical instruction. Proper organization of individual work. Observance of cleanliness and orderliness on the job. Economy in the use of materials, instruments and electricity; productive use of working time, caution in the use of equipment, and observance of safety measures.

Rationalization of working methods and processes; use of modern equipment and apparatus in the workshop and on the school experimental plot.

135

Practical knowledge and experience in conducting experiments

Physics. Knowledge and experience of the techniques of conducting experiments in a physics laboratory with simple apparatus.

Chemistry. Similar practice in conducting chemical experiments: solution, precipitation, filtration, evaporation, distillation, crystallization, etc.

Biology and manual and technical instruction. Techniques of conducting biological experiments in the laboratory and agricultural experiments on the school plot.

The work of imparting practical polytechnical work skills is continued in grades IX–XI. As a result of the broader basis of their scientific, mathematical and polytechnical education and their more advanced age, the pupils at this stage acquire in considerable measure the skills involved in mechanized labour.

The practical knowledge and skills acquired by the pupils over and above those imparted at the eight-year school are as follows:

Mensuration

Mathematics. Determination of distances and heights which cannot be measured by direct means. Measurement of area of polygons and the volume of polyhedrons and spherical bodies.

Physics. Measurement of the specific heat, fusion temperatures, thermal capacity and coefficient of linear expansion. Measurement of atmospheric humidity; use of the thermometer, hygrometer and psychrometer. Measurement of electrical discharges, potential, current, voltage, resistance and strength of current; use of the electrometer, voltmeter, ammeter, ohmmeter and wattmeter. Measurement of the refractive index of various materials, the focal length of lenses, and wavelengths.

Chemistry. Measurements with burettes, measuring-glasses, scales and chemical balances.

Technical drawing. Measurement of objects in the form of pyramids, cones, spheres and tores, using rulers, internal calipers and beam compasses.

Production training. Mensuration, with the aid of rulers, beam compasses, micrometers, gauges and clamps, in the course of processing materials.

Calculation and graphical and geometrical construction

Mathematics. Solution of equations, calculations by means of logarithms, and the solution of inequalities.

Finding the areas and volumes of polyhedrons and spherical bodies. Solution of oblique-angled triangles.

Construction of graphs for equations and trigonometric functions.

Physics. Calculations, from formulae, of energy, power, efficiency and other physical values; use of tables and graphs. Construction of various graphs for dependence between physical values.

Chemistry. Calculations, from formulae and equations, of reactions involving gaseous substances or substances which evaporate without decomposition.

Production training. Miscellaneous calculations and computations connected with the selection of processing conditions, (e.g., speed of cutting and feed), determination of the characteristics of mechanisms and machines (transmission ratios, efficiencies, rotation speeds, rating fuel consumption), using equations, graphs and tables. Construction of geometric figures (planes and solids) in marking out objects from sketches and drawings.

Practical knowledge and experience of drawing and design

Drawing. Use of templates. Tracing of ellipses. Joining up of lines. Practice in the execution and reading of sketches and drawing of technical parts of rectangular, cylindrical or prismatic shape, as well as objects whose shape includes that of the pyramid, cone, sphere, tore, prism, cylinder or frustum, using cross-sections, joining up lines and using the conventional representation of screw threads. Reading of simple assembly drawings.

Machine operation and production training. Execution of simple sketches, designs and drawing in connexion with the processing of parts, and simple diagrams in connexion with the assembly, finishing, and dismantling of parts, mechanisms, machines or machine units. Reading of simple sketches and drawings necessary for executing practical work.

Introductory practical knowledge and experience of assembling and processing

Physics. Setting-up and utilization of physics appliances (with particular emphasis on electrical, electronic and remote-control equipment).

Chemistry. Setting-up of various appliances for obtaining substances and studying their properties.

Machine operation, electrical engineering and production training. Dismantling, assembly and adjustment of simple machine parts and mechanisms. Simple work on the repair of machine tools, motor vehicles, tractors etc.

Manufacture of parts by hand and machine. Assembly and finishing of simple parts, using various materials.

Execution and reading of wiring diagrams; handling of basic instruments used in electrical fitting and technical electrical measuring appliances.

Operation of machinery and equipment

Machine operation, electrical engineering and production training. Simple setting of metalworking machines, and their operation in the production of simple parts. Elementary technical servicing and maintenance of a motor vehicle or tractor. Driving, operation of various machines in connexion with production training, in a factory or on a collective farm (using handles, flywheels, levers, knobs, steering-wheels and other devices).

Handling of a.c. and d.c. electrical equipment—transformers and three-phase electric motors with starting gear and relay protection of the motor.

Practical knowledge and experience in agricultural technology

Plant growing. Determination of the mechanical composition and other properties of local soils; tilling of the soil with ploughs and cultivators. Determination of the quality of seed material—cleaning and sorting of seeds in seed-cleaning machines. Machine sowing in rows and square clusters. Calculation of the amount and type of fertilizer to be used for the main field crops. Mechanized inter-row cultivation and crop thinning. Watering and feeding of plants by hand and by plant-feeder. Determination of the ripeness of the main field crops. Mechanized harvesting of grass, grain and fodder crops. Principal methods of combating weeds and pests.

Animal husbandry. Visual assessment of the build, productivity, and live weight of cows. Cleaning out the stockyard. Determination of the quality of various feedstuffs by visual means. Composition of daily feed rations for various types of productivity. Preparation of feed by hand and by machine. Observation of diets. Measuring-out and distribution of feed. Milking by hand and by machine. Calculation of milk yield, determination of quality, and calculation of the productivity of the herd per 100 hectares of farm land.

Agricultural-machine operation. Coupling the plough to the tractor and setting it to cut the first furrow. Setting a cultivator to work between rows at various distances from each other. Setting a row or square-cluster seed drill to the desired conditions for seed-dropping, and setting coulters to the required width between rows. Changing the screens on a winnowing machine and regulating their action. Setting the reel of a combine harvester to suit various conditions of stand. Regulation of the first dresser and the clearance between the pins of the drum and concave. Starting the engine and operating the tractor. Tractor work, using different farm machines.

Practical knowledge and experience of technical organization

Production training. Planning of work and formulation of technical plans and work charts. Proper organization of individual work. Cleanliness and orderliness on the job. Economy in the use of materials, equipment and electricity. Productive utilization of working time. Caution when using machinery and observance of safety regulations during production work.

Rationalization of work methods and processes, and of the instruments and implements used, whether in the factory, on the farm or on the building site.

Practical knowledge and experience of experimentation work

Physics. Knowledge and experience of the technique of conducting physics experiments.

Chemistry. Knowledge and experience of the technique of conducting chemical experiments. Obtaining substances with and without passing through the stage of intermediate products. Distinction between the series of anions and cations.

Biology and production training. Practice in the techniques of biological and agricultural experimentation both in the laboratory and in the field.

The principle is that the pupils in the process of practical and socially useful work will acquire a sound technical culture. The essential features characterizing a socialist industrial culture are:

A scientific understanding of the labour performed, its place in production, and its general role and significance in the construction of communism.

The ability to work in an organized manner, in a team, in accordance with plans, drawings and technical charts.

Observance on the job of the scientifically established working procedures—setting of stands, attachment of instruments, working movements.

Rational organization of the work-place, and maintenance of perfect order in it throughout the working day.

A careful approach to tools, equipment and materials, and observance of strict economy in the use of materials.

Rational alternation of work and recreation.

A thoughtful, inquisitive, constructive and inventive approach to the work in hand.

Mutual assistance and comradely co-operation.

Socialist emulation.

Conscious discipline.

A high level of labour productivity and quality of production.

Low production costs.
A combination of manual and intellectual work.

SOCIALLY PRODUCTIVE WORK BY PUPILS

The polytechnical work skills and technical culture in question are formed in the course of the practical educational work and socially useful work, a decisive factor in that respect being the socially productive work carried out by the pupils. Productive work is outstanding as a method of inculcating practical skills and technical culture and as a form of incorporation of the pupils in communist construction, and developing a communist attitude to work as the basis of their moral training. In other words, the incorporation of the pupils in productive work is at once the aim and means of their polytechnical education and communist upbringing.

How is this incorporation carried out in the Soviet schools?

The process begins as early as grades I–IV, where the pupils, during handwork lessons (two periods a week), make useful things for themselves and the school from paper and cardboard (envelopes, writing-pads, toys, etc.), repair and cover school library books, mend clothes and do simple jobs on the school experimental plot (growing beans, peas, aubergines, etc.).

These classes are supplemented in grades III–IV by two periods of socially useful work a week, during which the children make things for their own use, prepare visual teaching aids, do various jobs for libraries and kindergartens, prepare medicinal herbs, collect paper, jam-jars, scrap iron, and so on. At rural schools, considerable time is devoted to work suited to their capacities in the school garden or orchard. These working processes are combined with the study of tools and materials and excursions to various production plants in order to compare manual and mechanized labour and get an insight into Soviet working life. The absence of a knowledge of natural sciences in grades I–IV precludes any explanation of production processes at that stage, so that the question of doing so does not arise. However, the excursions on which the children are taken arouse their interest in production, and a desire to construct mechanisms and machines, make models (even though they may be extremely crude) and play at work-simulating games; this desire is satisfied during the periods of manual training and in the course of socially useful work. They also accumulate first impressions of the work of people in various trades, thus building a foundation for future vocational guidance.

140

A beginning is made in these grades in inculcating respect for work and the habit of socially useful work.

In grades V–VIII, the weekly number of periods on manual and technical training is increased to three and an extra two are devoted to socially useful work. The children in these grades are familiarized with workshop practice (woodwork and metalwork, electrical fittings), and help to grow vegetables and keep rabbits and poultry, while the girls follow domestic science.

The pupils begin in the school workshops by making teaching equipment for their own use or for the school experimental plots as well as teaching aids for the primary classes; gradually, they go on to execute orders from various organizations and undertakings, from whom they receive the necessary materials and implements. Toys and furniture are produced for kindergartens and crèches, packaging stands for machine parts are produced for the supporting undertakings and simple instruments (keys, dividers, calipers, etc.), electric heaters and other domestic appliances repaired, and so on. The sums received by the school are kept in a special account and spent on improvements in teaching facilities, material assistance to individual pupils, and cultural services in general. The articles to be produced are so selected that the children, in making them, acquire proficiency in production, assembly and electrical fitting, as well as a knowledge of tools and materials, and how to convert the latter into finished products. From this point on, the syllabus gives greater weight to the practical study of machine parts and mechanisms, electric lighting, generators and electric motors, domestic electrical appliances and equipment and the elements of radio technology. More time is spent on dismantling and assembling mechanisms, installing electric wiring, preparing models and equipment for technical, physics, chemistry and other work, and so on.

When it comes to preparing articles in large numbers, the work is organized on the basis of the division of labour, with the pupils changing places throughout the operation. In time, they master the technical requirements which the articles produced have to meet, their work gradually reaches the necessary standard, and socialist emulation develops among them. Organized workshop effort thus develops into an important teaching and educative factor, and in combination with excursions to plants and factories brings the pupils to an understanding of various aspects of large-scale socialist production.

Work on agriculture is also broadened and intensified in those senior grades. The pupils carry out agricultural experiments on the school plot and on collective and State farms, grow vegetables and maize, work in nurseries and orchards looking after fruit trees and bushes, and tend young cattle and poultry. The experimental work consists mainly of applying new farming measures recommended by local agricultural experimental stations. In this way, the pupils not only acquire a sound biological and agricultural knowledge and experimental and working skills—so vital for the future leading workers in agriculture—but also learn the latest methods of producing high yields in their area and creating new hybrid plants, harvesting the seeds and distributing them to collective farms.

In organizing this work, the line taken is to avoid making extensive use of mechanization, the pupils being led as far as possible to plan and carry out a complete cycle of experiments, analyse the results and popularize their successes.

The girls, in their domestic-science lessons, are taught how to sew and mend clothes, prepare meals and look after clothing, footwear, etc.

During the socially useful work periods, the children do things for themselves, and for the school amenities, the school garden, the neighbouring streets, parks, execute orders for various undertakings and organizations, collect scrap iron, medicinal herbs, and so on.

The practice of socially useful work serves to consolidate the scientific knowledge acquired in the classroom, impart new knowledge, develop a communist attitude to work and prepare the pupils psychologically for work when they leave the eight-year school. Together with the excursions to production plants, it helps to broaden the basis of work in respect of vocational guidance.

As already stated, the boys and girls, after finishing their eight-year schooling, either undergo training at trade schools and then finish off their secondary education at evening (shift) schools, or else they pass on to grades IX–XI of the secondary schools, where they get production training.

The socially useful work performed by evening-school pupils as workers and employees at undertakings and on collective and State farms and building sites is combined with general and polytechnical education and the improvement of their production rating at the school.

The pupils in grades IX–XI at the secondary schools providing production training get instruction in one of the general mass trades of vital economic importance for the area, are involved in socially useful work and receive a complete secondary education closely linked with that work. These schools train workers for all branches of production, agriculture, building construction, transport and communications, as well as culture and social work.

One-third of the total teaching time in grades IX–XI (i.e., about 1,350 periods) is spent on production training, about 25 per cent of that time being taken up by theoretical training in the pupil's speciality and the rest by practical instruction and work, the practical instruction being given in the course of socially useful and productive work in the selected speciality. In urban schools, two days a week (or three months a year) are normally set aside for production training, while in the rural schools the pupils study and undergo practical training in the winter and work for fifty-four days (in grades IX and X) or eighteen days (in grade XI) in the spring, summer and autumn on arable, fruit or stock farms.

As stated, the production training at schools is organized in accordance with the decisions of the June 1959 Plenum, which stressed the need for an all-round improvement in the general educational level and technical qualifications of the working class. 'The saturation of modern production with complex machines and mechanisms makes it imperative for every worker to have comprehensive general and specialized knowledge. Hence the production training of the workers can no longer be limited to the programme of the technical minimum but must include elements of technical engineering training.'

In the theoretical part of production training, the pupils are familiarized with a particular undertaking as a whole, and receive instruction on safety techniques, the construction and principles of operation of the machines and machine tools employed in their speciality, the properties of materials and their technological processing, the organization of labour, the establishment of work norms and pay rates, the communist form of labour, the obligations of workers in socialist production, and the way in which those obligations have been fulfilled by the foremost workers in a communist manner. They are also familiarized with new techniques, technological developments and the complete automation of production. The theoretical training is so arranged that full use is made of the general educational and polytechnical training given in grades IX–XI, so that by the time the pupils leave school it is solidly grounded on a complete general secondary education.

Meanwhile, the practical production training based on socially useful labour continues for all three years of the course, and is designed to prepare the pupils as quickly and as thoroughly as possible for independent paid work during which their education is continued and their trade proficiency improved. Subject to age-limits, practical training and work may begin in grade X, with corresponding changes in the schedule, while maintaining the proportion of time devoted to trade training.

The first trade tests are normally carried out in grade X, while the second and final tests are carried out in grade XI. In the case of trades, subject to age-limits, the tests are not carried out until a pupil completes his trade training in grade XI.

CHAPTER VII

METHODS AND FORMS OF ORGANIZATION OF POLYTECHNICAL EDUCATION

by S. G. Shapovalenko

METHODS AND FORMS OF ORGANIZATION OF TEACHING IN SOVIET SCHOOLS

By 'methods of teaching and education in Soviet schools' we mean the ways and means by which the *teacher* imparts to his pupils scientific knowledge, cognitive and working abilities and skills, organizes their independent work, fits them into social and practical activities in the building of communism, and brings about their communist education, and by which the *pupils* acquire knowledge, abilities and skills, become accustomed to working and combining physical and intellectual work, and develop in themselves the characteristics of the men and women of a communist society.

The history of the development of science shows that the results of scientific cognition become a method, if they are consciously used in the investigation of new phenomena. The method of cognition therefore depends on the state of scientific knowledge, and is born of its results. Lenin was sympathetically disposed towards the definition of a scientific method of philosophy given by Hegel—and Hegel defined it as a form of the inner dynamics of the content of philosophy.

In teaching, as in science, the method is also determined by its content, as becomes obvious if a comparison is made between the methods of teaching mathematics and physics, physics and literature, literature and history, and so forth. The closer the content of scientific subjects to each other, the closer are the methods of teaching them. It is therefore no accident that the methods of teaching natural sciences have much in common. The relationship between the method of teaching and the content of the subject taught has been excellently expressed by P. N. Gruzdev. In one of his published works he writes:

'The acquisition of knowledge is not only the object or task of instruction: it is also a means of instruction. When knowledge becomes an instrument for gaining further, wider, and deeper knowledge, it is transformed from the object into the means. Knowledge is therefore at once the subject and the method. Knowledge is the prerequisite and the essential condition for comprehending new concepts and new impressions.

'The most vital and inherent feature of the process of learning is that our minds work in such a way that earlier knowledge which has been stored up in the mind becomes the means and the method of gaining further knowledge.

'. . . Consequently, the task of education is essentially a single one, namely, to acquire knowledge in such a way as to assimilate it. *The assimilation of knowledge includes the use of knowledge as a method and instrument for futher study and for assimilating knowledge and improving practical activities.*'[1]

This means that methods of teaching the sciences depend on the content of the subject; the nature of the methods may vary according to the extent to which the pupils assimilate new knowledge and are able to proceed further. Major and decisive changes in the content of a subject entail major and decisive changes in the methods of teaching and assimilating them. Teaching methods are a form of the inner dynamics of the content of the subject of instruction and education. As the contents of a scientific subject develop into a method, so the methods of scientific perception and the methods of teaching depend on the methodology of science.

In Soviet schools, the methods of teaching are permeated with Marxist-Leninist methodology and a dialectical-materialistic concept of the world, in order to train the pupils in this concept.

The syllabuses include such scientific facts and laws as serve as a basis for familiarizing the pupils with the objective dialectics of material reality, the correlation and interdependence of its phenomena, their change and development, and the part played by socially productive practical experience in the cognition and transformation of the world. Thus, in studying history, the pupils learn about the origin and evolution of social structures, the disappearance of those based on exploitation and the building-up of communism in the U.S.S.R. In natural sciences, the pupils study the various forms in which matter exists and the theories and laws governing their origin, change, and development. In connexion with history, natural and technical sciences, the pupils learn about the origin and development of tools, machines, mechanisms, and technical processes, the basic lines of technical develop-

---

1. P. N. Gruzdev, *Problems of Education snd Teaching*, 1949, p. 123–4.

ment, and the various forms of labour and their development. In economic geography, they learn about the connexion between the various branches of the national economy and their development. The syllabuses and textbooks also provide for elucidation of the most important developments in science under the influence of the social experience of the people.

Every teacher, in teaching his subject, and in familiarizing his pupils with the facts of science, makes a Marxist-Leninist analysis and generalization of the facts, and leads his pupils towards assimilating the objective dialectics of material reality.

Having given his pupils information on the mutual relationship and laws of development of the phenomena of the world, the teacher stimulates and encourages his pupils to apply this information in the subsequent study of the subject (particularly in the senior grades) and teaches them to regard natural and social phenomena and their evolution and interdependence in a concrete manner. The teacher explains to the pupils that human beings gain knowledge of the world by practical study of it, that they do not always perceive the truth immediately, but become aware of it gradually (at this point, details taken from the history of science and technology are of great value), and that the experience of society is the criterion of truth. Man learns about the world in order to change it. Soviet science serves the cause of the building of communism in the U.S.S.R.

By doing all this in the terms of the subject being taught, and using the material of his subject, the teacher gradually leads his pupils towards the Marxist-Leninist dialectical materialistic conception of the phenomena, processes and transformation of the world, and the development of science.

The history of education shows that instructional and educative methods used in schools change under the influence of the requirements of society, which depend on the development of industry, technology, science and culture. The new requirements in regard to upbringing, education, and instruction lead to changes in the tasks of the schools; these lead to changes in the content of their instructional and educative work and, finally, these in turn lead to the further development of methods of instruction and education.

The fact that the U.S.S.R. has entered the period of all-round communist construction has made fresh demands in regard to the education and upbringing of the rising generation, and these demands have been proclaimed in the resolutions of the Twenty-first Conference of the Communist Party of the U.S.S.R. and the Law 'On the strengthening of the ties of the school with life and on the further development of the public education system in the

147

U.S.S.R.', which was adopted by the Supreme Soviet of the U.S.S.R. The new demands of education and upbringing have necessitated changes in the content of education, and these are reflected in new syllabuses and curricula. Besides changes in the content of education, there have been changes in educational methods. The theses of the Central Committee of the Communist Party of the U.S.S.R. and the Council of Ministers of the U.S.S.R. on strengthening the ties of the school with life, and further developing the system of public education in the U.S.S.R., indicate the general lines along which the methods of teaching must be changed. The methods of teaching must be changed 'with a view to the maximum development of the independence and initiative of the pupils. Visual methods of instruction should be applied more extensively; the cinema, television, etc., should be widely used; abstract teaching of the fundamentals of science and production must be done away with. It is particularly important to promote on a wide scale in the schools technical inventions and work encouraging the pupils to make new instruments, models and technical devices; experimental agricultural work should also be encouraged.'

In the preceding stages of the development of Soviet schools, various teaching methods have been developed, all of which are permeated with Marxist-Leninist methods. Depending on what is the main source of cognition of the pupils, when any particular method is used, all the methods of teaching are divided into three groups: teaching by the oral and written methods, teaching with visual aids, and practical teaching. Table 6 shows which methods relate to each group.

Obviously, the use of visual aids in teaching is not possible without the use of oral and written instruction, and the use of practical methods is impossible without the use of the oral method or methods using visual aids. Similarly, the oral and written methods are not used in practice without some visual aids and practical work by the pupils. Therefore, the above classification of teaching methods, which shows that the main source of cognition of the pupils in one group of methods is speech, in another visual aids, and in the third the practical work of the pupils, at the same time presupposes the existence of other sources of cognition in each group of methods.

Before the reorganization of the schools, teaching was based on oral and written methods; visual aids were used to a small extent, and practical methods still less, as the schools were without the necessary ties with life, nor was there any proper preparation of the

TABLE 6. Teaching methods

Method	Main source of cognition
Group of oral and written methods	
Oral exposition: explanation, description, lectures. Discussion. Written work: dictation, written accounts, reading, bookwork	Speech and the written word
Group of methods of teaching with visual aids	
Demonstration by the teacher and observation by the pupils, during lessons, excursions, practical training in production covering objects, phenomena, and processes of nature, production, social life, language, historical monuments, works of art, etc. Demonstration by the teacher, and observation by the pupils of films, slides, tables, geographical and historical maps, models, relief models, and other two- and three-dimensional visual aids. Carrying out various observations over a long period such as phenological, meteorological, or hydrological observations, etc.	Objects, phenomena and processes of reality and their representations
Group of practical methods of teaching	
The composition of theses, abstracts, and reports. Carrying out various practical exercises. The solution of problems. Experimentation and the solution of experimental problems. Experimental work by the pupils in the study room, the laboratory, and on the experimental plot. Measuring work. Surveying. Operational and objective methods in the teaching of working and experimental skills; practical experience in productive work. Planning, designing and development of labour-saving devices and other means for gaining experience in constructive and technical work; practical work in the workshops, experimental work on the agricultural experimental plot, or at the school meteorological station. Work by the pupils in the fields of production, culture, and social work	Practical activities of the pupils

pupils for work. Little use was made of the film in education, and radio and television were hardly used at all. Nor was there any wide use of the various forms of independent creative work by the pupils, such as experimental agricultural work, the construction of technical instruments, models, etc. No proper attention was given to developing the active interest of the pupils in their work. The independent work carried out by the pupils was on a very limited scale.

It should not be assumed from the above that it is necessary to discard entirely the established methods of teaching. They must be retained, but improved, taking into account the new tasks and content of education and the great importance of education and training for work in the new syllabuses. The use of oral and written methods of teaching must be restricted, while the use of visual aids, and still more of practical methods, must be extended. All these methods are essential, however, and they must all be used, each at the proper time and in the proper combination with the others, in order to carry out with the greatest degree of success, while observing economy in time and facilities, the new tasks of the schools, the new syllabuses and curricula.

The task of the schools is to give the pupils a proper knowledge of scientific methods and practical productive work. The teaching methods used must arouse the active interest of the pupils, and develop in them the spirit of inquiry, initiative, independence, a creative approach to any subject, and a communist attitude to work. The methods used should also inculcate in the pupils the habit of self-improvement, strengthen the ties of the school with life and with the practical work of communist construction, and should improve the ideological and political education of the pupils. The independent creative work of the pupils must be developed in every way.

Teaching methods must be freed from everything that has detached the school from life and from production and that has caused it to take the direction of cramming, dogmatism, and formalism. They must be supplemented by everything that links the school with life and helps to prepare resourceful, industrious, active, and ideologically trained members of a communist society.

The development of socially useful and other forms of independent work by the pupils has had, and will continue to have, a powerful influence on the organization of the scholastic work in the school. The system of education which consists solely of lessons in class is already outmoded. Of course lessons in class are the most effective way of organizing the study of the natural, technical, and humane sciences, and they therefore remain the basic form of instruction, but stereotyped methods in giving lessons cannot be tolerated (questioning, expounding of new subject matter, homework, and consolidation of the subject matter). Of course lessons may be given in the above manner, but side by side with them there should be lessons in which only new subject matter is expounded, or only consolidation of previous subject matter takes place, or only independent creative work by the pupils is carried out, or in which there is only checking of the degree to which the pupils have mastered the subject matter studied, etc. Checking the degree of progress must be made by various independent means, which not only stimulate the activity of the pupils, but also make it easier for the teacher to check their knowledge, ability, and skill.

Side by side with lessons, homework and discussions, wide use must be made of practical activities; practical productive experience by the pupils, and socially useful work in production; excursions (productive, cultural and historical, and scientific); lectures, debates, competitions and exhibitions; optional class and group activities, etc. Besides working in classes, which is the basic form of grouping the pupils for work, various other ways of grouping them should be used, e.g., in teams consisting of pupils from various grades.

The concept of extra-curricular work has to be reconsidered. Hitherto, extra-curricular work meant any voluntary work by the pupils carried on outside the classroom. Now, however, much obligatory work is done outside the classroom. Extra-curricular work now covers the following: (a) obligatory work by the pupils (socially productive work, practical activities, practical training in production, excursions, etc.); (b) optional and voluntary creative work by the pupils (study and social groups, social evenings, holiday trips, etc.).

As the pupils take a wider part in productive work, the system of obligatory extra-curricular activities will play an increasingly important role in the educative work of the schools, and is bound to have its effect on the system of lessons in class. This effect will be that extra-curricular work will lead to more and more educative subject matter from actual life and production being added to the work in the classroom.

Polytechnical education makes use of all the methods which are accepted in the teaching of general subjects and in training for work and production. The main tasks of polytechnical education are: (a) to impart knowledge of the main branches of modern production and its general scientific bases; (b) to teach the pupils how to use the basic instruments of production and to fit them into socially useful work. We will therefore examine below the

151

methods and forms of organization of education which are used in carrying out these two tasks.

METHODS AND FORMS OF ORGANIZATION OF THE STUDY OF THE MAIN BRANCHES OF PRODUCTION AND ITS GENERAL SCIENTIFIC BASES

Oral and written methods

Oral and written methods occupy, and will continue to occupy, an important place in polytechnical education, as thought and work are linked with speech, and books remain the principal source of scientific knowledge. Moreover, oral explanation by the teacher and the pupils, written work, and bookwork, which are independent methods of communicating and consolidating knowledge, are at the same time, as partial methods, a component part of all the other methods used in polytechnical instruction. The teacher must systematically explain the bases of the knowledge of production, using also other methods such as visual aids, independent work in the study room, the laboratory, the experimental plot, and the library, and combine all this with fitting the pupils into socially useful work.

In order to make the subjects as clear as possible, instruction follows the pattern of introduction, exposition and conclusion.

The task of the introduction is to state the problem and the purpose of the exposition which is to follow; to set forth the practical, social, and logical reasons for studying the problem; to awaken the interest and attention of the pupils; and to explain to the pupils the plan for studying the problem, which, for purposes of exposition, is divided into the particular questions forming component parts of it. These are linked together in a strictly logical form.

The subject matter is expounded, passing systematically from one question to another in the order in which the general problem is divided. First, each question is stated by the teacher, in order to draw attention to it; then the subject matter relating to each question is expounded logically and, finally, the degree to which the pupils have understood and assimilated what has been expounded is checked by the teacher and the knowledge imparted is consolidated in the pupils' memory. The previous experience of the pupils (particularly practical experience) is utilized in this connexion, and the importance of the expounded scientific data for the practical work of communist construction is explained.

The task of the conclusion is to generalize and systematize the expounded subject matter, including its significance for practical work. The exposition must begin and end from the standpoint of social and working practice; this rule is observed in order to link instruction with life.

In expounding questions of technique, technology and organization of production, reference is made to the experience of factories, collective farms, State farms, and the practical work of communist construction in the pupils' own area.

The active interest of the pupils is increased if the exposition follows the question-and-answer method, i.e., the teacher states one question after another and shows how they are resolved in science. Here, subject matter is adduced from the history of science, technology and production and from the pupils' observations of production and working methods.

Dialogues in which the pupils try to find the answers to problems increase their mental activity. Searching for answers to problems considerably stimulates the pupils' minds, and when they do find the answer, they enjoy a feeling of satisfaction. But this approach achieves its aim when the pupils have acquired, in their previous studies, the necessary stock of knowledge for the solution of the problems put to them and when the solution itself requires an effort within the competence of the pupils. The exposition of the subject matter studied is also made more effective by the pupil's independent work accompanying or supplementing the exposition. This may be either the preparation of answers to questions, minor written work, or minor work on material given out by the teacher, etc.

Finally, an important method of increasing the interest of the pupils when expounding subjects regarding production is to make use of the elements of planning and design. The manner in which this is done will be shown by taking the example of the study of chemical production.

The study of the technology and techniques of the manufacture of chemical products always presupposes a knowledge by the pupils of the chemical reactions on which the production process is based and of the laws to which they are subject. When this is the case, the teacher usually goes straight on to explain the subject matter relating to the manufacture of products in a factory. In that case the pupils' minds fail to become very active. Their minds become very active, however, if the teacher invites the pupils to reflect upon and resolve by themselves the question of how the chemical reactions they are studying can be brought about technically in a factory for the manufacture of a product, that is to say, when the teacher first organizes the independent 'planning and designing' of the production process by the pupils.

153

But are the pupils in a position to carry out successfully such 'planning'?

It has been observed that, when studying the chemical reactions on which production is based, some pupils successfully construct even fairly complicated apparatus, provided that the idea of the experiment is clear to them and provided that from their previous studies they have acquired a certain amount of knowledge of the parts of the apparatus and the way in which it is assembled. When constructing apparatus, the pupils naturally have some difficulty, mainly because they lack knowledge of some vital part of the apparatus (three-necked bottles, absorption towers, etc.). The pupils however do find their way out of such difficulties by being allowed to watch the assembly of various vessels and parts of complicated apparatus in the laboratory.

In the process of experimental investigation it was observed that, after studying and experimenting with chemical reactions on which the production of chemicals is based, the pupils were capable of anticipating certain aspects of the technology of production. It was therefore decided to carry out some individual teaching experiments including the elements of the planning of production technology by the pupils.

Here, for example, is a short description of an individual teaching experiment with one particular pupil.

The pupil was shown, and had thoroughly explained to him, an experiment for obtaining synthetic hydrochloric acid in the laboratory. He was then asked to find the answers, unaided, to the following questions: What raw material is used for the production of synthetic hydrochloric acid? What are the stages into which the production process is divided? What apparatus is needed for each stage of production? What processes take place in this apparatus?

The pupil replied that the raw materials for the production of synthetic hydrochloric acid are hydrogen and chlorine, that the production process is divided into two stages (the preparation of hydrogen chloride and its absorption by water), and that the apparatus needed consists of a furnace for burning up the hydrogen in the chlorine and an apparatus for absorbing the hydrogen chloride. Proceeding from the arrangement of the laboratory apparatus for burning up hydrogen in chlorine, and with only very slight help from the experimenter (in the form of additional questions), the pupil arrived at the conclusion that the furnace for burning up hydrogen in chlorine in a factory should consist of a cylindrical vessel with pipes led into the base for the supply of hydrogen and chlorine and a take-off pipe at the top.

The pupil was asked to consider what material the furnace

should be made of. He made several suggestions, and after discussing them with the experimenter he came to the conclusion that the furnace must be made of a material capable of withstanding high temperatures and not corroding under the action of hydrogen chloride. Judging from the design of the absorption tower used in the experiment, the pupil drew the conclusion that the factory apparatus for the absorption of hydrogen chloride must consist of a high tower made of acid-resistant material and filled with an acid-resistant packing through which a liquid is made to flow to absorb the hydrogen chloride, in the same manner as, in the laboratory apparatus, the column was packed with broken glass through which the water flowed.

The lower part of Fig. 1 shows the design of a factory installation for obtaining hydrochloric acid made by the pupil in the way it appeared to him as the result of his independent 'planning'.

The more the pupils accumulate concepts and ideas about individual types of production and their general principles, the better they are able to 'plan' the technological process, thus demonstrating their success in developing the ability to reason in technical terms. Fig. 1 also shows the first and subsequent 'projects' devised by another pupil. It was observed that the better the pupils master the details of experiments for obtaining substances in the laboratory, the better they plan the technological schemes of production. The success of 'planning' depends also on a carefully thought-out system of questions stimulating the mental activity of the pupils, and on the calm discussion of all suggestions in order to show whether they are correct or impracticable.

Lessons carried out according to this method are followed with interest and creative enthusiasm. Guidance on the planning is given during the class by means of a system of questions prepared by the teacher beforehand. The pupils make a large number of suggestions, which are discussed in detail and then accepted ro rejected. When, at the end of the planning, the teacher demonstrates the scheme of production and gives a short explanation of its technical details, the pupils quickly take it all in and express their satisfaction with the work. Questions put to the pupils in subsequent lessons show the permanent and intelligent manner in which the pupils have mastered the subject of production.

The elements of 'planning', used in the process of studying the bases of production in the schools, are undoubtedly a most important means of developing scientific and technical reasoning ability in the pupils.

As the years go by, many technological schemes learnt in school become out of date, and it is no longer of any practical value to know them, but the sound knowledge of the main principles and technical methods of production and the ability to reason in scientific and technical terms remain a firm basis for the success of former pupils in their work in production.

In preparing pupils for social life and work, Soviet teachers pay attention to the development of the pupils' abilities in speaking and writing. In every lesson, they include something designed to develop the pupils' power of expression.

Observations carried out in the last few years show that, in teaching pupils about production, it is advisable to keep to the following plan: products (composition, properties, uses); raw materials (composition, properties, preparation for manufacture); the natural and scientific bases of the transformation of the raw materials into finished goods; the organization of the main stages of the production process, its technology and techniques; and the organization of the main stages of the production process. If production is studied according to this plan, the pupils gain a complete idea of it as well as of the relationship between the object of the work, the equipment and the work process.

Another plan is also used in the schools: the raw materials, the technological process and its natural and scientific bases, production techniques and the finished products.

Experience has shown that the use of the first alternative teaching plan gives better results than use of the second plan, as may be seen from Table 7, in which data regarding the pupils' mastery of information concerning metallurgical production, when using the first and the second plans, are placed side-by-side for purposes of comparison.

Teaching on the subject of metallurgical production according to the first alternative plan gave better results because the pupils learned immediately what products were obtained in metallurgical production and what their composition and properties were. Knowledge of the composition and properties of the products enabled them to understand why specific raw materials are used in a given case, and thus facilitated their understanding of their composition and properties.

The study of the natural and scientific bases of the transformation of the raw material into a product revealed the principles and nature of the production process, and this, in its turn, helped them to understand and quickly master its technology, techniques, and organization. As a result, theory is linked in the closest possible manner with practice, and the natural sciences with techniques and technology. The explanation of each question

TABLE 7. Percentage of correct answers given by pupils regarding metallurgical production

Question	First alternative plan	Second alternative plan
Production of pig-iron		
Pig-iron (composition and properties)	56	21
Iron ores	72	68
Chemical reactions in blast-furnace production .	69	57
Main stages and processes in blast-furnace production	96	40
Construction and principles of operation of a blast furnace	66	47
Production of steel by the Bessemer process		
The properties of steel	56	21
Raw materials	46	—
Chemical reactions	68	14
Technological processes	73	52
Construction and principles of operation of a Bessemer converter	67	37
Disadvantages of the Bessemer process of making steel	46	52
Production of steel by the open-hearth process		
The properties of steel	56	21
Raw materials	76	10
Chemical reactions	82	18
The construction and principles of operation of an open-hearth furnace	73	23
Advantages of the open-hearth method of making steel over the Bessemer method	77	56

served as the basis for the understanding of each successive question.

Instruction according to the second alternative plan did not have this advantage—it is not consecutive, and therefore does not achieve the requisite effect.

Teaching concerning production by the oral and written method alone in class, without observations, experiments, and visual aids, or observations, experiments and visual aids without teaching by the oral and written method, cannot successfully provide the pupils with a proper knowledge of production. Why is it that oral and written teaching alone fails to provide specific, sound and clearly understood knowledge?

157

All our ideas, conceptions, judgements and inferences, are derived from sensory data, perceptions and visualizations. The richer the sensory data which forms the basis for the formation of ideas, the more successfully such ideas are formed, other conditions being equal. If a stock of sensory data has been accumulated by the pupils in previous cognitive experience by means of excursions, experiments, etc., then verbal explanation is provided with a material basis. It is from previous observations and practical activities that the pupil draws material for analysis and synthesis, abstraction and generalization, i.e., for the formation of ideas.

The more figurative the verbal explanation, the easier and more correct is the regrouping and reintegration of old relationships, the tightening of some and the loosening of others, which leads to the formation of new systems of temporary relationships subjectively experienced as new ideas created by the imagination. These visualizations of the imagination also serve as a point of support for the formation of ideas.

If, however, in the earlier cognitive experience of the pupils, there is no basis for the sprouting of new ideas connected with the material explained by the teacher, then the pupils will remember the words but will not assimilate properly the idea expressed by the teacher. This is how formalism arises in teaching.

On the other hand, underestimation by the teacher of the value and importance of verbal expression raises serious difficulties for the reasoning process of the pupils, for it exists as verbal reasoning.

The formation of new concepts and ideas regarding production, on the basis of existing words, phrases, concepts, and ideas, demands the consolidation of new ideas in new scientific terms and formulae. The assimilation of new terms and formulae assists the further development of the processes of abstraction and generalization and, hence, the further development of ideas.

Verbal methods must always be combined with visual and practical methods of teaching. The utilization of visualizations of the memory in the formation of visualizations of the imagination and of concepts is one of the ways of using visualization in the wide sense of the word in which this term was used by K. D. Ushinskii.

Visual methods

The use of visual methods in teaching provides for direct perception by the pupils of the objects, phenomena, and processes of production, or plane and three-dimensional visual aids representing these objects or phenomena. More often than not, these methods take the form of observations. On the basis of these direct perceptions, visualizations of the memory are composed, concepts are formed and theoretical generalizations are made. By perceiving plane and three-dimensional representations of objects and phenomena, the pupils build up a picture of them with the help of the imagination.

An idea of teaching with visual aids is given by Table 8, which lists the various forms and means to be used and the activities of the pupils, which are used in the study of production.

The independent work carried out by the pupils with collections of raw materials, semi-finished and finished products, with a view to describing their properties, is of great importance for the successful assimilation of information concerning production. The best results are obtained when collections of materials are used which are so arranged that they can be given out to the pupils, who can handle the materials, examine them thoroughly, and carry out simple experiments which enable them to determine their physical properties.

Two types of demonstration are used in the teaching of physics, chemistry, biology, machine construction, electrical engineering, and technology: first, demonstration experiments which, in a bare form unburdened with practical details, familiarize the pupils with physical, chemical, and biological phenomena and the laws which govern them, and secondly demonstration experiments which show how scientific knowledge is applied in practice; these explain the scientific bases of the corresponding production phenomena or technical apparatus and thus lead the pupils directly to full comprehension of the production processes. For this type of demonstration, appropriate sets of equipment are assembled (instruments, mechanisms, dynamos, electric motors, etc., or working models of machines, apparatus, and production processes). Examples of such working models are those used in teaching physics or machine construction (model steam boilers, steam turbines, radio-control installations, etc.), those used in the teaching of chemistry and chemical engineering (model installations for the production of synthetic sulphuric acid, model installations for the production of sulphuric acid by the contact method, models of plant for the production of alkalis and chlorine by the electrolytic method), and so forth.

In teaching about production in schools, wide use is made of the demonstration of various aids representing diagrams of production processes, machines, and apparatus. Without these aids, it is impossible to create the visual images in the minds of the pupils that serve as the point of support for abstract reasoning in the formation of scientific concepts of production. Plane representations

TABLE 8. Forms and means of teaching with visual aids, and activities of the pupils in the study of production

Elements of production	Recommended	
	For studying separate elements of production	For studying all elements of production
The product (its composition, properties and economic importance)	Demonstration of specimens of the product, tables of its uses, and experiments showing its composition and properties. Independent work with material distributed by the teacher. Laboratory experiments and practical activities concerning the composition and properties of the product.	Projection of films and slides, and collections of drawings and photographs shown by means of an epidiascope. Excursions: 1. To power stations, works, factories, collective and State farms, and tractor stations. 2. To museums. 3. To the technological laboratories of higher educational institutions and scientific research institutions.
Raw materials (composition and properties)	Demonstration of collections of raw materials and of pictures and tables illustrating the manner in which the raw materials are obtained. Independent work with materials distributed by the teacher, for the study of the products, the raw materials, the technology, techniques, and organization of production.	Independent observations of production by the pupils for the aforesaid purpose.
The scientific basis of the transformation of the raw material into the finished product	Demonstrations of how the product is obtained in the laboratory, the workshop, and on experimental plots. Practical activities to discover the scientific bases of production.	Socially useful and productive work in production.

160

Elements of production	Recommended	
	For studying separate elements of production	For studying all elements of production
The technological process and techniques in the main stages of production	Demonstrations: 1. Of diagrams of the production processes and the construction of machinery and equipment. 2. Of models of machinery and equipment (both solid models and dismountable models.) 3. Of collections of semi-finished products. Independent work by the pupils with drawings, plans, and models.	
The organization of the production process in its main stages	Demonstration of diagrams of the organization and management of production.	

alone, however, do not give the pupils sufficiently clear and precise ideas of the machines, apparatus, and factory installations, as many pupils find it difficult to associate the three-dimensional object with its plane representation on paper. It is for this reason that models, whether working or non-working, are used in addition to plane drawings. Experience has shown that the pupils obtain cognitive results when models of machines and apparatus (Fig. 2) are used in conjunction with schematic diagrams of the same machines (Fig. 3). The effectiveness of this combined method of visual teaching is explained by the fact that the models help the pupils to create images in the imagination of the machines or equipment, while the diagrams and drawings help the pupils to find the basic and vital parts of the machines. When, by making use of a model, the teacher has given the pupils an idea of a machine or factory installation, he goes over to the diagram in order to help the pupils to generalize these ideas. If the pupils experience any difficulty in abstracting and generalizing, the teacher returns to the model in order that the pupils can draw from their perception of it the empiric material that would facilitate the process of reasoning. By giving the names of the machines and equipment and of their parts in both their spoken and written form, the teacher helps to form in the pupil's mind the links between the word and the image, thus giving him the necessary point of support to enable him to pass from idea to understanding through the processes of abstraction and generalization.

Although the above aids (collections, machines, installations, diagrams, models) do much to facilitate the formation of ideas concerning production, they nevertheless do not create a real picture of it. These aids are to some extent approximate abstractions of concrete production, but like any abstraction, they are close enough to reality, and help comprehension. For this reason an important role is played by films in acquainting the pupils with production in a concrete manner.

Although films contain, on the whole, all the elements of information concerning production, watching them results in a good knowledge of production only when the pupils are prepared for the showing by a full, systematic explanation of all the instructional material, aided by the use of diagrams and models and experiments. The film cannot replace explanation by the teacher. The effectiveness of the film is increased if, before it is shown, the teacher puts questions to the pupils which they must answer as they watch it; if, during the film, the teacher draws the attention of the pupils to individual aspects of the objects shown and explains them; and if, after watching the film, the pupils are questioned and are given marks for their answers.

The projection of films serves as an alternative to excursions to power stations, factories, or collective farms if, for some reason, the pupils cannot go there. The showing of films on all kinds of subjects also serves to widen the polytechnical horizons of the pupils in a manner which it is hard to overrate. This is why a large number of modern films on production have already been made, and work is going on to produce further films to assist the teaching of physics, chemistry, biology, machine construction, electrical technology, agricultural science, etc.

Nevertheless, the showing of films cannot of course take the place of observation visits to actual sites.

Excursions and observations during these excursions are an extremely effective method of familiarizing the pupils with production. They give the pupils a direct opportunity of acquainting themselves with production and forming vivid impressions and ideas. No verbal descriptions or visual aids can take the place of excursions. Satisfactory results are obtained, however, only by those excursions in the preparation and carrying-out of which, as well as in generalizing the results, provision has been made for the creation of certain conditions to facilitate and make more precise the analytical and synthetical reasoning of the pupils. Such conditions are:

1. The preliminary familiarization of the teacher with the production in question through the study of technical literature and a personal visit to the enterprise; working out, with the excursion leader, the programme of the excursion, including acquainting the pupils with the history of the enterprise, its economic importance, its products and raw material, the main stages of the production process, the general principles and techniques of the processes, the main trades of the factory personnel, and the achievements of the enterprise in fulfilling production plans; the establishment of a short (one-and-a-half to two hours) itinerary for the excursion, together with an indication of which places in the enterprise are to be visited (they should not exceed seven or eight), for how long, and for what purpose (observation, explanation by the excursion leader, conversations with the workers), and so on.

2. The familiarization in class, before the excursion, of the pupils with the products, raw materials, scientific bases, technology, and techniques of production of the enterprise to be visited, using for this purpose the various forms and means of visual teaching. Explanation to the pupils of the programme and itinerary of the excursion. Writing-down by the pupils in their notebooks of the questions to be borne in mind when making observations at the enterprise and which must be answered in class after the excursion.

3. An opening talk, at the beginning of the excursion, in order to familiarize the pupils with the history of the factory and its importance in the economy of the country. Observation by the pupils, at every point of the itinerary, of the operation of the machines and apparatus, the technological processes, and the work of the staff, and listening to the explanations given by the guide. A closing talk at the end of the excursion, with the aim of summing up the pupils' observations, explaining the organization of labour in production, and answering any questions.

4. The questioning of all the pupils in class, after the excursion, on the topics given to them before the excursion in order to correct, render more accurate, and consolidate the ideas about production gained by the pupils during the excursion. The organization of independent work by the pupils, both at home and at school after school hours, in forming collections of products, part-finished products and raw materials, and the execution of diagrams of production processes, sketches

of machines and apparatus, and written accounts of the excursion.

In the last two or three years, in carrying out Lenin's instructions regarding polytechnical education, every school has worked out its own system of excursions to production places so that, during their school career, the pupils visit, if possible, a power station, metal and machine-building works and chemical factories, an industrial building site, collective or State farms, market gardens, and stock farms, a machine-repair station, a railway station, a telephone exchange, a radio station, and so on. In every area, depending on the types of production found in the areas, the local education authorities and the heads of the schools, with the active assistance of the Councils of National Economy and the agricultural administrations, decide on the places to be visited by the schools; the district education advisory bureau, assisted by engineers and agriculturalists, works out the programme and procedure of the excursions. Dates and times for the reception of excursions at the undertakings are fixed and the excursion leaders chosen.

Some excursions are conducted in a combined way, that is, the pupils simultaneously receive information on production in accordance with the teaching programmes for physics, chemistry, biology, geography, technology, etc., while side by side with these excursions there are, of course, some which merely meet the requirements of the programme in respect of a single subject.

On the basis of the list of places and subjects for excursions, the administrative part of each school, with the help of the teachers, prepares an annual plan of excursions for each class, laying down not only the subjects and places for the excursions, but also the dates. Excursions to the undertakings officially linked with the school (works, factories, collective and State farms) naturally figure much more frequently in the lists than visits to other undertakings (Fig. 4).

Pupils often become very tired on excursions, and moving about to the places of the excursion takes up a considerable time; in order not to overstrain the pupils the Ministry of Education has decided to allocate six school days a year (three days per half-year) for excursions in grades V–XI inclusive. This does not mean, however, that the whole of any week in the course of the year will be spent on excursions. Depending on their subject, excursions are carried out at various times of the year. The excursions take place on various days, so that each teacher 'loses', in the course of the year, only the lessons of six separate days. In other words, the plan for excursions envisages the use for excursions of one Monday, one Tuesday, one Wednesday, one Thursday, one Friday and one

Saturday—six days in all, but at different times of the year.

Experience has shown that two excursions each lasting one-and-a-half to two hours can be made to the same production enterprise on the same day, but only on condition that, in the interval between the excursion, the pupils are given the chance to rest and fortify themselves in the canteen of the enterprise. Thus, when the excursion is to a nearby enterprise, the first part of the excursion is devoted, let us say, to questions of power, while the second part is devoted to technological questions. The first part of an excursion to a collective farm might be devoted to questions on agricultural biology, and the second part to questions on the techniques of agriculture, etc.

For an excursion, the class is split into two groups, as it is not possible to carry out an excursion properly with more than twenty pupils. While one group is on an excursion under the guidance of, for example, a biologist, the other group goes on an excursion under the guidance of a physicist. Later, the teachers change groups.

The enterprises designate special persons to conduct the excursions. Aided by the teachers, these persons acquaint themselves with the preparatory work performed by the pupils and with the requirements of their curriculum.

In addition to excursions, touristic trips in the surrounding area and to distant parts are used to broaden the polytechnical horizon of the pupils. On these trips, the pupils visit works, factories, power stations, collective and State farms, building sites, scientific institutions, etc., and collect material for collections regarding production exhibits which are used in school as teaching aids.

Practical methods

Although the use of visual methods in teaching envisages working with objects and the phenomena of reality, it does not imply their modification in order to understand them. However, a profound knowledge of the laws of nature and their use, the assimilation of knowledge concerning technology and production techniques, and the acquisition of working abilities and skills can only be achieved by practical means, that is to say, when teaching is based on the practical (educational or socially useful) activities of the pupils, organized and directed by the teacher.

In carrying out practical work, the pupils make use of the knowledge they have previously acquired, see the changes which take place, analyse them, reach definite conclusions and decisions, gain new ideas, concepts, abilities, and skills, and develop new

165

traits of character. Practical methods are in complete harmony with the active nature of the pupils themselves.

In the study of the properties of materials, the scientific principles of the construction and operation of machines and mechanisms, and the scientific bases of technological processes, more and more use is being made of the experimental method, in the form of practical work in the study, the laboratory and on experimental plots. The schools are at this moment developing an interesting system for making use of the experimental method, the basis of which is to strengthen the ties with life and to develop the activities of the pupils.

Before setting the experimental work, the teachers try to start from the corresponding phenomena of nature and production and show that it is necessary to carry out an experiment in order to understand the laws of science and their use in production. Conclusions are drawn from the experiment carried out, and then, on the basis of the scientific data obtained, the teacher once more returns to the phenomena of production or nature, and explains these from the scientific point of view.

In order to increase the activities of the pupils during an experiment, the teacher demonstrates, explaining everything, and then asks the pupils to repeat the same experiment themselves, using the equipment laid out on the pupils' desks. He also asks them to write down in their copybooks the data observed and the conclusions reached which he also writes on the blackboard. This method ensures that the pupils, under the direct supervision of the teacher, acquire their first practical skill in experimenting and observing and in explaining the results of experiments.

Later, the teacher trains his pupils in how to carry out experiments on the basis of written instructions. This demands a higher degree of activity from the pupils.

An even more active and independent form of experimentation is the solving of experimental problems. In this case, only the details of the problem are given, and the pupil must work out the experiment himself, carry it out mentally, and then in practice. In the more complicated cases the pupil is given an experimental problem to solve, for which he only has part of the necessary knowledge and ability. Using books, he independently makes good the gaps in his knowledge, then develops his ideas for the experiment, designs the apparatus, carries out the experiment, makes all the necessary observations, analyses them, and prepares diagrams and drawings and a written account.

It is not difficult to see that each new type of experiment demands from the pupils increasingly greater effort, independence and initiative, and inculcates the characteristics of the scientific approach, which is of incalculable value in the training of creative, active members of society, with plenty of initiative.

All these forms of experiments are introduced one after the other in teaching, so that they are within the pupils' capacity and assist their development. The higher the degree of training of the pupils in a particular branch of science or production, the greater is the possibility of using more active forms of experimentation for teaching purposes.

One of the ways in which pupils can be made more active in studying production by the experimental method is the use of hypotheses. This awakens and maintains interest in the subject, stimulates the development of scientific imagination and reasoning, familiarizes the pupils with the methods and means of gaining scientific knowledge, and develops the ability to foresee phenomena and make creative use of knowledge. The pupils can put forward hypotheses independently only after they have accumulated the necessary knowledge. But this possibility can be brought about more quickly if the teacher, in explaining his subject matter, himself puts forward hypotheses for explaining observed facts and tells the pupils how, in the history of science and technology, hypotheses have been put forward, reasoned and proved.

The experimental method, the use of hypotheses, and the creative scientific approach are now widely used in teaching about work and general technical and specialized subjects. Production-study rooms have been established in enterprises and schools. These rooms contain materials and equipment for testing them, instruments, parts and units of machines, individual machines, plans for the organization of work, specimen methods of acccounting for and control of production, material relating to the advanced experience of production experts, etc. In such rooms it is possible to carry out demonstrations and laboratory work, creative experimental work, and to use the knowledge acquired in connexion with general-education subjects, thereby equipping the pupils with the technical knowledge and abilities required in order to develop inventiveness and a rationalizing approach to work, which are important for the training of creative workers in socialist production.

In familiarizing the pupils with the main branches of production in order to develop their creative activity and independence, their initiative and keenness, and their technical intelligence and resourcefulness, use is made of the designing and planning of the easier production processes and techniques, and the solving of problems relating to production. These problems are linked with the pupils' practical work in the study rooms, on experimental plots, and in workshops and enterprises. Solving these experimental and practical problems is a method used both in the process of imparting scientific and production information, and in the process of consolidating and testing the knowledge thus imparted.

A factor of enormous importance in familiarizing the pupils with the fundamentals of production is their practical work (see Fig. 5). Practical work gives the pupils a great deal of information about production if, during such work, the following conditions are fulfilled:

1. The pupils must learn all about the undertaking as a whole (by means of visits, observations, and discussions), stress being laid on the familiarization of the pupils not only with the specific characteristics of production at the enterprise, but also with the points which it has in common with other branches of production.
2. Theoretical and practical familiarization of the pupils with the factory shop in which they will carry out their practical productive work (using for this purpose visits, observations, lectures, and laboratory activities).
3. Familiarization of the pupils with the construction and operation of the machines on which they will be working.
4. Instruction of the pupils in production operations.
5. The organization of the productive work of probationers at their work places, and the carrying-out of their various tasks in the operation of the machines, production processes, etc.
6. The use, in their production training, of the pupils' training in physics, chemistry, biology, and other general-education subjects in connexion with machinery and electrical engineering.

Practical production experience helps the pupils to gain a deeper insight into the scientific principles of modern industry and to gain a closer acquaintance with the work of factory hands and engineering and technical staff.

In order to summarize knowledge about production in general and to separate the general and the specific into its various branches, it has become customary in the schools to arrange conferences of the pupils of the senior classes with the participation of the teachers of mathematics, physics, chemistry, biology, drawing, geography, and the fundamentals of production. At these conferences, the pupils read papers on polytechnical subjects. Engineering and technical personnel from the enterprises and collective and State farms officially linked with the school take part in the work of these conferences; the reports are illustrated with visual aids prepared by the pupils themselves; the reports presented are discussed by those present, and at the end of the conference one of the teachers sums up.

A very important part in familiarizing the pupils with the main branches of production is played by the work done outside the classroom, which widens and deepens the polytechnical knowledge obtained by the pupils in their lessons on physics, chemistry, biology, practical work, and the fundamentals of production.

Physical, chemical, young naturalist, mathematical, technical and other groups have become widespread in schools. Groups are formed to study electrical engineering, radio, machinery, automobiles, tractors, agriculture, building and other subjects. These groups study a wide range of production questions and thus widen and deepen the knowledge acquired in class. Production questions are studied in these groups by reading scientific and technical literature, by experimental work, and by devising technical projects and carrying them out in the school workshop (see Fig. 6), by making visual aids for the school, producing newspapers, and so forth. These study groups organize excursions to enterprises, to laboratories of higher educational establishments and research institutes and polytechnical museums. These groups also organize mass polytechnical work in the schools such as lectures, evening meetings, readers' conferences, and competitions, under the direction of the teachers.

Lectures by engineers and agricultural scientists, leading workers in industrial undertakings and experts on high-yield crops, and members of the scientific staff of research institutes and higher educational establishments are organized for the pupils both in school and outside. The subjects of these lectures relate to the main branches of production.

Evening meetings on production subjects organized in the schools are attended by engineers, agricultural scientists, leading workers from industrial enterprises, experts on high-yield crops, and scientific specialists. The theme of the meeting could cover 'Great Soviet power stations', 'Achievements in Soviet machine construction', 'The modern nitrate industry', etc. The pupils prepare visual aids and experiments for these evening meetings as part of their group work. These evening meetings serve as a form of propaganda for the theoretical, experimental, technical, and excursion work of the groups, and also as a means of attracting new pupils to constant systematic work in the technical field. The talks given are of great educational value.

In many schools, evening meetings devoted to the enterprise or collective farm sponsoring the school are held every year. At these gatherings the pupils talk about the results of their study of the enterprise in question, its leading workers, the successes of the enterprise in carrying out the resolutions of the Twenty-first Congress of the Communist Party of the U.S.S.R., and about their desire to use their knowledge and abilities for work in industry and agriculture. Exhibitions are prepared for the meetings. Members of the management and of the party and trade-union organizations of the enterprise are invited. Such evening meetings serve to reinforce the link between the school and the sponsoring enterprises.

Readers' conferences, devoted to the discussion of popular scientific and technical literature, occupy an important place in work outside the schoolroom.

One way of showing the standard reached by the pupils in their theoretical and practical mastery of the fundamentals of science and production is the holding of competitions, which may be organized for one school, a town, or a whole region. These competitions usually have two parts: (a) written answers to questions; (b) practical work in laboratories and workshops. Higher educational institutions and enterprises are invited to take part in the organization of these competitions, which are preceded by lectures to the pupils.

The extra-curricular work is so arranged as not to overburden the pupils. It is closely linked with the work of institutions for out-of-school education.

The Pioneer and Young Communist organizations of the schools are forces that enable the pupils to increase their creative activity out of school.

Well-organized extra-curricular scientific and technical work helps to develop the propensities and talents of the pupils and to promote a steady interest in a definite field of science or technology, which is a most important condition for the correct choice of a career. It is well known that young scientists and technicians usually choose their careers very successfully, because in class and in the technical groups after school they acquire the necessary knowledge and skills, together with a steady interest in the relevant field of work.

The knowledge of production gained by the pupils is appraised in Soviet schools by various methods: by oral examination of the pupils in class, compositions on production subjects, written tests consisting of questions and problems, reports presented by the pupils in class and at conferences, creative work in preparing drawings, sketches, instruments, models, collections, etc., and by means of the planning and carrying-out of agricultural experiments, etc.

170

CHAPTER VIII

METHODS AND FORMS OF ORGANIZATION OF POLYTECHNICAL EDUCATION (*continued*)

by S. G. Shapovalenko

METHODS OF TEACHING POLYTECHNICAL WORKING SKILLS AND OF INTRODUCING THE PUPILS TO PRODUCTIVE WORK

Basic principles

As has been shown, the teaching of polytechnical working skills to the pupils is carried out during the process of teaching general-education subjects, general technical subjects and in teaching about work and production. In studying these subjects, the pupils are also introduced to socially useful and production work. This takes place to the fullest extent during the process of training in production as the formation of working skills takes place, as a rule, while carrying out socially useful and productive work and is directed towards acquiring the knowledge and ability to carry out such work with the accuracy, speed, and productivity attained in society. In the process of work training, skills are also developed, as a rule, while carrying out socially useful work, but the pupils are not expected to reach the standard of a highly-skilled worker in mastering each type of work. To a lesser degree, the pupils' introduction to socially useful work is carried out during the teaching of skills at lessons on general-education and technical subjects, but here again the pupils sometimes make instruments and models, and carry out productive agricultural work which has a socially useful value.

The teaching of working skills and the introduction of the pupils to work is carried out in such a way that the pupils understand the scientific bases of work operations and of work as a whole. Nevertheless, the teaching of the scientific basis of the carrying-out of work processes does not always take place simultaneously with the teaching of skills. It sometimes precedes training in work and production and is even carried out during lessons on general-education and technical subjects. In that case, the scientific information previously imparted is merely refreshed and used in the teaching of working skills. Sometimes it takes place after the pupils have already been taught certain production processes because it was impossible, both before and during the practical work, to give scientific explanations, and it was necessary to wait until the required level of general scientific training in the relevant subjects was reached.

The following forms of organization are used in Soviet schools in the teaching of working skills to the pupils: lessons, practical activities (in study rooms, laboratories, workshops, and on experimental plots), instruction in productive work and practical training in production.

Depending on the nature of the working skills and the objects of the work, the teaching is carried out either with the full class, or with only half a class at a time (fifteen to twenty pupils). All the pupils in a class or group simultaneously go through the subjects of instruction according to the same curriculum under the direction of a teacher or instructor. In addition to the class and group forms of organization of work and instruction, the pupils are also taught individually and in teams.

Individual instruction takes place when the pupils go through the subjects of instruction individually under the guidance of a worker or collective farmer, to whom they are assigned for a certain period of time. In the team method of instruction the pupils learn by working as a group attached to a team of workers or collective farmers for a certain length of time, doing the same work as the regular members of the team. A special form of instruction is attaching pupils to 'Teams of Communist Labour', where they not only acquire working skills, but also assimilate advanced experience in living and working communistically. The instruction given in the teams is supervised either by the team leader, or by workers or collective farmers designated by him. Teams consisting solely of pupils from various classes are also formed in agriculture, where socially productive work and the learning of working skills is carried out under the direction of teachers and agricultural scientists.

Group instruction in working skills is preferred to individual instruction or instruction in teams. However, when the pupils who have acquired the necessary working skills are introduced to independent productive work, the schools make every effort to organize such work in a community of workers and especially in a 'Team of Communist Labour', so as to take advantage of the influence of the workers on the pupils.

172

Methods of training in working skills

At the present time, successful working skills are acquired through the following:

Preliminary explanation of the construction and principles of operation of the instruments and machines which the pupils will use, the layout of the workshops where they will work, and the properties of the materials which they will be working on.

Explanation of industrial safety principles.

Demonstration of the actions and movements which make up each industrial operation, and explanation of their significance.

Scientific explanation of the principles of execution of each movement.

Where manual skills are concerned, a comparison of manual and machine work.

Warning the pupils about the mistakes which may occur in the execution of the various operations.

Exercises in carrying out individual movements and operations according to oral and written instructions, and correct working arrangements.

The manufacture by the pupils of articles demanding the utilization of the operations taught by the teacher according to the corresponding instructions.

The teaching of operations in gradually increasing order of complexity.

Exercises in progressively more complex combinations of operations used in productive work, by making various selected articles involving these operations.

The correct distribution of work and rest periods.

Stimulation of the pupils to carry out their work in a creative manner—to improve it and carry it out more efficiently.

Until recently, there were three basic methods of training in working skills: training by operations, training by combinations of operations, and training on the basis of the objects to be produced.

The characteristic feature of the first method (training by operations) was that it was carried out by teaching the pupils operations which gradually increased in complexity. In order to do this, a corresponding system of exercises was used, in the course of which various useful objects might or might not be produced.

The particular feature of the second method (training by combinations of operations), compared with the first, was that it envisaged exercises not only in single operations of increasing complexity, but also in increasingly complicated combinations of operations used in productive work. This method stressed the necessity of separating the operations used in productive work into working movements and teaching the pupils the correct way to carry them out. It also entailed a greater need for the pupils to produce useful articles.

The characteristic feature of the third method (training on the basis of the objects to be produced) was that it was based on a selection of articles which the pupils had to produce in order to acquire working skills.

In fact, however, none of these methods was ever used in its pure form. They were always combined in such a way that, in practice, the methods which existed were the operation/object and the object/operation method. In those cases where it was not possible to use these methods, the method of practical factory experience was used. These three methods are now used for the teaching of polytechnical working skills.

The operation/object method. Under this method the teaching of working skills takes place through the execution of operations of gradually increasing complexity in carrying out specially selected combinations of socially useful work in which each succeeding type of work requires, as a rule, the mastering of a new operation and the consolidation of previous skills which are used either separately or in combinations.

The teaching of these methods is planned and specified according to Table 9, where the vertical column lists the names of the operations according to their increasing complexity and difficulty, and the horizontal lists the types of work and the number of times each must be repeated. The types of work are numbered according to their increasing complexity and difficulty. The number of times they are to be repeated is planned with a view to providing a sufficient amount of time for exercises in the corresponding operations. The work is arranged so as to provide sufficient time for exercises in the use of both new and familiar operations, both singly and in the combinations used in production.

The squares formed by the intersection of the vertical and horizontal columns are divided in half by diagonal lines. If, when carrying out work of a certain number (e.g., number 3), certain operations (e.g., numbers 2, 3 and 4) are used, then the squares formed by the intersection of the corresponding horizontal and vertical columns are traversed by a diagonal line (e.g., the squares formed by the intersection of the third vertical column and the second, third, and fourth horizontal columns). The amount of time apportioned for a given operation when the work is carried out once is entered in the upper left-hand half of each square, and the

174

TABLE 9. Form for planning and checking the training of pupils in working skills

No.	Name of operation	Number of types of work used (*upper left*) and number of times such work is repeated (*lower right*)							Amount of time expended
		1	2	3	4	5	etc.	etc.	
1									
2									
3									
4									
5									
6									
etc.									
	Amount of time spent on work								

Names of types of work:
1. . . . . 4. . . . .
2. . . . . 5. . . . .
3. . . . . etc. . . . .

number of times the work in question is to be repeated is entered in the lower right-hand half. The diagonally crossed squares give a visual idea of which operations are used in carrying out the work, and the figures in the squares make it possible to calculate the amount of time spent on executing each type of work once, and on executing it the number of times specified in the plan. The figures in the squares also make it possible to calculate the amount of time to be spent on the exercises in the use of each operation, both when carrying out all the types of work once only, and when carrying them out according to the number of times specified in the plan. It is absolutely essential that the time should be calculated, in order to be sure that all the operations will be mastered by the pupils in the proper manner.

In the above connexion, 'work' means both a given production process and the complete or partial manufacture of an article. The semi-finished articles obtained in manufacture are used for

175

subsequent operations, but such work is entered in the table under different numbers. The making of separate parts of an article (if it consists of several parts) is also entered under different numbers. At a certain stage in the training, these component parts are assembled, and this assembly constitutes new work, which is entered in the table again under a new number.

A preparatory analysis of complicated articles is made in order to establish: (a) whether the process of manufacture of the article includes the operations which are covered by the programme of the present class or of previous classes; (b) whether each operation takes up as much time as is necessary or permissible for exercising the corresponding skills; (c) whether the article is within the capabilities of the pupils, from the point of view of its construction and the accuracy and neatness of its finishing; (d) whether it is possible, in the process of making the article, to develop the technological knowledge of the pupils, and whether they will be able to use any knowledge thus gained for general-education purposes.

For the analysis of objects, it is recommended that tables arranged in a manner similar to the example given (see Table 10) should be used. The names of the parts of the object in question are listed vertically on the left, while the names of the operations are given in the horizontal column. On the basis of his experience, the teacher writes, in the corresponding squares, the time (in minutes) required for carrying out each operation in the manufacture of each part, and calculates how much time is required for the production of all the parts. In this way, the time required for the production of each separate part is accurately established. The teacher then calculates how much time is required for, say, filing all the various parts, and for rough cutting, threading, etc., and finally for the manufacture of all the parts making up the complete object.

When he has made up such a table, the teacher has all the particulars to enable him to decide whether or not the object is suitable for manufacture during the practical training.

The operation/object method can be used in workshops of schools and enterprises, on experimental plots, in experimental farming, in collective gardens and farms. This is the most appropriate method of group teaching for it requires the least expenditure of time to enable the pupils to acquire technical knowledge and take up socially useful work.

The type of instruction given to the pupils can be preliminary, concurrent, or concluding.

'Preliminary instruction' consists of acquainting the pupils with: the workplace, its arrangement, and the maintenance of order

TABLE 10. Analysis of manufacture of parts of a support (grade VII)

Name of part	Setting-out	Rough cutting	Hack-sawing	Filing	Drill-ing	Thread-ing	Riveting and bend-ing	Time required to make one part (in min.)
Base	7	—	10	25	18	20	—	80
Upright . . .	5	—	5	8	10	17	—	45
Lug	4	3	—	10	8	—	20	45
Sleeve . . .	7	—	10	15	15	18	—	65
Arm	—	—	2	5	10	18	—	35
Hinge . . .	5	—	10	30	20	—	—	65
Fork	3	2	—	10	15	—	10	40
Stem	5	—	—	13	10	12	—	40
Thumbscrew .	5	—	—	15	—	—	—	20
Stop spindle. .	10	—	5	15	—	15	—	45
Casing . . .	5	2	—	8	5	—	10	30
Tightening screw	—	—	—	—	—	—	—	—
Angle bracket .	15	—	10	20	20	—	25	90
TOTAL . .	71	7	52	174	131	100	65	600
As percentages .	11.8	1.2	8.7	29	21.8	16.7	10.8	100

during working hours; the construction and operation of the instruments, mechanisms, and machines, their adjustment, and the repair of minor faults arising during use; the properties of the materials to be worked; the manufacturing process and the documents used in the course of this process; checking of the work carried out; and safety procedures. It is also part of the preliminary instruction to demonstrate the methods of carrying out the operations. The operations are divided into movements, and each movement is demonstrated separately. Care must be taken to give the correct working methods and to warn the pupils against the danger of adopting incorrect methods. This involves showing the pupils the correct way to hold tools, the correct position of the body and stance, and the correct order in which the movements must be carried out. Afterwards the pupils should perform exercises in carrying out the operations while making a useful object.

'Concurrent instruction' involves the correction of errors which may have occurred in the pupils' work. For this purpose the teacher or instructor gives a demonstration of the correct method; concurrent instruction also involves helping the pupils to attain the necessary degree of accuracy, speed, and productivity, and to avoid rejects in their output; demonstrating new labour-saving methods; and explaining displays of socialist competition, helping in their organization and getting the pupils to take part in such competition.

Practical instruction is rendered much more straightforward and simple for the teacher if he makes use of instructional charts, which may be of two types: (a) operational charts showing how to carry out an operation; (b) working charts providing instructions on how to make a given object. An example of the first type of chart is one on electricity, showing how to make a connection from an electric cable to a lamp, while an example of the second type is an instructional chart showing how to make wooden bars in the school workshop. These charts are reproduced below and opposite.

Operational chart: 'How to make a connection from an electric cable to a lamp'

1. Place the insulator at the spot where the connection is to be made.
2. Mark on either side of the insulator the places where the insulation is to be cut away from each of the wires. Take the cord from the insulator and clean away the insulation at these places.
3. Remove the insulation from the ends of the wire to be connected to the main cable.
4. Connect the cleaned ends of the wire to the main cable, solder them in place, and insulate with insulating tape.
5. Thread the cord on the insulator, tighten and bind it.

Tools required: Screwdriver, knife, cutting pliers, and flat-nosed pliers.
Materials: Insulating tape, solder, and binding thread.

'Concluding instruction' is carried out on the basis of analysing the work done by the pupils and totalling up the results of socialist competition. It consists in showing the positive aspects of the work and its shortcomings and in explaining and demonstrating the best methods to ensure a further increase in productivity and an improvement in the quality of production.

The following methods are used for increasing the activity and independence of the pupils in their work: unaided planning of the production of articles; independent preparation and utilization of sketches, drawings, working plans, or instructional charts; independent observations during work; the drafting of proposals for improving the work, etc.

Evaluation of the pupils' success in mastering skills is carried out by observing their work, inspecting the articles made by them, imposing practical tests (the pupil is asked to carry out certain assignments, and the results of this—time spent, quality of produc-

Working chart for making wooden bars

Name of articles: 'Wooden bars—semi-finished articles to be made in practical instruction periods by grade IV'. Dimensions of wooden bars: 500 × 15 × 10 mm.
Materials: Pine or fir wood.

Name of operation	Tools required	Norms	
		Time (min.)	Accuracy (mm.)
Measurement, setting-out and cutting of material	Metre rule, straightedge, set-square, and frame saw	45	—
Planing of first broad edge and checking against straightedge	Straightedge and plane	25	—
Planing of second (narrow) edge, using straightedge and set-square for checking	Plane, straightedge and set-square	20	—
Planing of third (narrow) edge, using marking gauge	Plane, marking gauge, set-square, and straightedge	25	1
Planing of fourth (broad) edge, using marking gauge	Plane, marking gauge, set-square, and straightedge	20	1

tion, etc.—are then evaluated), by creative constructional work, and by examinations for determining the pupils' standard of qualifications.

In the teaching of manual skills in the school workshops, care must be taken to prevent the development of a mechanical attitude. This happens when there is an absence of the technological explanations which result in the scientific understanding of the operations to be carried out, show the connexion between technology and natural sciences, make the comparison between the manual and the machine processing of materials and develop industrious working habits in the pupils.

The object/operation method. It is obvious that the number of lessons required before an operation can be mastered by the pupils varies according to the different operations. When it is impossible to use the operation/object method, the object/operation method must be used.

When a metalworking enterprise, for example, has no training workshop and the pupils are taught by individual or team methods, they execute the same orders as the workers. If the methods of carrying out the separate operations are shown and explained to them every time, the pupils gradually master both the separate operations and combinations of them. Of course, in this case there is not the same strict sequence in mastering the operations as when the operation/object method is used. Moreover, a considerable time may elapse before the pupils come across certain operations and this will have a bad effect on their training. Nevertheless, this method can be improved in two ways: (a) by selecting articles whose manufacture involves the mastery of a full range of operations, and (b) by moving pupils from one workplace to another with a view to their mastering the full range of operations. The experience of a number of enterprises and schools shows that this can be done. In order to check their training the whole range of skills specified in the programme, the pupils are supplied with control tables, where, as in Table 9, the names of the operations are given in the vertical column, while the names of the objects are shown on the horizontal and in the squares formed by the inter-section of the horizontal and vertical lines are noted the amounts of time spent on practice in the various operations while carrying out the work in question.

The object/operation method has a rather special form when the pupils are working in a part of the factory where continuous-flow or conveyor-belt working is being carried on. In this case, the pupils learn the simplest operation, then move to another place to learn a more difficult one, and so on, until such time as they have learnt the whole range of operations.

A control sheet like that already referred to is necessary in this case also.

The above method can also be used in training workshops where the pupils take part in the manufacture of articles on the basis of the division of labour, passing gradually from one operation to another. In this case, rapid mastery of the operations and a sharp increase in the productivity of labour are achieved.

The object/operation method is also used in the teaching of polytechnical working skills during practical activities in physics, chemistry, biology, machine construction, electrical engineering, etc. In this case, the objects of the instructional work are those corresponding to the laboratory work. They follow a sequence determined by the programme of scientific knowledge, and the skills are developed at the same time; these can be analysed by means of the tables referred to above.

Polytechnical skills in these subjects begin to develop during the demonstration of experiments, provided the teacher arranges for the carrying-out of the corresponding experimental and working operations, and explains the purpose and scientific basis of each operation. The development of experimental working skills is continued further in carrying out experiments accompanied by the teacher's explanations. Here the pupils, under the direction of the teacher, acquire the ability to carry out separate operations. Finally, the skills are developed through independent practical activities. For the skills to be mastered quickly and well, they must be acquired on the basis of sound and systematic assimilation of scientific knowledge.

The practical training course method. In metallurgical, chemical, and many other enterprises and in the training of motormen for construction work, etc., neither the operation/object nor the object/operation method is suitable. Here the only way is to give preliminary training in the theory of the question, using for this purpose the observations made by the pupils at production centres, and then give the pupils a period of practical experience under the direction of a worker or expert; thus they can master a range of practical skills and knowledge by the practical training course method.

The work of a crane-driver on a construction site could be taken as an example. First of all, the pupils are familiarized with the crane and the work of the crane-driver by observation. Then, in school, they study in detail the construction and principles of operation of the crane, gain a theoretical knowledge of its parts, ways of driving it, and ways of adjusting it for different types of work, study the rules of industrial safety, and so on. After this theoretical training, accompanied by observations, the pupils go through a period of training with a worker, who gradually allows a pupil to carry out separate operations, then combinations of operations and, finally, allows him to do all the operations involved in driving the crane, under his supervision. The worker is supplied with a chart showing what operations and combinations of operations the pupil should carry out, how many times, and in what order.

FORMS OF ORGANIZATION OF THE TEACHING OF WORKING SKILLS AND THE INTRODUCTION OF THE PUPILS TO PRODUCTIVE WORK

In describing teaching methods, reference has also been made to the forms of organization of the teaching of working skills to pupils

181

and their introduction to productive work. Let us now consider these forms in greater detail.

Practical activities in study rooms and laboratories

Practical exercises in drawing account for more than 80 per cent of the total time allocated to the teaching of this subject in the syllabus. In physics, chemistry, and biology, the time devoted to practical activities is 20 to 25 per cent of the total time, and in mathematics and geography it is about 10 per cent of the total time. In each subject, the schedule of the practical work for each class is so arranged as to achieve three purposes: (a) to ensure a sound knowledge, by the pupils, of the main questions dealt with in the course; (b) to inculcate in the pupils polytechnical working skills, and a creative approach; (c) to teach them to make use of their knowledge in practice.

Depending on the content of the work and its technical aspects, and on its requirements, each type of practical work can give different instructional and educative results. Therefore each teacher, when making use of the list of practical activities in the schedule and their description in the textbooks used, works out his own plan for the pupils' practical work, in which he determines more precisely the content of each type of work and the method of carrying it out, the requirements which must be fulfilled, and the list of teaching aids and equipment required. In order to check to what extent this plan will contribute to the successful training of the pupils in polytechnical skills and labour culture, the teacher prepares a table in which he details the amount of time allocated by the plan to each type of work and to each operation (see Table 9). This table is used in preparing the practical work and in drafting instructions.

In addition to the work which is obligatory for all pupils, the teacher also provides for optional work. This work is of various degrees of difficulty, so that poor, fair and good pupils can, according to their knowledge and inclinations, choose for themselves appropriate additional work. Large or important projects are begun in practical classes and finished off in the pupils' own time.

Practical activities in physics, chemistry, biology, mathematics, geography, and drawing are carried out with all the pupils in the class, while activities in machine construction, electrical engineering, and agriculture are carried out with half the class. In the next few years, classes will also be halved for practical activities in physics, chemistry and biology.

The teachers endeavour to conduct as many as possible of the practical activities on the lines of a single front, that is, all the pupils carry out the same work simultaneously, either individually or in small groups of two or three. The decision whether to let them work individually or in small groups depends on the nature of the work and the number of sets of equipment available in the room or workshop. Work requiring expensive or complicated equipment cannot, of course, be carried out on the lines of a single front, but must be carried out in turn. The teacher lectures on each type of work for a certain length of time, and in each exercise the pupils carry out various kinds of work, so that by the end of the time allotted, each pupil (or each small group of pupils) will have carried out all the types provided for.

All the equipment required for carrying out the work in question should be already prepared before the lesson and laid out at the pupils' workplaces, while all the equipment intended for common use should be laid on the demonstration bench. As the same premises are used for discussions, lectures, and practical activities in Soviet schools, the pupils' workplaces are provided only with the essentials. For physics and electrical engineering, the benches are supplied with electricity; for chemistry, with gas, water, electricity, and drains; for machine construction the benches are equipped with removable wooden planks which are placed on top of the benches when heavy items are being used, so as to avoid damaging the surface of the benches; for drawing, the benches are provided with raising and tilting tops so as to serve as drawing-boards. All the remaining equipment (reagents, materials, glassware, instruments, and so on) is kept in a storeroom and laid out on the benches before the lesson. A card index covering every type of work and every experiment gives details of the equipment required. The teacher makes out these cards when arranging the practical work.

As a rule, the pupils make use of written instructions when doing practical work. These instructions are contained in their textbooks, and are published in various collections. If the teacher is not satisfied with the published instructions, he prepares and prints his own instructions.

Before practical work is begun, the pupils' knowledge of the working instructions, working techniques and safety precautions is checked, after which they set about the practical work.

The teacher supervises the work, gives the pupils assistance, makes sure that they keep their workplaces clean and tidy and that they carry out the operations correctly, and corrects any errors which he may notice. When the work is finished, the pupils make out a written report in the following form:

Work done (Notes and sketches)	Points observed (Notes and sketches)	Explanation of points observed, and conclusions

If the pupils do not succeed in finishing their reports in the work-room, they finish them at home. The reports are checked by the teacher and marked according to a five-point system.

The teacher selects as assistants one or two pupils are specially interested in the subject and makes use of their services in preparing and carrying out practical work.

Practical activities in the worshops and on experimental plots, by pupils in grades V–VIII, are intended to develop the pupils' skills in the working of wood and metal, electrical fitting, agriculture, and other occupations. As a rule, the work in the workshops is carried out according to the operation/object system, while work on the experimental plot is carried out according to the object/operation system.

In the work training programme, these activities take up about 80 per cent of the time. The remainder of the time is spent on teaching the pupils about the technology of materials and the conditions of agriculture. In planning work for the purpose of developing working skills, Table 9 is again used. Similarly, in addition to the work which is compulsory for all the pupils, optional activities are also arranged, of which the most important are combined construction work in the workshops and experimental work on experimental plots. For this kind of work, again the class is split into two parts, each of which carries on its activities separately, the pupils performing the work all at once or in turn, with or without the division of labour.

The instructional workshops for woodwork and metalwork and for instruction in electrical fitting are provided with a raised workplace for the teacher, equipped with a table, a bench with a set of tools, and a blackboard; workplaces for the pupils, provided with benches, clamping appliances and sets of tools for woodwork and metalwork (according to the age of the pupils), and with measuring, checking, and fitting tools and instruments; lathes and drilling machines for wood and metal (see Fig. 7); and places for the setting and sharpening of tools. The workplaces are supplied with electric power, or several workplaces are separately equipped for electrical fitting work. Spare tools, tools and instruments of general use, materials and finished and unfinished articles are stored in cupboards and on racks in a separate room.

In arranging experimental plots, the first thing to make sure of is that there is sufficient ground space (about fifty square metres) for each pupil, that there is a supply of tools of a size suited to the age of the pupils, that there is a supply of fertilizers, seeds, etc., and that a greenhouse is constructed.

The subjects of experimental work in agriculture are selected in accordance with the requirements of the district, the region, province, and the Republic.

The pupils make observations of the growing of plants, enter the results of these observations in their notebooks, and later analyse these observations and report the results to their teachers.

In order to develop a communist attitude to work, socialist competition is organized among the pupils in regard to the following main points: high productivity of labour and quality of production, good appearance of articles, absence of faults, maintenance of absolute tidiness of the workplace during work, economy in the use of materials and tools, and great care in the use and maintenance of machinery. The results of this competition are worked out every month with the help of the pupils, and the names of the winners are announced in the wall newspapers, or by the issue of special bulletins.

The practical activities in the workshops or on experimental plots are carried out regularly for two hours each week, and for the two weeks' practical training in productive work.

The socially useful work which is carried out for two hours each week is planned by a school committee consisting of the headmaster, two or three school teachers, teachers doing training in work, representatives of the Young Communist and Pioneer organizations of the pupils, and representatives of the enterprise officially linked with the school. The committee determines the work for each class for the week or month ahead, taking into account the requirements of the school, the patron enterprise, and the local administration, bearing in mind the educational value of the work in question. The execution of this work is organized by the class teachers in conjunction with the pupils' representative group, on the basis of the pupils' independent activity.

Practical production work carried out in grades V–VIII.

This is an important form of organization of socially useful work and of training the pupils in working skills. On the days for practical work, the pupils do socially useful work for three hours if they are in grade V, and four hours if they are in grades VI–VIII. There are no lessons during this time. The type of practical work for each grade is decided in the school on the basis of the teaching programme and local conditions.

Practical work is so planned that some classes work in the workshops and on experimental plots, some work on collective and State farms, some (the senior classes) work on building sites or in industrial enterprises, carrying out work suited to their abilities, and a number of classes work on improving the school amenities, planting trees and flowers along the streets, looking after the public walks, caring for public flower beds, and so on.

The practical work is directed by a teacher designated by the head of the school. The work may be carried out in any month, but preferably at the end of the school year.

During practical work, the pupils compete among themselves, striving to obtain the best production and quality rating. The pupils' work is combined with excursions to production centres for purposes of observation, and with various recreational and cultural activities.

Instructional and productive practical work in enterprises is organized for pupils of grade VIII. First, the pupils get acquainted with the enterprise by means of excursions, observations, conversations with the workers and staff, and then they work there for three hours a day. As a rule, workplaces in several shops, in which straightforward work is carried out, are selected, and during his period of practical training each pupil works at one or two different operations. The pupils are introduced to socially useful work, and gain their first concrete impressions of work at a production centre.

Training and experimental plots have now been set up at many country schools (e.g., the experience of the schools of the Ryazan province). On these farms, socially useful work is carried out all the year round in plant-growing and stock-raising and practical training is given to the pupils at the same time. All the work on these farms (including the planning, accounting and checking) is carried out by the pupils under the direction of the teachers. For this purpose the collective farms put at the disposal of the schools areas of fifteen to twenty hectares of ground, together with the necessary seeds and implements, and organize stock farms also. These training and experimental farms do work on seed-growing, the development of maize hybrids, fruit-growing, poultry-rearing, etc. The experimental trend of these farms has obliged the schools to strengthen the ties between theory and practice and between instruction and productive work, as the experiments on these farms demand a scientific approach and scientific knowledge. The experimental work develops in the pupils a creative approach to matters, a spirit of inquiry, a search for new ideas, an ability to overcome difficulties, to break previously established records, etc. For their work, the pupils are paid by the collective farm according to the number of work-days at a reduced rate in comparison with that for adults, and the entire harvest is handed over to the collective farm. From the income received, the collective farms allocate a certain amount of money to the school for the purchase of implements and for training expenses.

Another way of organizing systematic socially useful work during the school year on collective and State farms and of carrying out training and productive practical work has been developed in the schools of the Stavropol area. This system consists of the formation of brigades of pupils for work on collective and State farms, and is widely used in schools all over the U.S.S.R.

The pupils' brigades are organized by the school in agreement with the management of a collective or State farm. The directors of the school, the collective farm or the State farm guide and systematically check the work of the brigade. Most of the members of a brigade come from the senior grades (VIII–XI), and they are all volunteers. Pupils from the junior grades (V–VII) take part in the work of the brigades from time to time. Enrolment in a brigade takes place at a meeting of the teaching staff, which is usually attended also by the chairman of the collective farm or the director of the State farm. This procedure helps the pupils to realize the importance of the step they are taking in starting work for the first time. From the very beginning the pupils feel a sense of responsibility for the work which they are about to carry out.

The brigade is headed by a council which includes the headmaster or deputy headmaster of the school, a representative of the collective or State farm, an agricultural expert who is attached to the brigade, an educational expert, and the leader of the brigade.

The leader of the brigade is chosen from its members, and is confirmed in his position by the headmaster of the school. Usually the leader is a pupil from grade X or XI who has prestige among the pupils and possesses organizational ability.

The members of the brigade are divided up into small groups or units led by group leaders selected from among the pupils. Usually each group carries out a certain type of work. The groups are often named after the type of work they do: field group, vegetable-growing group, maize group, stock-breeding group, and so on.

The productive work of the brigade takes place under the

187

direction of an agricultural expert, who also carries out with the pupils work in connexion with the agrotechnical treatment of agricultural crops. He also organizes experimental work.

The working day for brigades engaged in practical productive work varies according to the pupils' grades. Pupils of grades V–VII work three hours a day, pupils of grades VIII–IX four hours a day, and pupils of grades X–XI six hours a day.

The work norms for schoolchildren who are members of a brigade are also established with due regard to their age. Usually they are approximately 25 to 30 per cent lower than those for adult collective farm workers (in the Stavropol, Krasnodar and Rostov areas, etc.), while the rate of payment is the same. The members of a pupils' brigade are paid for their work on a collective farm according to the number of days worked, at the same time as the adult workers.

The agricultural products obtained as a result of the work done by a pupils' brigade belong to the collective or State farm.

A great incentive to raise productivity in the pupils' brigades is socialist competition, which is organized both between the different groups and between the individual members of a brigade.

A collective or State farm sets aside a plot of land for a pupils' brigade, on which the brigade members build a field station consisting of a dining-room, kitchen, dormitories for boys, dormitories for girls, rooms for rest and for cultural activities, and an agricultural-biological laboratory. The plot is usually assigned for the whole time the brigade is in existence. The existence of a separate assigned plot is of great importance. On their own plot, the pupils carry out the whole range of agricultural operations, from the preparation of the soil for sowing to the gathering of the harvest. As a rule, the schoolchildren obtain better results on their plots than the members of adult working teams.

On many collective and State farms there are also pupils' brigades for animal husbandry.

The productive work of the pupils is under the constant and systematic control of their teachers. It can thus be used for deepening and widening the pupils' knowledge, giving them the necessary practical skills, and inculcating in them a love of work, a sense of the community, and a spirit of conscious discipline. Collective work plays a great role in improving the entire process of training and education in the schools of the U.S.S.R.

The work of the pupils on the training and experimental farms and their organization in brigades makes it possible to prepare a new complement of highly qualified workers for agriculture. Training and experimental farms and pupils' brigades are positive ways of linking the schools with the collective farms and State farms. First-class organizers capable of leading young people are formed in the brigades. The organizational and agricultural skills developed in the pupils' brigades are used in practical work on leaving school. The leaders of pupils' brigades are often chosen as leaders of youth teams on collective farms when they leave school.

Production training

It has been pointed out above that the main trend in the organization of the production training of youth was laid down in the decision of June 1959 of the plenum of the Central Committee of the Communist Party of the U.S.S.R. The Plenum stated that, in order to carry out the Party's plans for technical progress, it was essential to raise the level of technical education of the workers, particularly the young workers. The Plenum's decision said that 'the saturation of modern production with complicated machines and mechanisms demands of every worker an all-round general and specialized knowledge. Under present conditions, therefore, the production training of the workers cannot be limited to the curriculum of primary-grade technical schools, but should also include elements of technical-engineering training.'[1] An important place in this training should be given to familiarizing the workers with modern equipment, with the means of complete mechanization and automation of production, and to enabling the workers to make efficient use of the latest techniques.

These statements by the Plenum have a direct bearing on the structure of production training in grades IX–XI of secondary polytechnical schools providing a general education. It is essential to bear in mind that pupils who are now studying in grade IX will be working in production in three years' time, that is to say, when considerable advances will have been made along the path of technical progress in production.

In the schools production training is divided into two parts: theoretical and practical.

In the theoretical part, the pupils learn about a specific type of production, the machines, tools and other equipment, the properties of materials and the technological processes for working or treating these materials, technical documentation, industrial safety, the organization of the workplace and the work itself, and experience in socialist competition.

---

1. Minutes of the June 1959 Plenum of the Central Committee of the Communist Party of the U.S.S.R., p. 41.

In the course of practical production training, the pupils are taught working skills (according to their knowledge and ability), and the craftsmanship of the pupils is raised to the highest possible level. Practical production training is carried out on the basis of, and in the course of, production work by the pupils according to their specialities. This training is carried out in the production shops of industrial enterprises (see Fig. 8), in the fields and farms of collective and State farms, in training workshops and on training plots in school workshops, on training and experimental farms, and in teams or brigades on collective and State farms.

In country schools, in training for all branches of agriculture, the training is likewise divided into two stages—the theoretical and the practical—but it is organized with due regard to the special features of agricultural production.

The linking of work and training is the decisive means of carrying out the main task of the school, namely, to give the pupils a good preparation for life, give them a trade, prepare them for work in production and develop their ability to combine their productive work with the process of learning.

The success of vocational-training plans and practical work schemes depends on the availability of workplaces in enterprises.

The plan of production training adopted for most specialities in grades IX and X (twelve hours of practical work per week) enables the following routine of production training and productive work to be followed: two days per week (four periods per day) spent on productive work and practical production training, and two periods per day spent on theoretical instruction. Using this system, with two-shift working it is possible to train up to twelve pupils at a single workplace. If the whole twelve hours per week in grade XI are assigned to work and practical production training, then it will be possible to train six pupils at a single workplace. This number of workplaces can well be allocated by the enterprises.

During their production training, the teachers and skilled workers (instructors) teach the pupils to use their general-education and polytechnical knowledge, to study the work carefully, to approach it in a creative spirit, to seek the answers to questions in regard to further increasing the productivity of labour and improving the quality of production, and to make corresponding suggestions for increasing efficiency. This makes it easier for the pupils to master the appropriate skills, increase their knowledge and abilities, achieve a sound basis for self-improvement, and helps to inculcate a communist attitude towards work and communist morality.

190

Optional activities are a means of developing the scientific and practical interests of the pupils, their capabilities and talents. These are organized both for individual grades and for groups of pupils from different grades. The school is authorized to combine groups of pupils for optional activities in mathematics, physics, chemistry, radio electronics, electrical engineering, machine construction, automatic control, etc.

METHODS OF ESTABLISHING A CLOSE LINK BETWEEN INSTRUCTION AND SOCIALLY USEFUL WORK

In order to establish a close link between instruction and socially useful work, it is necessary first of all to accustom the pupils to work, i.e., to bring into the school the second component of the link, since the first (instruction) was and is already present. As productive work in Soviet schools is important not so much for the goods produced as for its value as a means of education and training, every effort is made to provide the pupils with work which is so organized and of such a type that, while being harmless to the pupils' health and well within their capabilities, it will also serve as a means of: (a) acquiring new knowledge and skills which are essential for the widening and deepening of the pupils' general and polytechnical education, or (in the senior grades) vocational training; (b) verifying the accuracy and soundness with which the pupils have learnt the information and skills which have been imparted to them in the course of their systematic study of general-education, polytechnical, and specialized subjects; (c) raising new theoretical and practical problems and giving the pupils an opportunity of finding the answers to them; (d) bringing up the pupils in the spirit of communist morality.

In the first years of the Soviet schools, great attention was given to socially useful work by the pupils, and this was considered an excellent method of education and of acquiring knowledge, abilities and skills. In order to show this value of labour activity, a combined method and also the method of carrying out projects were introduced into school practice. Eventually, these methods came to be recommended as being the only ones suitable for use. They did not, however, give the pupils a systematic knowledge of the fundamentals of science, as the pupils were only given just enough information to enable them to carry out a certain set of operations or a certain project. Moreover, this procedure did not give the pupils the necessary preparation for life. All this led to well-founded criticism of these methods. They began to be

191

considered unsuitable for establishing the link between instruction and work, and they ceased to be used in school.

At the present time, work in schools is linked with the systematic and consecutive study of the fundamentals of science and with polytechnical education, work training, and vocational education. In other words, the basis of the preparation of pupils for life is now instruction, education, and upbringing. This is not to set instruction against work, nor does it lower the prestige of work, but rather raises it and makes it what it should be in schools of the U.S.S.R.—a means of education, training, and upbringing, bringing the pupils into the field of communist construction.

But instruction in general-education and general technical subjects on the one hand, and work training and socially useful work on the other, have their own logic and consistency. It is not possible to establish a simultaneous link even between work which is subordinated to the training and educational purposes of the school and education itself. In practice there are three kinds of links between instruction and practical work:

1. The antecedent link: some time before the pupils begin to carry out socially useful work, the teacher, in the course of the systematic explanation of his subject, imparts to the pupils knowledge which reveals the scientific bases of the work, and teaches them the skills which help them to carry it out; in the process of working, the pupils use this knowledge in order to comprehend the work, and the skills in order to carry it out properly.

2. The simultaneous link: the teacher imparts the above information and skills to the pupils during the time they are carrying out socially useful work; here theory and practice are intermingled for a short time both in dealing with general-education subjects and with practical work.

3. The subsequent link: the work task is carried out first, empiric knowledge is accumulated and then, in the course of the systematic study of the fundamentals of science, the scientific basis of the work is revealed.

Obviously, in the process of instruction it is necessary to make use of all these kinds of links. In order to link instruction with work, the school selects socially useful work, which is of importance in the national economy and most valuable from the educative and instructional point of view; it organizes socially useful work for the pupils after full consideration of its educative content, and special programmes of work are made up for each class.

Each teacher makes a profound study, from every viewpoint, of the content of the work which has been done by the pupils in previous years, the work which is planned for the present school year, and the work envisaged for future years, and acquaints the pupils with the scientific bases of this work in the course of the systematic exposition of his subject.

The link between general-education subjects and practical work is established mainly through the elements of technology which are dealt with in physics, chemistry, and biology courses, through the technical and technological information imparted in work and in production training, and through machine construction, electrical engineering, and the fundamentals of agricultural science.

The basic elements of physics, chemistry, and biology, which are essential for the understanding of technology and techniques, should be taught to the pupils before the technological subjects. This point is covered in the teaching plans and programmes. When studying technological subjects, the pupils make use of their general-education knowledge, which is thus consolidated, and at the same time they learn how to carry out their work at a high rate of productivity and with full awareness of what they are doing. In the process of practical work, the pupils comprehend more thoroughly, consolidate and supplement their technological and technical information, and through this, of course, their mathematical knowledge. Education is thus linked with practical work, and this link becomes a method of improving education and productive work.

The main lines of the method of linking socially useful work with work and production training are as follows:

1. Giving the pupils tasks involving socially useful work and the improvement and widening of their scientific knowledge and working skills as a result of such work.
2. Instructing the pupils in questions of the preparation and execution of socially useful work.
3. The independent familiarization of the pupils, under the direction of their teachers, with the directives of the Communist Party and the Soviet Government on questions of practical work; study of the scientific side of the question in lessons and out of class; familiarization of the pupils with the experience of leading workers.
4. The development by the pupils of a plan for carrying out their tasks, and justification by the pupils of their plan before their teacher and the pupils' representative group.
5. The carrying-out of the work.
6. A final summing-up of all the work done—the holding of conferences at which the pupils give their reports, the organization of displays, and so on.

SELECTION OF TEACHING METHODS AND THEIR CREATIVE APPLICATION
BY THE TEACHER

In practical school work, the methods used are never exactly the same as those found in books. The specific conditions of teaching and education always make it necessary to apply these methods in a concrete manner and the teacher always creatively selects and adapts them to the teaching conditions, taking into account their general educational, psychological, and methodological nature.

While they contribute to the development of the pupils, at the same time the teaching methods themselves depend on the age and development of the pupils and their level of education.

For the pupils to develop successfully, it is essential to ensure the following in the process of teaching: first, the pupils must be given knowledge and skills, the mastery of which demands a level of development slightly higher than that already attained by the pupils, but which is nevertheless within their capabilities if they make the necessary effort; secondly, the pupils should be introduced to types of work for the execution of which a higher level of development is also required; and thirdly, knowledge and skills should be made to form the basis and method of further knowledge and activities and the methods should be turned into a means of acquiring new knowledge and turning knowledge into ability and skill.

As soon as pupils are given qualitatively new knowledge and skills and are introduced to new types of work, they show a corresponding development. This development takes place because qualitatively new knowledge, skills and work demand still further development from the pupils in order that they may be mastered. The level of development previously attained no longer corresponds to the requirements of cognition and practical activity that have arisen. A contradiction arises between the level of development which was attained before and the requirements connected with the mastering of new knowledge, skills, and types of work. This contradiction causes a change in the nature of the instructional and working activity, i.e., in the adaptation of the whole personality of the pupils, in the exercise of the various psychic functions, and in the methods of thinking and acting. Provided the pupils receive the necessary guidance from their teacher, they can reconstruct their activities on new lines and cope with any difficulties that may arise. An advance in the pupils' development is then observed.

Changes in the nature of the activities of the pupils, originating in the mastering of qualitatively new material or in the carrying-out of work with a new content, do not immediately become a component factor in the development of the pupils. In order to become a new factor of development, the new items of knowledge or forms of activity must be used and repeated many times, and must be turned into a method of acquiring new knowledge and working skills. Knowledge and practical activities which have become a method already constitute a certain peculiarity or feature of the thought and practical activity of the pupils, and, consequently, become factors in the development of the pupils, and the existence of this feature subsequently has a beneficial effect on the acquisition of new knowledge and working skills by the pupils.

The education and development achieved in previous stages of a pupil's upbringing and instruction make it possible to teach the pupil about more complicated questions of science and to introduce him to more complicated forms of socially useful work involving changes in methods or their use in a more complicated form.

Thus, for example, in grades I–IV from the logical point of view, the teaching methods are characterized by the use of analysis and synthesis, comparison, induction and deduction and demonstration. In grades V–VIII, analysis and synthesis become more complex and are directed towards finding the regular links which exist between phenomena, and, in some cases, towards showing the origin, change, and development of phenomena and their transformation into new phenomena. In grades IX–XI all phenomena are studied from the point of view of their links with each other, their change, movement, and development.

As more and more new knowledge and working skills are mastered, the more they become part of the methods of teaching, thus extending and enriching them. In this connexion, there is a change in the nature of the visual and technical means which the teacher includes in the pedagogic process. In grades I–IV, simple visual aids, very simple measuring instruments and hand tools are used; in grades V–VIII, balances, microscopes, calorimeters and other apparatus, all the hand tools, and simple machines are already being used, while grades IX–XI use different forms of electrical measuring apparatus, radio apparatus, complicated equipment for physics and chemistry, and various machines and technical devices. The pupils are constantly being introduced to new types of work—manual work in the workroom or on the experimental plot in grades I–IV, more complicated manual work in grades V–VIII, together with simple fitting and machine work, and finally various skilled manual and machine jobs and fitting work in grades IX–XI, carried out in industrial enterprises, on building sites, and on collective and State farms. Because of their

195

high standard of general-education preparation, pupils in grades IX–XI even know how to assemble radio and electrical equipment and how to assemble and repair calculating machines. The nature of the drawing work done by the pupils changes: drawings in grades I–IV; drawings, diagrams, sketches, and simple designs in grades V–VIII; complicated plans and designs in grades IX–XI. All this makes it possible gradually to increase the demands on the pupils' mental ability and on their independence in the teaching process; this takes the form of increasing use of the research approach, more and more complicated independent work, and ever wider use of the methods of planning and design in school work.

In grades I–IV, lectures are not used as a method, in grades VII–VIII lectures are used occasionally, while in grades IX–XI they are used systematically. In grades I–III the experimental method is little used, in grades IV–V it is used more extensively, and in grades VI–VIII even more so, as more and more natural sciences become the subject of study. The nature of the experiments also changes as increasingly complicated and profound questions of science are studied.

In evening schools, the success of the instruction depends on the ability of the teacher to explain to the pupils the main essential questions of the course, to teach them the methods of carrying out independent work, and to instruct them how to go about independent work at home or in the library. In selecting the teaching material, account must be taken of the pupils' knowledge of life and of their production experience. N. K. Krupskaya said of economizing the pupils' time: 'Anyone who would teach adults in the same way as children are taught, obliging adults to waste time on what they have learned long ago, would be doing something that is inadmissible if the pupils' time is not to be used unprofitably. It is the duty of a teacher of adults to save as much time as possible.'[1]

In evening schools particular importance is attached to analysing, systematizing and repeating what has gone before, and to the wide use of consultations among the pupils on what has been done.

What has been stated above shows that the methods of polytechnical education have a qualitative peculiarity in grades I–IV, V–VIII, and IX–XI. But the system of teaching methods remains the same. Just as the presence of certain chemical elements, plants, or animals in a certain locality does not change the periodic system or classification, so the qualitative peculiarity of the method of teaching does not change the general classification of teaching

---

1. N. K. Krupskaya *Teaching in Secondary Schools for Adults*, Uchpedgiz, 1939, p. 73.

methods in a general-education or polytechnical school. The methods are the same, but their use varies according to the various levels of instruction and the various subjects.

The selection of the methods and the way in which they are used vary according to the pedagogic task which they should help to carry out; according to the content and nature of the material which the pupils have to learn and the methodology of the science which is the subject of instruction; according to the development of the pupils and the amount of scientific, cognitive and working experience which they have acquired in previous lessons; according to the nature of the stages by which the pedagogic process proceeds and through which the pupils are to be conducted; according to the amount of time which can be spent in training the pupils and building up their knowledge, abilities and skills, and in carrying out socially useful work; according to whether the necessary teaching equipment is available in the school and whether there is any production in the environment of the school.

This means that the teacher must not only know the system of teaching methods and their general characteristics, but must also know the methodology of his subject, and be able to choose correctly the teaching methods for each specific case, develop them in a creative manner and give them a concrete form. To achieve this, the teacher should: (a) set the next school task (the acquisition of certain knowledge, the training of the pupils in certain skills, and the carrying-out of certain socially useful work, etc.); (b) take into account the general development of the pupils, their physical and psychological characteristics, the amount of general-education, polytechnical, and vocational training received by the pupils so far, the peculiarities of the content of the forthcoming work, the training equipment available in the school, the production environment of the school, local conditions, and the amount of teaching time available; (c) in accordance with the pedagogic task and with due regard to the conditions mentioned in (b) above, the teacher should select the methods and develop them further in a concrete manner:

He must analyse the material to be taught, establish its link with what has gone before, and determine exactly what, how, and in what order the pupils must learn.

He must consider how to link the material to be taught with production and the work of the pupils, and he must select material from practical communist achievements for his teaching work.

He must determine what needs to be consolidated and developed among the work already done by the pupils.

197

He must determine the stages of the pedagogic process through which the pupils must pass, the carrying-out of socially useful work, and so on.

He must work out the sequence of teaching in all its stages, going from ignorance to knowledge and from knowledge to mastery and skill (the use of analysis and synthesis, induction and deduction, comparison and demonstration and, in the middle and senior grades, the use, in addition, of the elements of the dialectical approach to the study of reality.)

He must determine what knowledge acquired in previous stages of learning is to be used as part of the methods for mastering new subjects and acquiring new knowledge and skills, and he must find out how fresh this knowledge is in the minds of the pupils.

He must determine the technical means (teaching equipment, teaching aids, etc.) required for successfully carrying out all the stages of the pedagogic process.

He must devise ways and means of arousing the interest of the pupils in the coming work.

He must determine the extent of the activities and of the independent work of the pupils, the content of their independent work in the process of acquiring new knowledge, abilities and skills and in the carrying-out of the stipulated type of work, and the nature of an individual approach to the pupils.

He must verify whether the methods devised are suitable for the implementation of the general tasks of the communist upbringing of the pupils with which the school is faced, including the task of their all-round development.

He must verify that there is enough teaching time available to carry out the appointed pedagogic task by the methods devised.

This creative use of teaching methods by the teachers is facilitated by the experience of leading workers in this field and by the study of works on pedagogics, methodology and psychology, which make a combined effort to discover the best conditions for the successful imparting to pupils of knowledge, abilities, skills, and working methods, and for the mastery by them of various types of work.

CHAPTER IX

THE ROLE OF OUT-OF-CLASS AND OUT-OF-SCHOOL WORK IN THE POLYTECHNICAL EDUCATION OF SCHOOLCHILDREN

by N. E. Tseitlin

Out-of-class and out-of-school work in physics, chemistry, biology, local lore, technology and agriculture is an important means of broadening the polytechnical horizon of school children, improving their working knowledge and skills and developing their technical creative abilities. By working in study groups, amateur groups, sections of children's clubs, Pioneer's Houses and at Young Technicians', Young Naturalists' and Young Tourists' centres and by taking part in excursions, competitions, technical contests, exhibitions and organized meetings with scientists, inventors and skilled workers, the schoolchildren broaden and deepen their knowledge in various fields of technology, industry, building and agriculture; they also acquire and consolidate practical knowledge and skills and develop their abilities. Out-of-class and out-of-school work gives children in the eight-year school an opportunity to test their abilities in a practical way and makes it easier for them to choose a career and subsequently to master the speciality they have chosen.

To further the polytechnical education of schoolchildren it is particularly important to encourage them to carry out electrical, radio and chemical-engineering work, to learn about agricultural machines, tractors and motor-cars and to work in Young Agricultural Experimentalists' groups and in groups specializing in nature study, land reclamation, aeromodelling, railways, amateur photography, etc.

GROUPS FOR PUPILS OF GRADES I–IV

Work with Young Naturalists begins in the lower school grades. Under the teacher's supervision the children arrange a 'nature corner' in the classroom, carry out simple observations of plants, animals and seasonal changes in nature and learn to conduct simple tests and make deductions from them.

Young Naturalists of early school age take part in holding a 'Bird Day' and a 'Forest Day', preparing seeds for sowing, sowing market-garden crops in beds and weeding them. The children make herbaria, collections of plant seeds and of the useful minerals of their district and prepare materials for object lessons at school.

The activities of work groups are organized in out-of-school time on the basis of the knowledge and skills acquired by the children in school. The interest of children of early school age in lessons about general work and technology is unstable and undifferentiated. Monotonous and laborious work, or being engaged in any particular form of work for a long time, quickly tires them and reduces their interest. Creative inclinations and abilities, technical flair and the desire to construct and invent merely begin to manifest themselves at this age. For this reason the general groups of Nimble Hands, extremely widespread throughout the Soviet Union, are the most suitable for children of early and middle school age. In these groups children work readily and with great interest at various forms of handicrafts within the range of their abilities; making objects out of pasteboard, wire and tinplate, bookbinding, sewing, knitting, fretwork and pokerwork, making scenery and props for the school puppet theatre, making simple models and maquettes out of paper, wood and tinfoil, making materials for classroom object lessons and decorating the school pioneers' room. Making objects of practical use in the children's home life, schoolwork and games in the Nimble Hands groups gives an active character to the children's work and raises its educational significance.

GROUPS FOR PUPILS OF GRADES V–XI

Out-of-class work with a polytechnical content assumes a wider scope in grades V–VIII and IX–XI. An extensive network of various groups has been created in the eight-year and secondary schools, and much is being done to develop the resourcefulness, independent activity and initiative of the pupils by way of mass out-of-school and out-of-class arrangements, such as excursions, lectures, 'science as entertainment' evenings, young technicians' competitions, sports festivals, exhibitions of creative technical work, etc.

Out-of-class work is conducted, as a rule, with pupils of one class only or with pupils of parallel or adjacent classes. The class teacher directs this work within each class. Various out-of-class occupations organized on the initiative of the Young Communist League, the Pioneers and pupils' organizations are co-ordinated within a single plan of educational work for the class, which is drawn up by the class teacher for each three-month term or half-year. This gives singleness of purpose to out-of-class work and assists in making its educational influence upon the school children effective.

In recent years many new elements relating to work and technology were introduced into the content and organization of out-of-class activities.

Pupils of all grades are systematically drawn into various kinds of socially useful work which is both within the range of their abilities and interesting in its form and content. Pupils' self-service activities are of considerable importance in schools. The pupils assume in full, or to a considerable extent, the responsibility for the upkeep of classrooms, study-rooms, school corridors and grounds. Some of the children look after the indoor plants and the school's flower-garden and become 'patrons' of nearby kinder-gartens, making toys for the younger children and helping to equip and maintain the playgrounds. Pupils of other grades collect waste paper and scrap metal, take an active part in the work of improving the town or village amenities and give labour assistance within their capacities to their supporting enterprises, State and collective farms.

As a rule, each teacher at the school organizes a group in connexion with his own subject for pupils who show special interest in any particular branch of knowledge. The purpose of these subject groups is to deepen the knowledge of the pupils and to widen their educational horizon in the field of a science the fundamentals of which are taught at school, as well as to encourage the pupils to engage in practical, socially useful activities.

Among the groups most widely found in Soviet schools, those of particular importance for the systematic widening of the poly-technical horizons of schoolchildren are the groups of Young Mathematicians, Young Physicists, Young Chemists, Young Naturalists, Students of Local Lore, Young Technicians, Agricul-tural Experimentalists, etc.

The content of the work of these groups and the subjects for technical and experimental activities are determined by the pupils under the teacher's direction. For these activities teachers and group leaders make extensive use of 'specimen programmes' and 'lists of specimen subjects' published by the public education authorities.

201

The entire work of the groups is built on the basis of stimulating and systematically developing the pupils' independent activity, resourcefulness, initiative and spirit of inquiry.

Various forms of activity are used in the work of the groups: lectures and talks, group attendance at public lectures, museums and exhibitions, group listening to broadcasts and viewing of television broadcasts and films, excursions, bookwork, discussions, nature and laboratory observations and experiments and research in local lore. Specialists—engineers, technicians, leading workers in production, tractor-repair-station workers, agronomists and skilled agricultural workers—are invited by the pupils to give talks; these specialists unfailingly respond to the needs of schools and are always ready to assist the children with their knowledge and experience.

The teachers strive not only to develop the pupils' interest in a particular branch of knowledge but also to impart to them the knowledge and skills for independent work in that field. For this purpose, socially useful practical work is carried out—making visual aids and equipment for the school's study-rooms, producing wall newspapers and school journals devoted to specific subjects, popularizing the various branches of knowledge, etc.

Other forms of independent educational work are also widely used in the activities of subject groups—the reading of books and the study of source materials, the use of reference books, the gathering and preparing of materials and arranging them into collections. The older the schoolchildren, the more widely and fully all these forms of independent work are practised. The leader enlists the co-operation of the pupils in organizing the work of the group, in the distribution of independent tasks among its members and in the examination and group discussion of papers, reports, experiments, models, etc.

The members of subject groups are also the teacher's active assistants: they help him in demonstrating experiments during lessons and in organizing laboratory work and excursions, address their fellow-pupils in the 'pupils' lecture-room', contribute items on popular science subjects to the school newspaper or journal. Members of subject groups organize school and inter-school competitions for young mathematicians, physicists, chemists and geographers.

The leaders of the groups make sure that the knowledge imparted in the classroom is utilized in the children's practical activities and that these pupils acquire fresh knowledge concerning the technical and technological bases of modern industrial and agricultural production. During their activities in the groups, the schoolchildren improve their 'technical literacy' by learning how to use instruction charts and drawings, and make simple technical calculations and master the working methods and the technique of operating the more common machines and mechanical devices.

Work in technical groups for pupils of the senior grades (IX–XI) is organized in such a way as to satisfy the specific interests in work and technology of that age-group in connexion with preparing them for practical activity and the choice of a career.

In these groups the pupils make fairly complex constructions, for which they need technical knowledge, solid working skills and an ability to organize their work. They design and build complex aircraft models, and working models of motor-cars, ships, self-propelled excavators, chemistry apparatus, and agricultural machines. They make an extensive study of motors, acquire practice in driving scooters, motor-cycles, cars and tractors and learn how to operate radio and film equipment. Optional courses for production grounds are organized under the direction of engineers, technicians or leading workers of the supporting enterprise.

Experience has shown that many young men and girls who have been active members of technical and production groups are remarkable for their thorough knowledge of physics, mathematics and drawing and the breadth of their general technical and practical knowledge. While learning at school, they thus become proficient in a technical aspect of production.

The groups of Young Naturalists and Agricultural Experimentalists in grades V–XI are intended to satisfy and develop the pupils' interest in the biological sciences and to improve their practical knowledge and skills in soil cultivation, plant-growing and animal care. In these groups the children are introduced to work which is commensurate with their abilities and valuable from the educational and training point of view at the school's experimental plot, in the fields and farm units of State and collective farms.

Intermediary and senior school pupils in these groups undertake activities which are of a more independent, serious and deeper nature and are differentiated according to the interests and inclinations of the pupils; separate sections cover study and conservation of nature, field-crop cultivation, vegetable-growing, flower-growing, gardening, bee-keeping, animal husbandry, Young Hunters and Young Foresters. They grow vegetables, fruit-bearing trees and decorative plants and flowers and conduct experiments involving the application of new scientific methods of farming. They make observations of insects, birds and rodents and carry out control measures against field, garden, forest and water reservoir pests.

Senior Young Naturalists participate in the investigation of the natural resources of their region, form herbaria and make collections of useful minerals, insects, fish and birds. They take part in socially useful agricultural work as far as they are able and assist in the work of collective farm laboratories. At livestock-raising farms belonging to collective farms the Young Naturalists look after the young animals and help the women caring for poultry, calves and pigs.

In connexion with their study of the principles of Darwinism, pupils of the ninth grade carry out experiments and observations on the phase development of plants, vegetative hybridization and modification of the nature of plants by the use of Michurin methods. They take part, as far as they are able, in experimental and research work in agriculture, agronomy and animal husbandry.

Many pupils, even before they finish the secondary school, make up their minds about what they are going to do in the future and decide to devote themselves to work in agricultural production. The number of pupils who exhibit at the All-Union Exhibition of Achievements of the National Economy of the U.S.S.R. increases year by year. Many are awarded medals and honorary diplomas for their achievements.

MASS OUT-OF-CLASS WORK

In close connexion with the above-mentioned out-of-class activities, there are mass educational and training arrangements such as competitions and 'olympiads' for young mathematicians, physicists, chemists, astronomers and technicians.

These olympiads are organized in two or three rounds, the first being generally held within the schools themselves, separately for the pupils of each grade. The winners of the first round from all schools in a given town, district, region or Republic participate in the second and third rounds. This method of organizing the olympiads makes it possible to get large numbers of pupils to take part in them.

An active part in organizing and holding the olympiads is taken not only by public education bodies and numerous out-of-school establishments but also by the relevant university schools and institutes, as well as museums, planetaria and local branches of the Society for the Dissemination of Political and Scientific Knowledge. Outstanding scientists, professors and teachers collaborate willingly with each other in setting the tasks for the participants in each round of the olympiad. The tasks set for participants in the olympiads differ considerably as a rule in their content and form from the problems which pupils are acccustomed to solve in the course of their school lessons. Participants in the olympiads are often invited to carry out independently a particular type of observation and make deductions from it, to assemble a piece of apparatus or to demonstrate an experiment or a method of performing some specific work. The solving of olympiad problems helps to single out those pupils who take their studies seriously and have a creative approach to the practical application of their knowledge.

Contests and competitions in making various types of models, apparatus and equipment, are another very widespread form of mass out-of-class and out-of-school work for pupils of intermediary and senior grades.

For example, competitions and contests for young aeromodellers, ship-modellers, radio amateurs, railwaymen and photographers are systematically conducted throughout the country. These contests are organized in several stages, school competitions being followed by district or town competitions, regional and Republic competitions and, finally, All-Union competitions.

Various mass contests, in which not only Young Technicians and Young Naturalists but all interested schoolchildren are invited to participate, are also systematically held. Among such mass contests on specific subjects are those involving socially useful work, such as Young Technicians for the Motherland, Let us beautify our Motherland with Gardens, and For the Motherland's Roads of Steel.

Exhibitions are also organized on a school, district, town, regional and Republican scale. All-Union exhibitions are also regularly held. At all these exhibitions there is extensive evidence of the children's independent activities in work and technology, of their creative technical ability and achievements and the results of their socially useful work. In some schools occasional exhibitions of children's creative technical work have been gradually turned into permanent exhibitions in the form of small school poly-technical museums.

School lecture-rooms represent a mass form of out-of-class work which deserves particular mention. Teachers, members of the Society for the Dissemination of Political and Scientific Know-ledge, scientists, engineers, inventors, production innovators and members of the staff of planetaria and museums give lectures on various subjects on fixed days for pupils in grades VI–VIII and

IX–XI. The lectures are given singly or in the form of courses. They are usually illustrated by the showing of films and slides.

The Young Communist League and Pioneer organizations play an important role in carrying out the tasks connected with the polytechnical training of schoolchildren. The Young Communist League organizations of the schools co-operate in the development of technical groups, organize competitions and exhibitions, take active part in equipping school study-rooms, organize meetings with leading personalities in industry, science and technology and help to install radio, electrical and film equipment in schools.

The Young Communist League organizations and Pioneer Brigades of the schools train children from an early age in a conscious and disciplined attitude to work and inculcate in them a love and respect for physical labour and the ability to perform any work suitable to their age.

Young Pioneers in detachments and units engage in many-sided work activities, making toys, assembling models from parts oi mechanical and electrical construction sets, learning to use magic lanterns and film cameras, replanting indoor plants and sowing flowers and vegetables.

In order to give a systematic character to the work of Young Pioneers in acquiring accomplishments and skills that are useful in life, the Central Council of the All-Union Lenin Pioneers' Organization has introduced a specimen list of accomplishments and skills ('Pioneers' stages') which the children acquire gradually during the time they belong to the Pioneer organization. Many of these accomplishments and skills are directly connected with polytechnical training. For example, the first stage (for Pioneers in grades III–IV) includes the ability to make simple objects for classwork, for the Pioneers' Room, for the Pioneer Detachment's Corner and for the home.

The second stage (for Pioneers in grades V–VI) includes the ability to do more complicated work, for example, making working models, toys, equipment for playgrounds, and toy collections, repairing agricultural equipment, growing vegetables and maize, raising ducks, chickens, geese, etc. The third stage (for Pioneers in grades VII–VIII) includes still more complicated work: helping to repair the school building and school furniture, installing electrical and radio equipment in the school, settlement or village, making teaching aids and instruments for school study-rooms, workshops, plot and sports ground. Pioneers at this stage learn to drive a tractor, motor-cycle and motor-car. They help workers in harvesting, building and other forms of socially useful work.

All this assists in broadening and deepening the children's

polytechnical knowledge, accomplishments and skills that are useful in life and for work in production.

THE WORK OF OUT-OF-SCHOOL INSTITUTIONS

Side by side and in close contact with the schools, various out-of-school institutions in the U.S.S.R. carry out different kinds of educational and training work with children. These institutions help the schools in consolidating and deepening the children's knowledge, broadening their horizons, developing their creative abilities and interests and carrying out their polytechnical training. They satisfy the children's interests in the fields of science, technology, literature, the arts, physical culture and sport and help to develop their abilities and talents.

During the years of Soviet rule numerous out-of-school institutions of different types have been created in the U.S.S.R.; they help to solve the problems involved in giving an all-round education to the millions of children. Children's out-of-school institutions such as Pioneers' Houses and Palaces, children's sectors in workers' and collective farm clubs and Houses of Culture, children's parks and 'children's towns' in Parks of Culture and Rest and Pioneer summer camps carry out educational and training work satisfying the children's many interests and requirements. Other institutions, such as children's libraries and reading-rooms, children's Houses of Artistic Education, children's theatres and cinemas, Young Naturalists' and Young Technicians' centres, children's stadiums and children's sports schools, children's excursion and touring centres and children's railways and river ports, carry out specialized work with children, organizing their activities and satisfying their interests principally within a single chosen field.

The work of Pioneers' Houses has recently assumed several new forms in connexion with the solution of the problems involved in training schoolchildren for practical activities. Young Mechanization Experts', Tractor Drivers', Combine Operators', Drivers', Fitters' and Turners' groups have become widespread. Young Communist League and youth summer camps are organized on collective farms; the activities of these camps are based on a combination of collective-farm work with sensible and healthy recreation for schoolchildren. Clubs for children in the senior-school grades are one of the new ways of organizing the older schoolchildren's leisure at Pioneers' Houses and Palaces. For example, more than twenty such clubs are already in operation in Leningrad, nineteen in Moscow and ten in Kiev.

207

Of considerable importance in the system of out-of-school work with children, are Young Technicians' centres ('Stations') which play an important part in encouraging a serious interest in technology among children and young people.

The Central Children's Technical Station (later renamed Central Station for Young Technicians), founded in Moscow in 1926, has developed into one of the country's largest centres for organizing out-of-school technological work.

The Central Station for Young Technicians (CSYT) carries out large-scale experimental work with children and adolescents, on the basis of which the programmes for various technical groups are drawn up. Local Young Technicians' Stations and technical groups in Pioneers' Houses, schools and clubs are guided by these programmes.

The Central Station for Young Technicians is a methodological instructional centre for technical propaganda among children. Its consultation department receives and sends out hundreds of letters a day, replying to questions from young technicians and from workers in out-of-school institutions. The Central Station and local Young Technicians' Stations give practical assistance to schools in carrying out polytechnical education by acquainting schoolchildren with the fundamentals of modern production in their own groups and in the groups at Pioneers' Houses and by organizing mass work in the form of lectures and excursions. They publish methodological literature to assist group leaders in schools. These centres have technical libraries of their own; they hold exhibitions of the work of young technicians and organize the work of groups in workshops and laboratories. They give methodological and practical assistance to teachers and Pioneer leaders in organizing out-of-class and out-of-school group and mass work. They arrange seminars, consultations, practical studies and conferences, and summarize and disseminate the best experiences of technological work in Pioneer Brigades, Detachments and school groups. They also organize, on a wide scale, the dissemination among schoolchildren of information concerning the achievements of world and Soviet science and technology.

Young Technicians' Stations also carry out all kinds of work aimed at acquainting schoolchildren with the scientific bases of agricultural production and fostering interest in it: they establish groups for young mechanization experts, supply these groups with programmes and aids and give them day-to-day methodological assistance. Rallies of young mechanization experts and competitions for best models of agricultural machines are organized during the summer holidays.

208

To enable schoolchildren to compare their experience of work at collective and State farms and training and experimental plots, the Central Young Naturalists' Station organizes annual All-Union or Republican rallies for young naturalists. These are held at the All-Union Exhibition of the Achievements of National Economy, Moscow, with the participation of scientists, teachers and leaders in agricultural production. Thousands of the best young naturalists in the Soviet Union have attended these rallies in the last few years and have presented reports on the work carried out at collective and State farms, in school gardens, and at school farms and training and experimental plots.

In order to raise the qualifications of persons working at the centres and to enable them to compare their work experiences, courses and seminars for directors of regional and town Young Naturalists' centres and for methodologists working at those centres are conducted every year.

The Central Young Naturalists' Station conducts seminars and individual and group consultations, both personal and by correspondence, for teachers, Pioneer leaders and workers at Pioneer camps. Participants in the seminars are given methodological literature, seeds and materials for planting. Every year, the Station sends out tens of thousands of packets of selected seeds for agricultural crops to schools and out-of-school institutions and hands over to them large quantities of high-grade material for planting (strawberry runners, roots, flower cuttings, flower, decorative-plant and vegetable seedlings, etc.). The Station has published a considerable number of methodological aids in connexion with the work of young naturalists.

The work of many Young Naturalists' centres is becoming important in the national economy. For example, the regional Young Naturalists' centre at Krasnodarsk has produced a new type of winter wheat named 'Yunnatka'; young naturalists of Mechetinsk (Rostov region) have produced a hybrid variety of wheat named *Mechetinskaya*, which is remarkable for its high crop-yield and large grains.

A considerable number of Young Naturalists' centres and groups successfully carry out experimental work at the request of collective and State farms and scientific research institutes. This type of work is done on a particularly wide scale in the Leningrad, Rostov, Kuybyshev and Krasnodarsk regions. A characteristic feature of Young Naturalists' work is the fact that it is not confined within the limits of a single plot, centre or school but that it leads to the results of agricultural experiments being adopted in the practical work of collective and State farms. For example, young naturalists at the Kutuzov eight-year school (Moscow region) have grown a new variety of maize called *Kutuzovka*.

Young Naturalists also do a great deal of horticultural work. They transplant fruit, soft fruit and decorative plants and start nurseries.

Interesting examples of the achievements of Young Naturalists are also shown at the Exhibition of Achievements of the National Economy of the U.S.S.R. The number of young naturalists who contribute to the exhibition increases every year.

The workers of many enterprises assist the schools in solving problems connected with polytechnical education. The Gorky automobile works, the Krasny Aksay works at Rostov-on-Don, the Moscow chemico-pharmaceutical works, the Avtopribor works at Vladimir, the Metiz works at Dnepropetrovsk, the Druzhkovo works, the Yaroslav Power Directorate and many other Soviet enterprises have established at clubs and Houses and Palaces of Culture children's clubs for creative technical work and young technicians' clubs, the work of which is directed by engineers, technicians and skilled workers on the basis of social-work principles.

The Ministry of Transport has established a fairly large network of Young Technicians' and Children's Railways' centres, the purpose of which is to develop the children's interest in railway transport, acquaint them with its technology and train them in the necessary practical skills. Children's railways, such as the Little Gorky, Little Erevan, Little Transcarpathian, Little North-Caucasian and Little Sverdlovsk railways and others, enjoy immense popularity among young passengers.

Hundreds of house management committees in Moscow, Leningrad and other large industrial cities, actively supported by parents' organizations, conduct continuous out-of-school work with children.

They organize various mass cultural events for children, such as evenings of creative artistic activities, readers' conferences, talks and excursions.

The extensive fostering of initiative, resourcefulness and independent activity in children by means of out-of-class and out-of-school work assists the harmonious, all-round development of schoolchildren and helps to consolidate and strengthen their interest in the branches of science and technology they have chosen and in their favourite forms of work. Children's talents and abilities develop in step with the growth of their general culture and the broadening of their polytechnical horizon.

This voluntary work has a lasting effect on the future generation. Many well-known Soviet inventors, efficiency engineers and production innovators remember with gratitude their childhood years and their spare-time work in technology and technical modelling. Many prominent innovators working in Soviet agriculture were in the past members of Young Naturalists' and Agricultural Experimentalists' circles.

CHAPTER X

THE EDUCATIONAL VALUE OF POLYTECHNICAL TRAINING

by M. N. Skatkin

Polytechnical instruction not only equips pupils with a knowledge of the scientific principles of production and with working skills but is also of great educational value as a means of promoting all-round development; in examining the educational value of polytechnical training we must bear these two aspects in mind—the theoretical (knowledge of the scientific principles of production) and the practical (acquisition of working skills).

It is in the process of activity that the child develops. Muscles develop only if they are active. Similarly, a child's mental capacity cannot develop unless the mind is made to work intensively; the all-round development of a child's personality can only be achieved through the organization of many-sided activity.

What forms of activity, then, are stimulated by polytechnical education, and how does this activity influence the development of the physical and mental characteristics and capacities of children?

THE SIGNIFICANCE OF POLYTECHNICAL EDUCATION IN THE PHYSICAL DEVELOPMENT OF CHILDREN

Polytechnical training involves schoolchildren in physical labour; and the work of the muscles, as we know from present-day physiology, invariably produces changes in the whole organism, either directly or indirectly.

What are the changes produced in the organism under the influence of physical labour? Let us first consider those of decisive importance in the case of a growing and developing child.

Strong muscular exertion, under conditions of purposeful activity, produces a qualitative functional change in the muscle cells and an improvement in their working capacity. Work helps to develop both the skeletal and muscular system and to increase the general working capacity and physical resistance of the organism.

But this is not the only positive effect. Active muscles are a source of powerful functional change in the whole organism: ordinary observations show that two closely allied processes of blood circulation and respiration are greatly intensified during work. The working muscles require an increased blood supply for feeding the muscle cells, and hence make a heavier demand on the cardiovascular system. Whereas the heart contractions do not exceed sixty-five to seventy-five a minute in a state of repose, even with light work the rate increases to eighty-five. The volume of blood pumped from the heart into the aorta substantially increases during this process.

To enable the blood to take the necessary amount of oxygen from the lungs and discharge the carbon dioxide, the breathing must become much stronger, breathing becomes more frequent and, which is far more important, more deep than usual. The lungs and the cardiovascular system begin to work at 'full capacity'. What takes place may be called an 'oxygen ventilation' of the organism. Stagnation phenomena are eliminated, especially from the brain; for deep breathing strengthens the outflow of venous blood and the inflow of 'fresh' (arterial) blood into the blood vessels of the brain, while metabolism is intensified, thus increasing the supply of nutrient substances to the brain and creating the proper physiological conditions for its normal development and an increase in its working capacity. All this is obviously of prime importance to the growing organism of the schoolchild who has to spend six or seven hours daily at a desk, either at school or at home, and the work he does in the school workshop soon restores the 'order' that has been upset by all these hours of sitting.

Physical exercises imposing an effort, particularly on the shoulder muscles, are an absolute organic necessity for a developing child. Work satisfies this need. Woodwork, metalwork and technical modelling are particularly valuable in this respect, for the processing of wood or metal involves broad and sweeping muscular movements performed according to a strictly defined tempo and rhythm.

As a result of such labour exercises, the child's hands become more dextrous and 'obedient', developing the ability to perform precise and well-co-ordinated movements over a relatively long period.

One of the healthiest forms of work is farm work, which takes place in the open and is characterized by a wide variety of movements. This greatly helps to develop the child's nervous and muscular system and produce close co-ordination between his movements.

As has already been shown, the alternation of mental and physical work creates more favourable conditions for mental work, and hence also for the mental development of children. Moreover, the strong emotional impulses produced in children by their creative labour stimulate the work of the cerebral cortex and improve its general tone—which in itself facilitates the process of developing new temporary connexions. And the creation of temporary connexions, as the famous Soviet physiologist Pavlov has shown, lies at the very root of training.

A great variety of 'analysers' come into operation during the labour process, and their systematic training helps to develop them. Let us take an example.

Suppose a child makes a model of a crane. In the process of work, he becomes acquainted with the various objects (materials and instruments), and their properties and interrelationships, through the medium of: (a) kinesthetic sense (resistance to breaking, bending, compressing, stretching and cutting); (b) visual sense (the outward appearance of the materials and instruments, their shape, colour, etc.); (c) auditory sense (the sounds produced when planing or sawing wood or cutting metal, the sound produced by blows, friction, etc.); (d) tactile sense (the hardness, roughness or evenness of surfaces, etc.); (e) olfactory sense (the smell of pinewood resin, glue, etc.).

In identifying a particular material, wood, for instance, a child uses all the senses in question; and their co-ordination, which helps him to get a deeper understanding of the nature of objects and phenomena, is accompanied by intensive mental activity. The co-ordinated functioning of the senses in the course of work presupposes, in fact, the co-ordinated work of the corresponding brain centres. In this way, well-directed labour activity helps to promote the harmonious development of the material substratum of intellectual activity—the brain.

The well-known Soviet educationist A. S. Makarenko gave an example in one of his lectures of the degree of precision attainable in the course of work, in the differentiation of stimuli.

'The other day, I received a visit from a doctor. I recall that he used to work here as a grinder, on a grinding machine which produced metal parts with the utmost precision—up to one-hundredth of a millimetre. The foreman would say to him: "Would you cut it down by one-hundredth?" And he would simply fix the part into the machine, and without doing any checking or using any measuring instruments, he would go ahead, and then announce: "Here you are—less one-hundredth it is!"

'His hand, his eye and the machine tool were so well co-ordinated that no checking was necessary. His sense of the machine-tool was absolutely perfect. And today this former master-grinder is a doctor; yet I am again conscious, in his philosophy, of his tremendous respect for precision.'[1]

Academician K. M. Bykov, in a paper presented at the scientific symposium on the problems of Pavlov's physiological doctrine, placed special emphasis on the importance of muscular movements in the upbringing of man in general and in the development of his brain in particular.

'Sechenov', he said, 'had already stressed the importance of muscular movements in the development of the cerebral activity of man. Without them, in fact, it is impossible to achieve cognition of nature let alone to transform it by means of human labour, or to perfect man himself in the process of education.'[2] In a later passage on the same theme, he added:

'The role played by the muscles in the cognition of the outer world is enormous. Sechenov used a striking image when he described the receptive machinery of the muscles as "tentacles"; he also referred to the tremendous part played by the work of the muscles in the activity of the brain.'[3]

Work helps to enrich a child's consciousness with concrete conceptions of the objects and phenomena of the objective world: it is with the help of the receptive machinery of the muscles and the sense of touch in the process of work that children grasp such qualities of objects as hardness, flexibility, elasticity, density, the nature of their surface, viscosity, resistance to breaking, compressing, stretching, cutting, etc., and get a grasp of the shape and size of objects and a better feeling of space.

It was already noted by Comenius long ago that a child's urge to acquire knowledge greatly increases the intensity of his intellectual effort and helps him in his studies: 'If we eat without

---

1. A. S. Makarenko, *Works*, Moscow, R.S.F.S.R. Academy of Pedagogical Sciences, 1951, Vol. V, p. 199.
2. *Scientific Symposium on the Problems of the Physiological Doctrine of I. P. Pavlov*, Verbatim record, Moscow, U.S.S.R. Academy of Sciences, 1950, p. 34.
3. ibid., p. 35.

appetite but nevertheless introduce food into the stomach', he wrote in *The Great Didactic*, 'the result can only be nausea and retching or indigestion and poor health at the very least. But if food is introduced into the stomach under the influence of hunger, it is taken in with pleasure, well digested and successfully turned into gastric juices and blood.'[1] And Comenius accordingly called on teachers to 'arouse in children by every possible means, a burning urge for knowledge and training'. Polytechnical labour instruction is designed to arouse this urge.

For example, the children are given the task of producing, on the school experimental plot, a better potato crop than the best local collective farm. To solve this problem, they have to know the exact requirements of this plant, and how to satisfy them. They listen very attentively to what the teacher has to say in the class about potatoes, and carefully study the relevant passages in their botany textbook. Still not being fully satisfied, they go on to discover more about the biology and cultivation of potatoes in the relevant sections of the more specialized books and periodicals in the school and collective-farm libraries. All this undoubtedly helps to stimulate their curiosity and broaden their polytechnical outlook. Again, in the process of work, the knowledge acquired during physics, mathematics and technical-drawing lessons becomes more concrete and deeply rooted. Professor S. M. Shabalov demonstrated this in his book *Polytechnical Education* by means of the following example:

A group of pupils are working on a lathe. It is literally impossible for them to take a single step forward without recalling and applying the mathematics or laws of mechanics they have learned during the physics lessons in class. The cutter is fixed into the holder; but how far should its working-end project? On the strength of what they know of levers, they decide that the less it projects the better; the smaller the load on the cutter, the less will be the vibration and the more regular, clean and accurate will be the work done.

Several forces act upon the cutter: one along its axis; another parallel to the axis of the material to be processed; and a third perpendicularly downwards. To understand these phenomena, we have to apply a knowledge of the laws of the parallelogram of forces.

Then the clipping profile has to be selected, and the choice of this will depend in the first place on the hardness of the material and the power of the machine tool. The equation of double the

1. A. Comenius, *Selected Pedagogical Works*, Uchpedgiz, 1939, Vol. I, p. 163.

rotating momentum of the spindle and double the cutting momentum will provide the solution to this problem. Here we see demonstrated that 'power momentum' which the physics textbooks usually refer to only in an abstract way. Here too we observe the vital importance of mathematical calculation.

The study of production shows pupils how men get to know the world in the process of work, and how the needs of production stimulate the development of science. Having learned the laws of nature, men apply them in practice in industry and agriculture, and change the properties of natural objects, in order to adapt them to human needs. Through direct participation in productive labour, pupils take a personal part in the transformation and conversion of natural materials and receive convincing proof of the power and accuracy of the human mind.

Polytechnical education familiarizes pupils with the fundamental scientific principles of production, gives them working proficiency and skills and lays the foundations for a general technical labour culture. As a result, pupils acquire that many-sided mobility ('functional mobility') of which Marx spoke—the capacity to find one's bearings quickly in any form of production, apply in practice the theoretical knowledge acquired at school, and to use the skills learned there in new situations. All this creates conditions in which a man can choose his profession freely and change over from one kind of work to another, without being tied to any one particular trade or profession all his life.

THE SIGNIFICANCE OF POLYTECHNICAL EDUCATION FOR THE MORAL UPBRINGING OF SCHOOLCHILDREN

Communist morality cannot be inculcated by means of sanctimonious preaching and discourses on morality. As Lenin pointed out: 'Only by working together with workers and peasant is it possible to become real communists.'[1]

The father of pedagogical science in the U.S.S.R., K. D. Ushinsky, saw in labour the source of human dignity as well as the source of morality and happiness. In his article on 'The Psychological and Educational Importance of Labour', which may rightly be called a 'hymn to labour', be brought out the tremendous significance of labour in the moral upbringing of the rising generation. 'Without personal work, man cannot advance, nor stay where he is: he can only go backwards',[2] for work is essential

---

1. V. I. Lenin, *Works*, 3rd edition, Vol. XXX, p. 416.
2. K. D. Ushinsky, *Works*, Moscow, R.S.F.S.R., Academy of Pedagogical Sciences, 1948, Vol. II, p. 339–40.

to the body, heart and mind of man. Deprived of it, he loses his way and falls into a state of black apathy and abysmal boredom, or else surrenders to childish whims or pleasures. 'In either case, he becomes a living corpse, because work—personal work, free work—is life itself.'[1]

The remarkable experiments of Makarenko and other leading educationists clearly demonstrate the enormous educative force of joint creative labour.

In organizing the varied work of pupils in the school workshop, on the experimental plot, on a collective farm or in a plant or factory, and in consciously controlling the mutual relations between children, and between them and adults, as well as their attitude to the tools, materials and products of labour, the teacher is able to shape the children's moral conscience and conduct in actual practice.

The educational significance of polytechnical training and of production experience acquired by pupils at industrial plants was described by N. D. Nelyubin, director of the Sverdlovsk Institute of Advanced Teacher Training.

The pupils got a closer insight into production processes and a better understanding of the workers' everyday activities, he said, and this experience developed in them a love and respect for productive labour creative of material values. The pupils came to the plants not as 'tourists' but as direct participants in production, and learned advanced methods of work. For example, pupils doing their practical training at the Verkh-Issetsk metallurgical plant learned about the high-speed processing of metals devised by the worker-innovator Kolyosov, while pupils at the Uralelektro-apparat plant were able to watch the work of the celebrated machinist Petrov turning the armature of a high-power generator.

It was an object lesson in how purposefully and efficiently leading workers went about their jobs.

At some plants, he continued, the pupils met children in an older age-group who completed the ten-year course at the same school, and could see with their own eyes how rapidly their ex-colleagues, thanks to the all-round training they had received, had mastered the correct working methods and were worthily holding their own in the factory team. Such meetings are of great educational value. The ex-pupils now working in production would give their juniors still at school an enthusiastic account of their own factory work, without forgetting to mention the good wages they were now receiving. At the same time, they would also point out that in

---

1. ibid., p. 240.

taking an industrial job, they had not abandoned the idea of receiving further education through correspondence courses. These meetings between present pupils and young workers who had completed their ten-year schooling, and the direct conversations to which such meetings give rise, have proved to be an effective form of propaganda in favour of taking up work in industry on completion of school studies.

The fact of associating with leading production workers presents pupils with shining examples of labour culture; and this acts as a spur: they begin to be more careful about their clothes, to cultivate the proper 'working stance' and working movements, and to maintain order and cleanliness at the bench. They also become infected with the urge to do better and better work, and produce more. They try to avoid spoilage and waste, to economize in raw materials and electricity, and to work accurately to drawings and blueprints so as to produce the 'cleanest' work possible. That is how polytechnical training helps to develop in young workers a sense of responsibility and a high general level of technical labour culture.

The conditions in production plants have a disciplining effect on the children. Our own experience was that they soon learned in practice that they had to be punctual in arriving at work, and that it was essential to prepare the bench promptly and properly. On the first day they spent at the Uralelektroapparat plant, they were surprised at first on being told that they were not to talk loudly or shout in the workshop. They had thought that amid all the din of machinery, it was useless trying to talk in a normal voice, and that the only way to make themselves heard was to shout. They soon realized that shouts and loud conversation distracted the workers and interfered with their work, and that the atmosphere should always be conducive to thoughtful and concentrated effort. In this way they were able to appreciate the importance of labour discipline and the rules prevailing at the plant, which were essential if productive work was to be successfully performed.

In the process of work, schoolchildren establish the most varied relations between themselves, as well as with the adult workers. As a result, they develop certain definite forms of behaviour. The teacher's main task is to organize labour relations between pupils in such a way that good habits are acquired and the development of habits in conflict with the rules of communist morality prevented. Experience shows that bad habits usually result from bad organization of work, whereas correct organization, including the clear-cut distribution of tasks and duties between all the members of the group—a group united in its determination to reach a

219

socially significant objective—creates most favourable conditions for establishing good rules of behaviour in keeping with the accepted standards of communist morality.

Socialist competition in the course of work is also extensively used as an aid in the moral upbringing of schoolchildren. In organized socialist competition the teachers inculcate in the children a sense of happiness and pride at their comrades' successes, a readiness to talk about their own achievements; and an urge to help the laggers so that the success may be as complete as possible.

In order to give proper educational guidance to pupils in the course of their work, the teachers resort to a variety of methods designed to encourage good habits and confirm them. For instance, they give praise for conscientiousness, initiative, good-quality work, team spirit and co-operativeness. The effect is particularly good when brighter teams or individuals who have done especially well are publicly praised by the school director or farm management in front of all the pupils, for joyful experience of harmonious work in common for the general welfare is a good means of instilling a warm and genuinely communist attitude to labour.

Through association with leading workers and farmers in the process of productive labour, the children are not only infected by their skill and experience but also acquire something of their collectivist psychology; they develop a new, communist attitude to work, to working people and to public property.

THE SIGNIFICANCE OF POLYTECHNICAL EDUCATION FOR THE AESTHETIC DEVELOPMENT OF SCHOOLCHILDREN

One of the aims of the school is to turn work into a source of pleasure and joy, into a natural necessity, indeed. It is therefore most important that the children's work should be accompanied by strong and positive emotional experiences. The aesthetic elements of work greatly intensify its emotional effect on the young; and this consideration has led some of the leading teaching staffs to pay special attention to this question.

For example, A. S. Zhukova, director of studies at School No. 1 at Obninsk (Kaluga Region) has described how the teachers at her school create frequent opportunities for the children to experience the joy of collective labour: working together with the children, they have planted a 'Garden of Youth', built a school greenhouse and organized annual flower shows and harvest festivals.

P. Y. Eidlin (Chernolesk School, Stavropol District), notes that collective farms afford particularly good opportunities for the aesthetic training of children's brigades. 'Aesthetic training can be made part of their work, in direct association with nature. . . . We teach the brigade members to make not only useful but also beautiful objects; to see in the natural scenery around them something not only useful but also beautiful; to work not only well, but beautifully.

'Teamwork by children helps to solve a number of educational problems,' he continues. 'The day's work starts with a morning parade, at which the results of the previous day's socialist competition are announced. The brigade pennant is presented to the best group, which performs a ceremonial march to music, and leads off the procession to work. It was a great day for the brigade when the representatives of the District Young Communist League arrived to hand it the challenge Red Banner. The children swore an oath that they would never let the banner go; and sure enough they kept their word.

'It is the practice of the brigade to encourage its members to do their very best. Significantly, the children themselves propose the names of the prize-winners—first, at the meeting of the brigade council, and then at the general meeting of the brigade and, although there is a good deal of heated discussion, those awarded the prizes in the end are really the best ones.

'When we told the children that they should "work beautifully", some of them were puzzled, and wanted to know what we meant. And so every day the teachers would say something like this: "Just look, Kolya, how you are doing your planting, and how Misha is doing it. With one stroke of the spade, he puts just the right amount of earth at the bottom of the hole, while you have to pick at the earth two or three times, and instead of putting the humus at the bottom and the clay on top, you often do it the other way round. And just look at the way you are holding the spade! It's awkward to work like that. . . ." And so the children gradually begin to understand what "beautiful" work means: it has to be co-ordinated, well organized, precise and well thought out. And now the children want their work to "look more beautiful" and every so often the teacher is asked, "Well, aren't we working beautifully?"

'. . . We attach special attention to the quality of the work. When the children were given the job of planting a hundred hectares of fruit-trees last spring, the manager of the State farm had grave doubts: would they not "spoil the picture", would they plant the young trees properly, in straight lines? But the children put their backs to it. The symmetry was perfect, and the rows of apple-trees, all as straight as an arrow, stretched right to the horizon. The percentage of trees that took root was above the target figures and the children are today keeping the orchard in splendid shape.'

Aesthetics is something that concerns not only material objects or products but also human relations. The teachers therefore stress the beauty of the mutual relations existing within every group or brigade and encourage those relations in the course of social labour.

Ceremonial parades, music, songs, festivals (for instance, the harvest festival which has become a tradition with many of the school brigades in Stavropol District), and the tempo and rhythm of the work itself all create a sort of poetry of labour to which schoolchildren are very sensitive. And wherever they may be—on a collective farm, or in a mine, or in a factory—they will always be conscious of the beauty of constructive and creative work, and they will make a point of working 'beautifully'.

Thus polytechnical education is an extremely important means of ensuring the all-round development of schoolchildren—a means which Soviet teachers are using with great skill in order to develop them physically, mentally, morally and aesthetically—to train the builders of a new society composed of fully-developed people 'able to do everything', as Lenin said, and 'people with great hearts and lofty ideals', as N. S. Khruschev put it.

CHAPTER XI

THE MATERIAL FACILITIES OF POLYTECHNICAL EDUCATION IN SOVIET SCHOOLS

by I. V. Kozyr

In the work done by the Soviet schools in solving the problems of general and polytechnical education, manual and technical instruction, production and vocational training, the material facilities are of particularly vital significance.

These consist of the school buildings, complete with the classrooms and auxiliary premises, open-air training grounds and training garages, experimental plots and farms, together with a host of plants and undertakings working on behalf of the national economy of the U.S.S.R.

In towns and workers' settlements, the material facilities are provided by industrial undertakings, building sites and transport services, with the training taking place in specially organized teaching workshops and on school plots. Sometimes, where these facilities are absent, the schools combine to set up production-training workshops of their own. In the countryside, they are provided by the collective and State farms, where practically all production processes are mechanized, and at tractor repair workshops.

SCHOOL BUILDINGS

Every year, thousands of new school buildings come into service and capital investment in school buildings increases, as does the part played by collective farms in supporting schools run by industrial plants or social organizations. Of the 30,160 school buildings for 5,059,000 pupils built in the U.S.S.R. during the ten-year period 1946–55, 19,996 (for 1,966,000 pupils) were built on the initiative of collective farms with funds supplied by them. In 1958, the corresponding figure for the R.S.F.S.R. was 1,433 schools (catering for 120,100 pupils) out of a total of 2,457 schools (catering for 436,900 pupils). In many cases, the school buildings

223

have been put up on the workers' own initiative, applying the *narodnaya stroika* or 'peoples' construction' method.

The main organization for planning school buildings in the U.S.S.R. is the Gipropros—the State Planning Institute of the Ministry of Education of the R.S.F.S.R. Others include the planning institutes and organizations of the various Union and Autonomous Republics. Experimental projects are handled by the Scientific Research Institute for Experimental Planning, which forms part of the U.S.S.R. Academy of Building and Architecture, and by other institutes and by Gipropros. Decisions on pedagogical and health problems connected with school buildings are taken with the participation of the R.S.F.S.R. Academy of Pedagogical Sciences and the Ministry of Health. Plans for school buildings designed to standard specifications are examined and approved by the State committee for building attached to the Council of Ministers of the U.S.S.R.

School buildings are constructed in accordance with modern methods and with the extensive use of new building materials. They consist either of a single block, or of two or more blocks connected by passages. New buildings are planned on the basis of no more than three floors (or four, in exceptional cases).

In planning school buildings, provision is made for the possibility of organizing school groups with an extended working day, and Gipropros is working on experimental projects where the extended working day could apply to both eight-year and the eleven-year courses.

The architectural design of school buildings, both in general and in their various details, reflects the socialist character of Soviet education and the aesthetic needs of Soviet society.

The school site is divided into several zones: the building sites proper, the area for training and experimental work; the sports area; the gardens; the administrative zones; the recreation grounds; and the access roads.

In line with the Education Law, and town-planning and demographic conditions, the following have been adopted as the basic types of school buildings:

General-education schools

1. The eight-year general-education and polytechnical school consisting of grades I to VIII (catering for 320 and 480 pupils in rural areas and small towns, and for 640 and 960 pupils in larger towns). (See Figs. 9, 10, 11*a*, 11*b*, 12*a*, 12*b*, 13*a*, 13*b*, 14*a*, 14*b*.)

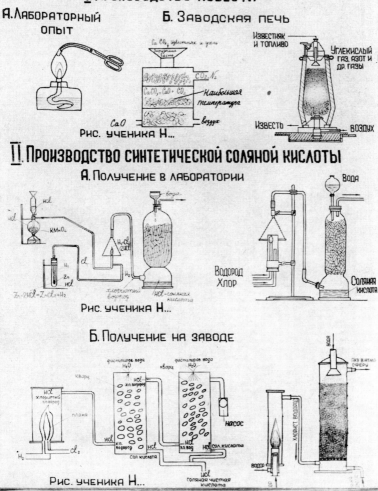

Fig. 1. Experiment in the construction of apparatus and design of factory installations by a pupil.

Fig. 2. Model of factory apparatus for the production of nitric acid.

Fig. 3. Diagram of factory apparatus for the production of nitric acid.

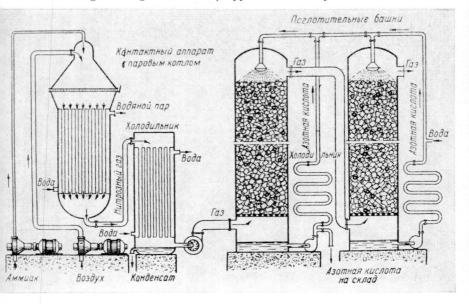

Поглотительные башни

Контактный аппарат с паровым котлом

Водяной пар

Холодильник

Вода

Нитрозный газ

Вода

Вода

Газ

Газ

Азотная кислота

Газ

Азотная кислота

Холодильник

Вода

Аммиак

Воздух

Конденсат

Азотная кислота на склад

Fig. 4. Pupils from the Zhdanov collective farm secondary school in the Alta-Aryksky district of the Ferghana region on an excursion (checking the regularity of square drillings for cotton-sowing).

Fig. 5. Pupils carrying out an experiment in artificial pollination.

Fig. 6. At School No. 69 (Moscow), pupils installed the school's automatic telephone exchange.

Fig. 7. Grade V pupils at work at drilling machines in the workshop.

Fig. 8. Pupils at work in a production shop assembling electrical equipment.

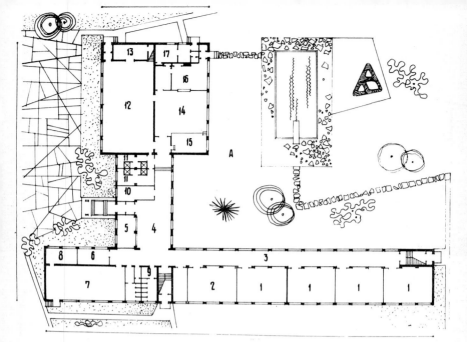

Fig. 9. Plan of ground floor of eight-year school for 320 pupils: (1) classrooms; (2) workroom for pupils in grades I to IV; (3) recreation room; (4) vestibule; (5) cloakroom; (6) library; (7) school workshop; (8) tools and equipment room; (9) toilets; (10) headmaster's study and office; (11) changing room with shower; (12) gymnasium; (13) apparatus room; (14) assembly and dining hall; (15) platform; (16) kitchen; (17) caretaker's room.

Fig. 10. General view of a design for an eight-year school for 320 pupils (prefabricated construction). Architects: K. D. Frenkel and I. L. Korobitsyna.

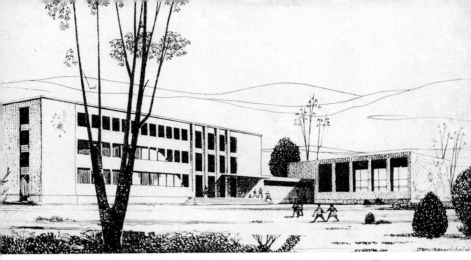

Fig. 11a. General view of a design for an eight-year school for 480 pupils. Architects: K. D. Frenkel and I. P. Kravchinskaya.

Fig. 11b. Plan of ground floor of eight-year school for 480 pupils: (1) classrooms; (2) recreation room; (3) cloakroom; (4) woodwork and metalwork rooms; (5) tools and equipment room; (6) assembly and dining hall; (7) kitchen; (8) caretaker's room; (9) platform; (10) office; (11) headmaster's study; (12) toilets; (13) changing rooms with shower; (14) gymnasium; (15) apparatus room; (A) playground.

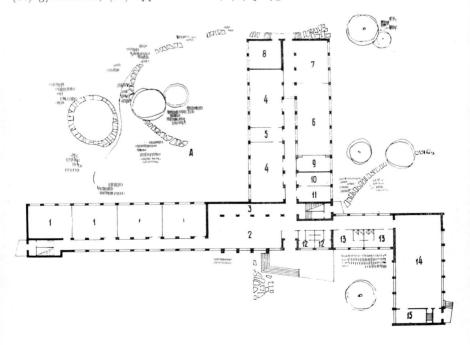

Fig. 12a. General view of a design for an eight-year school for 640 pupils. Architects: K. D. Frenkel and N. S. Shcherbakova.

Fig. 12b. Plan of ground floor of eight-year school for 640 pupils: (1) classrooms; (2) vestibule; (3) recreation room; (4) cloakroom; (5) school workshops; (6) tools and equipment room; (7) library; (8) office; (9) headmaster's study; (10) caretaker's room; (11) toilets; (12) assembly hall; (13) kitchen; (14) radio announcements room; (15) changing rooms with shower; (16) doctor's office; (17) gymnasium; (18) apparatus room; (A) playground.

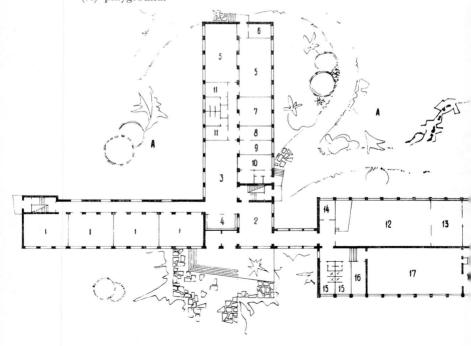

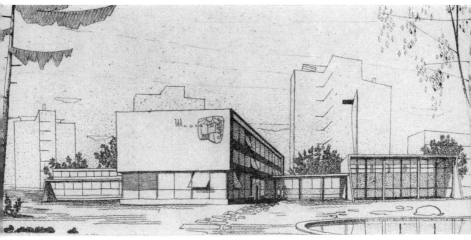

Fig. 13a. General view of a design for an eight-year school for 640 pupils (prefabricated construction). Architects: K. D. Frenkel and N. A. Mordbintseva.

Fig. 13b. Plan of first and second floors of prefabricated eight-year school for 640 pupils: (26) classrooms; (27) recreation rooms; (28–29) teachers' room on second floor and domestic-science room on third floor.

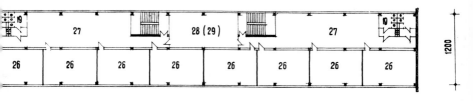

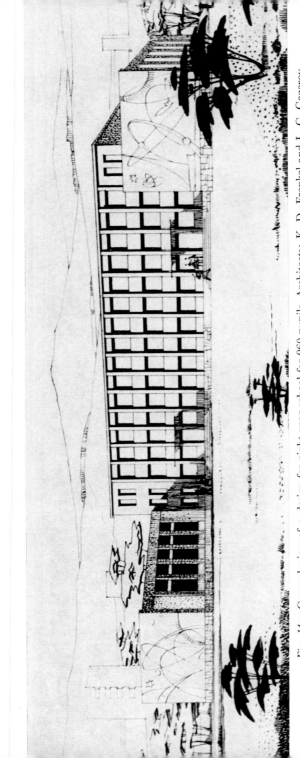

Fig. 14a. General view of a design for eight-year school for 960 pupils. Architects: K. D. Frenkel and L. G. Gazerov.

Fig. 14b. Plan of ground floor of eight-year school for 960 pupils: (1) classrooms; (2) recreation rooms; (3) woodwork and metalwork rooms; (4) tools and equipment room; (5) toilets; (6) library; (7) office; (8) headmaster's study; (9) workroom for pupils in grades I–IV; (10) caretaker's room; (11) doctor's office; (12) radio announcements room; (13) assembly and dining hall; (14) kitchen; (15) platform; (16) gymnasium; (17) changing rooms with shower; (18) apparatus room; (A) playground.

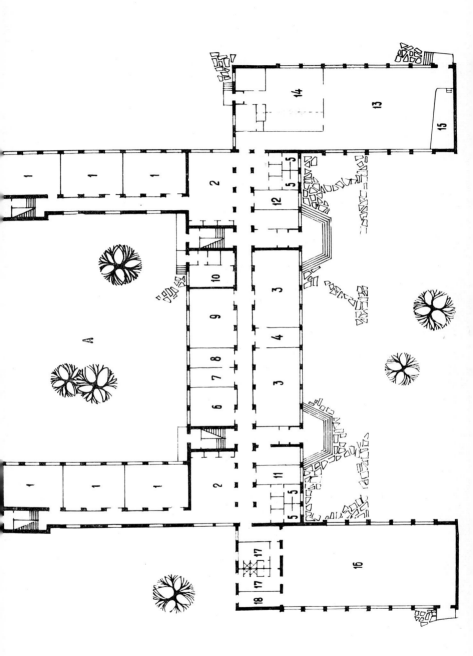

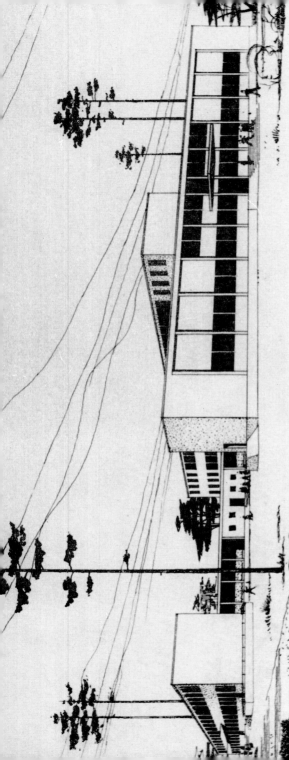

Fig. 15a. General view of a design for a secondary polytechnical school providing industrial training for 1,000 pupils, in Dubna, Moscow District. Architects: K. D. Frenkel and L. G. Gazerov.

Fig. 15b. Plan of ground floor of the Dubna Secondary School, Moscow District: (1) classrooms for junior classes; (2) vestibule and cloakrooms; (3) recreation rooms; (4) toilets; (5) staff room; (6) radio announcements room; (7) dining room; (8) kitchen; (9) wash rooms for dining room; (10) doctor's office; (11) headmaster's study; (12) office; (13 and 14) biology room; (15) domestic-science room; (16) engineering room; (17) specialized technology room; (18) woodwork and metalwork rooms; (19) tools and equipment room; (20) lobby; (21) assembly hall; (22) platform; (23) changing rooms with shower; (24) apparatus room; (25) gymnasium; (A) recreation ground.

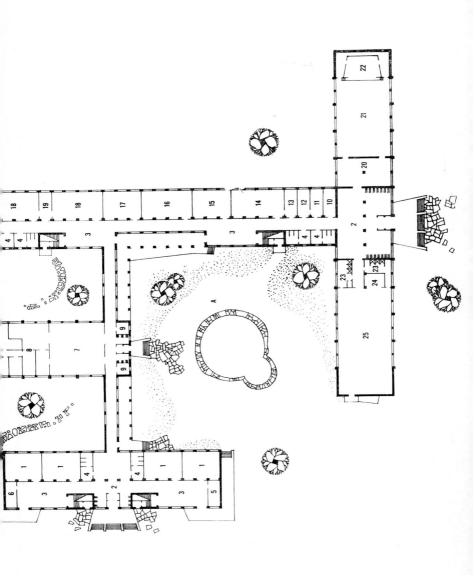

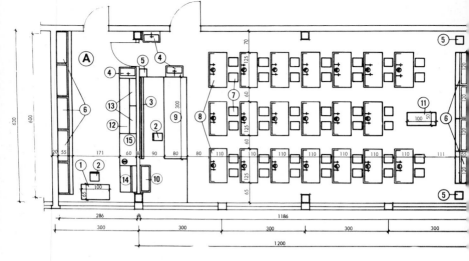

Fig. 16. Plan of physics room, with places for 40 pupils. Area, 74.5 square metres; area of laboratory annex, 18 square metres. (1) Teacher's table; (2) teacher's chair; (3) raised blackboard; (4) sink; (5) waste box; (6) section cupboards; (7) stools; (8) twin laboratory tables; (9) demonstration table; (10) electricity control panel; (11) projection table; (12) work bench; (13) shelves; (14) commutator; (15) work bench fitted with clamps; (A) annex.

Fig. 17. Pupil's laboratory table in the chemistry room (detail of equipment).

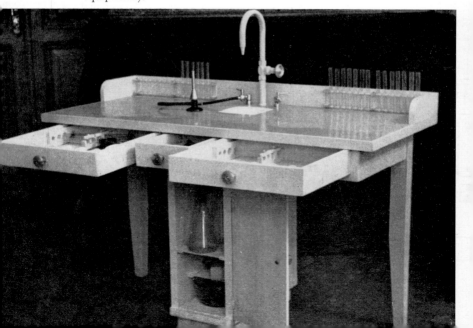

Fig. 18. Pupil's drawing-board desk.

Fig. 19. Plan of woodwork room, with places for 20 pupils. Area, 74 square metres; area of tool room, 17.6 square metres. (1) Raised blackboard; (2) sink; (3) waste box; (4) section cupboards; (5) work benches; (6) lathe; (7) drilling machine; (8) multipurpose lathe; (9) grinding lathe; (10) assembly bench; (11) rack for timber; (12) table; (13) electric heating element (for glue, etc.); (14) stools; (A) tool room.

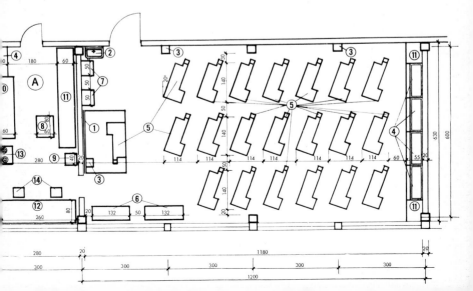

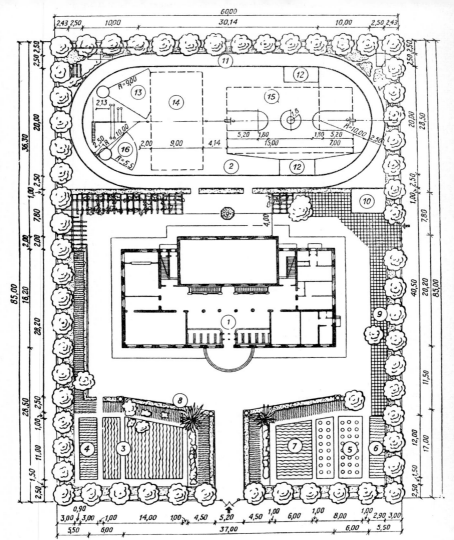

Fig. 20. Training and experimental plots at eight-year school (area 0.5 hectares): (1) school building; (2) sports field; (3) vegetable plot; (4) field crops; (5) nursery garden for fruit, berries and decorative plants; (6) plant collection; (7) primary-school plot; (8) flowering plants; (9) protected plot; (10) equipment shed; (11) running track, 125 metres; (12) sand-pit, 6 × 3 metres; (13) shot put area; (14) volleyball pitch, 18 × 9 metres; (15) basketball pitch, 22 × 12 metres; (16) discus area. Area distribution (in square metres): buildings, 700; training and experimental plot, 500; sports fields, 1,500; plantations within school grounds, 750; equipment storage, 250; recreation grounds and pathways, 1,300; Total, 5,000 square metres.

2. Secondary general-education and polytechnical school providing training in production, consisting of grades IX to XI (for 432 pupils).
3. Secondary general-education evening shift school consisting of grades IX to XI (for 480 and 820 pupils).
4. Secondary general-education and polytechnical school providing training in production, consisting of grades I to XI (for 536 and 964 pupils). (See Figs. 15a, 15b).

The general appearance and layout of the ground floor of these buildings are shown in the above figures.

Boarding-schools

1. Eight-year general-education and polytechnical boarding-school consisting of grades I to VIII (for 240 and 480 pupils).
2. Secondary general-education and polytechnical boarding-school providing production training, consisting of grades I to XI (for 330 pupils).

The organizational and architectural structure of the buildings is governed by the educational and training aims of Soviet schools. The main teaching premises are the classrooms, laboratories, study rooms, workshops and gymnasiums. The rest of the buildings consist of auxiliary premises such as the laboratory assistants' rooms, recreation rooms, school halls, libraries, rooms for the pupils' social organizations, teachers' rooms, the director's and headmaster's studies, the medical rooms, canteens, etc.

The main and auxiliary premises are closely connected organizationally and correspond to the school's clearly established functional needs and established hygienic standards.

A very important part in general and polytechnical education, labour training, and production and vocational training is played by the study rooms and workshops. Under the provisions laid down by the government for general-education schools, these consist of the following:

In the eight-year schools: rooms for physics (Fig. 16); chemistry; biology and domestic science; and wood and metal workshops.

In secondary polytechnical schools providing production training: rooms for physics and electrical engineering, chemistry, biology, technical drawing, principles of industrial production (in urban schools), principles of agricultural production (in rural schools); workshops for production training (where necessary).

The physics, chemistry and biology rooms usually consist of a laboratory classroom with the laboratory assistant's room attached. In many schools, the physics room also has additional premises

225

for practical work in physics and electrical engineering and for out-of-class physics work on the construction and manufacture of instruments, models, etc. The biology room contains separate premises for work with living objects—the 'live nature' corner. These rooms contain special furniture (Fig. 17) and a variety of technical equipment for demonstrations, experiments and laboratory work. Water, gas and electricity are laid on. The chemistry rooms are fitted with draught chambers.

The laboratory assistants' rooms attached to the classrooms are auxiliary premises where visual aids, instruments, laboratory equipment, reagents, etc., are kept and the equipment required for experiments and laboratory work is prepared.

There are also special rooms for technical drawing equipped with all the necessary material and instruments, including drawing-board desks adjustable for angle and height (Fig. 18), so as to provide suitable conditions for teaching pupils the correct working methods.

For the younger children, manual training is given in the classrooms or in special workrooms complete with tables, joiner's benches, tools, store cupboards, stocks of raw materials and objects manufactured by the pupils themselves.

There are special premises for two types of school workshops —for woodwork (Fig. 19) and metalwork, with workplaces equipped for individual and group work. These workshops contain lathes, drilling machines, planing machines, grounding machines and other equipment.

The domestic-science room usually consists of a kitchen-canteen and a sewing room. The former is equipped with gas and electric stoves for cooking, refrigerators, kitchen tables, sinks, material for washing and drying plates and dishes, a large dining table, and sideboards for keeping kitchen utensils, crockery, cutlery, table linen, as well as the foodstuffs required for practical work. In some schools, the foodstuffs are kept in a separate storeroom. The sewing room is equipped with sewing machines, sewing tables, a large cutting table, fitting mirrors and a cupboard for keeping the material and finished and unfinished garments on which the pupils have been working.

In many of the urban schools where machine operation is taught, there are study rooms equipped with metal-cutting machine tools, stands bearing large machine parts, etc. Rural schools have similar rooms for the study of agricultural machine operation.

In the urban schools providing production training, production rooms are installed for the purpose of theoretical training and practical laboratory work in the vocational subjects. In rural schools, there are similar rooms for studying the principles of agricultural production.

TEACHING EQUIPMENT

The structure and composition of the teaching equipment depends on the educational purposes for which it is intended, the subjects taught, the methods of work and the organization of studies. It includes specimens of natural objects, visual aids, instruments and apparatus for school experiments, optical appliances, equipment for labour training, laboratory equipment, kitchen utensils, etc.

Apart from the teaching aids produced by the school equipment industry and publishing houses, an important element is the material made by the pupils themselves. In addition, a considerable amount of the teaching equipment is supplied free of charge by industrial enterprises, tractor-repair stations and State and collective farms.

In the primary grades I to IV, the children acquire the elements of polytechnical knowledge and certain practical skills. The material used for practical work includes very simple calculating and measuring devices and simple drawing equipment such as rulers, set-squares or compasses; very simple weather-observation devices such as rain gauges, precipitation gauges, anemometers, weather-vanes, thermometers; and simple surveying instruments for measuring distances such as field compasses, cross-staffs, measuring chains, tape measures, sextants, etc.

Hand work in these lowest grades is done with the aid of sets of tools and other equipment for work on paper, cardboard, wood and metal (wire, tinplate, etc.).

On the school experimental plot, the children work with spades, hoes, rakes and other implements which are made to size for children aged between seven and ten in accordance with the models designed by the Scientific Research Institute of the R.S.F.S.R. Academy of Pedagogical Sciences.

In the explanatory reading and natural-science lessons, use is made of pictures, illustrated tables, lantern slides and filmstrips illustrating the nature, economy and working life of the people of the Soviet Union; herbariums of agricultural plants and collections of seeds; samples of soils, fertilizers and useful minerals; and technological collections.

Many of the visual aids, devices, instruments and articles of auxiliary equipment used in these grades are made by the older pupils in grades V to VIII during their labour lessons or out-of-class work.

227

For each subject, the Scientific Research Institute has devised regular sets of laboratory apparatus and auxiliary equipment for work covered by the syllabus, all this material being produced by enterprises coming under the Ministry of Education. The sets are in special containers convenient for distribution and collection in the classroom, and also serving as a protective covering.

The material used for practical work includes demonstration apparatus, general laboratory equipment and special instruments designed by the Institute. The equipment used for laboratory work and practical work is also used by physics pupils during out-of-class work.

Much of the equipment and apparatus used relates to recent advances in physics, technology and production, and helps to familiarize the pupils with the principles of heat engineering, jet propulsion, automation, telemechanics, electronics, and so on.

Other aids used in physics teaching include tables, diagrams, films, filmstrips, models, etc.

In chemistry teaching, as in physics teaching, an important place is occupied by school experiments—demonstration experiments and independent experiments by the pupils. But unlike physics, where ready-made equipment and sets of equipment are used, practically all the chemistry equipment (especially that used by the laboratories) consists of laboratory apparatus, vessels and containers, and glass and rubber tubes which are dismounted when the work is finished.

The chemistry equipment thus covers individual instruments, apparatus, and fittings, measuring instruments, laboratory accessories, vessels and containers, chemicals, reagents and other materials. In addition, there are a number of visual aids: tables, diagram slides, films, filmstrips, models, collections, material for distribution, etc.

Home-made devices, including electrolysers, ozonizers, retorts, automatic devices for producing gases, acids, alkalis, salts, plastics, artificial fibres, etc., as well as pupils' collections, also play a large part.

Of particular importance are the materials and visual aids which emphasize the close bonds between studies on the one hand and the life and economy of the country on the other—samples of chemical products, collections of plastics, technological collections, films acquainting pupils with the main branches of the chemical industry, etc.

In biology teaching, the essential feature is the use for demonstration purposes of live plants and animals, physiological experiments and various visual aids such as objects preserved in liquids, stuffed animals, skeletons, collections of natural objects, casts, models, tables, pictures, photographs, slides, films, etc. Also important is the pupils' laboratory work based on experiments discussed in class, or on the biological material issued, or on experiments conducted on plants or animals in the 'living nature' corner, or on the school experimental plot. Use is made, in the course of this work, of magnifying glasses, microscopes, simple physiological appliances, instruments for preparing experiments, and other laboratory equipment.

In practical biology teaching, great stress is laid on excursions to biological and health institutions and museums, to the country-side and to farms. During excursions to the countryside the special equipment used includes herbarium nets and folders, butterfly nets, pail for specimens, secateurs, etc.

In mathematics teaching, the emphasis is on mensuration, calculation and graphs, modelling, work with calculating machines and tables, and the solution of problems relating to physics, chemistry, technical drawing, etc., as well as on practical field work. The school equipment includes the usual material for all mathematical subjects (rulers, set-squares, compasses, protractors, pantographs, etc.), as well as aids for each separate subject (arithmetic, algebra and geometry). The aids used for classwork include tables for linear, square and other functions; tables for the study of axial and central symmetry; tables illustrating examples of the practical application of geometry or certain geometrical conversions; models for demonstrating the characteristics of the principal geometrical figures or the rules for constructing representations, etc.

A point is also made of supplying schools with calculating devices (such as abacuses, arithmometers, slide rules), and other instruments which help pupils to do independent practical work at school or in the field.

In technical drawing, pupils learn how to read and make drawings, sketches and blueprints of the simpler parts of machines and machine tools, as well as of simple assemblies, attention being focused on developing their ability to do independent drawings, and to model or construct from blueprints.

The teaching equipment accordingly includes tables, models for projection drawing and technical drawing, models of geometrical bodies and technical shapes, machine parts, machine tools, simpler assemblies and completed machine-made articles.

In geography, the pupils learn about the natural geographical conditions under which the populations of the various States and countries live, complete with their economy, productive activity, etc. Great weight is placed on independent work on maps, topographical charts, collections of natural and manufactured objects, weather observation and practical field work.

Extensive use is made of cartographic material, representational devices and other visual aids. In addition, various instruments are used for the observation of natural phenomena, such as meteorological equipment. In practical field work, simple geodesic instruments are used, as well as astronomic instruments for observing the sky.

In history, the pupils are familiarized with the main instruments of labour and the improvements made to these by the masses in the course of their daily work, and learn about the development of productive skills in the various fields of production. They also acquire an understanding of the division of labour and the consequent increase in labour productivity, the relation between the latter and the development of technology and the improvement of production methods; and the effect of labour productivity on the increased output of goods from which society benefits. Concrete examples are given to show the part played by the practical work of the masses in scientific progress. Use is made of visual teaching aids in history classes. These include historical maps, atlases, charts, diagrams, pictures, slides, filmstrips, models, dioramas, etc. The maps reflect the geographical conditions under which the productive activity of man took place, while the pictures, slides and filmstrips give a vivid and concrete idea of the work of people during different historical periods and of the implements they used. Home-made visual aids, and especially models made by the pupils, also play an important part.

Practical work in the school workshops develops the labour training begun in the junior grade, and provides the pupils with initial experience of woodwork and metalwork. The workshops are accordingly equipped with sets of the necessary carpenter's and metalworker's tools specially designed to suit the age and physiological development of the children. Lathes, drilling machines, grinding machines and the like are provided in order to familiarize the children with machine tools and the rudiments of their operation. Visual aids are also used in the workshops, instructional tables on the treatment of wood and metals, on the assembly of machinery and electrical equipment, and on safety precautions; collections of species of wood, samples of metals and alloys, etc. In addition, wide use is made of models, slides and films.

The pupils in grades V to VIII do experimental and practical work in agriculture. This work is an important element in their labour training and polytechnical education, since it gives them an insight into agriculture, and develops their practical knowledge and manual skills in growing plants and raising animals; it also enables them to apply their knowledge of biology in practice and promotes their labour culture, their creative attitude to work and their interest in agricultural production.

In explaining the agrobiological requirements involved in the performance of individual tasks, the teachers use visual aids such as tables, pictures, slides, films and models of farm machinery and implements. For studying soils or the quality of seeds and fertilizers, or for calculating crop yields, simple instruments or laboratory devices are used such as plane-tables for sorting grain samples, trays for determining the germinability of seeds; instruments for analysing fertilizers, etc.

In view of the fact that most of the tilling, sowing, planting, plant-tending and harvesting operations are done manually, the schools are given sets of agricultural implements specially made for children. At the same time, extensive use is made of so-called 'small-scale mechanization' equipment—simple instruments, implements and machines such as winnowing and sorting machines, presses for making peat-compost feed pots, hand-operated seed drills, and cultivators, simple water sprinklers, small threshing machines, etc., which facilitate the children's work, increase its productivity and also serve as a stepping stone in acquiring a mastery of advanced machine technique.

In urban schools, the material training for practical and experimental agricultural work is provided by the school experimental plots (Fig. 20), with separate allotments for field crops, vegetables, hotbeds and greenhouses. In rural schools, this training is provided at experimental plots, collective and State farms and fields, or school experimental farms. These last generally consist of an experimental plot, an orchard and arboretum of from two to three hectares; a productive area for field crops (ten to eighteen hectares); and an animal farm (twenty to twenty-six calves, three or four pigs, two horses, chickens, rabbits).

For the study of machine operation, the children use tables describing the construction of machine tools, machines and mechanisms, as well as reference tables and instruction tables, slides, films, models, machine parts singly and in combination, machine tools, machines, implements and technical devices, miscellaneous metalwork instruments and apparatus, etc. For the practical work, wide use is made of operational and dummy metal-cutting lathes (screw-cutting lathes, milling machines, boring machines, etc.), the latter being assembled and taken down by the pupils for teaching purposes. To provide the schools with the necessary machine-tool equipment, the government has given plants and factories permission to provide them, free of charge, with equipment suitable for polytechnical training. As a result, during the five-year period 1954–59, school in the R.S.F.S.R. alone received a total of 35,750 metalwork lathes, 8,950 electric grinders and much other essential equipment. In addition, the schools buy new machine tools out of their own funds.

For electrical engineering, the equipment includes (apart from that also used for physics teaching) such measuring instruments as electromagnetic and magneto-electric ammeters, ohmmeters, transformers, electric generators, electric motors, selenium rectifiers, electronic oscillographs, sound generators and electrical and radio-engineering tables.

On the basis of the knowledge, proficiency and skills acquired at the eight-year school, the pupils at rural secondary schools are taught the fundamentals of agriculture and trained as specialists in plant-growing, animal husbandry, or agricultural-machine operation. While still at school, they join the adults in productive work on collective and State farms. The theoretical studies at school are combined with productive work either in production brigades, or on school experimental farms. This practice in productive work makes it possible to combine theoretical training with first-hand experience in socialist agriculture. A variety of visual aids are used in the course of the theoretical studies—tables, photographs, slides, films, models of agricultural machines and implements, of hotbeds, greenhouses, stock yards, silos and other farm buildings and equipment.

Practical laboratory work on plant-growing and animal husbandry play an important part in the study of the fundamentals of agricultural production, extensive use being made of special agricultural devices for the mechanical analysis of the soil and of its aqueous properties, instruments for studying the quality of seeds, instruments for analysing milk and dairy products, etc.; visual aids, including herbariums of the most important kinds of agricultural plants, samples of soils, seeds and fertilizers, large collections of insects including pests; and of laboratory equipment, containers and other materials.

In the practical work on agricultural-machine operation, the visual aids include specimens of the various parts and working mechanisms of farm machinery and implements; aparatus for applying insecticides and fungicides, and component parts of tractors and motor-cars.

The practical work of studying machines and implements in operation—ploughs, harrows, cultivators, grain cleaners, seed drills, harvesters, machines for fodder ensilaging or preparation —takes place in the special sheds or 'training areas' of the schools or collective or State farms.

In the electrical-engineering classes at rural schools special attention is focused on a proper understanding of the electric-drive system for agricultural machines and installations; and on the study of tractor-drawn generators and the electrical equipment of cars and tractors, the charging of accumulators and the use of electricity in agriculture, whether in plant-growing or animal husbandry, the electrical equipment used being that of the agricultural undertakings supporting the particular school.

MEASURES TAKEN BY THE STATE TO STRENGTHEN MATERIAL FACILITIES

The Communist Party and the Soviet Government are keenly interested in strengthening the material facilities of polytechnical education. A special branch of the State school-equipment industry has been set up in order to produce teaching equipment and visual aids in all the subjects taught in the general-education schools, and teaching aids, instruments and textbooks are now being turned out in vast quantities. The school textbooks most commonly used are reprinted every year, or at even shorter intervals, and to supply schools with all this material, a specialized sales organization has been set up, complete with a network of shops, stores and wholesale warehouses.

Every provincial centre has its school-equipment shop to supply the local schools. In addition, to supply schools with films, slides and filmstrips and projectors, a network of film libraries has been created. They issue educational films, sets of slides, filmstrips and cinematographical equipment on loan free of charge, repair projectors and give advice and instruction on the use of films in schools.

The Ministries of Education decide and issue periodical directives on the standards of equipment for use in each subject by the different types of schools; while their Teaching Methods Councils exercise idealogical and methodological control over the issue of textbooks intended for schools. Meanwhile, to encourage invention in the field of teaching aids, the Ministries of Education run 'invention bureaux'.

Scientific research work on designing new school apparatus and visual aids and improving those produced is mainly centred in the Institute of the Academy of Pedagogical Sciences referred to earlier, which has a special School Equipment Department and an experimental workshop for making prototypes of new teaching aids. The department also designs new types of school furniture, blackboards and auxiliary devices for demonstrating or storing visual aids.

CHAPTER XII

THE TRAINING OF TEACHERS FOR POLYTECHNICAL EDUCATION

by P. R. Atutov and A. E. Stavrovsky

TEACHER-TRAINING ESTABLISHMENTS

The provision of polytechnical education in combination with productive labour has imposed new and greater demands on natural-science teachers; at the same time it has also become necessary to supply schools with qualified teachers for labour and polytechnical instruction and the teaching of vocational and technical subjects.

The training of teachers for general-education schools is done by teacher-training, technical and agricultural institutes, and by the universities. The bulk of the teachers of polytechnical subjects for eight-year and complete secondary schools are provided by the teacher-training institutes, whose structure and curricula have been correspondingly revised so as to impart the knowledge and skills required for carrying out the programmes of labour instruction and polytechnical education successfully. Faculties of industrial pedagogy have been organized and two new faculties created in place of the single faculty of biology, chemistry and the fundamentals of agriculture; one for biology and chemistry; the other for biology and the fundamentals of agricultural production. The industrial pedagogy and physics-mathematics faculties train teachers of physics, mechanics and electrical engineering for urban and rural schools. All of these faculties have a five-year course.

The polytechnical bias in teacher-training applies to all subjects, but is particularly marked in the training of teachers of natural sciences, mathematics and general technical subjects. This bias is developed without any lowering of the level of general or pedagogical training. On the contrary, the introduction of a number of technical disciplines into the physics-mathematics and other faculties has the effect of actually raising the theoretical and practical standards, whereas the production practice obtained at industrial and other undertakings equips the trainees with practical knowledge and skills.

THE TRAINING OF LABOUR INSTRUCTORS AND TEACHERS OF MATHEMATICS, PHYSICS AND GENERAL TECHNICAL SUBJECTS

The proportion of technical disciplines has been increased in the curriculum for the physics-mathematics and industrial-pedagogy faculties, as can be seen from Table 11.

TABLE 11

Teacher's special subject	Curricula	Proportion of time spent on polytechnical and technical disciplines in relation to the curriculum	Number of weeks devoted to production practice at industrial undertakings
		%	
Mathematics and physics	1957	11.3	2
	1959	12.3	12
Physics and the fundamentals of production	1957	20	7
Physics, electrical engineering and machine operation	1959	26.6	12
Machine operation, technology of materials, and training in secondary-school workshops (industrial pedagogy faculty)	1957	—	—
	1959	29.5	31

The timetable covering the curriculum for training labour instructors and teachers of general technical subjects for secondary schools can be quoted as an example of how the subjects are divided (see Table 12, p. 238).

As stated above, the introduction of technical subjects helps to raise still further the scientific and theoretical level of training, as can be seen from a brief analysis of the syllabuses of some of the polytechnical subjects.

Thus, the syllabus for technical mechanics (350 periods) at the engineering faculties of teacher-training institutes lays the scientific and theoretical foundations for studying the subjects of the polytechnical cycle, and includes the following sections: resistance of materials, theory of machines and mechanisms, machine parts, transport and hoisting machinery, etc.

In accordance with the curriculum, applied mechanics is studied during the fifth, sixth and seventh semesters, i.e., after the students have already studied higher mathematics, general physics, descriptive geometry and technical drawing, theoretical mechanics, and the technology of materials, and after they have acquired essential skills in the manual and mechanical processing of machine parts.

Buttressed on the general scientific and theoretical grounding in the above subjects, the applied-mechanics course is conducted as a single composite discipline in which the scientific logical and methodical logical links between the various sub-divisions are maintained. In the study of the resistance of materials, for example, the students solve problems relating to the expansion, compression, transverse flexure, shearing and crushing under conditions of complex tension, longitudinal flexure and dynamic resistance of machine parts.

Again, in the section on the theory of mechanisms and machines, a study is made of geometrical parameters, kinematics, the statics and dynamics of transmission for achieving rotatory movement; mechanisms for turning rotatory movements into progressive, oscillatory, intermittent and other movements; hydraulic and pneumatic drives in machine operation, etc. In studying a particular subject, therefore, the students become familiar with the most general laws and principles used in all branches of mechanized and automatic production.

The same principle is applied to the syllabuses on the technology of metals, wood, plastics and other materials and the theory of cutting, machine tools and other implements. The purpose of these courses is to give students a sound and systematic knowledge of techniques and of the theory and practice of technological processes in the treatment of metals, wood, plastics and other materials, commonly used in production. At the same time, the course on the technology of these materials gives the students an insight into their properties and uses and provides the basis on which they acquire practical skills in treating the materials, in the shops and in the course of technological production practice at industrial plants, and on which they pursue their studies of other general technical subjects and the technology of the branch of production most characteristic of their area.

Special attention is paid during this course to the problems of the vocational training of prospective manual and technical instructors and teachers of general technical subjects who will be teaching grades V–VIII in school production workshops at eight-year and secondary schools and of prospective teachers who will be organizing technical and production training in grades IX–XI. In studying all the technical subjects and in doing practical work, the emphasis is on questions bearing directly on the school syllabuses for these subjects.

By the time the trainee has completed his course, he has the trade rating of a joiner, a turner and a metalworker. Those who had already become specialists in any of these trades before entering the institute work on their own during the practical work on the subject, and either acquire another speciality or improve their qualifications.

The teaching of technical subjects is based on a knowledge of physics, chemistry, mathematics and technical drawing, and hence the general physics and chemistry courses at the industrial-pedagogy faculty are organized in such a way as to facilitate that teaching.

TABLE 12. Special subjects: general technical subjects and labour instruction (industrial-pedagogy faculty). Five-year course

Subject	Number of periods			
	Total	Lectures	Laboratory work	Seminars and practical work
History of the CPSU	220	120	—	100
Political economy	150	80	—	70
Dialectical and historical materialism	140	70	—	70
General and age-group psychology .	88	68	—	20
Pedagogy	100	50	—	50
History of pedagogy	72	54	—	18
School hygiene	36	18	—	18
Methods of manual and technical instruction and the teaching of technical subjects	160	50	90	20
Special seminar on pedagogy, psychology or the methods of manual and technical instruction and the teaching of technical subjects . .	36	—	—	36
Higher mathematics	410	220	—	190
General physics	318	160	110	48
General chemistry	108	64	44	—
Descriptive geometry and technical drawing	204	34	170	—
Theoretical mechanics	150	90	60	—
Applied mechanics	350	180	140	30
Electrical and radio engineering . .	210	100	110	—
Technology of metals, wood, plastics and other materials	130	86	44	—

Subject	Number of periods			
	Total	Lectures	Laboratory work	Seminars and practical work
Theory of cutting, machine tools and other implements	80	56	24	—
Practical work in manual and machine processing of metals, wood and other materials	526	—	526	—
Technology of actual production . .	114	70	32	12
Machine operation (including engineering)	240	112	116	12
Practical work on automobiles, tractors and agricultural machinery, and their repair	204	28	176	—
Educational cinema topography and photography	48	—	48	—
Safety techniques	38	30	—	8
Fundamentals of organization and economics of production . . .	36	36	—	—
Physical training	140	—	—	140
Foreign language	140	—	—	140
Specialized training	48	—	—	48
TOTAL (hours)	4 496	1 776	1 690	1 030

A very important feature in the polytechnical training of teachers is the course on general electrical engineering, the syllabus for which includes the following sections:

1. Fundamentals of electrical engineering covering the theory of d.c. and a.c. circuits and methods for working them out; theory of electromagnetic phenomena and magnetic circuits, as required for the subsequent study of the principles and structure of electrical measuring instruments and electrical machines; and questions concerning the insulation of electrical installations and equipment.

This section also includes electrical measurements of electrical and non-electrical quantities.

2. Electrical machines as sources of electric power, and the main example of the practical application of electric power to industry and agriculture.

3. Industrial electronics—a new field of technique in outfitting industrial plants with electrical equipment and introducing new methods for controlling and directing production.

As can be seen from the industrial-pedagogy faculty's curriculum, the teaching of polytechnical subjects includes not only lectures but also practical and laboratory work. This enables prospective teachers to acquire the necessary skills in handling modern machines and appliances and also helps them to absorb theoretical knowledge in the most effective manner.

The third-year course on machine operation, technology of materials and workshop training provides for twenty-one weeks of technological production practice at industrial undertakings, combined with evening classes at the institute and, in the fifth year, the students do ten weeks' operational productive work at an industrial undertaking. All this provides them with sufficient production experience and a practical knowledge of the techniques, technology and organization of labour in a given undertaking; and the work done on the job deepens and broadens their theoretical knowledge and improves their vocational and technical skills. They see with their own eyes the trend of development of socialist production and the new attitudes that are being created among the workers in Soviet plants and factories.

In this way, the study of polytechnical and technological subjects, together with production practice at industrial undertakings, gives them the necessary polytechnical training which enables them, in turn, to give secondary-school pupils a polytechnical education and vocational training.

THE TRAINING OF TEACHERS OF BIOLOGY AND THE FUNDAMENTALS OF AGRICULTURE

Eight special subjects are included in the curriculum of the new faculty of biology and the fundamentals of agricultural production (see Table 13, p. 242): soil science; general agriculture, including agro-chemistry; meteorology; plant-growing (field crops, vegetables, fruit); plant protection; animal husbandry (cattle, pigs, sheep, horses, poultry, rabbits); mechanization and electrification of agricultural production; economics and organization of agriculture.

The timetable allots 1,006 teaching periods out of 4,188, (or 24 per cent) to the theoretical, practical and laboratory study of these subjects. The curriculum of the former faculty of biology, chemistry and the fundamentals of agriculture included only two agricultural disciplines: fundamentals of agriculture and mechanization of agriculture; and for these only 340 periods, (or 8 per cent) were allotted.

Thus the timetable of this new faculty devotes three times as many periods to the scientific and theoretical agricultural and zoo-technical training of teachers of biology and the fundamentals of agricultural production than the former faculty of biology, chemistry and the fundamentals of agriculture. At the same time, the course has been extended from four to five years. It should be noted, incidentally, that the teaching time for subjects of the biological cycle has remained unaltered, since the extra time for agricultural disciplines has been derived not only from the increase in the length of the course but also from a reduction in the time spent on chemistry, chemical technology and chemical methods, the training of chemistry teachers having been transferred to another faculty (biology and chemistry).

The new faculty also provides for a great improvement in practical field instruction, to which fourteen days are devoted during the second year, twenty-two days during the third year and 126 days during the fourth year, all combined with theoretical instruction by correspondence.

In the former faculty the amount of time spent on practical productive work was only sixteen days during the third year, and thirty-two days during the fourth year.

This increase has had the effect of considerably broadening and deepening the scientific, theoretical, practical laboratory, and production training of students in the fundamentals of agricultural production.

The first-year subjects include meteorology, covering general atmospheric features; solar radiation and the heat régime of the soil, air and water reservoirs; elements of meteorology, the weather and weather forecasting; weather conditions unfavourable to agriculture and the means of counteracting them; and the fundamentals of climatology and agro-climatology. The study of the theoretical principles of meteorology is accompanied by practical laboratory work and is completed during the second year by four days' field practice.

During the second year, the students study soil science, together with general agriculture and agro-chemistry. The soil-science syllabus falls into two parts: (a) formation, development, composition and characteristics of soils; and (b) soils of the U.S.S.R. (their genesis, characteristics and geography). Special attention is given to the study of soil-forming strata and to soils of the particular regions or districts in preparation for local soil-science teaching at the schools. Half of the soil-science study time is spent in laboratory work, while ten working days are spent in practical field work.

TABLE 13. Timetable of the faculty of biology and the fundamentals of agriculture production. Five-year course

Subject	Periods				Semester in which examinations and tests are held	
	Total	Lectures	Laboratory work	Seminars	Examinations	Tests
History of CPSU . .	220	120	—	100	2,4	1,3
Political economy . .	150	80	—	70	6,7	5,7
Dialectical and historical materialism . . .	140	70	—	70	7,9	—
General and age-group psychology	88	68	—	20	3	0
Pedagogy	100	50	—	50	4	—
History of pedagogy . .	72	54	—	18	5	—
School hygiene . . .	36	18	—	18	—	4
Special seminar in pedagogy, methods of teaching or psychology (at student's choice) . .	36	—	—	36	—	7
Inorganic chemistry and elements of analytical chemistry	200	80	120	—	2	1,2
Organic and biological chemistry	72	36	36	—	3	2
Fundamentals of physical and colloid chemistry	72	36	36	—	3	3
Botany	260	130	130	—	2,4	2,3
Zoology	260	130	130	—	2,4	2,4
Histology and embryology	72	36	36	—	1	1
Plant physiology and principles of microbiology	140	80	60	—	6	5
Human anatomy . .	90	38	52	—	5	5
Human and animal physiology	180	100	80	—	6,9	7,9
Darwinism	72	52	20	—	7	7
Geology	160	110	50	—	1,3	—
Soil science	60	30	30	—	4	4
General agriculture and agro-chemistry . .	150	60	70	20	5	5
Meteorology	60	30	30	—	1	—
Plant-growing . . .	260	130	130	—	6,8	6,7,8
Plant protection . . .	60	30	30	—	—	5
Animal husbandry . .	170	80	90	—	9	8,9
Mechanization and electrification of agriculture	190	80	110	—	8	5,6,8

Subject	Periods				Semester in which examinations and tests are held	
	Total	Lectures	Laboratory work	Seminars	Examinations	Tests
Economics and organization of agriculture .	56	26	30	—	—	9
Methods of teaching biology and fundamentals of agricultural production.	170	60	110	—	7	6
Specialization in accordance with geographical area	180	80	100	—	9	9
Educational cinematography	36	—	36	—	—	6
Foreign language . .	140	—	—	140	3	1,2,4
Physical training. . .	140	—	—	140	—	1,2,3,4
Specialized training . .	48	—	—	48	—	1
TOTAL (study hours) .	4 188	1 918	1 540	730		

Number of special projects, 2; number of examinations, 34; number of tests, 44.

Disciplines subject to state examinations: history of CPSU; botany or zoology (at student's choice); plant-growing or animal husbandry (at student's choice); pedagogy, with one of the special methods of teaching, or special project on pedagogical or methodological subject (at student's choice).

Among the main questions dealt with in the course on general agriculture and agro-chemistry are the following: conditions of life of agricultural plants; systems of cultivation; system of crop rotation; weeds and how to combat them; treatment of soil; seeds and the sowing of agricultural plants; tending of crops; principles of agro-chemistry; land and forest improvement; and experimental work.

In addition to practical laboratory work, seminars are held at which the subjects discussed include integrated agricultural measures to improve acid podsols in other than black-earth areas, or saline soils in steppe areas, and formulation of methods for conducting field experiments at experimental school farms under varying soil and climatic conditions. The course ends during the first half of the third year, when the students go on to study plant-growing (field crops), plant protection, and the mechanization and electrification of agriculture.

Under the heading of plant-growing, they learn about cereals, pulses, oleaginous plants, fibre-plants, tubers, root-crops, gourds, fodder grasses, etc., and their respective importance in the national economy, their agro-biological characteristics, and their main varieties and grades, as well as the agricultural techniques for raising large crops. In addition, they study the principles of the selection and cultivation of field-crop seeds.

Under the heading of plant protection, they learn about agricultural pests, the peculiarities of their structure and mode of life, their ecology and rates of development, and the means of combating them; characteristics of the main groups of pests (rodents and insects, including orthoptera, lepidoptera and coleoptera); the pests attacking cereals, pulses, root-crops, industrial crops, vegetables, fruit, berries, and grain products, and the means of combating them. They also study agricultural plant diseases and the ways of treating them; and the organization of school excursions to farms with a view to determining the degree of infection of crops and the pest-population density in a given agricultural area, and arranging for participation by the schoolchildren in socially useful labour to aid collective and State farms in combating these pests.

The syllabus of the course on the mechanization and electrification of agriculture includes theoretical studies and practical laboratory work in the following subjects: basic data on materials, machine parts and mechanisms; machinery and implements for soil cultivation, crop-tending; sowing, planting and fertilizer-spreading machinery; machinery for combating plant pests and diseases; hay-harvesting machines and ensilage harvesters; grain-cleaning and grain-sorting machines; grain harvesters; machines for harvesting industrial crops, potatoes and vegetables; mechanization of production processes in animal husbandry; mechanization of water supply and internal farm transport; tractors and automobiles and their operation; stationary internal combustion engines, locomobiles, wind motors; and principles of agricultural electrification.

The courses on these three subjects are completed by twenty-two days of production practice on a collective or State farm (Fig. 21), in addition to which the fourth-year students put in 126 days of production practice in all subjects.

The courses on plant-growing (in so far as it relates to vegetables and fruit) and on the mechanization of agriculture are completed during the fourth year, when the study of animal husbandry begins. The latter is completed in the fifth year, when the economics and organization of agriculture are also taught.

The syllabus for animal husbandry covers the fundamentals of feeding, the tending and breeding of livestock, the elements of veterinary science and animal hygiene, and the main branches of animal husbandry; stockbreeding (large cattle); and the raising of pigs, horses, poultry and rabbits. The course is rounded off by production practice on collective or State farms (see Fig. 22).

It will be seen from this brief description of the theoretical and practical studies in the agricultural disciplines that the prospective teachers of biology and the fundamentals of agricultural production acquire a fairly extensive knowledge at the institute of agricultural mechanization as well as of zoo-technical, agronomic, economic and organizational matters, and sufficient practical skill in all these fields to qualify them to teach the elements of plant-growing and animal husbandry and to combine this teaching with production work by pupils on school experimental farms or as members of school production brigades on collective or State farms.

Furthermore, the comprehensive body of knowledge acquired by students in scientific agronomy and animal husbandry has the effect of considerably raising their general scientific standard in the biological disciplines, thanks to their direct and first-hand experience of everyday production material. This helps them, when they begin to teach, to link their instruction with life and practice.

In order to provide students with scientific knowledge of the theory of education and training and an insight into modern teaching methods, they are taught the following subjects during their first three years: psychology, pedagogy, history of pedagogy, school hygiene and educational cinematography. During the third and fourth years they study the methods of teaching physics, mathematics, general technical disciplines, biology and the fundamentals of agricultural production, the studies being accompanied by practical teaching practice at schools. The time-table for the first three years allocates 300 periods to this practical work, eight weeks during the fourth year and twelve weeks during the fifth year.

Thus the content and organization of teacher training at the two new faculties set up at the institutes (industrial pedagogy, and biology and the fundamentals of agricultural production) ensure the production of well-qualified teachers with a good knowledge of physics, technology, biology and agricultural science as well as productive skills and a knowledge of modern methods of teaching polytechnical, vocational and technical subjects at school.

Teachers responsible for production training at general secondary-education schools are also produced by a number of technical and agricultural higher educational establishments which have set up special pedagogical departments.

245

IMPROVING THE QUALIFICATIONS OF TEACHERS

Equally important for the provision of polytechnical education in schools have been the steps taken to raise the theoretical, poly-technical and methodological level of existing teachers.

The work providing teachers with additional training and improving their qualifications is carried out by advanced training institutes, by the district and urban education departments and by the polytechnical committees at individual schools.

The object of additional training is to help teachers and school directors to see their way clearly in the reorganization of school work, to familiarize them with the new curricula and syllabuses; give them basic information on the principles of industrial and agricultural production; and to help them to take stock of rational teaching and training methods designed to meet the new tasks confronting the schools (see Fig. 23).

The curricula for those additional training courses accordingly cover the following: (a) raising of the theoretical and ideological level of teachers and other education workers; (b) study of directives and other programmatic documents defining school reorganization

TABLE 14

Subject	Number of teaching periods		
	Lectures	Practical work	Total
Questions on Marxist-Leninist theory . . .	8	4	12
Selected questions on pedagogy and psychology .	14	6	20
Achievements of science, technology and art in the U.S.S.R.	26	—	26
Principles of machine operation	24	30	54
Questions on the content and methods of teaching and training in connexion with the reorganization of school work	24	16	40
Fundamentals of technical drawing	16	—	16
Practical briefing on production. Excursions to local industrial, agricultural, transport, building and other undertakings in order to obtain first-hand knowledge of the functioning of machines and mechanisms, and the organization of power basis and safety techniques of production .	—	12	12
Principles of school hygiene, and prophylaxis of infectious diseases	10	—	10
Work on specific questions	4	—	4
Seminar for exchange of working experience . .	—	6	6
TOTAL	126	74	200

methods; (c) exchange of experience; (d) further improvement o teachers' qualifications in their special subject or subjects; (e) lectures on current achievements of science, technology and art in the U.S.S.R.; (f) study of the principles of industrial, agricultural and other branches of production; (g) improvement of teaching and training methods, and improvements in the internal management, control and inspection of schools.

The reorganization of educational and training work in schools in accordance with the principle of forging close links between school and everyday life makes one subject (regional studies) particularly important; and provision is accordingly made, in the syllabuses and relevant sections of the curriculum, for the inclusion of material covering the content and teaching methods for this subject, and for acquainting teachers with the history, economy and natural features of their own areas.

The timetable (Table 14) for the further training of teachers in machine operation (a 200-period course at an advanced training institute) will serve as an example. Teachers have the option of leaving work to take the complete course or of following one part of the course at a time without leaving work.

This work assumes a variety of forms: in some cases there are study groups which run for one-and-a-half to two months and consist of members who have discontinued their regular work; other courses, covering a whole year, are taken by teachers continuing to work (in towns where teacher-training and advanced training institutes exist); then there are five- to ten-day seminars and practical study groups, series of lectures, conferences where practical experience is exchanged, and so on. Additional training is compulsory for all teachers, school directors and employees in education.

Large numbers of engineers, technicians, skilled workers, agricultural and zoo-technical experts, and agricultural mechanics are drawn into the work of teaching general technical and vocational disciplines at secondary school and directing the labour of pupils in workshops and industrial and agricultural undertakings, and the district education departments and school directors organize seminars on general educational, didactic and methodological problems for their benefit.

Model curricula and syllabuses for requalifying or improving the qualifications of teachers are drawn up by the R.S.F.S.R. Academy of Pedagogical Sciences in concert with the Central Administration of the R.S.F.S.R. Ministry of Education. Alongside with this, considerable efforts are made by the local education departments to raise the polytechnical level of teachers through the organization

247

of seminars, manual training for teachers of the junior grades, conferences for exchanging experience on labour and polytechnical education and excursions designed to familiarize teachers with the techniques and technology of industrial and agricultural production. A great deal is also done inside the schools themselves to improve the teachers' qualifications.

POLYTECHNICAL COMMITTEES AT SCHOOLS

The provision of polytechnical education involves the introduction of much that is new into the methods of work employed by teachers of subjects in the natural-science, mathematics and polytechnical classes. Hence considerable attention is given in every school today to improving the formulation of polytechnical education methods —quality of the teaching of the fundamentals of science, of manual and technical instruction and of the study of the principles of production, improving the vocational training of pupils, and establishing interdisciplinary links between natural-science, mathematics and polytechnical subjects as well as links between school instruction and productive work.

To solve these questions successfully, polytechnical committees have been set up at schools consisting of the school principal or director of studies (chairman of the committee), the deputy-director for production training, the manual and technical instructor and the machine and electrical engineering teachers, the director of production practice, the physics, chemistry, biology, mathematics, technical drawing and geography teachers, and workers from the supporting undertaking.

Apart from trying to solve the above-mentioned problems, the committee helps teachers to familiarize themselves with the techniques, technology and organization of industrial and agricultural production and with new developments in science and technology. An important aspect of its work is the exchange of experience and the elaboration of long-term plans for developing further the polytechnical aspects of the school.

It also deals with traditional problems of general methodology— preparation of lessons, collection of methodological material, analysis of the lessons to be learned from the experience of leading workers, teachers' attendance at one another's classes, discussions of questions of didactics, solution of specific questions of method in the various subjects, discussions of questions regarding the pupils' progress, discussion of works on methodology, etc.

The committee meets once a month to discuss the general

questions concerning teachers of all subjects of the polytechnical classes, while in between meetings the measures it has decided upon are carried into effect and other meetings are held between teachers of related subjects to discuss the specific links between them, as well as the links between instruction and manual work. For example, the physics and chemistry teachers discuss methods of teaching about the structure of the atom; the chemistry and biology teachers discuss teaching about fertilizers, and so on.

The committee may invite teachers of history, say, or other subjects to attend its meetings in order to discuss specific problems. However, the meetings do not constitute its main work. The latter consists rather of the execution by committee members of the decisions taken at those meetings.

The above-mentioned measures for the training and further training of teachers of polytechnical subjects are by no means the only forms of work done in this field. However, they cover the main aspects of the question and give an idea of the essential relevant data.

PART TWO

POLYTECHNICAL EDUCATION AS ILLUSTRATED IN THE TEACHING OF INDIVIDUAL SUBJECTS

CHAPTER XIII

POLYTECHNICAL EDUCATION AS ILLUSTRATED IN PHYSICS, CHEMISTRY AND BIOLOGY TEACHING

by *A. S. Enokhovich, L. A. Tsvetkov and M. I. Melnikov*

PHYSICS

The aims of the secondary-school physics course are: first, to give the pupils a framework of knowledge in the main branches of this science (mechanics, vibrations and waves, sound, heat and molecular physics, electricity, optics, atomic structure); second, to provide a certain range of polytechnical information and in particular to show the physical basis of some of the more important branches of the national economy, such as power production, mechanical engineering and transport; third, to develop in the pupils certain practical skills and accomplishments which they acquire in the process of performing laboratory work, experimental household tasks and other forms of work with the ability to do things for themselves, and the qualities of technical creativeness and imagination; and fourth, to develop in them a materialist outlook and an understanding of the physical pattern of the world on the basis of physics.

The course is given in two stages: the first at the eight-year school (grades VI–VIII, 249 periods), the second in the senior grades at the eleven-year secondary school (grades IX–XI, 382 periods). Grades VI and VII have two lessons a week, grades VIII and IX three, grade X four and grade XI three.

Eight-year school. Grade VI: elementary physical phenomena; physical quantities and their measurement; properties of solids, liquids and gases; rudiments of the structure of matter, elementary heat. Grade VII: mechanical motion (uniform) and friction; composition of forces and equilibrium; work (when the direction of the force coincides with the direction of displacement) and energy; mechanisms; heat and work; transition of matter from one state to another; thermal engines. Grade VIII: sound and light, rudiments of electricity, current, resistance and voltage, work and power of electric current, electromagnetics, rudiments of radio reception, principles of atomic structure.

Eleven-year school. Grade IX: mechanics (uniform motion, Newton's laws of motion, elements of statics, parabolic and circular motion, universal gravitation, work and energy, mechanical vibrations and waves, motion of liquids and gases). Grade X: molecular physics and heat (fundamentals of molecular-kinetic theory, structure of matter, heat, work and internal energy, properties of gases, liquids and solids in relation to their internal structure, fusion and crystallization, evaporation, boiling and condensation, properties of steam and thermal engines); electricity (electrical charges and electrical field, electric current in metals, electrolytes and gases, semiconductors, magnetic fields and electromagnetic induction). Grade XI: electricity (alternating current, electromagnetic vibrations and waves, production and use of electric power); optics (photometry and geometrical optics, wave and quantum properties of light); atomic structure, atomic energy (the electron envelope of the atom, radioactivity, composition of the atomic nucleus, nuclear transformations, peaceful uses of atomic energy—atomic power, tracer atoms, radiation, radioactivity).

The course is designed to link up with other school subjects. What the pupils learn in grade VI for example, about temperature, the various methods of heat transfer and the thermal expansion of bodies enables them to do their spring work on the school plot and on the farm with a clearer understanding of what they are about. They will use the knowledge they have gained about the structure of matter in grade VI for their chemistry work in grade VII. What they learn about sound and light can be applied when they learn about the organs of hearing and vision during the human anatomy and physiology course. Their knowledge of electricity will be used for work in the school's electricity workshops, and so on.

The ground covered during the second stage is not a repetition but an extension and more thorough coverage of the eight-year syllabus. For example, whereas the pupils in grade VII learn the rudiments of mechanics (force, mass, work, energy, etc.), in grade IX these concepts are used to examine the laws of dynamics; Ohm's law for part of an electrical circuit is learnt in grade VIII, whereas in grade X Ohm's law for a complete circuit is learnt.

During both these stages, the pupils receive instruction on phenomena, concepts, laws, theories and their practical application in nature, daily life, and industrial and agricultural production, with emphasis on the physical content of phenomena and laws and the use of physics in technology and production. The physics work covers only the physical principles underlying technological processes and the construction of machines and machine tools: the technical details are learnt in classes on machine operation and electrical engineering and in the course of production training. To enable them to understand the nature of these phenomena, the pupils are familiarized with the molecular-kinetic theory of the structure of matter, electron theory, electromagnetic fields and the wave and quanta theories concerning the nature of radiation, the theories being explained in terms of specific discoveries and experiments and applied to the forecasting of phenomena and processes. In addition, they are extensively used as a means of developing a materialist outlook among the pupils.

The secondary physics course has an experimental bias, the syllabus and the physics-room equipment being designed to stress experimentation and the application of physics to technology and production. This work takes the following forms: experiments by the pupil during the lesson, laboratory work in all grades (all the pupils performing the same work at the same time); practical physics work in the senior grades at the end of the school term or year (the pupils perform various tasks at the same time but change places during subsequent lessons); experimental tasks and observations at home; solution of experimental problems on the basis of data collected through tests, and verification of the results by means of experiments; and the staging of experiments during lessons (with the pupils giving answers based on current teaching material) and during examinations. Experimentation thus becomes an integral part of the systematic and consistent exposition of the course. In addition, educational films are shown and excursions organized (see Table 15) as the course proceeds.

The material is explained by class talks and discussions and in some cases—especially in the top grade—by lectures. These are

TABLE 15. Teaching aids and methods used in physics

	Number of occasions	
Type of aid or method	Eight-year school	Eleven-year school
Demonstration experiments.	146	149
Laboratory exercises, including practical work .	31	33
Films (excerpts and sequences)	16	28
Visits and excursions	6	6

usually given when conclusions have to be drawn from the material learnt in class or when technological information has to be imparted. A number of periods are set aside for laboratory work by the pupils, including the measurement of various physical quantities and the efficiency of mechanisms and of chemical and electrical heaters; the verification of physical laws; the observation of phenomena (Brownian movement, movement of spectra, scintillations in a spinthariscope, tracks of charged particles in a Wilson chamber); and the assembly of models (various relays, electric motor, microscope and telescope).

The physics teacher, sometimes assisted by other subject teachers, takes his pupils on excursions (twice a year) to building sites, mechanized farms, factory workshops, automobile or agricultural-machinery depots, railway depots, electric-power stations, telegraph offices and telephone exchanges.

During the lessons films are shown on sluice construction and operation, metal-casting, the physics of aeronautics, the jet aeroplane, pneumatic instruments, the electromagnetic crane, the principle of telephony, Brownian movement, the nature of an electric current, the mechanism of transversal and longitudinal wave propagation, the mechanism of electrolysis, the photo-electric cell and its use and nuclear energy for peaceful purposes.

Much emphasis is placed on physical problems requiring various methods of solution. These include problems involving calculation (computation), qualitative problems, including those without numerables (not involving calculations), experimental problems (involving the staging of experiments), graphical problems (involving the reading and construction of graphs and the construction of geometrical shapes), and set tasks, including drawings. These tasks cover a wide range of phenomena dealt with in the physics course, and their allocation within each topic is geared to the pupil's training in the concepts of physics and to the gradual consolidation and deepening of his knowledge, their physics content being placed in the forefront rather than being wrapped up in long textual explanations or concealed behind mathematically complicated methods of solution and protracted calculations.

Physics is one of the most important school subjects as far as polytechnical education is concerned, for it concerns the commonest forms of the motions and properties of matter, which means that its laws cover a very wide range of problems directly related to production and technique. Physical laws are in fact the basis of modern technique, and the content and teaching methods of the school physics course are organically related to the pupil's familiarization with the natural and scientific bases of the main branches of modern industrial and agricultural production and his acquisition of polytechnical labour skills.

In learning physics, he becomes familiar with the physical principles of power engineering, the construction and operational principles of the most important prime movers and working machines, and the devices, apparatus and installations used in the different branches of industrial production, transport, tele-communication, agriculture and building. He learns something of the physical principles underlying technological processes and how these processes are checked, regulated and controlled.

In these days of rapid technical progress, when the nature of labour in production is steadily changing, physics is becoming an ever more important factor in polytechnical education. As the machine takes over such jobs as adjusting, regulating and tuning machine tools, the task of checking performance and using inspection and measuring instruments becomes an increasingly important part of the worker's function, and correspondingly greater demands are made on his knowledge. Above all, he has to know more physics, without which it will be impossible for him to do a proper job in many of the labour processes that call for a high level of skill.

Again, in learning physics, the pupil becomes familiar with its application to modern production and develops the aptitude to apply his knowledge in practice. But since its field of application is so vast and it would be quite impossible for a school course to cover all types of machines, mechanisms and technical equipment, the teacher's main task is to provide examples which will illustrate how physical phenomena and laws apply in the main branches of modern production and in the commonest machines. The examples used are closely tied in with the subject matter, so that they become an integral part of the course without disturbing the arrangement or overtaxing the pupils. The emphasis is placed on the central, typical and basic features of a series of machines, leaving complicated and burdensome details aside.

The pupils acquire a good deal of knowledge during the course about the scientific principles of the main branches of production and the national economy, the most important of which are as follows:

Power production: the various types of power used in modern production, the law of conservation and transformation of energy; the physical principles governing the production and long-distance transmission of energy, its distribution and use; the physical properties of working bodies—steam, gas, water;

257

the constructional and operational principles of hydraulic and steam turbines, internal combustion engines, steam engines, electric generators of various kinds, electric motors; thermal, hydraulic, wind and atomic power plants; and transformers.

Machine construction: concept of the machine as an assembly of very simple mechanisms; different forms of transmission; roller bearings; physical principles of different types of relay used in automation; main physical properties of solids; processes of metalworking; and elastic and plastic properties of metals.

Metallurgy: physical properties of bodies, in ralation to the technological processes employed in metallurgy; physical principles of casting, rolling and wire-drawing.

Transport: physical principles of the construction and operation of transport equipment of various kinds: diesel and electric locomotives, aeroplanes and motor-cars.

Communications: principles of telephony, telegraphy and radio; radar.

Building construction: elastic and mechanical properties of bodies; pressure and the calculation of pressure; elastic modulus of the main building materials; safety factors; use of simple machinery on building sites; central heating, electric lighting and lighting standards for rooms.

For the purpose of polytechnical education the pupils are also given instruction on a number of technical and technological problems and on the technical applications of the physical phenomena and laws studied.

The syllabus provides for instruction on a number of electronic instruments such as the two-electrode and three-electrode tube and the use of these as a.c. rectifiers and amplifiers respectively, and on the construction of the electron tube with various types of relay. Other points covered include the main properties of semiconductors and a number of the most important transistor devices, this providing an opportunity for explaining the constructional and operational principles of the automatic and remote-control instruments which are becoming more and more widely used in the automation of industry and agriculture. The electrification of the country bulks large in the syllabus while the principles of district heating from a central source—the development of which is considered as a matter of great importance in the U.S.S.R.—are also dealt with.

In addition, the course covers the physical principles of technological processes such as electric welding, electrolysis, flotation, the mechanical and thermal processing of metals, modern methods of production control (ultrasonic, gamma and X-ray detection of defects), spectral analysis, the use of labelled atoms. Jet engines, artificial earth and sun satellites, the refrigerator and pneumatic instruments are likewise studied.

The pupil begins by having his attention drawn to the general features of the construction and operation of a whole series of machines. When he studies water and air pumps, the hydraulic press and compressor, for example, he sees that the work is affected by the compression of gas or the raising of a liquid by means of a cylinder, a piston, valves and working body (liquid or gas). He sees the same general principles at work when he studies a water pipeline or a liquid manometer operating in accordance with Pascal's law, or water or underwater transport equipment operating in accordance with Archimedes' principle. Levers and blocks, inclined planes, wedges and screws, various types of rotary transmission—devices widely used in the design of every machine—operate on the basis of the golden rule of mechanics: they do not deliver more work than is put in. Similarly, electric generators, electric motors, transformers and other electrical devices have much in common in their construction and operation.

Simultaneously with his discovery of the main features of the various technical devices, the pupil also discovers the differences between them. He learns, for example, to distinguish the constructional differences between a steam engine and an internal combustion engine, or between an internal combustion engine and a jet engine, between friction drive and belt drive, between steam and gas turbines, between a generator and a d.c. motor, between electric motors working in series and electric motors working in parallel, and so on.

An important part of the polytechnical education of the pupil is that he should be shown how every machine, mechanism or instrument that he is studying is used in different branches of technology and production. A steam engine, for example, is a component part of steam locomotives, steamships and stationary steam-powered installations alike. The internal combustion engine is used in motor-cars, tractors, self-propelled combines, aeroplanes, motor-cycles, diesel locomotives and diesel-engined ships. Electric motors are used to operate machine tools, excavators, trolley-buses, trams, electric locomotives and so on.

Modern production and production technique make it necessary for every worker to have not only the theoretical knowledge essential for mastering different types of work but also a number of practical accomplishments and skills of a polytechnical nature. Among these, measuring and calculating skills are of major importance. The worker in any branch of modern production must be able to measure weight, length, volume, force, pressure, temperature, electric current, voltage, resistance, illumination and so on; and the training in these skills is largely acquired during the school physics course.

Provision is made in the syllabus for the acquisition of the following practical skills and accomplishments of a polytechnical nature.

Eight-year school (grades VI–VIII): measurement of bodies with scale-rule; measurement of force with dynamometer; use of spirit-level; weighing with balance; measurement of pressure with manometer; graphical representation of force measurements; use of levers and blocks; measurement of temperature with thermometer; familiarity with heaters; determination of the coefficient of friction; use of stop-watch; familiarity with sources of current (galvanic cells, accumulators) and electrical heating instruments (plates, soldering irons); construction of very simple electric circuits according to set plans; inclusion of an ammeter and voltmeter in a circuit, and reading of the current and voltage; measurement of the resistance of conductors; inclusion of a rheostat in an electric circuit; determination of the power used by an electric bulb; location of the poles of a magnet and an electromagnet; assembly of working models using an electromagnet; selection of measuring instruments for constructing an electrical circuit suitable for given conditions; determination of the ratio between units of work: the joule and the calorie; taking readings from an electric meter; use of transformers.

Eleven-year school (grades IX–XI): length measurement with beam-compasses and micrometer; handling a gauge knob; use of revolution counter or speedometer; construction and reading of graphs showing the variation of certain mechanical quantities in time; use of band brake for measuring the power of an electric motor; determination of the efficiency of simple mechanisms working from models in the construction and operation of a carburettor and a water-jet pump; determination of types of electrical measuring devices and their purpose (d.c. and a.c., ammeter and voltmeter, range of measurements); working with more accurate laboratory ammeters, voltmeters and galvanometers; determination of the e.m.f. of a source of current; assembly of apparatus from a set plan (with branch circuits), using a resistance box; handling a thermocouple; determination of the capacity of a condenser and an induction coil; the use of shunts for ammeters and auxiliary resistances for voltmeters; choice of rheostat for measuring current in a circuit within given limits and as a potentio-meter; use of semiconductors; assembly of a working photo-relay from ready-made parts.

In addition to these skills, the pupil acquires a number of accomplishments which are of great importance in the system of secondary polytechnical education, i.e., computation of various physical quantities and calculation of work, energy, power and efficiency from formulae, using physics and other technical reference books, tables and graphs.

A sound and systematic knowledge of physics is the bedrock for gaining an understanding of technical questions and acquiring practical skills: the scientific principles of power production can be studied only on the basis of a knowledge of the fundamental phenomena and laws of mechanics, heat and electricity; for a proper understanding of communication media there must be a thorough study of vibrations, waves, electricity. The right approach to polytechnical education through the physics course, therefore, is to give the pupils a concrete, lucid, sound and realistic knowledge of theory. This in turn means using methods and forms of instruction from which bookishness is banned.

A persistent and systematic drive is being made in schools to establish the experiment as the basis of the course. In particular, great importance is attached to demonstration experiments by the teacher, and in particular to those designed to acquaint the pupil with physical phenomena and laws in 'pure' and 'naked' form without any 'colouring' resulting from instrumental design or as far as possible from secondary reactions (for example, Archimedes' bucket, production of an induction current in a closed circuit, etc.). At the same time, greater and greater use is being made of demonstration experiments which illustrate the application of scientific knowledge to practice and explain the physical principles of production processes.

Technical objects are often presented during the lessons. After the class has studied the lever and the rules of momentum from demonstration equipment, for example, the teacher will show a series of simple tools which work on the principles of the law of levers, (shears, pliers, pincers, etc.). He will often make use of 'distribution material': during a talk on the transformer or on the electric motor, say, he will distribute standard models of these objects to the class, and the pupils thus become more familiar with them and master the explanations more readily.

Such teaching aids as the film are becoming particularly important. Nevertheless, the film cannot replace direct, live observation through excursions to production points. These are one of the most effective forms of polytechnical education at school provided they are well prepared and properly conducted. Every effort is made to ensure that the physical principles of the construction and operation of the equipment and technological processes are clearly revealed during the visit. And beforehand, during an introductory talk in class, the pupils will go over certain points which they need to know in order to have a proper understanding of the processes and equipment they will see, apart from which they are given assignments to fulfil during the visit itself. These are commonly designed not only to ensure that the teacher's explanations are carefully followed but also to give the pupils a certain amount of work to do on their own (making measurements, determining a physical quantity, etc.). They are subsequently questioned in class about the visit.

The effectiveness of excursions largely depends on how they are conducted. Experienced teachers use active methods which ensure that the pupils have to think for themselves when examining a technical object, so that instead of being a passive audience listening to the teacher's explanations they take part under his guidance in analysing various points. The direct talk, during which the teacher exploits the pupils' knowledge in order to explain the phenomena they are observing and the principles on which the various machine parts and units operate, enables him to set their minds working more actively and gives him a chance to see how far they are absorbing the information obtained during the visit and how clearly and accurately they understand his explanations.

One of the main methods of physics teaching in general and polytechnical education in particular is to set the pupils practical exercises. Side by side with laboratory work designed primarily to familiarize them in the most graphic way with physical phenomena and laws, they are set work which gives them an idea of the scientific principles of technology and production. Laboratory work plays a leading part in inculcating the practical skills enumerated above.

In practical physics the pupils learn how to work on their own; the skills they have already acquired are further developed; and they become familiar with the more complex technical measuring instruments and appliances in current use in modern production. Below, by way of example, are the details of an exercise on assembling and checking the operation of a photo-relay. It entails learning the properties and application of a semiconductor photo-resistance, using it in assembling a photo-relay and testing its operation in the most common automatic installation.

Assembling and checking the operation of a photo-relay

Equipment. Photo-resistance on stand, electromagnetic relay, ammeter, electric bulb on stand, electric motor, accumulator, torch battery, connecting wires, flat glass dish, retort containing pure water, beaker containing saturated solution of potassium permanganate, pipette.

1. The circuit with the photo-resistance is assembled and its voltage measured. The milliammeter with a limit of 0.5 milliamps is then connected in series and the current measured with the photo-resistance at various degrees of illumination, the light-sensitive layer being rotated first towards the window and then away from it. The resistance of the semiconductor (photo-resistance) is calculated in each case, and the variations established. Shutting and opening the photo-resistance (rotated towards the window), the variation of current in the circuit and hence the variation of the resistance are observed from the oscillations of the milliammeter pointer and the corresponding variations in illumination.

   By varying the distance from the window and the angle of rotation of the photo-resistance, it is found that the current is not less than 50 to 60 microamps.

2. Instead of the milliammeter, an electromagnetic relay winding is cut into the circuit, adjusted to work at a current of 50 to 60 microamps and to cut out at a current of 20 to 30 microamps (attention being drawn to the polarity of the terminals). Opening and shutting the photo-resistance, the pupils check whether the electromagnetic relay is working by listening for the knocking sound of the armature inside the relay housing.

   An operating circuit is assembled, consisting of the bulb and accumulator and plugged into the rear terminals of the relay. By adjusting the illumination of the photo-resistance, rotated towards the window, as described above, the pupils can observe that the bulb is automatically switched on and off.

   The circuit is then wired for tripping and an experiment is made illustrating how street lighting is automatically switched on. As the illumination is gradually reduced, simulating the onset of dusk (for this purpose the photo-resistance is rotated away from the window or the window is gradually covered), the pupils see that the artificial lighting (the bulb) is switched on; conversely, as the illumination increases (daybreak) they see it switched off.

3. The electric motor is cut into the operating circuit and the pupils verify that its operation can be controlled with the help of light.

   An experiment is performed illustrating the automatic safety device used on lathes. The operating circuit is wired for tripping, and when the light is intersected by hand (that is, when the photo-resistance is covered) the electric motor is cut out.

4. Using the ammeter, the pupils measure the current in the operating circuit and find out how many times greater the current in the controlled circuit is than that in the controlling circuit containing the photo-resistance.

Lastly, the pupils are given an exercise to show them the working of an automatic device for keeping track of the concentration of a solution. Using a photo-relay, they select a concentration of potassium permanganate solution; that is, they determine how many drops of the saturated solution must be added to the glass dish containing pure water in order to operate the relay (cause the bulb to light up), the dish being placed near the photo-resistance.

The pupils are also required, in order to make them familiar with the main branches of production and acquire practical skills, to solve physics problems having a production content drawn from real life and their own production environment.

Out-of-class work in physics and technology, including study groups, plays an important part in this respect in extending and deepening the polytechnical knowledge acquired in class (see Fig. 24).

At the group meetings the pupils present papers and reports on the achievements of modern science and technology and about particular branches of production and their prospects of development, and there are frequent group visits to plants and factories, the laboratories of university technical institutes, research establishments and polytechnical museums.

Great importance is attached to the children's technical creativeness and inventiveness, and to their acquisition of the ability to work by themselves in designing physics instruments, equipment and working models. At Moscow Secondary School No. 694, for example, the pupils in the electrical engineering groups made model traffic-lights, simple automatic signals and a simple telegraph station. The senior pupils' groups, under the guidance of engineers, designed models of a crane, a dump-truck and a rocket chariot. At Secondary School No. 98, Kratovo Station (Moscow Region), the pupils designed separate parts and complete instruments after the teacher had set them the task of making an instrument with which he could demonstrate a particular physical phenomenon. A great many useful instruments and technical models were designed and made at the Perevozskaya School (Gorky Region), Secondary School No. 18 at Raevka Station, Secondary School No. 28 at Batraki Station, Secondary School No. 65 at Ulan-Ude, Secondary School No. 32 at Taganrog, and elsewhere.

Designing and making physics instruments and technical models and equipment at school has become a common practice, in fact, and in many cases is a form of socially useful labour employed for equipping physics rooms.

Other socially useful activities include instrument repair,

keeping the physics room in working order, wiring the benches for electricity, equipping the school with radio and telephone, equipping dark-rooms and constructing astronomical and meteorological observation sites attached to the schools. In addition, the pupils look after the school electrical, broadcasting and telephone systems under the teachers' guidance and with due regard for safety regulations.

The polytechnical knowledge acquired in the physics class provides a scientific basis for a number of technical subjects taught at schools, and especially for electrical engineering and machine operation.

The correct dovetailing of physics and electrical engineering and machine operation is something more than a one-sided process with physics as the sole starting point. Instruction in the two technical subjects is linked up with physics by making use of the pupils' knowledge of that subject and showing how what they know is embodied in actual technical phenomena.

CHEMISTRY

The science of chemistry deals with the study of matter, the components of natural bodies—their composition, structure and transformation into other substances. Applying the laws governing the transformation of matter, and under the impetus of the demands made by life and production, chemistry artificially creates new substances enabling man to produce industrially on a vast scale, from natural sources, the substances and materials he needs.

The study of chemistry, together with that of other natural sciences, gives pupils an objective picture of the world and helps to train them in a scientifically correct materialist outlook while at the same time equipping them with knowledge of practical use in daily life and production.

The secondary school chemistry course covers five years: grades VII and VIII at the eight-year school and all grades (IX, X, XI) at the eleven-year school.

The eight-year school course (144 periods) is to some extent complete in itself, its coverage being sufficient to provide a proper understanding of the most important chemical phenomena occurring in nature, production and daily life, a mastery of a particular production job or a thorough insight into the principles of chemistry at a higher educational stage.

It includes such fundamental concepts as the chemical formulae and their signs, the main types of chemical reaction (composition, decomposition), the division of substances into elements and compounds, the chemical elements as component parts of matter, the valency of elements in compounds, the molecular and atomic structure of matter, and the conservation of mass during chemical reactions. While learning these concepts through easily understandable chemical phenomena, the pupils also master the language of chemistry and the use and construction of chemical formulae and equations. They study oxygen, hydrogen, water and the commonest oxides, bases, acids and salts, a knowledge of which is important from the practical standpoint and also for later systematic study of the chemical elements.

To strengthen the practical bias of the course and give it a certain completeness, the course includes a study of the main fertilizers, carbon and its compounds (including the main types of fuel) and combustion processes, as well as elementary data on metals.

The order of topics is as follows: (1) substances and their changes; (2) rudiments of the structure and composition of substances; (3) oxygen, air; (4) hydrogen; (5) water, solutions; (6) oxides, bases, acids, salts; (7) main classes of inorganic compounds; (8) mineral fertilizers; (9) carbon and its compounds; (10) metals.

The eleven-year school course (265 periods) is designed to provide systematic instruction on the principles of inorganic and organic chemistry. After a brief review of the fundamental concepts of chemistry, it begins with a study of the natural groups of elements—alkali metals, halogens, and the oxygen and sulphur groups—as a necessary preliminary to a study of the periodic law of chemical elements. The latter, together with the periodic system of elements and the study of atomic structure and the theory of electrolytic dissociation flowing from it, constitutes the theoretical basis for the inorganic chemistry course. The pupil learns about the successive chemical elements, starting with the non-metal group and passing to the metals, in the light of this knowledge.

The sequence of the inorganic course is as follows: (1) fundamental chemical concepts; (2) alkali metals; (3) halogens; (4) sulphur; (5) Mendeleev's periodic law and the periodic system of chemical elements; the structure of matter; (6) fundamentals of the electrolytic dissociation theory; (7) nitrogen and phosphorus; (8) carbon and silicon; (9) metals (magnesium, calcium, aluminium, copper, chromium, iron); (10) general review of the elements by groups in the periodic table.

The organic course is given in grade XI. Taking the main substances as examples, the basic classes of organic compounds are studied in their genetic link from the simplest to the more complex, so that the pupils have an opportunity of understanding the process whereby inorganic substances in nature develop into organic substances and thence to organisms, the study of these substances enabling them to appreciate the growing practical significance of organic chemistry today.

The course is based on A. M. Butler's theory of the chemical structure of substances and is constructed as follows: (1) subject matter of organic chemistry; (2) saturated hydrocarbons; Butler's theory and the structure of organic substances; (3) unsaturated hydrocarbons; (4) aromatic hydrocarbons; (5) alcohols and phenols; (6) aldehydes; (7) carbonic acids; (8) esters, fats; (9) carbohydrates; (10) nitro compounds; (11) amines; amino-acids; (12) proteins; (13) synthetic high molecular substances; (14) further development of chemistry in the Soviet Union.

As stated, chemistry is the basis of a wide range of production processes supplying the national economy with a great variety of products, and its importance for modern technical progress is steadily increasing; and the school course contributes towards the pupils' polytechnical education by providing ample opportunities for acquainting them with the scientific principles of the various branches of production based on applied chemistry.

The latter include the chemical industry proper, which produces mineral acids, alkalis, salts, agricultural fertilizers, and a variety of organic products including plastics, rubbers, chemical fibres; the ferrous and non-ferrous metal industry, including metals and alloys from ores by making use of the chemical reactions of oxidation and reduction; the oil- and coal-processing industries, including the various types of fuels and lubricants, solvents and a large number of other substances providing the raw material for all sorts of products; the wood-chemical industry, which processes timber products to provide ethyl alcohol, acetic acid, acetone, resin, turpentine; the building-materials industry; the food industry, in which chemical processes play a considerable part in transforming agricultural products; the pharmaceutical and a number of other industries also coming into the category of chemical industries.

The branches of production enumerated are based on the use of chemical processes and are essentially chemical even though they are not always so called; for the chemical industry proper accounts for only part of chemical production. It is impossible, in fact, to understand the scientific principles of these branches without a study of the chemical processes on which they are based—outside the context of chemistry.

But the significance of chemistry in modern production is far wider, even, than this: chemical products and processes are finding increasingly wide application in still other branches of production which are not classified as chemical on account of the fact that these products and processes play a subordinate rather than the leading role in them.

In engineering, which makes extensive use of a great variety of metals and synthetic materials produced by the chemical industry, chemical processes are used to preserve metals from corrosion, improve their surface properties, provide an electrolytic coating, etc. In agriculture, where all biological processes are inevitably connected with the conversion of substances in the organisms of plants and animals, the use of chemical fertilizers and chemical means of combating plant pests, growth stimulants and other products of the chemical industry is steadily growing.

As the pupil progresses systematically through the chemistry course, he becomes familiar with: (a) the general scientific principles of chemical production; (b) its main branches; (c) the use of chemistry in other branches of production.

The polytechnical element is not mechanically added to the course but forms an integral part of it expressive of the didactic principle of linking science with life and theory with practice. In compliance with this principle, the substances studied are considered not only in terms of their composition, structure and properties but also in terms of how they are used in the national economy and industrially produced. This approach, properly pursued, constitutes the essence of polytechnical education.

In order to ensure that the pupil's introduction to the general principles of chemical production is not abstract but specific and convincing, it is linked up with a study of particular branches. It is obviously impossible to acquaint him with all of them, nor is there any need to do so, since the polytechnical principle does not call for instruction in everything but only for instruction in production principles in general.

To meet its general requirements, the branches studied must be: (a) those which produce the products most important for the national economy; (b) those which are most suitable for giving the pupil a clear idea of the general principles underlying the chemical processing of materials and advanced chemical techniques and technology; and (c) those which will be most readily understood by him from the standpoint of chemistry.

The secondary school syllabus accordingly provides for a study of the following branches: (a) the basic chemical industry; (b) the heavy organic synthesis industry; (c) the metallurgical industry;

(d) the petroleum-processing industry; (e) the coal-processing industry; (f) the silicate industry.

These industries are studied not as special topics but as and when they become relevant during the course. The pupil learns about sulphuric-acid production, for example, under the heading 'Sulphur', about ammonia production when studying ammonia under the heading 'Nitrogen'; about metal production under the heading of 'Metals', about the silicate industry as an extension of the topic 'Silicon', and so on.

Similarly, the applications of chemistry to other branches of production are examined in the course of studying the chemistry of substances applied in a particular way. The nature of corrosion and methods of combating it, for example, are studied under the heading of 'Metals'; the use of different types of fuel in power production are studied under 'Carbon', and so on.

In learning about how the different products are made, the pupil gains an insight into the general principles of chemical production. Accordingly, he is taught about the main aspects of each branch in such a way as to permit a fairly full description of it together with an idea of the general concepts of production.

Every production process—the point has been made earlier—involves three main elements: the materials which have to be processed; the instruments of labour used in processing these materials into the finished product; and human labour, consisting of the direction of the production process.

To ensure that these three elements are reflected in the study of chemical production the following group of concepts is covered: (a) the composition, properties and economic significance of the product; (b) the composition and properties of the raw materials; (c) the chemical reactions whereby the original materials are converted into the finished product, and the conditions under which this is done; (d) the main stages and processes of production; (e) the apparatus used in the main stages of the production process, their construction and operation; (f) the principles whereby the production process is effected during the main stages, and the principles of production as a whole; (g) the trades and labour functions of the workers engaged in production.

In addition to the methods common to all branches of production (integrated mechanization, automation, electrification, continuous flow, etc.), chemical technology has developed its own specific methods, often referred to as the scientific principles of chemical production.

On the basis of what physical chemistry teaches about chemical equilibrium, chemical-reaction speeds and the conditions affecting

269

changes in equilibrium and speed, chemical technology has shown that for obtaining optimum reaction speed and full utilization the following principles have to be observed:

Higher concentration of substances with surplus concentration of one low-cost reagent: there are various ways of achieving this, e.g., by enriching the raw material, by using high pressures for gases, high concentrations for solutions, counter flows, circulation processes, etc.

Use of optimum temperatures: various methods of heating or cooling are used, including the heat exchange of substances normally used in production.

Use of catalysts.

Optimum development of the surface areas of substances: this is achieved by crushing, use of precipitates in the reaction apparatus (towers), etc.

All these principles are used to a greater or lesser extent in the various branches of production and can therefore be explained progressively as the pupils come to study them.

The development of the pupil's polytechnical knowledge through the study of chemistry can be briefly described as follows.

In the eight-year school he becomes acquainted first and foremost with the way in which hydrogen, oxygen, acids, alkalis, salts, mineral fertilizers, various types of fuel, pig-iron, steel and other metals are used in ordinary life and production, and gets an initial idea of how pig-iron is produced and of blast-furnace construction and operation.

It is in grades IX–XI, at the second education stage, that he learns the scientific principles of chemical production on a broader basis.

The first main branch of production he learns about, under the syllabus, is that of synthetic hydrochloric acid. He is given a very brief account of the obsolescent method of obtaining it by the action of sulphuric acid on sodium chloride, followed by a fairly detailed account of the synthetic method, and a description of the construction of the furnace for the combustion of hydrogen in chlorine and the use of an absorption tower for capturing the hydrogen chloride. The construction of the tower and its working principles (counter flow, surface development) are also dealt with, in consideration of its very wide use in the chemical industry.

Under the heading of 'Sulphur' the pupil learns about the production of sulphuric acid. Of the two methods of production (the old chamber [or tower] method and the newer contact method), only the latter is covered, as being technically better and more readily understandable, and at the same time enabling

270

attention to be focused on such general aspects of technology as the use of catalysts, the principle of heat exchange, the purification of primary materials from catalyst-poisoning admixtures, the various types of industrial furnace, contact apparatus, absorption devices, etc.

Under the heading of 'Nitrogen' comes the study of the production of synthetic ammonia, synthetic nitric acid and nitrogenous fertilizers—a group on which considerable emphasis is placed not only on account of their great importance in human life but also because nitrogen production plants can be used as an example in illustrating many branches of chemical production, such as the synthesis of methyl alcohol and liquid fuel and the production of formaldehyde. Under this heading, too, the pupil learns about high-pressure apparatus, the principle of the circulation of reactants used in cases when the reaction cannot be completed, the standard apparatus for producing salts (neutralizer, granulation tower, etc.).

Under the heading of 'Silicon', the production of glass and cement is studied and the pupil learns about new types of furnace, methods of preparing the materials, optimum conditions for conducting the different processes, etc.

Later in the course comes a fairly detailed study of steel-casting and aluminium production, coal-coking and the processing of petroleum and natural fuel gases, and a briefing on the production of polymers (resins, fibres and plastics).

In this way the pupil gets a fairly broad idea of individual branches of production and of chemical production as a whole.

Provision is made, at certain stages in the syllabus, for summing up the knowledge acquired. The first summing-up comes after the study of ammonia and fertilizer production: it is shown, from a comparison of the branches studied, how general scientific principles are used in chemical production to increase labour productivity and reduce production costs.

The second comes after the study of metals, when the pupil knows something about the metallurgical industries (pyrometallurgical, electrothermal, electrochemical, etc.).

The last comes at the end of the organic chemistry course (following the inorganic course), when all the knowledge acquired about chemical production is summarized: the main products and their economic importance, types of raw materials, main chemical processes used in production, typical apparatus, scientific principles, etc. This simultaneously provides an opportunity for revising what has been learnt about the individual branches.

In the course of study and summarization, considerable attention is focused on questions relating to Soviet economic development. The pupils are told about achievements in the field of chemical production and the chemicalization of the country under the Soviet régime, the tasks set by the Communist Party for the further development of particular production branches, and the outstanding work of production teams doing pioneering work in chemical techniques and technology. This gives them a deeper understanding of the growing role of chemistry in communist construction in the U.S.S.R. and helps those who have a bent for the subject to decide where to use their abilities when they leave school.

The next question that arises is that of the polytechnical teaching methods used in the chemistry course.

In familiarizing the pupils with a particular branch of chemical production the teacher first decides the content and scope of the information to be given about it, in the light of the pupils' knowledge of chemistry and related disciplines on which he can rely in expounding the new material, and plans the sequence in which this will be taught. The experience of leading teachers and the results of S. G. Shapovalenko's research on the matter have shown that the information is best given in the following order: product→raw material→chemical reactions→main stages in the production process→principal apparatus→general principles of production→human labour. Shapovalenko also indicated the methods to be used for this purpose.[1]

The first necessity is for the pupils to see actual samples of the raw materials and finished products and to become familiar through experiments with the chemical reactions on which production is based. Once they have understood the essence of these reactions and the conditions under which they proceed, they will be better able to grasp the technology involved.

To help them understand the chemical reactions, they are taught the theory involved, made to design an apparatus in which the chemical process can take place and are shown an experiment in an apparatus similar in design to one used in production. In addition they make drawings of the apparatus on the blackboard and in their exercise books, and make a detailed analysis of the experiment.

The 'planning' element is an essential factor in chemistry-teaching methods. Once the chemical reactions have been learnt, the teacher suggests to the pupils that they think out how these reactions can be technically realized under production conditions,

---

1. *Polytechnical Instruction in Chemistry*, ed. S. G. Shapovalenko, Moscow, Academy of Pedagogical Sciences, 1957, p. 88–132.

and he directs the 'planning' of a flow sheet by means of question and answer. The various suggestions made by the pupils on the basis of their analysis of the production experiment are discussed, the valid ones being accepted and the others rejected. In this way, the pupils reach conclusions about the shape and relative size of the production apparatus, the material it is made of and the scientific principles involved—enrichment of the raw material, optimum development of the surface area of the reactants, use of optimum temperatures and pressures, use of catalysts, counter flow, circulation and so on.

When the pupils study their first chemical-production branch in the secondary school (hydrochloric acid), they find considerable difficulty in 'planning', and need basic assistance from the teacher; but as they gradually master particular branches and the general principles of chemical production, they get better at 'planning' the flow sheet.

Another teaching aid is the class demonstration of selected models of chemical apparatus used in the factories, together with diagrams showing their construction (see Fig. 25). The models help pupils to visualize the apparatus, while the diagrams and charts help them to discover its essential features. Production models and diagrams of this kind have been prepared by D. A. Epshtein and issued for school use by the Ministry of Education.[1]

A number of educational films on production have also been issued in recent years. These give the pupils a convincing picture of chemical production and an idea of the latest techniques and of the construction and working principles of apparatus, of automation, of the technological process as a whole, and of phenomena and objects not accessible to direct observation.

Experience has shown that these films are most effective if the following conditions are met: (a) that only part of the film or excerpts strictly relevant to the subject are selected for class demonstration; (b) that the pupils are made receptive in advance by having questions put to them to which they must find the answers in the film, or being set problems linking the new material with what they have already learnt (in the case of a film on sulphuric-acid production, for instance, say, the teacher will suggest that they compare the construction of the apparatus and the scientific principles of sulphuric-acid production with what they have already learnt about hydrochloric acid); (c) that the film is accompanied by a commentary (if only in the form of brief remarks) synchronized with the frames projected on the screen;

1. D. A. Epshtein, *Visual Aids in Secondary School Chemistry Teaching*, Moscow, Academy of Pedagogical Sciences, 1958.

(d) that the work is rounded off in class by clearing up any points not understood, and that the knowledge imparted by the film is consolidated.

But while the film show is an important way of making ideas and concepts concrete, it is still only an image of reality: hence the special value of excursions to factories and plants to supplement class lessons. Two types of excursions are commonly organized: (a) visits conducted by the chemistry teacher to familiarize pupils with an entire plant or with particular workshops; (b) combined visits organized by the chemistry teacher in conjunction with other subject teachers (physics, biology, geography, etc.), the content of these visits being determined by the teaching material for a group of subjects but the places visited being selected in the light of the chemistry syllabus and the school's production environment.

The eight-year school chemistry syllabus, for example, recommends visits to a water-purification plant, an oxygen plant, a carbon-dioxide plant, a factory laboratory, a lime-kiln, a blast-furnace shop in a metallurgical factory and a mineral-fertilizer factory. The eleven-year school syllabus recommends visits to a hydrochloric- and sulphuric-acid factory, an ammonium and nitric-acid synthesis plant, a gasworks, a glass factory, a cement factory, the workshops of metallurgical factories, electrolysis shops, an oil refinery, a coke chemical works, a soap factory, margarine and sugar-beet factories and synthetics plants (alcohols, carbonic acids, synthetic rubber, plastics, chemical fibres, etc.)

Polytechnical education, in chemistry as in other subjects, involves a mastery of practical accomplishments and skills to enable the pupils to understand the scientific principles of chemical production; they are familiarized with the chemical reactions on which production processes are based but they cannot, of course, perform the appropriate experiments and make the necessary observations until they have mastered certain experimental methods. Even the simplest experiments involve accomplishments and skills in handling laboratory equipment and reagents apart from which there is the fact that they recur in every branch of modern production (power, engineering, chemical or agricultural) with its analytical laboratory for testing incoming raw materials, controlling the production process and testing the finished product.

The acquisition of practical skills is of great educational importance, also, for they involve the development in the pupils of the qualities essential for labour activity: perseverance, shrewdness of judgement, concentration, promptness, accuracy, carefulness in the use of materials, and so on.

They are inculcated in the course of demonstration experiments by the teacher or by the pupils themselves, of the laboratory experiments made in unison in studying new material in class, and also of the special practical exercises which follow the study of particular points or sections of the course, designed to consolidate what has just been taught. The syllabus includes a list of demonstration and laboratory experiments and a list of practical exercises.

Gloriozov's research[1] has shown that the best results in teaching practical skills and accomplishments in chemistry are achieved when the following conditions are observed:

Verbal explanation by the teacher regarding the order in which the operations will be performed, accompanied by a demonstration of each.

Explanation of the nature of the processes taking place during the performance of the operations.

Demonstration of drawings giving a detailed picture of individual aspects of the operation to be performed.

Warnings against possible errors which may occur during the performance of the operations.

Performance of an adequate number of exercises by the pupils under the teacher's observation and guidance.

Systematic check on how the pupils are mastering practical accomplishments and skills in the process of their work.

A great deal of out-of-class work is conducted to satisfy the pupils' curiosity about chemistry and develop their bent for it at school. This makes it easier to select the most advanced pupils for admission to the chemistry faculties of the universities and technical colleges.

There has lately been a considerable expansion in out-of-class work in chemistry laboratories at plants and factories where the pupils acquire a wide knowledge of analytical chemistry as well as proficiency in experimental technique. The laboratory work encourages the pupils to study the technological process carried out in the plant concerned, and many stay on to work in its laboratories and workshops.

BIOLOGY

Biology as a science deals with the properties of living bodies, and the laws governing their life and growth, and formulates methods for applying those laws in practical human activity. The past and present development of this discipline is linked with practical

---

1. P. A. Gloriozov, *Development of Skills and Accomplishments in the Process of Chemistry Teaching*, Moscow, Academy of Pedagogical Sciences, 1959.

requirements in agriculture, medicine, veterinary science and a number of branches of industry.

Biology teaching is of great importance for polytechnical education, for it is essential for pupils to know the principles of agronomy and the physiological principles of labour; conversely, scientific agronomy and the intelligent organization of various forms of labour acticity are based in their turn on the laws governing the life and growth of plant, animal and human organisms.

The first stage in learning about nature is in grades I–IV. Beginning with grade I, the pupil observes natural objects and phenomena, is taken on excursions and does practical work on the school experimental plot; and these observations and practical tasks are linked with sections in the school textbook. This first stage is completed in grade IV with the introduction of the preparation subject, 'Nature study', which covers the rudiments of physical geography and elementary instruction about water, air, useful minerals and soil.

The work done in the junior grades provides a basis for an elementary biology course in grades V–VIII covering botany (grades V and VI), zoology (grades VI and VIII), and human anatomy, physiology and hygiene (grade VIII).

The grade V syllabus covers the structure, life and individual development of flowering plants, local species being used as examples. Grade VI goes on to the plant world in its various forms, and the pupils are familiarized with the biological characteristics of the most important local agricultural crops and the Michurin methods of raising new varieties (the simplest and clearest examples being chosen). The study of the main plant groups, from bacteria to angiospermae, concludes with a general review of the historical development of the plant world.

As zoology appears in the timetable in the last quarter of grade VI, the general topic 'Forests and forest plant life' deals not only with plants but also with harmful and useful animals inhabiting forests, the interrelationship between plant and animal organisms and the importance of forests in the national economy. If there are no forests in the neighbourhood, the pupils learn about other plant societies, for example, meadow vegetation.

The elementary zoology course takes the form of a survey of the main classification groups in the animal world starting with the simplest and ending with mammals. The final topic covers the main stages of development of the animal world. The entire course is linked closely with practical matters, with the main emphasis on agriculture, and the pupils are familiarized with the biological principles governing the raising, feeding and tending of animals.

276

The survey is followed by a study of the selective breeding of animals by man and the development of new breeds of livestock. Great attention is paid to animals harmful to agricultural plants, local examples being taken, and to agents and carriers of diseases, and methods of combating them.

The eight-year school course ends with elementary work on human anatomy, physiology and hygiene, with instruction on how to maintain and improve health, and organize work and recreation. There is also instruction on first aid. This part of the syllabus ends with the 'Origin of man' and 'Public health in the U.S.S.R.'

Of the three periods a week set aside for socially useful work, one period in grades V and VI and half a period in grade VII in urban schools, and one a week in grades V, VI, VII and VIII in rural schools, is devoted to practical agricultural work on the school experimental plot.

In grade IX of the eleven-year school the pupils take a concluding course on general biology and the principles of Darwinism (three periods a week).[1] The first part includes material summing up and deepening the pupils' knowledge of the features common to all organisms and the fundamental laws governing the individual development of plants and animals, while the second part deals with aspects of Darwinism, and is based on a study of the laws of development of the organic world, the theories propounded by their discoveries and the ways in which man uses these laws in his practical activity. The syllabus is so arranged that the pupils not only learn the laws governing the structure, life and development of plants and animals but also the methods by which these laws are used in the practical work of plant-growing, animal husbandry and certain other branches of the national economy.

Originally, the biology syllabus dealt not only with the practical application of biology but also with agro-technics and zoo-technics, but to some extent this acted as a diversion from the task of providing a training in biological concepts. Agro-technical and zoo-technical questions in the narrow sense have now been transferred to the syllabus for practical agricultural work on the school plot, leaving the biological principles of raising agricultural crops and animals in the biology syllabus so as to maintain the essential link between biology on the one hand, and real life and production on the other.

For the purpose of comparison, particulars concerning the past and present structure of the section of the grade V botany course dealing with seeds and sowing are given below by way of example:

---

1. In the ten-year school, the course on the principles of Darwinism covered two periods a week.

1956 syllabus	New syllabus
... preparation of seeds for sowing : determination of germinability; cleaning, sorting; importance of these measures for increasing crop yield. Sowing. Sowing times for various plants. Bedding depth in relation to seed size and germination characteristics. Sowing in rows and square clusters.	...germination and non-germination of seeds. Sowing times in relation to biological characteristics of the crops. Bedding depth in relation to seed size and germination speed.

The inclusion of material linking biological theory with practice enables the pupils to master the biological principles of agriculture and gives the syllabus a polytechnical character; while in the process of practical work on the school plot, in the rabbit and poultry yard, the pupils not only apply but also extend the knowledge they have gained in class and on biology excursions, and develop their manual and technical education. Getting the children appropriate experiments with the plants and animals to be raised is a very important means of developing their powers of observation and creative initiative as workers, and helping to develop their inclinations and talents in that particular direction.

With the proper combination of theoretical syllabus material and practical work on the school plot and socially useful work, the polytechnical value of school instruction in biology is greatly enhanced. The better the pupils' grasp of the fundamental biological laws governing the structure, growth and development of plants and animals, the more clearly and fully will they understand the significance of the methods used in agriculture and animal husbandry. The practical application of what they learn makes them more intelligent in their work in that connexion—a point which is of particular importance for senior pupils at rural schools, as a preparation for combining instruction with productive agricultural work.

Familiarity with the application of biological knowledge to agricultural practice and other branches of economic activity is also good for the pupils' general education, for it helps to give them a clearer insight into the nature of plant and animal life and growth and to understand the general biological laws governing the organic world, as taught in the general biology course in grades IX or X.

Since the botany course precedes that on chemistry, the mineral nutrition of plants and mineral fertilizers, which are touched on in grades V and VI, are dealt with more thoroughly in grades VII and upwards, when the corresponding topics in the chemistry course are studied. Similarly, the pupils' knowledge of plant life and growth and nature's methods of controlling plants is to a large extent filled in during the general biology course (grade IX).

The entire zoology course is also closely tied in with practice. The connexion between zoology and various branches of the national economy, particularly agriculture, is explained, and the pupils are familiarized with the biological principles governing the raising, feeding and tending of livestock. Even when they begin by learning about the silkworm and the bee, they are introduced to the idea that it is necessary to satisfy the requirements of these creatures, and this idea is developed and treated more thoroughly when they learn about tame carp, fowl and agricultural mammals. Following a review of the most important groups of animals, attention is paid to the specific topic of how man can alter animals and produce new breeds of livestock. This topic is treated biologically, and as far as possible with the use of local examples, and thus provides the pupils with a theoretical basis for performing practical tasks in tending livestock and going on to study the principles of animal husbandry during the second stage of secondary education.

Other questions covered include the conservation of nature (conservation and stocking of fishing grounds, and habitats of birds and fur-bearing animals; hunting seasons, fishing regulations, etc.). In addition, the pupils have to be taught to treat such useful animals as frogs and toads, grass snakes and bats with respect and to get rid of any prejudices or superstitions they may have about them.

The pupils begin the general biology course by going more thoroughly into what they have already learnt about the general properties of all organisms (cell structure, metabolism, sensitivity, reproduction, growth and development) and about the individual growth of plants and animals, and then learn about the historical laws of development of the organic world, the methods by which man uses those laws in his practical activity, the processes by which life originated and developed on earth, and the origin of man.

All these studies are vital not only for developing in the pupils a scientifically correct approach to living nature but also for practical activity, particularly in agriculture and a number of branches of industry. Without a knowledge of aerobic and anaerobic bacteria, for instance, it would be impossible to have a proper understanding of the processes of soil formation, the nature of plant-feeding by the soil, the importance of pulses in crop rotation, fodder-ensilaging methods and so forth.

A knowledge of how metabolism proceeds in autotrophic and heterotrophic organisms is essential for an understanding of the methods used to control the conditions for successful formation of organic substances in plants, the role of vegetation in human life, the rational feeding and raising of livestock and methods for controlling the nature crops and domestic livestock.

In the second part of the general biology course, the pupils learn about the laws of heredity, mutation, artificial and natural selection, the struggle for existence and mutual assistance in nature, and the main methods and achievements of plant and animal selection, at the present time.

The course on human anatomy, physiology and hygiene has no direct connexion with polytechnical education. Nevertheless, it provides the pupils with information on matters of health and labour protection which is vital for practical work in production; they learn the importance of a correct working stance, proper lighting, ventilation, noise prevention, protective devices and the rational organization of work and recreation.

Such, in broad outline, is the range of polytechnical knowledge covered during the biology course in both urban and rural schools.

The requirements as regards basic agronomical studies are the same for urban and rural schools, but as far as practical agricultural skills are concerned the requirements vary according to natural and agricultural conditions, the locality in which the school is situated and the existence or otherwise of appropriate material facilities (school plot, greenhouse, rabbit or poultry yard, relations with a local agricultural undertaking, and so on).

The skills developed by the pupils vary according to the type of plant they are growing and the animals they are tending. In the central regions of the U.S.S.R., for example, they learn to grow wheat, potatoes, vegetables, fruit and berries; in the south-eastern Republics (Uzbekistan and Turkmenia), where cotton-growing and viticulture predominate, they concentrate on those. In the former area they learn how to grow crops without irrigation, whereas in the latter their studies include irrigation projects and so on. In the same way, they learn the skills proper to the various regions as regards the types of livestock raised locally.

In urban schools remote from farms and possessing either no experimental plot or one which is too small to permit all the pupils to grow plants or tend animals, the work usually consists of ornamental gardening in local parks and boulevards, or in the grounds of patron undertakings, children's institutions and so on.

In parts of the country where other branches of the economy such as fishing, hunting or sericulture are more important

Fig. 21. Students from the Orekhovo-Zuevo Institute of Education thinning out tomato seedlings in the seed beds on a collective farm.

Fig. 22. A livestock farm where students do practical work.

Fig. 23. In the Moscow District Advanced Teacher-Training Institute. Physics teachers are given advice on how to explain the functioning of an electronic time relay to their pupils.

Fig. 24. Pupils taking part in a physics study group.

Fig. 25. A pupil assembles a model of factory apparatus for the synthesis of ammonia.

Fig. 26. Pupils at the Bolshe-Troitsky Secondary School carefully tend the sugar-beet crops on their practice farm.

Fig. 27. Pupils at School No. 315 (Moscow) at work in the 'live nature' corner.

Fig. 28. Sketching technical details.

Fig. 29. Pupils checking the regularity of the depth of planting of maize seeds by a square cluster seeding machine on their brigade's allotment on a collective farm.

Fig. 30. Practical work in engineering.

Fig. 31. Practical work in engineering.

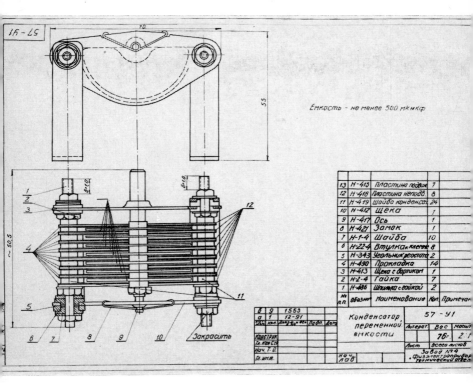

Fig. 32. Condenser (diagram).

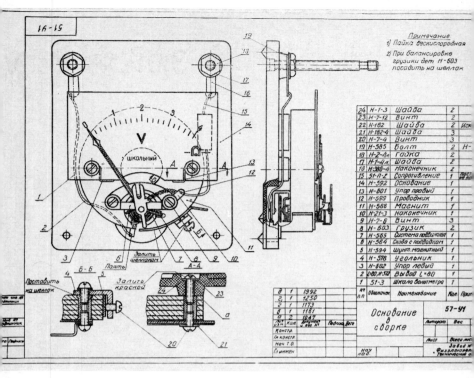

Fig. 33. Ammeter (diagram).

than agriculture, instruction in those branches is more intensive.

The content of the biology course is so devised that the pupils are able to do a thoroughly sound job in growing plants and raising animals on the school (or inter-school) plot and to broaden, intensify and vitalize their knowledge of agrobiology thanks to the experiments and observations carried out there.

Of great importance in polytechnical education are the excursions to farms and to agricultural exhibitions which are arranged for under the syllabus for biology and practical agricultural work (see Fig. 26). The former usually involve socially useful work, and it is found that grade VI and VII pupils at rural schools are very keen to take an active part in agricultural work alongside their older comrades (they form groups within the school agricultural brigades). This is of major significance for polytechnical education, for only on a basis of familiarity with large-scale agricultural production and its machine technique can the pupils get an idea of the basic principles of modern agriculture. Later, the children acquire a more thorough knowledge of these matters when they come to study the special subjects in the senior grades.

By linking biology instruction with creative agricultural work and participation in urban tree-planting and the preservation of nature, the schools help to accustom their pupils to labour and develop in them endurance, expertness, an interest in agriculture and a knowledge of how to stage simple experiments; and this work, especially when combined with out-of-class group activities, helps them in choosing a trade.

The solution of tasks involved in giving schoolchildren poly-technical work experience depends not only on the content of the course but also on the way it is organized and the teaching methods used. The biology teachers make extensive use of active methods to stimulate the pupil's perceptivity, and do their utmost to develop their ability to work on their own in staging experiments in the classroom, in the 'live nature' corner (see Fig. 27), on the school plot or on a plot provided by a local farm. Nor do the teachers confine themselves to expounding the syllabus material: they also tell their pupils easily understandable facts about local practical achievements in plant-growing and animal husbandry, for material drawn from the life around them makes a particularly deep impression on schoolchildren. Many schools, for example, have made display stands showing the progress made by local agriculture under the seven-year plan for agricultural development.

Practical work on the school plot and the pupils' participation in socially productive agricultural work take various forms. In the case of the former, the children in grades V–VII work in accordance with the syllabus approved by the Ministry of Education. If the size of the school plot or farm permits, part of the work (hoeing, autumn harvesting, sowing of trees and shrubs, etc.) is performed by all members of the class,[1] and part by individual brigades or groups (sowing, planting out on experimental beds, care of the plants, harvesting, evaluation of the yield, etc.). To ensure that the work of tending plants and animals suffers no interruption during the summer months, a work chart is drawn up in advance, in agreement with the children and parents (so as to allow for visits to camps or relatives during the holidays, etc.) and in conjunction with collective-farm managements.

As to the organization of socially useful work, it takes the form of youth camps, school production groups and agricultural brigades.

The camps are mainly for pupils in the senior grades of schools in towns and on workers' estates, and are located near the farm with which the school has established relations. Well before the camp is opened, the school is familiarized with the farm's production plan and enters into firm commitments to help in agricultural work according to its capabilities. During the stay in camp, which lasts from two to four weeks, with three to four hours work a day, the children take part in various types of work, and this helps to develop their agricultural knowledge, accomplishments and skills. The work is combined with recreation, and the stay in camp has an excellent effect not only on the general educational and poly-technical training of the pupils but also on their health.

A more thorough way of combining instruction with productive farm labour is provided by the integrated school brigade operating on collective and State farms and on experimental training farms, where work goes on all the year round. These brigades have well-equipped field camps. A special plot for cultivating a fruit orchard and doing experimental work is made over to the school brigade or experimental training farm for an extensive period (ten to fifteen years), and the pupils perform all operations from preparing the soil and sowing to harvesting the crop. The plot is regarded as part of the grown-ups' collective farm, and the children therefore take their commitments very seriously, and plan beforehand at a meeting of brigade members.

Experimental work is a compulsory part of that plan, as it is one of the most successful forms of combining theory and practice and developing the children's powers of observation, initiative,

---

1. If there are more than twenty-five pupils in the class, the regulations stipulate that it must be divided into two halves for this work.

creative approach to agricultural techniques and perseverance in achieving the objectives set.

In grades V–VII, the experiments are mainly of an educational nature, but even there the interest in them becomes greater when they are linked with practical jobs of economic significance. The senior pupils perform experiments aimed at increasing crop yields and livestock productivity, and in this way the scientific achievements of research institutes and experimental stations are introduced into agricultural practice. To work out the programme of topics and co-ordinate experimental work, *ad hoc* committees consisting of leading biology teachers, school directors, teachers at agricultural and teacher-training institutes and agricultnral experts have been set up under the auspices of the regional and district education departments.

High priority is given in experimental work to the growing of seeds of various species of hybrid maize and comparing their productivity; the study of new varieties of agricultural crops and the best time for sowing and planting in the locality concerned; the invigoration of wheat seeds by intervarietal crossing; experimentation with various systems of feeding and stabling agricultural livestock, and so on.

The brigades, groups and individual pupils compete with one another, and the results of their socialist competition are systematically evaluated and tabulated, and brought to the notice of all the brigade members. In the Stavropol territory, a new form of collective cross-check on results has been introduced, known as the territorial relay race. In each area the mutual check concludes with an assembly of brigade members at which the results of their work are announced, and which is addressed by leading workers in the area. The relay race ends with a territorial congress of brigade members at which a big exhibition, illustrating the productive, teaching, experimental and mass-education work done in the brigades during the agricultural year, is staged with the help of youth organizations and the territorial institute of advanced teacher training. This form of collective check on socialist competition is not only a powerful stimulus in improving the labour discipline of the brigade workers but is also an important means of uniting them into a single, friendly work community.

It was some time before the methodological experts and practical teachers found the most rational way of combining the theoretical syllabus material on biology with teaching and experimental work and socially useful agricultural work by the pupils. There were cases, for example, where teachers tried to prompt the children artificially at every lesson on botany, zoology or the principles of

Darwinism to reach certain conclusions an agronomy or animal husbandry; and there were also cases where the syllabus material on biology and the practical agricultural work done by the pupils were treated as two unconnected parallel processes. But these shortcomings have now been overcome in most schools: while taking care not to establish artificial connexions between biological and agricultural material, the teachers stress the link where this naturally follows from the subject matter, through exercises which allow the biological knowledge acquired to be used in practical work on the school plot or in farm production. The pupils' reports on their performance in these exercises, illustrated by herbaria prepared by them along with their log-books and records of experiments and observations, are the subject of very lively discussions in class.

The Young Naturalists' and agricultural experimenters' groups have come to play an increasingly important part in the poly-technical education and labour instruction, and their members are the biology teacher's best assistants in organizing practical work of all kinds. In the experience of many schools class work and out-of-class activities are intimately linked, each enriching and supplementing the other; and out-of-class naturalist and agricul-tural experimentation work helps to reveal and develop the pupils' bent for these branches of knowledge.

CHAPTER XIV

POLYTECHNICAL EDUCATION AS ILLUSTRATED IN THE TEACHING OF MATHEMATICS AND TECHNICAL DRAWING

by A. I. Fetissov and L. M. Gossudarsky

MATHEMATICS

Mathematics is a powerful instrument for learning about the world, helping man to achieve the rational control of natural phenomena and to dominate the forces of nature.

Mathematical sciences, which teach about the spatial forms and the quantitative correlations of the material world, comprise a very extensive field of the most varied objectives and their interrelationships. Because of the comprehensive nature of mathematical concepts, it is possible to express the correlations between the most diverse phenomena in a single short formula.

For instance, one and the same exponential function represents both the law of organic growth (the reproduction of bacteria, the increase in the number of trees in a forest), the speed of a chemical reaction, the cooling process of a heated body, the speed of disintegration of a radioactive substance, the absorption of light in a semi-transparent medium, and so on.

What methods does mathematics employ for learning about the world around us, foreseeing phenomena and controlling events?

The process may be described in the following terms. Suppose for a moment that we have to study a set of objects and the mutual relations between them. The mathematician uses certain objects (figures and numbers) linked together by specific laws. If he is able to establish a one-to-one correspondence between the concrete objects and the mathematical units, and in such a way that to every mutual relation between the objects of the first set corresponds a similar mutual relation of the corresponding objects of the second set, then the two sets are isometric.

Mathematicians therefore operate on units with which they are thoroughly familiar (numbers and figures) knowing that to these operations correspond certain transformations in a concrete set with the corresponding material objects. To explain what we mean, let us take a few examples.

To start with the simplest: let us suppose we are moving into a new flat. We have at our disposal a specific set of objects: the flat itself, and a specific aggregate of movable objects of furniture—chairs, tables, cupboards, etc. The question arises as to how this furniture is to be distributed in the best possible way in the space available. The most effective way of solving this problem will be to take a plan of the flat, drawn to scale, then cut out paper dummies of the pieces of furniture, according to the same scale, and move them about (in accordance with specific rules determined by the purpose of the objects) until we find the best solution of our problem. This is an example of two isometric sets, one concrete, the other geometrical.

Another example is that of a book-keeper who has to distribute wages between manual workers and office workers. On the one hand we have a concrete set: people, time, the produce of labour and money; on the other, an isometric set of symbols, in the hands of the book-keeper: lists of manual and office workers, tables and figures, determining the wages. By operating on the given symbols in accordance with certain rules, the book-keeper finds the appropriate solution.

And, lastly, a third example. Everyone knows about the great triumph of mathematical thought in the middle of the last century, when a new planet—Neptune—was discovered, through the work of Le Verrier and Adams, on the basis of calculations alone. In this instance the concrete object was the solar system with all the planets and their satellites, revolving round the central luminary, the sun. All that the mathematicians had at their disposal was an isometric set of 'material points', each with its spatial co-ordinates and numbers representing its masses and speeds. In short, all that the mathematicians had at their disposal were figures. The movements of the material bodies of the solar system are subject to the law of universal gravitation; for the mathematicians this corresponded to the well-known formula; the figure expressing the force of attraction is directly proportional to the figure equal to the product of the masses and inversely proportional to the square of the distance.

Guided by this principle, and taking account of general numerical laws, astronomers succeeded in solving an exceedingly complex problem—that of finding the co-ordinates of a hitherto unknown material point; they thus enabled man to see the real object corresponding thereto—the planet Neptune.

Whenever a set of concrete objects has to be represented in a set of numbers, there arises the problem of measuring the corresponding quantities. Experience has shown that direct measurement is often very difficult, sometimes completely impossible. Hence there arises a new and extremely important mathematical problem —that of the indirect measurement of quantities. This problem is so vital that some scientists have even defined mathematics as 'the science of the indirect measurement of quantities'. This is, of course, too narrow a definition, but it does nevertheless show how important this problem is. In fact, when we remember how many vitally important numerical values we have obtained by means of indirect measurement, we realize its great importance.

It is, after all, by indirect measurement that we have calculated the dimensions and mass of the earth, the distance to the moon, the sun and the planets, the dimensions of the Milky Way, the distance from the earth to the furthest stellar systems, the dimensions of the microcosm—atoms and atomic nuclei, the mass and charge of the electron, and the mass and charge of other particles. In all these cases, a wide variety of mathematical laws had to be applied for working out the data obtained by measurements, observations and experiments.

The multiform quantitative mutual relations between the objects of the material universe have been represented in a variety of numerical symbols. Thus for the representation of discrete quantities, the comparison of which is carried out by means of their confrontation, natural numbers (the result of calculation) began to be used. Subsequently, the need for expressing a part of an object which is divisible led to the introduction of fractions. In order to represent continuous quantities irrational numbers were introduced. The correlations between directed numbers (vectors) began to be represented first by negative numbers, then by complex numbers and finally by quaternions. All possible connexions and relationships between quantities found their representation in the mathematical concept of functional dependence—the most important concept of modern mathematics.

As regards spatial forms, their representations are, primarily, basic geometrical concepts, the mutual relations between which are determined on the basis of axioms, and the deductions from these axioms on the basis of theorems. The mutual relations between concrete spatial objects and the changes occurring in them are represented in the basic geometrical concept—transformation, comprising the correlations of symmetry, equality, similarity, affinity and collinearity. All changes to which spatial forms are subject, such as parallel displacement, revolution about an axis and a point, change of size without change of form, and deformations of all kinds (contractions, shifts, twisting, etc.), are also represented as transformations. The present century has seen the development of a new branch of mathematics, namely, topology, in which a study is made of the very profound transformations of spatial figures.

Thus, generally speaking, the process of learning about reality with the help of mathematics may be described as follows: first we have to select the objects of the set we wish to study and elucidate the laws to which it is subject. These laws are revealed and studied by means of natural, economic and other sciences. We then construct an isomorphous set of mathematical objects, representing as accurately as possible the particular objectively existing set. By carrying out mathematical operations on our objects it becomes possible for us to describe the given state of the set as a whole, as well as to forecast its behaviour when we introduce changes into the mutual relations of its elements. It is easy to check that any practical or theoretical problem to be solved by mathematical methods will fit into this scheme.

In this connexion it must be pointed out that in mathematics itself there is a tendency to make very broad generalizations embracing isometric sets of objects of an exceedingly varied nature. An example of this is the concept of groups and the concept of mathematical structure, which is of very recent origin.

Equipped with these very general and comprehensive concepts representing objective reality and with powerful methods, modern mathematics penetrates into the most diverse and sometimes most unexpected spheres of human activity. The discovery of the secrets of the atomic nucleus, the mastery of the inexhaustible stores of energy it contains, flights into space, the invention of calculating machines which outstrip even the most skilled reckoners—all these results have been achieved through mathematics.

Let us now consider what methods can be used for teaching people to handle this amazing mathematical instrument. Training begins with the very first activities of children in school, from the moment they begin to count objects, that is, bring several concrete objects of a given set into one-to-one correspondence (sticks, beads, balls on the abacus, etc.) with the words one, two, three . . . and then with the symbols 1, 2, 3 . . .

They then learn the operation of uniting several such aggregates into one, and how to represent them by numerical symbols with which they are already familiar, that is, in the written form: $3 + 5 = 8$, and so on.

However, as the study of mathematics becomes more and more advanced, so the connexion between concrete objects and the abstract concepts taught in class becomes less and less obvious. But the connexion always exists, and it is the teacher's job to help his pupils to see it. They often have difficulty in understanding that concrete objects or their correlations are represented by complex numbers, and they are genuinely astonished to learn from the teacher, for example, that Professor N. E. Zhukovsky's research on the lifting power of an aeroplane wing, which marked an important stage in the development of aviation, was based on the theory of the function of the complex variable.

It is obvious that the teaching of mathematics, as a science in isolation, is essentially abstract, divorced from real objects and phenomena and from the social and productive life of man. But teaching along these lines is not scientific.

We know how great a role is played by mathematics in everyday life and in production, and mathematics teaching in schools should do everything possible to make the pupils understand its significance. It should start from a set of several concrete objects which we can see, feel, measure and with which various operations can be carried out, and end with mathematical objects (numbers or figures) on which similar operations can also be carried out. If all the concrete objects are production objects or operations, then the teaching of mathematics will contribute to polytechnical training.

It must be remembered that polytechnical training is not merely an expansion of the syllabus or an incidental addition to the school course; it is a fundamental basis determining both the content and the methods of teaching.

Polytechnical training in mathematics must not be regarded as the preparation of pupils for any specific profession. It helps them acquire the knowledge and skills which are essential for all professions and all types of practical work. It is precisely from this angle that we must regard the content and methods of teaching mathematics in schools.

From the point of view of the subject matter, school mathematics is usually divided into arithmetic, algebra, geometry and trigonometry. To treat trigonometry as a separate subject, however, cannot be regarded as appropriate, since the material it covers consists partly of geometry and partly of algebra. Table 16 overleaf shows the number of periods spent on each subject, class by class.

In this division of school mathematics into separate subjects two basic trends are to be distinguished, corresponding to the dual content of the subject of mathematics. The first trend (the study of quantitative correlations) relates to arithmetic and algebra; the second (the study of spatial forms) to geometry. In the study of quantitative correlations, several basic lines determining the fundamental content of the school course in arithmetic and algebra are also distinguishable. The first of these lines is arithmetical and is mainly concerned with the evolution of the concept of numbers. This theme runs through the whole of the school course, from the first grade to the last, beginning with counting and ordinary numbers and ending with complex numbers. From the point of view of polytechnical education it is extremely important that pupils should understand at every stage the development of the concept of numbers, that numbers represent the quantitative correlations of the material world, including technology and production; and that operations on figures correspond to specific operations on real objects.

This is taken into account in the arithmetic of integers and fractions. The position is, however, much less satisfactory as

TABLE 16.   Number of teaching periods spent on each subject, by class

Grade	Arithmetic	Algebra	Geometry
	Periods and subject	Periods and subject	Periods and subject
I	210 Integral numbers and operations on them		
II	210		
III	210 Solving arithmetical problems		
IV	210 Simple measurements		
V	40 Real numbers. Divisibility 66 Ordinary fractions 90 Decimal fractions. Operations with fractions		
VI	34 Approximate calculations. Percentages 34 Ratios and proportions	36 Algebraic expressions. Rational numbers. Equations 44 Transformation of integral algebraic expressions	16 Basic concepts. Triangles. Parallelism
VII		24 Linear equations 60 Transformation of expressions 32 Graphs and systems of linear equations	20 Quadrangles 30 Areas. Volume of prism 34 Periphery

290

Grade	Arithmetic	Algebra	Geometry
	Periods and subject	Periods and subject	Periods and subject
VIII		9 Logarithmical slide-rule 44 Quadratic equations 36 Functions and graphs	44 Similarity of figures. Trigonometrical functions 12 Inscribed and circumscribed polygons 20 Area, surface and volume of geometrical bodies
IX		24 Linear equations 20 Real numbers and quadratic equations 66 Goniometry	20 Loci and transformations on a plane 26 Metrical correlations in triangles and circles
X		14 Numerical sequence 30 Power functions 20 Exponential and logarithmic functions	22 Straight lines and planes in space 16 Dihedral and polyhedral angles 16 Polyhedrons 24 Spherical bodies
XI		16 General notions on functions 36 Investigation by means of derivatives 16 Complex numbers	26 Measurement of volumes 25 Revision and solution of problems

regards irrational and real numbers, when it is essential to show the pupils that these represent the aggregate of points on a straight line, for instance, or the quantity of moments of time, and so on. The concepts of positive and negative numbers represent quantities having two opposite directions. The concept of complex numbers is best defined as the ratio of two vectors belonging to one and the same plane. Given this definition, the part played by complex numbers in the study of various vectorial fields becomes quite clear. Parallel with the study of numbers pupils also learn about the processes whereby these numbers are found, namely, direct and indirect mensuration. The pupils have to carry out all kinds of mensurations themselves, learn to check their degree of accuracy, and perform all the necessary calculations on the results, using the method of approximate computation. The material for these mensurations is obtained in the course of field work, practical work, excursions, and so on.

Schoolchildren start measuring work from the first class at

school. They learn how to use the simplest measuring instruments, and how to read their scale. At the same time, they are taught how to judge distances by eye, on paper, on the blackboard, in the classroom and outdoors. Later, when they reach the intermediary grades, they learn to handle more complicated and more precise instruments, such as sliding callipers, inside callipers and micrometers. In addition to making direct readings on the scale, they also make readings using a nonius and a vernier; in grade VIII, they study the diagonal scale, and how to use it for the measurement of lengths. In grade VI, they are already learning how to measure angles with the help of protractors and astrolabes. After measuring angles and lengths, children then go on to learning how to make indirect measurements, so as to be able to measure inaccessible angles, altitudes and distances. The special techniques used in making these measurements are taught in the senior grades, in connexion with trigonometry.

They also learn how to measure areas and volumes. The main task of mathematical theory in this case is to reduce the measurement of these quantities to the measurement of lines. In the senior grades, however, the pupils have to learn how to make indirect measurements of areas, using the graticule, Amster's planimeter and the hatchet planimeter.

The task of polytechnical education is to combine these measurement studies effectively with the pupils' practical work in workshops and factories, solving specific practical problems. As a general rule, the results of measurement are checked, in the process of which pupils acquire a number of practical skills, the most important being the ability to operate with approximate numbers; they also learn to handle the simplest calculating instruments such as the abacus, the slide-rule and the arithometer.

The measurements carried out by schoolchildren are not, however, restricted to the narrow range of geometrical quantities; depending on the pupils' practical work, they may learn how to measure time, with a chronometer or a stop-watch; temperature, with thermometers of all kinds; pressure, with a barometer or a pressure gauge; specific weights of liquids, with a hydrometer; the strength and tension of an electric current and the resistance of conductors, with the appropriate instruments.

Here the polytechnical orientation of the mathematics course is ensured by the fact that all these measuring operations are included as an integral part in the subject matter of the pupils' exercises. Instead of taking examples from a textbook, pupils are asked to solve problems the data of which they provide themselves. For instance, they may be required to find the area of a plot of ground.

They will measure the sides of the plot with a measuring tape, and the angles with a goniometer. Using the theorem of the sum of the interior angles of a polygon, they then check the accuracy of the results they have obtained, and correct the error, if any. They make a scaled plan of the plot, and then determine the area either by trigonometrical means, with a graticule, or with a planimeter (or best of all, using all these methods and comparing the results).

Even this comparatively simple operation possesses features which are important from the point of view of pedagogy and teaching method. The pupils see how real objects, through the process of measurement, are represented by specific numbers; how these numbers are then used for constructing an isometric chart; and how, finally, the operations on that chart are transferred back to the original object.

The second basic line of quantitative correlations—the algebraical line—relates to the study of the most general laws governing operations on quantities. In this course, schoolchildren learn how to handle transformed algebraic expressions, and how to carry out direct and inverse operations, which in turn enables them to solve equations. The process of working out and solving an equation according to the terms of the problem illustrates very clearly the basic principle of the mathematical cognition of reality, namely, the representation of concrete sets of elements and of their mutual relations by means of mathematical symbols, so that by carrying out operations on these symbols, it is possible to discover new, hitherto unknown mutual relations in the corresponding concrete set. In this connexion, it is very important that the terms of the problems should be carefully selected, and represent sets actually existing in life, production and related sciences. Exercises in which the children are able to find the numerical data for solution of the problem themselves, by making their own experiments, observations and measurements are particularly useful. To give an example: a method fairly frequently used in chemistry is that of indirect analysis. Let us suppose that we know the weight of a mixture of two substances AP and BP, where A, B and P represent atoms all having the same valency. Let us suppose also that we can isolate the substance P from this mixture, and find the weight of the remainder. We are required to find the quantities, by weight, of the substances AP and BP respectively. If we take g to denote the weight of the mixture, and x and y to denote the unknown weights AP and BP we obtain the first equation:

$$x + y = g.$$

If we then take a, b and p to denote the corresponding atomic or molecular weights of the substances A, B and P, and q to denote the weight of the isolated substance P, we obtain another equation as follows:

$$\frac{x}{a+p} + \frac{y}{b+p} = \frac{q}{p}.$$

By solving these equations, we obtain the value of x and y. By this means it is possible, for instance, to find the composition of a mixture of sodium chloride and potassium chloride by isolating the chloride contained in the two mixtures, and the composition of a mixture of calcium carbonate and strontium carbonate, by isolating the carbonic-acid gas.

A second example of a problem, leading to a set of linear equations, may be taken from the field of electrical engineering. Let us suppose that we have a network of wires which the current enters at one point and leaves at another. The problem is to find the strength of the current in each section of the network, the force of the resistance being known.

When working out the corresponding equations, Kirchhof's well-known laws are used. By this means it is possible, for instance, to find the resistance of the conductor, using a Wheatstone bridge.

Finally, the third line in the study of quantitative relations is analytical. The most important concept here is that of functional dependence, which reflects the multiple links existing between the objects and phenomena of the material world. It is absolutely essential that pupils should understand that all the diverse events occurring in the world around them and in production are subjects to laws establishing a causal relationship between these events, and that the task of mathematics is to represent these relationships in terms of functional dependence, in mathematical symbols.

It is important not to skimp the time spent on this subject, and to give plenty of examples of all sorts of relationships, taken from everyday life, science, technology and production.

Let us take a few examples. The relationship between the quantity of a commodity and its value is expressed by the simplest linear function (simple proportionality). A more general example is the relation between the length of a metal rod and its temperature.

Quadratic functions express the dependence on time of the path traversed by a freely falling body at the surface of the earth; also the relation between the temperature of the conductor and the strength of the current (Lenz's law).

Fractional functions of the first degree are used to express the relation between the volume of gas and the pressure (law of Boyle and Mariotte). Fractional functions are used also to express the law of gravitation and Coulomb's law regarding the force of electrical attraction between two charged bodies being proportional to the square of the distance between them.

Irrational (quadratic) functions are used to express the relation between the speed of flow of a liquid through an aperture in the bottom of a vessel and the height of the level of the liquid above the aperture.

The second trend of mathematical theory (geometry) deals with the spatial properties of our universe, in other words, the properties which determine the shape and magnitude of objects, and their position in relation to one another. The primary task of poly-technical education in the teaching of geometry is to give pupils the fullest possible understanding of the concept of an object's shape. They learn to recognize, differentiate between and name the shape of all kinds of different objects in their home surroundings, in the classroom, in the workshop and on excursions to the country and to enterprises. When, for instance, a child learns about the triangle and its main property (rigidity) he must then learn to pick out this shape in the rafters of roofs, in wicket gates where the diagonal bar introduces the shape of a triangle, and prevents deformation, and in the frame of a bicycle.

Schoolchildren continue their study of geometry by learning about the correlations between spatial forms. It is necessary to explain to them the correlations of equality, symmetry, parallelism, perpendicularity, similarity; and here again, they have to distinguish all these relations in the objects around them—the idea of symmetry, for instance, can be grasped by observing the symmetry of the leaf of a plant, a flower, the wings of a butterfly, by observing a crystal, technical appliances, things in the home, ornaments, etc.

A concept particularly important in geometry is that of transformation. It is essential to draw attention to the fact that, in the vast majority of cases, the main technical operation is to confer on objects a specific shape. This is precisely the purpose of all kinds of machine tools—planing machines, cutting machines, turning machines, grinding machines, and so on. In all these cases one and the same task is carried out—that of transforming one geometrical form into another and this is what schoolchildren, too, must learn to do with the help of the instruments at their disposal. They must be made to grasp the fundamental idea that symmetrical, identical, and similar shapes do not arise spontaneously, but are the result of purposeful action. For this reason, considerable attention must be devoted to exercises in transforming given figures into identical, symmetrical and similar shapes. The entire geometry course, from beginning to end, is planned on the basis of 'constructivism', in the sense that children are constantly required to construct the geometrical figures. For instance, for the theorem of equilateral triangles we must begin by constructing a triangle equal in regard to some of its elements to the one given; and then proceed to demonstrate that all the other elements of the triangle are correspondingly equal. The question of the similarity of figures must be dealt with in the same way.

The concept of transformation acquires particular significance in the process of representing solid bodies by projectional drawing on a flat plane. All the stages of this process, starting with the operation of projecting and ending with the reconstruction of the corresponding geometrical figure and its projection, are of the utmost practical significance. We only have to remember that any kind of technical construction whatsoever—instruments, apparatus, machines, architectural structure, etc.—is first conceived in the mind of the constructor, then transferred to paper in the form of a projectional drawing, and it is from this drawing that it is translated into reality in the form of the corresponding object. Hence the ability to draw plans, to decipher technical drawings and to reconstruct solid objects according to such drawings is an essential part of polytechnical education.

It must not be supposed, however, that polytechnical education relegates the second important aspect of geometry teaching—the method of deduction—to the background. It is extremely important in everyday life, in production work and in science alike to be able to make correct deduction from established facts. Pupils must learn to think clearly, to analyse and synthesize, and to spot mistakes and errors. Having established the fact that the basic geometrical concepts and axioms are derived from the working experience of all mankind over many centuries, we can then show, from numerous examples that, given the ability to make correct deductions from the knowledge we possess, it is possible to use one set of facts in order to forecast other, new facts. Herein lies the key to the power of the human intellect with its ability to dominate and bring natural phenomena under its control. The importance of deductive conclusions is that they can be used for establishing general, universally applicable truths. The theorem regarding the sum of the internal angles of a triangle was true in ancient Egypt, is true now, and is equally true on the moon and on Mars.

Another very important aspect of geometry is the measurement of geometrical quantities. After starting by direct measurement of lengths and angles, pupils go on gradually to grasp the idea of making indirect measurements of geometrical quantities. They may start by measuring inaccessible altitudes and distances, using the axial or central-symmetry method. Then the theorem of Pythagoras provides an example of dependence whereby the length of some segments can be calculated by measuring the length of other segments. The whole of the study of the solution of triangles by means of trigonometrical functions centres round the problem of indirect measurement and the whole of the theory of the measurement of area and volume is concerned with reducing the measurement of these quantities to measurement of certain segments, that is, to measurement of lengths.

It is essential that pupils should do exercises and solve problems of every kind—problems of computation, construction and demonstration. It is also essential that they should learn to solve problems directly connected with their practical work in workshops and production, learning from the standpoint of geometry, about the shape of the machine part being made and of working tools. A number of construction problems can be solved in the process of making a machine part according to a given sample. This involves carrying out both elementary construction operations (cutting off a segment identical with the one given, tracing the perpendiculars and parallels, dividing the segment and angle into two halves, and so on) and also more complicated operations, such as determining the centre of gyration when bringing the given component into a new position.

What then are the conclusions to be drawn regarding the methods to be employed in carrying out polytechnical education? The first and most important point is that teachers must endeavour, in mathematics lessons, to make the children play as active a part as possible. They must learn to regard the classroom as a laboratory where they are always at work. At the same time, the teacher must make sure that the children never lose sight of the fundamental significance of mathematics and that, both in the workshop and on excursions, they are constantly on the look-out for applications of mathematical laws, and observing geometrical shapes and the relations between them.

Polytechnical education imposes serious responsibilities on teachers. First of all, they have to remember that their main task is to teach children mathematics and that mathematics lessons should not become merely an adjunct to lessons on mechanics, electrical engineering or any other technical subject. The main principles of mathematics should be explained to the children as fully as possible, and they should fully understand the vital importance of the part played by mathematics in technology, production and related disciplines. There should be co-ordination between the various subjects in the school syllabus. Every subject, including mathematics, should be regarded as part of a single, integrated body of knowledge directed towards one and the same general purpose.

In order to make the teaching of mathematics more active, it is essential to adopt methods and practices involving the maximum participation of the pupils themselves, such as heuristic methods, inductive-genetic methods and laboratory work.

Let us consider, for instance, the process of teaching children to understand mathematical concepts. In the traditional form, the teacher simply gives a logical definition of each new concept, which the children then have to study and memorize. The result is that a large proportion of the pupils, though they may be able to repeat the teacher's definition word for word, do not in fact understand what it means. The position is entirely different if the teacher, when introducing a new concept, gradually reveals the content of this concept by means of examples, and then finally, when he is sure the children understand it correctly, asks them to give their own definition of the concept. The same method should be used in formulating other propositions as well. Intensive measures must be taken to train children to demand demonstration, and to teach them that demonstration gives to a proposition the universality and necessity by which mathematical knowledge is characterized.

TECHNICAL DRAWING

Without technical drawings, normal work is impossible in contemporary industrial and agricultural production, transportation, communications and building enterprises. Without the ability to interpret and execute simple production drawings, it is difficult, and sometimes even impossible, to carry out any work or to acquire technical knowledge. Hence the importance attached to technical drawing in polytechnical education.

The purpose of teaching technical drawing in Soviet secondary school is:

1. To give pupils a knowledge of the principles of the method of right-angled projection on one, two, or more reciprocally perpendicular planes of projection, and the construction of visual representations in axonometric projection (right-angled isometric and oblique-angled frontal diametric projection).

2. To promote the development of the pupils' spatial concepts and imagination, which are of great importance in production and creative technical work; to teach pupils how to analyse

the form and design of objects, and to reconstruct similar objects from drawings (to read or interpret a drawing).

3. To teach the independent use of textbooks and reference sources in the practice of interpreting and executing drawings, sketches and technical designs; to acquaint pupils with the most important rules, conventional signs and designations used in technical drawing, as laid down by the State All-Union Standards (GOST).

4. To assist the training of pupils in habits of proper organization of their workplace, rational methods of work with drawing and measuring instruments, accuracy and precision in their work, the execution of drawing exercises in a set period of time, etc.

The drawing syllabus also provides for familiarizing pupils with some production techniques. For instance, when the drawing of components, assemblies and manufactured articles is set as an exercise, the pupils become familiar with their names, their uses, the materials from which they are made, and with some data on their manufacture. This is not, however, the main purpose of the course.

Drawing in the secondary school is a general-education subject; its teaching is not aimed at the training of students as draughtsmen-copyists. Secondary-school leavers employed in production are required not so much to make drawings as to interpret them. Instruction in the interpretation of the simplest technical drawings therefore takes first place. All drawings are executed in pencil only.

The teaching of technical drawing begins in grade VII and ends in grade IX. A summary of the syllabus for this subject is given below.

GRADE VII (*one period a week, 36 periods in all*)

INTRODUCTION

Drawing. The importance of drawing in people's practical work; the purposes of drawing in the school.

Summarizing of the knowledge of drawing and technical design acquired in work lessons by the pupils in grades V and VI.

The instruments, materials and other equipment needed. The choice of pencils according to their degree of hardness and preparation of pencils for work. Rubbers. Drawing-boards and T-squares or rulers. Drawing triangles. Compasses and the attachment of pencils. Dividers. Paper. Sizes of drawings.

Understanding of the State All-Union Standards (GOST), with special reference to 'Drawings for mechanical engineering'.

Organization of the work place. Preparation of scaled frames for technical drawings, with inset for specifications.

Learning of standard lettering. Lettering in the specifications inset and on the drawing itself.

SUBJECT 1. WAYS OF REPRESENTING OBJECTS IN DRAWINGS

A. *Right-angled projections*

Right-angled projections as the principal method used in technical work for making drawings of objects.

Making projections of an object on two or three reciprocally perpendicular planes of projection. Arrangement of projections in a drawing and their terminology—main view (frontal projection), view from above (horizontal projection), view from the left (side-on projection).

Building-up of a drawing. Construction lines, lines of the visible contour, lines of the invisible contour, axial and centred lines.

Analysis of the geometric form of an object. Splitting-up of an object into simple geometric bodies (cube, parallelepiped, prism, cylinder, cone, pyramid and sphere). Finding in a drawing of the apexes, edges and surfaces making up the object.

The interpretation and execution of sketches, drawings, visual representations and technical drawings of objects containing rectilinear and curved elements which must be represented by means of standard geometrical construction methods; division of a segment and a circumference into equal parts; the conjugation of angles by means of arcs; the conjugation of two circumferences by a straight line and by an arc with a given radius; the conjugation of a circumference by a straight line with the help of an arc having a given radius. Finding the points of conjugation and the centres of conjugate arcs.

The marking of dimensions externally by extension. Rules regarding the different lines for writing the figures indicating dimensions. Symbol for the diameter, for the radius and for a square. Written indication of the thickness and length of any component. The scaling of drawings and the relevant terminology.

The order of operations in sketching a component (from life) and the execution of a drawing from a study.

B. *Visual representations in axonometric projections*

The idea of axonometric representations and their use in technical drawing.

The execution of plane figures and components having prismatic and pyramidal forms in oblique-angled dimetric and right-angled isometric projections. The direction of the axes, indices of distortion. The marking of dimensions.

Visual representations of components having a cylindric and conical shape: (a) in oblique-angled frontal dimetric projection (showing the circumference in a frontal plane); (b) in right-angled isometric projection (replacing the ellipse with an oval consisting of the arcs of the circumferences).

Execution of technical drawings of components.

N.B. It is recommended that the study and execution of visual representations and technical drawings should go hand in hand with the study and execution of drawings of right-angled projections.

SCOPE OF THEORETICAL AND PRACTICAL KNOWLEDGE AND OF SKILLS

At the end of the academic year, pupils in grade VII should:
1. Have an understanding of the methods of projecting objects adopted in technical drawing (method of right-angled projection and of axonometric projection).
2. Have an understanding of designs, sketches, visual representations and technical drawings and their purpose.
3. Be acquainted with the basic rules for constructing designs.
4. Be able to interpret and execute sketches, designs, visual representations and technical drawings of simple objects which form the basis of the main geometric bodies.
5. Know the correct methods of handling drawing and measuring instruments and rational methods of work.

GRADE VIII (*one period a week, 36 periods in all*)

SUBJECT 2. INTERPRETATION AND EXECUTION OF SKETCHES, DESIGNS, VISUAL REPRESENTATIONS AND TECHNICAL DRAWINGS OF COMPONENTS, BY USING SOME OF THE CONVENTIONS OF TECHNICAL DESIGN

A. *Sections and segments*

Understanding of working drawings of components and their purpose. Purpose of sections. Simple sections. Horizontal and vertical sections (front and side views). Combining a half-view of an object with half-section thereof. Local sections.
Understanding of segments. Difference between sections and segments. Segments drawn as part of and separated from the whole. Hatching in sections and segments. Marking of sections and segments on drawings.

B. *A few conventions and simplifications*

Representation of a screw-thread viewed axially and from the screw-hole. Designation of screw-threads according to the metric system.
The use of conventional lines to indicate part of an object not represented in full. Supplementary views of individual parts. Designation of the component parts of a square segment.
Inclination and study of cones.

SUBJECT 3. GENERAL ASSEMBLY DRAWINGS

Understanding of general assembly drawings and their purpose. Specifications. Sections on general assembly drawings. Hatching of contiguous components.
Detailed interpretation of a general assembly drawing of an article consisting of 4 to 8 components.

301

SCOPE OF THEORETICAL AND PRACTICAL KNOWLEDGE AND OF SKILLS

At the end of the academic year, pupils in grade VIII should:
1. Have an understanding of a working drawing of a component and its purpose; of sections and segments, of the conventional representation of a screw-thread and of other simplifications adopted in technical design. Be able to turn their knowledge to practical account in interpreting and executing sketches and designs.
2. Be able to use reference books on drawing.
3. Be able to interpret and prepare sketches and working drawings of simple components of machinery, equipment, fittings, etc.
4. Have an understanding of general assembly drawings and their purpose.
5. Be able to interpret simple general assembly drawings of manufactured objects consisting of four to eight components.

GRADE IX *(two periods a week, 78 periods in all)*

SUBJECT 4. APPLICATION OF THE METHODS OF DESCRIPTIVE GEOMETRY TO TECHNICAL DESIGN (26 PERIODS)

Repetition and summarizing of the knowledge acquired in the eight-year school. The drawing of prisms, pyramids, cylinders and cones as intersected at different projection planes. Determination of the actual magnitudes of segments and their development, marking the end of each segment on the developed plane.

Execution of a complex drawing of a sphere. Drawing of two geometric bodies with intersecting surfaces in their simplest positions and forms (e.g., two prisms, a prism and a cylinder, two cylinders, a cone and a cylinder).

Conventional representation in drawings of the convergence of surfaces.

Practical work in the interpretation and execution of drawings of machine parts containing intersecting and contiguous lines.

SUBJECT 5. SKETCHES, TECHNICAL DESIGNS AND DRAWINGS (12 PERIODS)

Complex drawings from six angles, their designation and distribution. The choice of the main viewpoint. Choice of the right number of views. Partial views.

Simple and complicated sections. Partial sections. Conventional representation of the path of intersecting planes and of the direction of projection.

The actual execution of sketches, technical drawings and drawings of components, together with the use of simple and complex sections.

Interpretation of working drawings.

SUBJECT 6. REPRESENTATION OF CONNEXIONS OF COMPONENTS (10 PERIODS)

Representation of connexions made by means of bolts, screws, studs, splines, dowel pins, rivets and welding.

Practical execution of drawings and sketches of detachable connexions.

SUBJECT 7. GENERAL ASSEMBLY DRAWINGS (22 PERIODS)

The general assembly drawing and its purpose. The numbering of the separate items of a drawing in correct sequence and compilation of the specifications. Execution of sketches of parts of a simple assembly, unit or manufactured article consisting of six to eight components.

Execution of a sketch of an assembly in one projection for the purpose of determining the relative position of the separate parts.

Execution of a general assembly drawing from sketches of the component parts.

Interpretation of a general assembly drawing by study of the separate parts. Execution of sketches and working drawings with four to six components.

Exercises in interpreting general assembly drawings by written answers to questions.

SUBJECT 8. BUILDING DRAWINGS (8 PERIODS)

The main differences between drawings of buildings and those of machinery. Scales. The various aspects and their designation. Sections and hatching in sections. The marking of dimensions. Conventional representations of door and window openings and of lighting, heating, sewage and household installations. The interpretation of building drawings. Sketching of a classroom or some small construction and execution of a drawing from the sketch.

Extra lessons in technical drawing are sometimes included in the grade X course, depending on the particular field in which the pupils are specializing. For instance, the following supplementary material will be included in courses for prospective building designers.

GRADE X

Subject 1. Graphic conventions used in drawings of buildings. Hatching in sections profiles and elevations. Constructional elements of buildings: apertures (windows, doors, gates), staircases, stoves, sanitary and technical installations.

Subject 2. Basic drawings of buildings. Plans, sections, elevations. Familiarity with sketches of buildings.

Subject 3. Conventions used in drawing the main components of buildings. Foundations, walls and partitions, floors, ceilings, roofing and roofs, staircases, etc.

Subject 4. Exercises in the execution of construction drawings.

Subject 5. Exercises in interpreting construction drawings.

303

In his lessons, the teacher is free to choose the order of presentation of the subjects and to decide on the matters to be dealt with, the degree of complexity and the character of the exercises and technical drawings.

Pupils taking drawing at school acquire a knowledge of the elementary principles of technical drawing, practical ability and skills in the interpretation and execution of technical drawings and sketches, and of simple components of machines, equipment and gear, typical of modern technology (see Fig. 28). Having acquired these abilities, the graduating pupils will be prepared for work in modern production, able to interpret and execute simple industrial drawings and to follow sketches contained in books and instructions. While studying drawing at school, pupils become familiar with new ways of getting to know and understand the real world and the world of technical knowledge through the aid of sketches and through visual representation. The drawing lessons develop the students' capacity for observation, comparison, and analysis of geometrical forms and their relative position.

Besides acquiring a body of ideas about space, the student develops a spatial imagination, the ability to synthesize and visualize (with or without an actual picture) the representation in space of a non-existent object from a design, or an object not directly visible, or, on the contrary, to visualize an actual object as a plane figure. This promotes in the students an ability and inclination for the study of technical subjects, technical work and invention of equipment, which is of special importance for the fulfilment of the objectives of polytechnical education.

The study of technical drawing at school speeds up the learning of all subjects in the school curriculum for which illustrations of any kind are required (e.g., drawings, visual representations, developments, diagrams, etc.). Drawing is of special importance for geometry, physics, mechanics and electrical engineering.

In teaching technical drawing, the teacher usually begins with a talk or explanation, during which objects, geometrical bodies, visual representations and drawings of them are shown. Particular attention is given to explaining methods of representation. A short time (about five to fifteen minutes) is set aside at the beginning of the lesson for theoretical explanations which are of limited scope in the lower grades. For the rest of the lesson, the theoretical knowledge is fixed in the pupils' minds by exercises in the interpretation of drawings, the execution of technical drawings, sketches and designs, first from life as a class assignment (the same for the whole class), and later as individual assignments not only from life but also from visual representations and drawings. These exercises are completed in the following lessons and may be very different from one another. Visual representations and drawings are executed not only from life or from other visual representations but also from descriptive accounts. An exercise frequently given is the preparation of a third or additional projection on the basis of two given projections, the execution of sections and segments, the bending of a surface into a plane (development), the execution of models, the detection of errors in drawings and the answering of questions on drawing.

Since the main purpose of teaching technical drawing is the acquisition of practical knowledge and skills by pupils, most of the time during the lessons is taken up with exercises and graphic work, particularly individual assignments.

The pupils' ability is judged mainly on the basis of the drawings and sketches they execute.

At the end of each term (four a year), half-year and year, the pupils' knowledge of all the subjects studied is tested. As a rule, pupils do individual tests or one of the four to six set tests.

High teaching standards are maintained not only through the use of correct methods but also through the material facilities provided for technical-drawing lessons. The schools have either separate rooms for drawing lessons or joint mathematics and drawing classrooms. They are mostly equipped with tables having movable drawing-boards. The machine parts, etc., needed for executing studies from life are usually procured by the school from nearby industrial enterprises that are patrons of the school. Apart from the drawing work done in the classroom, out-of-class activities such as hobby groups, competitions and exhibitions of drawings are also organized.

CHAPTER XV

POLYTECHNICAL EDUCATION AS ILLUSTRATED IN HISTORY AND GEOGRAPHY TEACHING

by N. G. Dairi and I. I. Samoilov

HISTORY

Schoolchildren receive their first notions of history from a reader in their native language in grades I–III. The school curriculum provides for a separate 'historical episode' course in grade IV. This consists of stories from the history of the U.S.S.R. concerning the life of working people before the Revolution, the October Socialist Revolution, the civil war and the intervention, the building of socialism in the U.S.S.R., the Great War of 1941–45 and the present intensive communist construction in the U.S.S.R. These are short accounts suitable to the children's age, arranged in chronological order. Seventy-two lesson periods are set aside for this course.

Children in grade V take an elementary course in foreign ancient history (72 periods). The course is divided into the following sections: life of primitive man, the ancient East (Egypt, Mesopotamia, India, China), ancient Greece, ancient Rome.

Children in grade VI take an elementary course in foreign mediaeval history (72 periods). This comprises the following sections: (a) establishment of the feudal system; Western and Central Europe; the Eastern Roman (Byzantine) Empire; the Arabs from the sixth to the eleventh centuries; (b) development of feudalism; development of crafts and trade, growth of towns in Western Europe; the Christian Church from the eleventh to the thirteenth centuries; the Crusades; formation of centralized States in Western Europe; the popular movement in Bohemia against the Catholic Church and German domination, the Peasants' War; the Ottoman Empire and national struggles against the Turkish conquerors; Western European culture from the twelfth to the fifteenth centuries; China in the Middle Ages; India in the Middle Ages; (c) beginnings of the decline of feudalism; development of technology in Western Europe—geographical discoveries, colonies;

development in sixteenth-century England; the Peasants' War in Germany, the Reformation in Western Europe; the absolute monarchy in France; the Netherlands revolution; European culture at the end of the fifteenth and in the first half of the sixteenth century.

Pupils of grades VII and VIII take an elementary course in the history of the U.S.S.R., including the most important facts about the country's social and political system, with some information about the modern and contemporary history of foreign countries (177 periods). This course comprises the following sections: Russia in ancient times; rise and development of feudalism (until the mid-eighteenth century); developments in Western Europe and North America; decline of serfdom and development of capitalist relationships in Russia (from the end of the eighteenth century to 1861); rise of the labour and national liberation in foreign countries; origins of scientific communism; Russia during the period of capitalism (from 1861 to the end of the nineteenth century); the transition to imperialism; the bourgeois-democratic revolutions in Russia; the victory of the October Socialist Revolution and the building of socialism in the U.S.S.R.; the second world war; the U.S.S.R. in the postwar years; foreign countries after the second world war; entry of the U.S.S.R. into the period of intensive communist construction; basic law of the Soviet Socialist State (social system, political system and State organs, fundamental rights and duties of Soviet citizens).

The syllabuses for grades IX, X and XI in general secondary polytechnical schools include systematic courses in modern and contemporary history and in the history of the U.S.S.R.

Grade IX covers the first period of foreign modern history, from the mid-nineteenth century to 1870 (63 periods) as follows: introductory revision of the principal features of the development of society in ancient times and in the Middle Ages; the world at the beginning of modern history; the revolution in seventeenth-century England; the beginning of the industrial revolution in England; the formation of the United States of America; the French Revolution in the eighteenth century; France from 1794 to 1815; the formation of independent States in Central and South America; France and England from 1815 to 1848; Utopian socialism; the origins of scientific communism, Marx and Engels; the revolution of 1848 in Europe (France, Germany, Austria); India from the seventeenth to the nineteenth centuries; China from the eighteenth to the nineteenth centuries; Japan in the nineteenth century; the United States of America at the end of the eighteenth and the beginning of the nineteenth century; the

307

unification of Italy, the unification of Germany; the First International; literature and art and the principal results of scientific developments during the first period of modern history.

In the first half of the school year, pupils in grade X begin to study the second period of foreign modern history covering the years from the Franco-Prussian war and the Paris Commune to the October Socialist Revolution and the end of the first world war (52 periods). The headings are: the Franco-Prussian war and the Paris Commune; Germany, England, France, the southern and western Slavs, the United States of America at the end of the nineteenth and the beginning of the twentieth centuries; the international labour movement, the Second International; culture at the end of the nineteenth and the beginning of the twentieth century; imperialism; the first world war, 1914–18.

Grades X and XI also cover contemporary foreign history (57 periods), as follows: (a) The Western world during the period between the two world wars: rise of the revolutionary movement and growth of national liberation movements in colonial and dependent countries after the October Socialist Revolution; the political developments following the Versailles Treaty; the United States of America, England, Germany and France from 1924 to 1939; the national movements of the peoples of China, India and other countries; the Communist International in the struggle for a single popular front against fascism and the threat of a new world war; the formation of two hot-beds of war; the struggle of the U.S.S.R. for peace and collective security; (b) The second world war; (c) The Western world after the second world war; transformation of socialism into a world system; collapse of the system of imperialism; the peoples' struggle for peace; People's Democracies in Europe and Asia: Poland, Czechoslovakia, Bulgaria, Hungary, Rumania, Albania, the German Democratic Republic, China, the Democratic People's Republic of Korea, the Democratic Republic of Viet-Nam, the Mongolian People's Republic; countries which have achieved national independence—India, Indonesia, Burma, United Arab Republic—and others which are struggling to achieve it; the principal countries of the Western world; the United States of America, the United Kingdom, France, the Federal Republic of Germany, Japan; the struggle between two trends in international politics; the peoples' struggle for peace; the principal features of the development of culture; the international communist and labour movement.

A systematic course in the history of the U.S.S.R. is taken during the second half of the school year in grade IX (54 periods), from the end of the first half of the school year in grade X (82 periods) and in grade XI (33 periods). The course consists of the following sections: primitive communal and slave-ownership system; rise and development of feudalism (Kievan Russia, the period of feudal fragmentation, the formation and consolidation of a centralized multinational State in Russia, the principal events of the seventeenth century, the formation of the Russian empire); decline and crisis of serfdom; development of capitalist relations in Russia; beginning of the revolutionary struggle against Tsarism; Russia in the period of capitalism; the revolutionary-democratic stage in the socialist revolutionary movement; the beginning of the revolutionary struggle of the proletariat; the period of imperialism; the transfer of the centre of the world revolutionary movement to Russia (Russia's entry into the period of imperialism, the emergency of the Bolshevik party, the revolution of 1905–07, the February bourgeois-democratic revolution); the victory of the October Socialist Revolution and the building of socialism in the U.S.S.R. (the victory of the socialist revolution, and the foreign military intervention and civil war (1918–20), the building of socialism in the U.S.S.R.); the U.S.S.R. during the period of completion of the building of a socialist society and gradual transition to communism (the U.S.S.R. from 1938 to 1941; the Great War of 1941–45; the U.S.S.R. from 1948 to 1959); the beginning of intensive communist construction in the U.S.S.R.

Pupils in grade XI take a course in 'The fundamentals of political knowledge' (70 periods). This covers the following topics: Marxism-Leninism, the theoretical basis of communist construction; ways in which socialism develops into communism; the forming of communist man; the development of a world system of socialism; the two major international political systems; peaceful policies of the U.S.S.R. and other countries of the socialist camp; inevitability of the triumph of the cause of peace and democracy throughout the world; the Communist Party as the guiding and organizing force of Soviet society in the process of building communism; communism as an equitable society.

In the Union Republics, the history of the Republic concerned is studied in addition to the courses described above.

In the reorganization of the schools, substantial improvement in the teaching of history has been brought about through some curtailment of the material relating to the early periods of history and expansion of contemporary history, both Soviet and foreign, making history teaching considerably closer to life. The pupils, including those attending eight-year schools, cover the whole course of world history from ancient times to the present day. They become acquainted with the history of many countries, with various aspects of their societies and with all important events.

All this helps to give the schoolchildren an understanding of history as a process of progressive development of society rather than a haphazard collection of events, and understanding of the objective laws governing that development, a scientific appreciation of past and present events in the life of society and the beginnings of a scientific outlook on the world.

All history courses include a detailed description of the means of production and their progressive development, transmitting to the children a volume of concrete, graphic and colourful factual material as well as general conclusions in a form they can understand.

It teaches the young to hold technical progress in high esteem and gives them a better understanding of the problems in the field of scientific and technical development which the Soviet Union is in process of solving. It aims at providing pupils with a profound understanding of the social significance of production and labour, the fundamentals of political knowledge and an understanding of their personal duty in the sphere of production.

The following forms of work which help the children to a better understanding of the social role of production and the immediate tasks of its development are widely used in polytechnical schools providing production training: (a) participation by senior pupils in production meetings at factories or State farms; (b) study of the history of industrial undertakings and collective farms; (c) lectures and amateur performances organized by schoolchildren for workers and collective farmers; (d) talks and essays at schools on subjects such as 'Why I chose a particular trade' (turner, animal farmer, etc.), 'What I have learnt from my work at the factory (or on the collective farm)', 'My apprentice master', etc.

The teaching of history makes an invaluable contribution to the polytechnical education of schoolchildren in that it acquaints them with the social aspect of production and labour and prepares them for later work. The reorganization of history teaching in the U.S.S.R. aims at reinforcing the element of communist education and in particular the element of labour education in the teaching of this subject.

GEOGRAPHY

In the U.S.S.R., geography is taught both in the eight-year schools and in full secondary schools.

The systematic geography course begins, in grade V, with an

310

elementary course in physical geography, with information about maps and charts, surface relief, inland waters and the oceans, the earth and its movements, weather and climate, and natural zones.

The geography of the parts of the world is taught in grade VI and the first half-year in grade VII; this course includes additional information on natural conditions in the most important States, their populations and the economic activities of those populations, and brief surveys of other countries on the map.

A course in the geography of the U.S.S.R. is taken in the second half-year in grade VII and in grade VIII. This includes the study of the seas, islands, peninsulas, surface, climate, rivers, lakes, natural zones, population, political and administrative divisions and national economy of the U.S.S.R., and of the natural conditions, population and economy of the Union Republics and of the region or autonomous Republic in which the school is found.

Economic geography is studied in the senior grades of secondary schools. This course covers the economic geography of foreign countries and of the U.S.S.R., which includes information concerning the geography of the principal branches of the national economy of the Soviet Union and a survey of the economy of the fifteen Union Republics (and, within the Russian Soviet Federal Socialist Republic, of each of the principal economic areas).

School geography, and particularly the courses in the geography and economic geography of the U.S.S.R., play an essential part in broadening the schoolchildren's polytechnical horizons.

Without a knowledge of the fundamentals of geography, the children cannot fully comprehend such production matters as the significance of natural conditions in economic development, the organization of socialist production, the geographical distribution of industry, the structure of the national economy, branches of production and the links between them.

Polytechnical education enriches the teaching of geography by the addition of material with a bearing on production acquired in other subjects.

The system of polytechnical education in geography teaching comprises the following basic elements: (a) a study of the scientific bases of production in class, particularly in lessons on the economic geography of the U.S.S.R.; and (b) an introduction to the economy and organization of production in the course of excursions to industrial and agricultural undertakings.

In the study of physical geography, natural objects and phenomena are considered from the point of view not only of their structure and development but also of their economic utilization. In this connexion, considerable attention is devoted to the economic assessment of favourable and unfavourable natural conditions found within the confines of a particular country or area and to the appraisal of the natural resources of the territory being studied. For instance, when studying the geography of the U.S.S.R., the children are told about the natural possibilities for agricultural development—soil and climatic conditions—these being of great importance for land cultivation, which is the basis of all agricultural production.

In economic geography courses, the children are taught about the geography of the principal branches of the national economy of the Soviet Union, and other countries, and gain an insight into the fundamental differences in their organization of production. Their knowledge of technical and technological matters is used in this connexion, since it helps to show the nature of the organization of production and to explain the geographical distribution of industry. Such knowledge is also used in imparting an understanding of the rate of development of individual branches of industry, agriculture and transport.

For example, facts concerning the technical equipment available to Soviet agriculture help the schoolchildren to understand the exceptionally rapid rates of developing virgin and long-disused lands.

In studying the economic geography of the U.S.S.R., the schoolchildren become conversant with the national-economic significance, structure, territorial organization, achievements, prospects of development and production links of the principal branches of the national economy and with the types of enterprises found in them.

As part of this course, the schoolchildren learn of the Soviet people's successes in fulfilling the seven-year plan for the intensive building of communism in the U.S.S.R. They also learn the national-economic significance and occurrence of natural conditions and of the country's natural resources which provide the basis for the operation and reorganization of the national economy, without which no form of production is possible. The subjects covered include the power industry, the ferrous metal industry, the non-ferrous metal industry, engineering, the chemical industry and agricultural production.

Side by side with the course in the economic geography of the U.S.S.R., the physical geography courses—particularly that in the geography of the U.S.S.R.—play an important part in acquainting pupils with the economic exploitation of natural conditions and of individual territories. In the course of these studies, the pupils learn how relief, climate, topsoil and vegetation are utilized in agriculture. While making a geographical survey of the U.S.S.R. area by area, as part of the course in the geography of the U.S.S.R., they assimilate information on the natural conditions of various areas which affect the development of agriculture; for instance, the climate of Central Asia with its long, hot, dry and cloudless summer which, with artificial irrigation, is well suited to the cultivation of long-staple cotton.

In making an economic appraisal of climatic conditions from the point of view of the possibilities of developing agriculture, account is taken not only of average temperature and precipitation but also of conditions over the year. This is essential in planning agricultural operations, since yearly conditions affect the schedule of field work. In the Krasnoyarsk region, for instance, the summer is short and the autumn rainy; there may be frost in May or June and sometimes in August. The harvesting period is accompanied by rains. Consequently, in order to avoid damage to crops, spring sowing has to be done within the shortest possible time (five to seven days), and the grain harvest has to be gathered in within seven or eight days at the most if the entire crop is to be saved.

Carrying out local observations of weather conditions over a period of years, in some cases with the help of school meteorological stations, reinforces the links between the study of geography and agricultural production. The pupils are convinced, by practical examples, of the economic importance of the weather for the organization of agricultural work.

Data concerning the direction of the dominant winds, collected at schools situated on the steppes, help to determine those areas where protective forest belts should be grown. In designing wind turbines, it is essential to take into account the dominant winds and their force. This kind of approach to the study and evaluation of local weather factors is practised at a number of schools.

The courses also include the geographical distribution of the principal cereals (spring and winter wheat, maize, rye, oats, barley, millet) and industrial crops (cotton, flax, hemp, sugar beet, sunflower, soya bean, etc.) and of the principal varieties of animal husbandry (meat and dairy, dairy, whole milk, pig-, sheep- and deer-raising). In teaching the geography of agricultural production, use is made of elements of ecology which explain the relationship between agricultural plants and animals and their environment.

For example, the schoolchildren learn that rye can be grown successfully in less fertile soils (e.g., podsol) and in a fairly cold climate. Rye cannot stand great heat and is therefore not usually grown in the extreme south of the country. Spring rye is grown where there are severe winters (in the north of the Soviet Union)

313

or where the snowfall is small (in Siberia); winter rye is grown elsewhere. Barley is the least particular of the cereals as regards climate. The usual varieties of barley need little heat for their entire vegetative cycle; at the same time, barley can also be grown successfully in hot, dry climates.

In the course of the economic geography of the U.S.S.R., the students are also taught about the concentration and specialization of agricultural production. The former means the concentration of production in larger enterprises. Small collective farms in the U.S.S.R. have been enlarged during the post-war period; this has led to further concentration of agricultural production. Under the heading 'geography of agriculture in the U.S.S.R.', concrete facts relating to specific regions are used to demonstrate the technical and economic advantages of large enterprises over small ones, favourable possibilities for the use of machines, including those of the latest design, the application of scientific achievements, the use of fertilizers and the reduction of administrative and management costs.

Instruction is also given about the specialization of agriculture, which takes the form of special combinations of principal agricultural crops and forms of animal husbandry.

The pupils learn that decisions on agricultural specialization are taken in the light of the requirements of the national economy, with due regard to local natural and economic conditions, in particular climate, soil and water conditions, relief, the distribution of food and light industries, transport, towns and other economic factors. Cattle-breeding goes on in almost all areas, but the natural and economic conditions affecting whole-milk, butter, beef, and veal production differ from area to area. For this reason, cattle farming in some areas takes the form principally of meat and dairy farming, while in others it may be dairy farming and in yet others, milk production.

In the course of their geography studies, the students acquire practical skills and abilities which help them to take part in socially useful and productive labour. These practical skills and abilities, which have to do with measuring, calculation and cartography, are the following: measuring distance (by pacing out, measuring cord, measuring tape or folding rule); measuring, on the terrain, the height of a hill, river bank, side of gulley, etc.; determining the height of the snow cover; measuring temperature, pressure, air humidity, cloud and wind strength with the help of instruments; measuring the width, depth and surface rate of flow of a river; calculating daily and monthly temperature, pressure and cloud averages on the basis of own meteorological measurements;

calculating river flow; plotting graphs of temperature, cloudiness and days with precipitation; drawing a wind rose; drawing a cross-section of a river (or lake basin); drawing diagrams and plotting graphs relating to economic matters; calculating the proportion of the country's area, population and national economy, represented by one's own region or autonomous Republic; field sketching of local terrain; determining distances on the map, in kilometres and degrees; estimating, with the help of maps, natural conditions and natural resources for the development of agriculture, industry and transport; making, with the help of maps of various kinds, an economic and geographical description of countries, areas, regions or autonomous Republics, towns and large industrial and agricultural undertakings.

The introduction of polytechnical education has made it necessary for geography teachers to adopt new active teaching methods which give the pupils a more vital grasp of what they are taught, arouse their interest and creative initiative, help to foster a love of work, and form habits of acquiring knowledge independently, analysing phenomena observed in life and seeing how they tie in with one another. This helps the schools in the U.S.S.R. to find a better solution to the problem of training future builders of a communist society, people whose abilities have been developed in all directions and who can find their bearings in any part of the production system.

The introduction of polytechnical education has increased the importance of local studies, which provide a well-adapted means of acquainting pupils with the principles of production.

The local-studies approach, i.e., the use, in teaching, of data relating to the pupils' own region, area, town or village, is essential for giving a practical impact to questions of the organization and location of production and acquainting the pupils with the economics of local enterprises.

Since most children, on leaving school, will work in local industrial or agricultural enterprises or local institutions, a thorough knowledge of their region—including local enterprises—has a practical value in preparing them for life and work.

Local studies help to draw schoolchildren into socially useful work. For instance, the meteorological observations made by pupils at rural schools very often serve a socially useful purpose.

The pupils supply collective and State farms with information concerning the weather over a ten-day period and compile basic agro-meteorological data (average monthly air temperature, height of snow cover, dates of frosts, number of bright and cloudy days, total amount of precipitation for each month and over the year, recurrence of different wind directions, sowing tables for collective farms, etc.).

To quote an example: pupils at Dondukovskaya Secondary School, Krasnodar Region (teacher R. F. Fokin) regularly carry out weather observations at the school meteorological station which is equipped with instruments and registered at the Central Directorate of Hydro-Meteorological Services. Teams of pupils carry out these observations three times a day (at 7 a.m., 1 p.m. and 7 p.m.) on a weekly rota. The results are carefully analysed and expressed in the form of graphs, diagrams, a wind rose, etc. Graphs and diagrams showing the annual movement of air temperatures, daily average and minimum temperatures, total precipitation, wind rose, and duration of snow cover at Dondukovskaya Cossack village are widely used for the study of climate in geography lessons in grades V–VIII.

As another example, when pupils are studying 'atmospheric precipitation', they learn that so-called 'blanket' precipitation falls over a prolonged period and is gradually absorbed by the soil. It plays a very important part in nourishing agricultural plants. Rain showers make the soil more compact. In sunny weather, a crust forms over the soil which makes it difficult for shoots to break through and intensifies the evaporation of moisture.

Frequent and abundant rains at harvest-time cause serious losses of crops and spoil the quality of agricultural production. The snow cover is an important source of moisture accumulation and a thermo-insulator which protects the soil and vegetation from freezing.

While going through the section on 'European forest steppe' and 'Krasnodar region', the teacher discusses the causes of drought, the harm it does, and methods of preventing it, and points out the part played by forest strips on the local collective farm's land (reduction of wind speed and retention of snow in the vicinity of the forest strips). A feature of R. F. Fokin's teaching is the fact that in the course of studying the soil and vegetation zone in which their school is located, the pupils are given a description of agricultural plants grown on the local collective farm with reference to their heat requirements at different stages of development.

In this way pupils at Dondukovskaya Secondary School receive, at their geography lessons, agro-meteorological information on local agricultural production which is of practical importance. The weather observation work done at the school helps to accustom the students to working with instruments, develops their powers of observation, trains them to precision, fosters a sense of responsibility and thus is socially useful.

Pupils at Novo-Kurlak School, Voronezh Region (teacher A. I. Scherbakov), when engaged in local studies in connexion with their polytechnical training, devote much attention to socially useful work for the needs of the local collective farm. For instance, the pupils, under the teacher's supervision, make observations of the depth of the snow cover and of the effect of high or low stubble on the distribution of snow over a field. They determine the extent to which snow accumulation depends on the presence of forest, and the amount of moisture stored in the soil on snow retention. For this purpose they ascertain the thickness of the snow cover in different sections of a field, different types of thawing, and the flow of melted snow. All the data concerning the distribution of snow and accumulation of moisture in the soil are transmitted to the collective farm, which in turn lets the school know the amounts of yield of cereal crops from different sections of its agricultural land. The example of their own collective farm convinces the pupils of the importance of snow retention in raising crop capacity; as a result, they show great willingness and conscientiousness in assisting the collective farm in snow retention work.

The work of G. A. Zapalov, teacher at Bolshe-Yanikovskoye Secondary School in the Urmary area of the Chuvash Autonomous Soviet Socialist Republic, also merits attention. He uses the study of the local collective farm under the heading of 'agricultural geography of the U.S.S.R.' (course in the economic geography of the U.S.S.R.) to explain the basic economic factors which characterize agriculture, such as total available lands, arable land, etc.

As a result of this study, the students draw up a topographical plan of the territory, a plan of the economic organization of land exploitation by the collective farm, and current and future plans for the development of the collective farm.

The solving of economic accounting problems is used for the purpose of inculcating skills and habits of practical use in real life. Some examples of such problems are given below: [1]
1. Examine the table and, having analysed the structure of total and commodity output and financial returns, determine the specialization of the collective farm's economy (Table 17).
   Analysis of the figures reproduced in the table leads to the conclusion that the collective farm specializes in livestock-raising, vegetable-growing and horticulture.

---

1. T. A. Basyuk, *Organization of Socialist Agricultural Production*, Moscow, State Political Publishing House, 1956, p. 89

2. In 1955, 20 per cent of the collective farm's sown area was planted with cereals and leguminous crops, 28.1 per cent with potatoes, 14.9 per cent with vegetables and 37 per cent with fodder crops.

Draw up a table of the structure of the sown areas and deduce the specialization of the collective farm's agricultural production.

In view of the fact that potatoes and vegetables take up 43 per cent of the sown area, the pupils conclude that the collective farm tends to specialize in vegetable-growing.

TABLE 17

Branches of the collective farm's economy	Total output	Commodity output	Financial returns
	%	%	%
Crop farming	50.5	13.9	49.9
cereals	1.3	—	—
potatoes	8.1	4.8	4.17
vegetables	38.3	6.0	29.22
fodder	1.3	—	—
horticultural	1.5	3.1	16.51
Livestock	49.5	86.1	44.38
cattle	45.5	80.1	36.33
pigs	3.5	5.4	6.24
poultry	0.5	0.6	1.81
Other income	—	—	5.72

3. Examine Table 18 and calculate, on the basis thereof, the over-all yield from each section of thirty hectares and make deductions as to the efficiency of separate harvesting as compared with direct combine harvesting.

TABLE 18

Date of harvesting	Harvesting area (hectares)	Method of harvesting	Date of threshing	Average yield per hectare	Over-all yield from 30 hectares
4 July	30	separate	20 July	21	
7 July	30	separate	20 July	19.8	
10 July	30	separate	20 July	18.86	
13 July	30	separate	20 July	18.83	
16 July	30	direct combine	16 July	14.23	

4. The distance from Leningrad to Rostov-on-Don is 2,003 kilometres by rail, 3,030 kilometres by river and canal, and 9,075 kilometres by sea.

Compare the cost of transporting 500 tons of freight from Leningrad to Rostov-on-Don by these different means of transport, if it is known that the cost per ton-kilometre is 1 kopeck by rail, $1/2$ kopeck by river and $1/16$ kopeck by sea.

Excursions to industrial and agricultural enterprises and to museums of local studies, together with practical field work, have come to occupy an important place in geography teaching as a means of putting polytechnical education into practice.

Geographical excursions to production enterprises aim at giving students an idea and understanding of: (a) a modern, highly mechanized industrial or agricultural enterprise; (b) the factors governing the geographical distribution of enterprises belonging to different branches of the national economy; (c) the production links of enterprises; (d) the organization of labour at enterprises; (e) the different trades of workers employed at factories and works, and the work of peasants employed on collective farms.

The following questions are thus studied through excursions to agricultural enterprises:

1. The geographical location of the collective or State farm. Area and dimensions of its territory from west to east and from north to south. Its position in relation to physical and geographical features (rivers, large forests, watersheds, etc.). Its geographical location in relation to transport (railways, roads, area and regional centres). Sketch map of the lay-out of the collective or State farm.

2. Natural conditions at the collective or State farm: relief, climate, water resources, soils, vegetation, economic assessment of natural conditions. Measures taken to improve natural conditions.

3. History and present situation of the collective or State farm. The peasants' life before the October Socialist Revolution. Date of establishment of the collective farm. Brief description of its lands. Land utilization plan. Life of the peasants on the collective farm at the present time (living conditions, cultural and educational activities, etc.).

4. Specialization of the agricultural economy of the collective or State farm. Dominant branch of agricultural production, evolved on the basis of the country's general requirements and responding most closely to local natural and economic conditions. Supplementary and auxiliary branches, the development of which, with the dominant branch, makes it possible

319

to utilize, fully and economically, the collective or State farm's labour resources, land and technical equipment. Economic structure of the collective or State farm.

5. Production links of the collective or State farm under the following headings: (a) its own production; (b) agricultural machines, fertilizers and electric power.

6. Prospects of development of agriculture on the collective or State farm. The principal objective of agricultural planning. What factors serve as the basis for planning the volume of production of every collective or State farm? How is the volume of production (crop-farming and stock-breeding) calculated?

7. Working conditions at the collective or State farm. Mechanization and electrification. Organization of leisure.

8. Leading personalities at the collective or State farm. Fulfilment of the production plan by the best people at the collective or State farm. Their suggestions for improving the collective farm's work. The organization of socialist emulation. Rewards and incentives for selfless work at the collective or State farm.

The value of excursions from the point of view of geography teaching lies in the fact that they broaden the polytechnical horizons of the students and link technical and technological knowledge with the organization, geographical distribution and economics of enterprises. These excursions develop a liking and respect for work of people employed in the sphere of material production.

Since the number of production excursions within the scope of economic geography studies is very limited, it is necessary, for the purposes of polytechnical education, to make extensive use of visual teaching aids (collections of minerals, raw materials, semi-finished and finished products, diagrams of technical processes, etc.). These familiarize the students with the organization and economics of industrial and agricultural production. Films have come to take a very important place among these teaching aids. Film showings are used alike as a means of preparing students for excursions and as a means of showing the general significance of things seen during an excursion, since films often make it possible to show production processes more clearly than can be done in the course of a production excursion.

CHAPTER XVI

MANUAL AND TECHNICAL INSTRUCTION AND THE TEACHING OF PRODUCTION PRINCIPLES IN POLYTECHNICAL EDUCATION

by N. E. Tseitlin

Practical experience has shown that it is impossible, in the process of teaching physics, chemistry, biology, mathematics and other general-education subjects to impart to the pupils all that they need to know in the way of polytechnical knowledge and skills without disturbing the specific character and logical structure of these subjects. For this reason, manual and technical instruction has been introduced as a separate subject in the school curriculum.

In this subject, the pupils acquire a progressively wider range of polytechnical knowledge and skills, proceeding from work with the simplest hand tools to work with electrical instruments and mechanical tools and ending with a study of various complex machines. On the basis of the elementary knowledge and proficiency acquired in grades V–VIII in constructing electrotechnical models and fitting up electrical lighting systems and domestic heating appliances, the pupils in the senior grades become acquainted with electrical machinery and technical measuring instruments. Similarly, from a study of the simplest technological methods of manual processing of the most widely-used materials and the preparation of technical models, they pass on to a study of modern machines and production processes and become acquainted with modern techniques and technology and the organization of present-day production.

Let us consider more closely the system of manual and technical instruction and its role in polytechnical education.

INSTRUCTION IN GRADES I–IV

The object of the work lessons given in the primary grades is to equip the children with work skills, promote their labour education, provide a successful solution for the tasks of polytechnical education and lay the foundations for the psychological preparation of the children for practical work.

During these lessons, the children acquire a concrete idea of the varied materials employed and of some of their characteristics (colour, weight, strength, etc.), of the tools used in working them, and of the simplest operations applied in the process. Their ideas of space and geometry are deepened and vitalized; they become used to applying their knowledge of arithmetic, natural history, drawing and other subjects; they get familiarized with various appliances, and master such material-processing methods as are within their ability.

From the very beginning of these studies, they acquire an elementary training in labour culture, i.e., they acquire the habit of keeping their workplace clean and tidy, arranging their materials and tools properly and taking care of them, using materials economically and carrying out operations accurately. They learn to work rationally and productively and not to waste time, to plan, arrange and check their work, and to make simple calculations. They become accustomed to observing conscientiously the rules of labour discipline, to meeting health and sanitation requirements and to observing safety regulations.

The work lessons create favourable conditions for the development and training of the pupil's personality, for work fosters the development of such positive traits of character as industriousness, curiosity, will-power, the ability to overcome difficulties, accuracy and attentiveness. The children learn to respect labour, their fellow-workers and the products of labour, and to work as a team and for the team.

In grade I, they work with paper, pasteboard, cloth, clay and plasticine, and do simple work on plant-growing. In working with paper, they acquire such basic skills as learning to mark out, bend and fold paper and pasteboard, cut them with scissors or knives along marked lines, and glue and paste them. This work is well within the scope of a seven-year-old, and in carrying it out, the child learns to work accurately with pencil, ruler, scissors and glue, to make simple articles for his own use (e.g., material for doing sums, bookmarkers, packets for seeds, notebooks for word-lists, Christmas cards, etc.). In working with cloth, the children learn to sew on buttons, to sew simple little objects (pen-wipers, hand-kerchiefs, etc.) and to look after their own clothes. The work with clay and plasticine has considerable educational value, for it develops their power of observation, creativeness and taste. In their modelling work, they develop co-ordination of movement, dexterity, the ability to measure by eye and the idea of space.

On the school experimental plot they learn to grow flowering plants in special beds, and both in class and at home they acquire the first practical skills in tending indoor plants.

In grade II, the children also work with paper, pasteboard, clay and plasticine and continue to learn sewing and work on the school plot, but the tasks are more complicated; the children cut out shapes from paper and pasteboard along marked lines, glue them together, and learn to use the graduated ruler and set-square for simple measurements and for checking the quality of their work, on the basis of the progressive development of their desire for accuracy.

In their work with clay and plasticine, they develop, as in grade I, the ability to recognize and reproduce accurately the shape of relatively simple and familiar objects; for example, they model from life (or from memory) fruits and vegetables. In their work with cloth, they do very simple and ordinary stitching, and learn how to embroider very simple designs on serviettes and sew little bags and other uncomplicated objects. They also learn how to use the tape measure and ruler for simple measurement, mark out rectangular shapes for making patterns, and become accustomed to looking after their own clothes, doing simple mending, etc.

On the school plot they grow pulses, and in class and at home they continue to look after indoor plants and grow flowers in jars, flower-pots and boxes. Working on the school plot, they dig beds, rake them smooth, use a marker-cord to align the drill-furrows in which they sow the seed and observe the growth of plants.

The task of developing proficiency in work with paper and pasteboard continues in grade III. The pupils make and mend simple visual aids needed for teaching Russian, arithmetic and natural history, and learn to mark out paper more accurately, to rule lines, to glue paper to pasteboard and to frame flat cardboard articles of simple shape with paper strips. They acquire skills in elementary bookbinding, making simple pads, notebooks and small file-cases, and binding pamphlets, etc. They perfect their knowledge of fabrics in grade III, continue to learn sewing and embroidery and begin to darn stockings and socks. They learn to cut out and sew very simple articles (aprons, mittens, small bags, etc.) and acquire an elementary idea of dressmaking and tailoring and learn simple methods of mending clothes.

On the school plot they cultivate beetroots, carrots and their seeds, and plant and tend strawberries. They dress the beds themselves, sow dry, wet and germinated seed, thin out root crops, transplant beet and cabbage seedlings, look after seed-plants, apply top-dressing and conduct simple experiments with the plants. As far as indoor plants are concerned, the children learn how to plant flower seedlings in pots, jars and boxes.

In grade IV, work is continued, and the proficiency acquired in manipulating paper and pasteboard is consolidated. The children make file-cases and pads, repair maps, diagrams and other visual aids made of paper or pasteboard, stick diagrams, photographs and reproductions on pasteboard backings and make models of simple geometrical forms.

They go on with their sewing, embroidery and knitting, and undertake more complicated dressmaking work: they take measurements on their own, note them down, make the rough sketch, cut out the patterns, cut out the cloth on their own and for the first time sew simply constructed articles. They also learn more about looking after their clothes and simple mending, and they crochet belts and small scarves. They also learn how to use sewing-machines and flat irons, and are taught to observe the basic safety rules in using them.

The object in grade IV of technical modelling work is to develop the children's technical-mindedness and powers of creative design. The syllabus accordingly provides for the preparation by the children of simple equipment for natural history experiments and simple models and mock-ups of various machines.

On the school plot, they grow potatoes and maize, learn how to plant currant cuttings and to tend and look after the plants. In class and at home, they learn how to propagate indoor plants from cuttings, and this work provides a good preparation for the systematic study of botany in grade V.

The knowledge, accomplishments and skills which they acquire in the work lessons in the junior grades (I–IV) are of major importance from the standpoint of polytechnical education, providing a thorough grounding for further manual and technical and polytechnical instruction in grades V–VIII. In addition, the knowledge, accomplishments and skills acquired by the younger children make it possible to initiate them progressively into socially useful work and housekeeping work at school and in the home.

INSTRUCTION IN GRADES V–VIII

The object of manual and technical instruction in these grades is to impart general technical, agricultural and domestic knowledge and skills; to develop technical thinking and creative capacities in the pupils; to foster in them a communist attitude to work and to labour conditions in general; to help them give expression to their own inclinations, find their bearings in the various spheres of human activity, and make a careful choice of their future vocation.

The instruction given in these grades at the eight-year school is polytechnical in character. It includes work in the school workshops, practical and experimental work in agriculture, and domestic-science activities, three periods a week being devoted to these in every grade (V–VIII).

In the school workshops, the pupils become knowledgeable and proficient in woodwork and metalwork with the use of hand tools and certain machine tools. Most of the metalworking operations in factories and plants are carried out, of course, with the help of a variety of machines, but manual work is also used to some extent in every branch of production for the successful operation of a machine, the elimination of breakdowns, and the assembly and adjustment of mechanisms. Hence the study and mastery of the methods of working these most commonly-used materials—metals and wood—with hand tools are of great importance for the pupils' polytechnical education and technical training, and the procedure employed is to get them to make various useful articles, including equipment, models, mock-ups, tools and implements for use in the school workshop and on the school plot, articles for use in pioneer activities or for the pupil's personal use, toys, etc., and component parts manufactured to the order of factories and of collective or State farms. These activities are chosen and carried out in a particular sequence, progressing from the simple to the more complex, so that their execution helps to consolidate and develop the skills which the pupils have already acquired in working the materials.

The eight-year-school pupils also acquire some knowledge of the mechanization of labour processes. They learn about the construction of the commonest simple machines and mechanisms and how to use them. The wide application of electric power in modern industry, agriculture, transport and everyday life makes it essential that every pupil who leaves the eight-year school should have acquired some elementary knowledge and skill in handling the commonest electrical equipment and electric appliances.

In the workshops, they learn to read and prepare very simple technical drawings, sketches and blueprints, and to transfer the data to the material. The basic method of instruction consists in interpreting the drawings of articles which have to be prepared in practice. The work with drawings at all stages of school workshop activity is organized in such a way as to make use of the knowledge and skill which the pupils have acquired in their studies of drawing, mathematics and (from grade VII onwards) technical drawing.

Various methods are used for instruction in the workshops; oral instruction (talks, explanations, discussions); demonstration of natural objects, visual aids and working methods; exercises; individual and group instruction; independent work from drawings or instructional charts; graphic work; special laboratory work for the practical elucidation of the properties and peculiarities of materials, the construction of tools, components and appliances, the interaction of tools and materials, and other technical and technological questions; excursions to industrial undertakings to familiarize the pupils with the organization of work at plants and factories, the mechanization of production and the construction of individual machine tools and appliances with the help of which the pupils carry out the operations which they have studied and mastered in the school workshops.

In grades VII and VIII, the pupils are given set tasks on their own, commensurate with their capacity, in making components and complete articles.

The technical and technological knowledge imparted to the pupils broadens their general technical outlook and is an essential factor in correctly developing their skill in the use of materials. In its turn, the acquisition of practical skills enables them to acquire a deeper appreciation of technology and an understanding of the working principles of machine operation in processing materials, and of mechanized production in general.

The teacher's explanations, with their marked technical bias, are based on the knowledge acquired by the pupils in their studies of the fundamentals of the various sciences. On the strength of what they have learnt in physics, for example, they can be given the scientific reasons for a number of technical phenomena and technological processes; again, in studying the mechanical properties of materials and machine parts, and the construction and operation of mechanisms, machines and machine tools, they make use of their knowledge of mechanics.

A prominent feature of this instruction is the comparison made between the processes and tools used in woodwork and metalwork, and the elucidation of their similarities and differences, depending on the characteristics of the materials processed. The pupils steadily enlarge their knowledge of the correct use of tools, correct working stance, proper rhythm of work and the essential technical and health measures to ensure high productivity and the necessary standard of workmanship with the minimum loss of energy.

Apart from wood and metals, the pupils in grades VII and VIII get to know materials such as plastics and glass, which are very useful for making items of school equipment or items ordered by factories and farms.

In order to broaden the pupils' polytechnical outlook, comparisons are also made between their work in the workshop and similar technological processes carried out under production conditions, and also between manual and machine processing, and the syllabus accordingly provides for excursions, demonstrations of diagrams, mechanisms and machines, and the showing of films and filmstrips. With the same object in view, some of the jobs are executed on the basis of a division of labour as regards particular items and operations, and this form of organization of labour gives the pupils an insight into how work is organized at an industrial plant.

The school workshops provide favourable conditions for conducting out-of-class technical work on a large scale; many school clubs have been organized in grades V–VIII so that they can engage in technical modelling, electrical engineering and radio engineering, or delve deeper into and become proficient in carpentry, light engineering, lathe work with wood and metal, wood-carving, fretwork, etc.

Workshop activities in these grades are different for boys and girls. Whereas the boys take both woodwork and metalwork the girls take only woodwork in grade V and only metalwork in grades VI–VII. They do less mechanical engineering than the boys in grade VIII, but the syllabus in electrical engineering is identical for boys and girls alike.

To take account of the special characteristics of technical instruction for girls, the eight-year school gives them a training in domestic science which provides them with knowledge and skills in housekeeping work. The main aims are to develop in them a conscientious attitude towards their obligations to share in the general domestic duties of the family and to be self-reliant at school and at home; to acquaint them with the principles of domestic economy, give them the necessary knowledge and skill to carry out various forms of everyday domestic work, and inculcate good taste and a constant desire and ability to keep a place tidy, clean and comfortable.

In the course of their domestic-science work they are familiarized with the social arrangements for everyday domestic work and the communal forms of public service such as communal catering, the work of domestic-service centres, the organization of communal sewing-rooms for making and mending clothing, underwear and footwear, and so get to realize how the everyday household work of the Soviet family is being systematically and steadily lightened. A special point is made of familiarizing them with the use of modern labour-saving devices and with new materials, fabrics, foodstuffs and so on. The result is that they learn to be tidy, thrifty and punctual, and develop a love of cleanliness and order

327

and the ability to make their homes and clothes attractive and sensible and use foodstuffs and materials economically.

The study of domestic science in these senior grades is based on the knowledge and skill acquired in the work lessons in the junior grades, and also on lessons in Russian (or the mother tongue) on the subject of 'The care of health' (in grades I–III) and on the natural-history lessons on the subject of 'The human body and its care' (in grade IV).

In studying the subject 'Cutting and sewing', the girls become acquainted with fabrics, with the preparation of designs and patterns for articles they are making, with methods of sewing and finishing, and with the construction and operation of the sewing-machine. They also acquire a basic knowledge of the care of clothing, of laundering, ironing and storing linen, of cleaning woollen garments, and of laundering knitwear containing synthetic fibres.

One important section of the syllabus is the elements of cookery, including instruction in dietetics, and in the foodstuffs required by the human body. The girls learn how to prepare simple vegetable dishes and cook simple and nourishing meat and fish dishes, handle kitchen equipment, crockery, and table linen and serve and behave at table.

Under the heading of 'Housework' they acquire a basic practical knowledge of home hygiene and sanitation and the essentials of housekeeping (daily, periodical and spring cleaning; ventilation, lighting and heating). In addition, they learn how to arrange furniture and handle tablecloths, curtains, carpets, pictures, photographs, reproductions and decorative tapestries.

To widen their horizon and enlarge their knowledge in various fields, excursions are arranged to public restaurants or food-processing factories (canteens, mechanized restaurants, canneries, butter factories, bakeries), garment-making establishments (tailoring and dressmaking workshops), or to domestic-service centres. These excursions are arranged during the school year in accordance with a timetable drawn up by the teacher.

All the pupils at urban and rural eight-year schools receive initial training in both agricultural and industrial labour, for familiarization with agricultural production is one of the tasks of polytechnical training. This work is closely co-ordinated with the biology course, and is of great educational significance. It is carried out both on the school experimental plot and under actual production conditions, and as it takes place for the most part in the open, it promotes the children's physical development and improves their health.

To meet local conditions, the school is empowered to spread the practical and experimental work evenly over the school year, or to concentrate it in the first and fourth quarters. And since it is of a seasonal nature and is to some extent governed by the weather, it is not included in the timetable but is carried out in accordance with a time-schedule approved by the school director.

In the course of this work, the pupils acquire basic practical skills in cultivating the main agricultural crops (vegetables, fruit and berries, field crops) and—in rural areas—in raising calves. At the same time, they acquire a knowledge, during their excursions, of mechanized cultivation and animal husbandry.

The work in grades V and VI is largely conducted on the school plot. In grades VII and VIII (at rural schools) the pupils work on collective and State farms and fields where they operate in groups on jobs suited to their capacity: looking after poultry, rabbits, and young farm animals, or doing suitable field work, depending on local conditions (the tilling of the soil, and often sowing and harvesting, are done by pupils in grades X–XI or by collective farmers with the aid of agricultural machinery).

At urban schools which have no school plots, the practical and experimental work in grades V–VII is carried out in greenhouses on grounds belonging to Pioneer homes, or Young Naturalists' Centres, in conservatories, parks and squares coming under the Greenery Trust and at specialized suburban agricultural undertakings. In addition, plots at Pioneer camps are made available to the children for educational and production work during the summer.

Their excursions to agricultural production points give the children an insight into the mechanized side of agriculture on collective and State farms. In grade V, for example, they study the mechanization of market-gardening, in grade VI they learn about mechanized work in horticulture, and in grade VII (in urban schools) they become familiar with the mechanization and cultivation of field crops and with heavy work in stock-raising. The grade VIII syllabus (at rural schools) provides for a more detailed study of soil-working implements, seed-drills and grain-cleaners and harvesters (see Fig. 29). The pupils get to know the local collective or State farm and the lines on which it is developing, and this generally acts as a factor in the vocational guidance of the school-leavers.

The content of the syllabus for practical and experimental work during the eight-year period of schooling ensures that the pupils conscientiously apply the knowledge acquired in their biology lessons.

Due account is taken, in following the syllabus, of local soil and climatic conditions and the main crops in the area concerned.

329

Some of the jobs, for example, can be replaced by other equivalent ones (for instance, the syllabus recommends the autumn sowing of fruit trees, but on heavy clay soil the seeds are stratified and the sowing is done in spring; or in southern areas, seedlings are cultivated in seed-beds instead of under glass).

The experimental bias is particularly important. Experiments on the school plot which have given the most productive and economic results are repeated on the plot the following year and then tried out on the collective or State farms, where the pupils carry out so-called 'productive' experiments. Where the results prove positive, they are incorporated into agricultural production.

Many eight-year general schools have started an original type of fruit and berry plantation stocked with the finest strains. The cultivation of seedlings of fruit trees and ornamental plants (in urban schools), the taking of cuttings of the finest strains of currants and other soft fruits, and the grafting and cultivation of the best strains of fruit trees are in fact an important element in practical school work.

The cultivation of seedlings and the work in the nursery garden plays a very important part in agricultural education in grades V–VII (and also in grade VIII at rural schools). In the latter, the pupils study the cultivation of apple trees, while in urban schools they study the propagation of valuable types of trees and of perennial flowering plants such as phlox, lilac, roses, etc. A substantial area (300 to 500 square metres) is provided at rural schools for nursery seed-beds; while urban schools can arrange for nurseries to be established in the gardens of dwellings in the neighbourhood.

An equally important item in grade V practical work is the cultivation of vegetable seedlings in greenhouses, under glass and on hotbeds. Where a greenhouse is available on the school plot, practical work can be carried out in early spring. Apart from growing vegetables, the children grow fruit trees from seedlings, propagate currant bushes, and learn by practical experience the best times and methods for thinning out seedling trees, the best method of taking cuttings of currant bushes, the best way of applying organic and mineral fertilizers to the various vegetable crops and seedling stock and the amounts needed, the best times to sow and plant vegetables and the correct amounts of mineral fertilizer to be used as a top dressing for vegetables. At the urban schools, experiments are conducted to find out the best methods of vegetative propagation of perennial flowering and ornamental plants, the best system of feeding and tending them, the best system of rooting cuttings, etc.

In grade VI, the pupils experiment on the accelerated propagation of valuable strains of raspberries (or trees, in schools in large towns); they learn about the best methods of grafting scions and discover the best means of preparing maize and potatoes for planting, the richest areas for arable crops, the effect of various methods of treatment in increasing the yield of maize, potatoes and seed-plants of biennial vegetables. These experiments, the object of which is to apply and develop the children's knowledge of biology, are carried out on sub-divisions of the experimental plot.

In grade VII at rural schools the experimental work is carried out under agricultural production conditions. The pupils grow maize, potatoes and industrial crops on plots provided for the school and divided up in accordance with the number of pupils in grades VII and VIII. They also tend farm animals on collective and State farms.

The points on which the work is focused, and the subjects of the experiments, are chosen to suit local conditions and lines of future agricultural development.

As stated, the children at urban schools plant greenery in the towns and on workers' estates, look after trees and bushes in the public squares, streets, etc., and help collective farms to look after tree belts and plantations along the main roads. The cultivation of ornamental shrubs and flowering plants, the planting of greenery in courtyards and squares, and work in parks and conservatories, is treated as a matter of major importance.

Included in practical work is the campaign against agricultural pests, which takes various forms—mechanical, chemical and biological. Special attention is paid, in the children's experimental and practical work during school hours, in their educational production practice during the summer and in their socially useful work, to the observance of health requirements and the inculcation of habits of hygiene in connexion with work.

All these arrangements for systematically raising the level of the children's agro-technical and zoo-technical knowledge, and familiarizing them with the principles underlying agricultural production are of great importance in training efficient workers who have an all-round education.

SOCIAL PRODUCTION PRACTICE

The work done by the pupils in the course of instruction is very definitely slanted in the direction of social usefulness, and two periods a week are devoted to socially useful work in every grade

(V–VIII) with the object of coping with the subject of manual and technical instruction more effectively and forging links between education and life. In addition, twelve days are set aside at the end of the school year for social production practice—three periods a day in grade V and four periods a day in grades VI–VIII. This socially useful work takes place outside school hours, and is therefore not included in the timetable. The general educational direction of this work is in the hands of the class teacher, who prepares a plan of work for each successive week, but the immediate handling of it may be entrusted to other teachers, depending on its nature.

Social production practice in urban and rural schools forms a continuation of the manual and technical instruction given in the school workshops and on the school plots, and is based on the knowledge and practical skills acquired by the pupils in the various grades. It includes doing work suited to the pupils' age in the school's training and production workshops, making various articles for use in the school itself and the kindergarten and fulfilling orders from industry. In agriculture, it constitutes a continuation and extension of the experimental and practical work prescribed by the syllabus, thus making it possible to arrange for the systematic tending and observation of plants sown in spring at the proper sowing times and bring in the harvest and evaluate the yield by the due date.

This work ensures the continuation and completion of experiments with vegetable crops and fruit-tree seedlings, conducted in grade V, and with fruit crops, maize, potatoes and the seed-plants of biennial vegetables on the school plots in grade VI, the pupils carrying out practical work and making the corresponding observations at the proper times in accordance with a schedule prepared by the school director.

In grade VII at rural schools, the work involves tending maize and other field crops on collective or State farms and conducting experiments relating to them, raising poultry and rabbits, and looking after fruit seedlings on the school plot. The pupils carry out these jobs in accordance with the director's schedule, working in groups (in view of the need to complete the experiments begun during school hours). At urban schools, the grade VII work is limited to tending field crops on the collective or State farm, or, where it is impossible to organize this in agricultural production, to tending tree plantations and ornamental flowering plants for parks coming under the Greenery Trust.

CHAPTER XVII

THE IMPORTANCE OF COURSES IN ENGINEERING PRACTICE AND ELECTRICAL ENGINEERING FOR POLYTECHNICAL EDUCATION

by M. A. Zhidelev and N. P. Bulatov

ENGINEERING PRACTICE

The essential common feature of all the diverse and complex branches of production is the use of various machines, mechanisms, appliances, equipment and instruments for the mechanization and automation of work processes. In every sphere, the worker has to deal with machines, mechanisms and electricity. Machines are used for the transformation of energy, the extraction of fuel and raw materials, the treatment of materials, in building, cultivation of the land, care of crops and harvesting; machines print books, they transport goods and people at tremendous speed, project satellites and space-ships into interplanetary space, and are used to carry out the most complicated calculations and other operations; electricity is not only a source of motive power for machines but is also widely used in modern industry; electronic instruments are widely used for the checking, regulation, control and adjustment of mechanical devices. Hence the factory worker, the agricultural mechanic, the building worker, the laboratory worker, the seamstress and the scientific worker—workers, in fact, in every field—must have a good knowledge of the basic construction, operation and application of machines, mechanisms, electrical equipment, electronic apparatus and instruments.

The study of machines and of the application of electricity is one of the most important features of polytechnical education in the school; it is essential for the training of young people for practical work in production and for their all-round development.

Hence it has been found necessary to introduce, into the syllabus of Soviet schools of general education, courses or subjects which would impart in a more or less systematic form a range of knowledge and practical skills connected with the application of machines and electrical and radio equipment to production. These courses are called 'Engineering practice' and 'Electrical engineering'.

'Engineering practice' as an educational subject is based on an analysis, by the teacher, of the field of knowledge systematized in present-day 'machine science'.

It is well known that generalized data concerning the design, manufacture and maintenance of machines and mechanisms enter into a whole series of technical sciences. These include:

The theory of mechanisms and machines, concerned with the study of the kinematic and dynamic properties of machinery. The theory of mechanisms and machines comprises the structural analysis and classification of various types of mechanism and the synthesis of new types of mechanism carried out in accordance with the laws of theoretical mechanics.

The resistance of materials and machine components, which it is necessary to know for the design of mechanisms and machines (the calculation of strength, determination of optimum shape and dimensions, etc.).

Mechanical engineering, which involves the study of the properties of engineering materials (e.g., metallography), the processes of working these materials by cutting, pressing, etc. (e.g., metal technology), and also the assembling, finishing and adjustment of machines.

The study of the methods of using machines (fitting, control, maintenance and care, etc.).

Engineering practice as a science is a derivative of theoretical mechanics, the theory of elasticity, aerodynamics and hydrodynamics, the physics of metals, thermodynamics, electrical engineering and other subjects, and includes the theoretical scientific bases of the most important branch of production—mechanical engineering.

At the same time, engineering practice is continually developing and improving, thanks to new achievements in the practical construction and use of more and more highly perfected mechanisms and machines.

It is well known that any developed machine assembly consists of four parts: motors, transmission systems, operational units and the technical equipment which provides the automatic checking, regulation, control and adjustment of the devices and machines.

Despite their variety, motors can be divided into three groups according to their mechanical characteristics: piston-operated, rotary and reaction.

In the construction of all piston engines, the same basic parts and mechanisms are repeated. Steam engines and internal combustion engines have the same main moving parts (crankshaft and connecting rod), steam and gas diffusion mechanisms (eccentrics and cams) and control mechanisms (hinged levers with centrifugal governors). Pupils must become acquainted with these mechanisms first and foremost.

In all rotary engines (turbines, electric motors, wind-driven motors) there are two parts (rotor and stator) which form a very simple twin-link lever mechanism. The same control mechanisms are used as in piston engines.

The construction of modern turbo-reaction motors involves gas turbines and centrifugal or axial compressors, the mechanisms of which are the same as in rotary engines.

The fuel-feed system of all motors using liquid fuel employs piston, plunger, diaphragm or rotary pumps; the lubrication system, regardless of the type of motor, employs gear pumps; the water-cooling system uses centrifugal pumps.

Among the piston engines which are available for study in secondary schools and which are most widely used in various spheres of practical work, mention must be made of the internal combustion engine, which combines all the mechanisms of the other types mentioned above. Most important among the rotary engines for school use is the electric motor.

Transmission systems of machines have undergone considerable changes during the years. The use of a separate drive in the operational unit, and very often in its separate mechanical parts as well, has had the result that the transmission systems have begun to function as part of the operational unit. Sometimes a transmission system may be entirely absent (if the motor is directly connected to the operational unit). Nevertheless, we find transmission systems wherever motion has to be transmitted from a motor to an operational unit and also within the operational units and engine units themselves.

The transmission systems employed in engineering can be divided into mechanical, hydraulic, pneumatic and electrical.

Mechanical transmission systems such as friction, belt, tooth or worm gearing or chain are the most widely used in machines. They are found in all industrial machines and all vehicles, not to mention complicated machine units in which they are of particular importance.

Pneumatic and hydraulic transmissions have gained a firm foothold in the machine-tool industry, and in recent years they have become widely used in building and agricultural machines and in motor vehicles and cranes. Various types of hydraulic transmission can be used under school conditions to acquaint pupils with this type of transmission, as they are simple in construction and operation and convenient as subjects for practical study. Electrical transmission systems are being used more and more widely. They are based on the use of electric power in machines. They have a relatively high efficiency factor, are reliable in operation, and facilitate economical and rapid remote control of machines.

It is thus of prime importance for schoolchildren to study mechanical transmission systems but they should also be acquainted with pneumatic, hydraulic and electrical transmission systems.

In speaking of operational units, it should be pointed out that, despite the enormous variety of types, it is possible to identify certain common factors in their construction and the principles of their operation, and to distinguish certain typical mechanisms.

All operational units can be divided into three groups according to their functional characteristics: productive, transfer and transport. Each of these groups has its own peculiarities of design which are most clearly shown in the differences between their operating parts.

In the operation of every machine connected with the working or transfer of a material, the operating parts must effect appropriate movements. The movements are determined by the corresponding combinations and couplings of parts which are common to all machines: spindles, shafts, bearings, cog wheels, couplings, cranks, connecting rods, cams, push rods, springs and other standard components. Also common to all machines are free couplings which allow the machine to effect certain movements. These common elements are kinematic pairs (rotatory, progressive, helical and rising), and the most varied mechanisms can be formed from them.

Since the basic movements in production processes are rotatory and progressive (or a combination of them), the typical mechanisms for all machines are those which transform and change one of those motions into the other. These mechanisms are: crank and connecting rod, cam gear, eccentric, screw, rocker. Many of these mechanisms are modifications of each other, such as crank and connecting rod, eccentric, rocker (articulated four-bar motion).

A knowledge of the general principles of the construction and functioning of the mechanisms for transforming motion is the most important item in the study of machines.

The study of the operating members of machines is carried out in connexion with the technological processes performed by the operating units. For example, in all machines for working solids most of the operating members are wedge-shaped, or a modified wedge.

The main items which can be used for the study of machines in schools of general education are the universal screw-cutting lathe, the motor vehicle, tractor or agricultural machine, since these items are available to ordinary schools and embody the above-mentioned complex machine parts, including mechanisms for the transmission and transformation of force; they contain such components as pumps of various types, control devices, etc., which are typical of the majority of machines; as they are very widely available they can be used not only for study but also for training in operation.

The internal combustion engine of the motor vehicle or tractor is of universal importance, as it is widely used in the most varied power plants and vehicles. The mechanisms used in the engine, the transmission, the steering and the chassis of the motor vehicle (crank and connecting rod, cams, clutch, gearbox and differential) are widely used in various machines—machine tools, presses, textile, printing and building machinery, mechanical handling equipment, etc.

To ensure a good knowledge of machines it is very important to acquaint the pupils with the basic technical processes of engineering, and above all with the basic technological processes of manufacturing machine parts and assembling them: working metals by cutting, pressing, casting and welding, the inter-changeability of components, the basic requirements in connexion with components and their assembly, and the processes of erecting and dismantling machines.

From the above brief analysis it can be seen that, in their course of engineering practice, the pupils must acquire a theoretical knowledge of the following branches of engineering:
Machine components and their combination.
The construction and working of mechanisms.
The construction and working of machines.
The basic technological processes for the manufacture of machine parts, the assembly and finishing of machines and mechanisms which are applied in engineering.
It is essential to have a practical as well as a theoretical knowledge of machines. For this reason, in the study of engineering practice and the execution of a specified range of practical work in the treatment of materials, the assembly and dismantling of mechanisms, the operation of machines, etc., the pupils must acquire certain manual and polytechnical skills, such as are used by workers engaged in the production, maintenance and operation of machines, e.g., machine-tool operators, machine fitters, mechanics, maintenance fitters and adjusters, engine-drivers, motor-men, etc. The following skills are involved:

1. The ability to measure, in marking up the blanks and working the machine parts, checking the working parts of mechanisms and machines, dismantling and assembling, etc.
2. The ability to calculate and construct, in determining the dimensions of the blanks, choosing the rate of machining (e.g., speed of cut and feed), determining the characteristics of mechanisms and machines (gear ratios, output, speed, power, fuel consumption, etc.), with the use of formulae, graphs and tables; and the ability to construct geometrical figures, marking out the blanks in accordance with sketches and drawings.
3. The ability to prepare simple sketches, plans and technical drawings and simple kinematic diagrams, to interpret sketches, plans and diagrams; to design simple parts and members; to work out simple designs from a rough draft, and also to work out independently plans and designs for simple articles.
4. The ability to carry out elementary fitter's work in dismantling, assembling and adjusting simple machine assemblies and mechanisms; to undertake simple repairs of machine tools, motor vehicles, tractors and other machines;
5. The ability to effect simple adjustments to metal-cutting tools (drills, lathes, milling machines, etc.), and to control their basic operations; to service and maintain motor vehicles and tractors, and to operate them and other machines with the aid of levers, pedals, fly-wheels, steering wheel, control knobs and other devices;
6. The ability to undertake the technical organization of work—to plan work efficiently, draw up production plans and machining programmes, and to organize work correctly (observing cleanliness and tidiness in the workplace, employ materials, tools and electricity economically, treating equipment carefully and observing safety precautions); to co-operate in rationalizing work processes involving the use of tools, appliances, machines and other equipment.

The above-mentioned branches of engineering practice are dealt with step by step, with due regard to the pupils' age, their level of general education, particularly in such subjects as physics, chemistry, technical drawing and mathematics, and the knowledge and skills acquired in practical work in the school workshops (grades V–VIII).

The syllabus for this subject was originally planned in the form of the so-called *practicum* or course of practical work which was introduced into the schools of general education in the 1954/55 academic year.

Following a review of experience with the *practicum* in engineering practice in the general schools, and on the basis of special research carried out in the experimental schools of the Academy of Pedagogical Sciences, the syllabus of the 'engineering practice' course is being steadily perfected.

At the present time, 'engineering practice' is taught in grades VIII–IX and proceeds along the following lines.

As an introduction, the pupils are told about the use of machines and machinery in various fields of human activity, and about the mechanization and automation of production, which form the basis of technical progress today.

The first section, 'machine parts and their combination', is devoted to the study of standard machine parts and their combination (moving and stationary, detachable and fixed). The pupils are given an idea of the various types of deformation and stress in machine parts, and the basic requirements of hardness and strength.

The second section of the syllabus, 'the construction and working of machinery', provides for acquainting the pupils with the transmission of rotary motion, with mechanisms for the transformation of motion (helical, rack-and-pinion, crank, ratchet), and with the construction of pneumatic, hydraulic and electrical transmissions. Information is given about standard machine units—reversing gears, reduction gears, gearboxes, brakes, etc.

In the third section, 'machines', the pupils learn about the classification of machines into motors and operational units, gain an idea of the construction and work of rotary, piston and reaction motors and of machines for production, transfer and transport. Information is also given about mechanical devices and other modern means of automatic control, regulation and checking of machines. The pupils learn about the basic trends of contemporary machine development—the application of unit construction, of machines with programme control, and of automatic production lines, shops and factories.

In the fourth section of the syllabus, 'machine production', information is given about the production of blanks for machine parts (casting, rolling, forging and stamping, welding and cutting), and about processes of working them by cutting on machine tools and by the latest electrochemical methods. The pupils learn about accuracy and cleanliness in machining parts, about tolerances and fit, about the production processes of assembly and dismantling, regulation and adjustment, testing and erection of finished mechanisms and machines.

The study of mechanisms and machines, and the basic processes of their manufacture, is based on the knowledge of physics which the pupils have previously acquired. Thus, the pupils become acquainted with the application of the laws governing the inter-action of forces, the transmission of effort and motion in machines, processes of friction, balancing and adjustment of machines, the application to operating machines of the law of conservation and transformation of energy, etc. In studying the processes of working materials by cutting and by pressure, they make use of their knowledge of the physical and mechanical properties of solids, of deformation, breaking loads and strength.

The various methods of teaching, applied to lessons in engineering practice, meet the basic requirements for the general methods which are used in teaching children in Soviet schools. Their selection and combination help to produce clear, comprehensible and systematic teaching, help the pupils to understand what they are doing and to acquire a sound mastery of knowledge and skills, and contribute to the achievement of the general tasks of communist education.

But the special content and organization of engineering practice and the special character of the pupils' work (in comparison with normal classwork in the study of basic subjects) have a strong influence on the nature of the teaching methods and give them a certain special character. This applies in particular to the demonstration of methods of working, exercises in practical laboratory work, the use of technical literature (sketches, drawings and instructional diagrams), visits to industrial undertakings, and also to methods of testing and appraising the pupil's knowledge and skills. Practical research work of various kinds is widely employed (in the study of the properties of materials, their structure, the study of mechanisms, machine parts and machine units, etc.), as are various kinds of work intended to inculcate practical skills and accomplishments in dismantling, in minor repairs and adjustments, in the assembly of various mechanisms and machine units, including metal-cutting lathes and motor vehicles (see Figs. 30 and 31). The syllabus for this work includes the preparation of lists of parts and their faults and of elementary kinematic diagrams of mechanisms, the determination of gear ratios, efficiency, etc. Practical work is a characteristic item in the teaching of engineering practice in the schools.

The teacher also brings into the practical lesson periods a demonstration of working methods, supervises the independent work of the pupils, checks their progress, assesses the results and draws conclusions. Practical work is carried out in accordance with written instructions. Where the purpose and nature of the work makes this necessary, the teacher intervenes actively in the pupils' work with supplementary oral explanations and the showing of detailed written instructions. In the research-type activities, pupils are given a written instruction chart and are allowed very great independence in their work. If the work is intended to teach the pupils particular skills, the teacher will give them active guidance in their work, showing them the correct methods of using tools, the correct sequence of working movements, etc.

For the pupils' independent work during class periods, use is made of educational aids for engineering practice brought out by the State Educational Publishing House and of reference books, albums and other literature. In their practical work of dismantling and assembling mechanisms, manufacturing and finishing articles, various set tasks, drawings and instructional charts are used, giving the names of items of practical work, set exercises, theoretical notes, a list of materials, appliances and tools required for the work, and the sequence of operations. The use of these instructional charts makes it possible to effect a substantial reduction in the amount of introductory and routine explanation given by the teacher, and to make greater calls on the pupils' ability to work independently.

In their practical work the pupils learn to carry out various checking and measuring operations, using rules, the calliper-square, micrometer, angle gauge, gauges, templates and other instruments, and to interpret and prepare sketches and drawings, to carry out simple technical calculations and to prepare production work plans. The pupils develop an ability to use materials and electricity economically, to observe safety precautions at work and to handle instruments carefully. They learn the fundamental methods of design, in which they are set exercises containing the most usual data for the preparation of articles, so that they themselves may determine the shape, form and dimensions of the required parts. The practical work is so arranged that the pupils may consciously use their theoretical knowledge, learn to solve production problems on their own, prepare their own workplace, select the required materials, tools and appliances, and ensure that the machine-tool equipment is ready for work.

The teachers prepare their pupils carefully for excursions to industrial undertakings in connexion with the study of engineering practice, by giving them preliminary explanations about the plant.

First of all, there is an introductory visit to the enterprise to give the pupils a general picture of the types of modern machine tools, after which excursions are arranged with more specific aims, e.g., to machine shops, to acquaint the pupils with the construction and working of lathes, milling machines, planing machines and other machine tools; to foundry, forging and pressing shops, to familiarize the pupils with the processes of casting and forging; to the heat-treatment shop to acquaint them with the hardening of parts; to the metal-testing laboratory and other departments of the undertaking.

As he supervises the progress and results of their practical work, the teacher assesses it on a five-point scale, taking into account the quality of the completed work, the correctness of the methods used, and the speed of the work, i.e., its 'productivity'. At the conclusion of each section of the course, the pupils' over-all progress is assessed by practical tests lasting from one to two hours. The results of these general practical tests not only make possible a correct assessment of the pupils' progress in engineering practice, but also throw light on common shortcomings in their knowledge and skills, and enable conclusions to be drawn about any deficiencies in the methods of teaching engineering practice and the necessary remedies for them.

The engineering-practice course requires the use of mechanical fitters' workshops and of an engineering study room.

The mechanical fitters' workshops, equipped with fitters' benches and operational machine tools, is used for practical work on metal-cutting lathes and for the manufacture, assembly and finishing of such articles as models, simple appliances, instruments and tools.

The engineering study room is used for work on the fundamentals of production engineering and engineering practice (including the construction and working of the motor vehicle) and also for practical work in the dismantling and assembly of mechanisms and machines, in the design, calculation and measurement, checking and verification of machine parts, etc.

As a rule, the teachers try to get through all the subject matter in class. Homework is set for engineering practice only in special cases.

The basic forms of teaching used in the engineering-practice course are lessons in which the pupils are taught theory and in which they carry out practical laboratory work; practical activities in the engineering study room, in workshops or in the engineering shops of industrial enterprises; and excursions to enterprises and other places.

The ratio of theoretical to practical work in engineering practice varies according to the subject. On the average, as has been shown by practical experimental work and by the experience of the general schools, the ratio of theory to practice should be approximately 2:1. With this ratio, it is feasible to teach engineering practice at the proper educational level, the necessary interest in the subject is awakened in the pupils, and excessive bookwork is avoided.

An important principle of the organization of work in engineering practice is that a considerable part of the work done by the pupils should be of practical use. The pupils frequently make metal objects such as fitters' hammers, angle bars, rules, inside callipers, outside callipers and other instruments, nuts and bolts, bits, centre punches and simple apparatus, technical models, visual aids for mechanics and engineering studies, and various appliances for use in work. Experience has shown that in following the syllabus the pupils can be successfully put on to minor repairs of mechanical devices used in teaching (repairing and replacing machine parts, cutting threads, replacing keys, pins, chains, etc.), of tools, and sometimes even of metal-cutting lathes. Assembly fitter's work (syllabus for grade VIII) is particularly useful on articles manufactured to the order of production enterprises (works or factory, machine and tractor station workshops, etc.).

The business link between the school and the production enterprise in the study of engineering practice may also take the form of practical production work by the pupils (for example in the machine shops, assembly shops and other parts of engineering and repair works). Considerable experience of such practical work has already been acquired, with the pupils operating metal-cutting lathes and carrying out the assembly and finishing of articles in the machine shops of enterprises, in accordance with plans which supplement and extend what is learnt in the engineering-practice syllabus. Similarly, the study of machines, which is begun at school, is continued in the factory. The pupils gain a sounder and wider knowledge and perfect their skills while taking part in machine operation and in the production process at the works.

ELECTRICAL ENGINEERING

The study of electrical engineering deals with the methods of utilizing electrical phenomena for practical purposes, and is useful in the technological field as it promotes the application of electricity in the national economy.

A distinction is made between theoretical, general and specialized electrical engineering. The theoretical branch deals with the characteristics and methods of calculating d.c. and a.c. circuits and voltages, and electromagnetic fields. In general electrical engineering, a study is made of electrical measurement, d.c. and a.c. equipment and machines, their construction and use. In the specialized courses of electrical engineering, a study is made of electrical engineering as applied to mining, agriculture, and other fields.

343

The course in electrical engineering in the secondary school is intended to acquaint the pupils with the construction, working principles, and application of typical electrical equipment which is met with in many factories.

In studying electrical engineering, the pupils come to realize that higher production and increased productivity of labour depend on electrification and on complex mechanization and automation of the productive processes, all of which are bound up with the application and use of electric power. Automatic electrical operation, with a highly developed system of regulation and control, is one of the important basic requirements for a rapid expansion of industry. Electric power is used not only for the operation of machines and various machine tools, but also for the smelting of metals in electric furnaces, for the heat treatment of materials, automation, communications, etc.

The electric motor, as almost the sole motive power in machines and machine tools, is already ceasing to have an existence separate from the machine; it is becoming part of the machine, being built into it, being incorporated with it at the design stage; hence, the machine or machine tool is often served not by one, but by several motors of varying power. Every metalworking, textile or other machine, every industrial or transfer machine, uses an electric motor, starting and controlling mechanism, and wiring, in which electric power is employed. Automatically operated machines use automatic regulating and control devices. Automation in industry is based mainly on the use of electric power.

The possibility of breaking down electric power, transmitting and distributing it over wiring, the ease with which its use can be controlled, and its high efficiency, all combine to make it universally applicable.

The Plenum of the Central Committee of the Communist Party of the U.S.S.R., in June 1959, planned a further development of the automation and mechanization of productive processes, which is being carried out on the basis of the use of electric power. Secondary-school pupils need to acquire a knowledge of the fundamentals of electronics, automatic electrical transmission, automatic regulation and control.

Lenin attached great importance to spreading the idea of electrification, and considered it essential that young people should have a basic knowledge of electricity, of the use of electricity in the engineering and chemical industries, and of the electrification plan of the Russian Soviet Federal Socialist Republic.

The pupils acquire a knowledge of the application of electricity in the physics course, during their study of the appropriate part of the syllabus in grades VIII, X and XI. But this knowledge is given only incidentally, not systematically, and is quite inadequate in amount. To include in the physics course a larger amount of technical knowledge might prejudice the logical and systematic presentation of the subject in teaching.

In their laboratory work in physics, the children acquire some skill in electrical measurements. But in the physics lessons it is impossible to teach them how to handle technical electrical equipment and electrical machines, how to dismantle and assemble electrical machines, how to test them, etc. Consequently, it has been found necessary to study electrical engineering in school as a polytechnical subject. Taking the children's knowledge of physics as a basis, electrical engineering should acquaint them with the scientific principles of electrical technology and its processes, and help them to deal with the commonest electrical equipment used in modern industry, and to prepare them for productive work in their chosen field.

Consequently, in their electrical-engineering course, the pupils are given a theoretical and practical knowledge of the following subjects: (a) the basic materials of electrical engineering, from which electrical machines and equipment are manufactured (conductors, insulators and magnetic materials); (b) technical electrical measuring instruments, used in the assembly of control panels, switchboards and other installations; (c) alternating current (single phase and three-phase), the wiring of current-consuming equipment (electric lamps, electric motors, etc.) in a three-phase circuit, and the power factor of alternating current, its importance for the national economy and the means of increasing it; (d) transformers, which are widely used in the transmission and distribution of electrical power and in electric welding, electric measurements, radio engineering, etc.; (e) three-phase electric motors (asynchronous and squirrel-cage) most commonly used in electrically driven equipment in industry and agriculture; (f) direct-current machines (generators and electric motors) which are widely used in lifting gear, cranes and transport (motor vehicles, electric locomotives and aircraft), in electric drives, where speed has to be adjusted within wide limits, in electromechanical transformers, etc.; (g) the principles of automation, automatic electric drive and control of mechanisms (the magnetic starter, thermal and electromagnetic relays, etc.); (h) the principles of industrial electronics (semiconductors and electronic equipment, electronic relays and photo-relays, amplifiers, etc.) which are of exceptional importance in the automation of production processes and hence in raising the productivity of labour.

Electromagnetic processes provide the essential basis for electrical machines. A course in electrical engineering gives the pupils a clear conception of the physical laws underlying the construction and operation of electrical machines and equipment.

One or more electrical circuits are installed in every electrical plant. In their study of electrical engineering, the pupils acquire an understanding of electrical circuits, construct their own, and read simple theoretical and working diagrams.

The general educational, polytechnical nature of the secondary-school course in electrical engineering is emphasized by the fact that the course is based on the explanation of the scientific principles of electrical engineering, on the application of a knowledge of physics and other subjects to electrical engineering, and on the familiarization of the pupils with the most usual types of electrical equipment. Machines and equipment are studied with an understanding of their operation and use in production.

The study of electrical engineering is begun when the pupils have been through the basic elements of electricity in their physics course, i.e., in grade XI.

The physics teacher acquaints his pupils with the physical basis of electrical equipment and machines, and explains the physical phenomena and laws which govern the operation of such machines and equipment, whereas the teacher of electrical engineering explains the construction, design, working principles and uses of electrical equipment, and teaches the pupils the practical handling of electrical machines and equipment.

There is uniformity, in physics teaching and the teaching of electrical engineering, in the definition of physical quantities, terminology, methods of preparing electrical diagrams, the sequence followed in practical work, the keeping of work records and notes and the handling of electrical apparatus and instruments. Both in physics and in electrical-engineering lessons the pupils learn to use technical terms correctly, to work on their own, and to use works of reference.

In presenting new material, or in revision, the physics teacher makes use of examples from electrical engineering. He also uses the equipment of the electrical-engineering room to give his lessons and general lectures; the teacher of electrical engineering, in his turn, uses the equipment of the electrical section of the physics study room.

Teachers of physics and electrical engineering may arrange joint excursions to factories for their pupils, on such themes as 'the application of electric power in modern industry', 'the production and distribution of electric power at the power station', 'the electrical equipment of the factory', 'the electrical repair shop', etc.

Theoretical studies on electrical engineering are accompanied by the showing of samples of machine parts and designs and demonstration of the operational methods of handling electrical equipment, by experimental demonstrations, the preparation of various electrotechnical diagrams, and the showing of tables, wall-sheets, slides and films.

The theoretical lessons on each item in the syllabus also provide an introduction to the practical work which is carried out during the course of study. If the practical work follows immediately after the theory, the two can be more closely linked, and the pupils' theoretical knowledge can be consolidated and deepened in the course of their work. The work itself is also a source of new knowledge.

To stimulate the pupils' powers of learning, and to develop habits of independent work, they are given various pieces of practical productive work to do, and exercises with materials for electrical distribution, taking ten to fifteen minutes each.

The pupils have to identify samples of various electrical materials, which are laid out on the tables in sets; to interpret the rating plates of electrical machines and equipment in accordance with previously prepared charts; to read the scale values of electrical measuring instruments and interpret the conventional signs on the scales; to draw and read electrotechnical diagrams; identify samples of radio parts, etc. Their practical work also includes such tasks as familiarizing themselves with the automation of electric drives, with various automatic devices and various relays: electromagnetic, thermal, electronic, etc. In such work, use is made of relays which are employed in automatic electric drives for metal-cutting lathes, of magnetic starters, magnetic amplifiers, relays and indicators used in motor vehicles, of automatic equipment employed in agriculture for the control of electric drives and electric heating, equipment for the control of temperature and incubators, and of the water level in water reservoirs.

In their practical work, the pupils proceed from one task to another in accordance with a fixed schedule. Two to three workplaces are provided for each practical job, depending on the number of pupils and the availability of equipment.

For practical work in electrical engineering, written instructions are provided, describing the purpose of the work and its content, setting certain tasks, indicating the basic working equipment, and providing test questions, in the answers of which the pupils show whether they have understood the essentials of the work concerned. Instruction charts are drawn up so as to ensure that the pupils

347

steadily acquire greater independence in carrying out their practical work. Here is a typical instruction chart.

Testing a three-phase induction motor with squirrel-cage rotor

Collect the equipment and electrical circuit for testing the electric motor.

In the equipment for testing an electric motor a braking device is employed, consisting of a wooden frame on which is mounted a torque meter, connected to the motor pulley by a belt, the tension of which can be measured by means of a screw. Examine the wiring diagram. State what voltage (line or phase) is shown by the voltmeter. At what voltage (phase or line) is the wattmeter switched into circuit? What is the reading? How is the current consumption of the motor determined from the reading of the wattmeter? How is the full single-phase and three-phase load determined from the ammeter and voltmeter readings? How is the power factor of the motor determined from the readings of all the instruments?

Select all the electrical measuring instruments required for your work, on your own, making use of the rating plate of the motor. The ammeter must have a current rating four to five times greater than the nominal rating of the motor in question. Show the selected circuit to the teacher. After obtaining his permission, connect the equipment to the three-phase circuit.

Many teachers make use of instructional charts with incomplete data, and the pupils themselves select the appropriate measuring instruments, make the diagrams or prepare their own work plan.

Double periods are allotted in the school timetable for electrical-engineering work. Normally these classes take place either in the laboratory of the physics room, or in the special electrical-engineering room, installed in premises adjacent to the physics room. The premises in which electrical-engineering studies are carried out are equipped with special work benches for the pupils' practical work. Beside each bench or on it, a small switchboard is installed with power points, and instructional sheets and drawings on electrical engineering and safety precautions are hung on the walls. If circumstances permit, some practical work is carried out under production conditions in the mechanical repair shops and electrical fitting workshops of factories, in electrical-instrument laboratories, etc.

An important factor in linking electrical-engineering studies with production is the organization of excursions to enterprises during out-of-school hours. These acquaint the pupils in a practical way with electrical equipment and the uses of electricity. Out-of-class studies at specialized technical clubs are organized for pupils particularly interested in electrical engineering. Electrical-engineering studies are linked up with participation by the pupils in productive work.

Schools have a great deal of experience in drawing school-children into socially useful work, such as installing electricity and radios at the school and in their district, installing electrical equipment in the school's physics and electrical-engineering rooms, making and installing electrical equipment for practical studies in physics and electrical engineering, making models and visual aids, etc. At some schools, the pupils build and service the school power stations, and this is of great help to them in acquiring a practical mastery of electrical engineering.

On the basis of experience at leading schools, it may be said that the teaching of electrical engineering becomes more effective and contributes more to the polytechnical and practical training of schoolchildren if: (a) the study of this subject is based on knowledge and skills acquired in the course of physics lessons; (b) care is taken, when technical objects are studied, to bring out the underlying physical and technical scientific principles; (c) during their practical studies in electrical engineering, the pupils work intelligently and find solutions, by themselves, to technical problems within the scope of their ability; (d) technical objects are studied in relation to each other, and their common features, which are shared by other technical objects as well, are pointed out; (e) the pupils are shown the practical application of acquired technical knowledge under industrial conditions and are drawn into socially useful work, subject to the educational and training requirements of electrical-engineering teaching at school.

HOW COURSES IN ENGINEERING PRACTICE AND ELECTRICAL
ENGINEERING HELP SCHOOLCHILDREN TO MASTER VARIOUS
FORMS OF WORK

Engineering practice and electrical engineering are studied, as general technical subjects, in the senior classes of secondary polytechnic schools. These schools, as already explained, offer production training with a view to preparing pupils for vocational work in production enterprises, in cultural and educational or commercial institutions. Production training in a particular trade cannot include this sort of general information about machines or the application of knowledge concerning electricity, since such training is, by its very purpose, limited to the specialized and fairly narrow study of the design and operation of certain specific machines and electric and radio devices.

School polytechnical courses in engineering practice and electrical engineering acquaint the pupils with standard machine parts and their connexions, the design and uses of the most common mechanisms for transmission and transformation of force, the materials, devices and machines used in electrical engineering, and the common and typical methods of automatic control, regulation and checking. The information conveyed is of the most general kind, having a wide polytechnical significance and enabling the pupils to grasp and assimilate, quickly and fairly thoroughly, the principles of the design and operation of special machines and appliances used in electrical and radio engineering, which are characteristic of different branches of production and aspects of technology and are used by workers in different trades.

As a result of the experimental teaching of engineering practice and electrical engineering in the general schools, and on the basis of research carried out at the experimental schools of the R.S.F.S.R. Academy of Pedagogical Sciences, it has been established that these general technical courses, occupying a place midway between physics and the specialized technology studied under the heading of production training, are a most important factor in polytechnical education and help the pupils in the successful mastery of their chosen trade. The teaching of engineering practice and electrical engineering gives the general technical grounding needed for any kind of working activity, acquaints the pupils with up-to-date technology and prepares them for work, not only in modern mechanized and automated production, but also in the sphere of everyday repairs and services and in the fields of science and culture.

Actual examples of production training at schools in Moscow, Novosibirsk, Sverdlovsk, Gorky, Saratov and other towns, and the comments received from schools and production enterprises, confirm that pupils who have completed the course in engineering practice and electrical engineering master the trades of fitter, turner, milling-, boring- or grinding-machine operator, etc., more successfully and more quickly than those who, for some reason, have not previously studied these subjects.

The close link between the study of engineering practice and electrical engineering on the one hand and, on the other, the productive work done in the school workshops, at factories and at collective and State farms, where the pupils make various articles and help to install electricity, radios, etc., enables them to acquire a number of practical skills and habits useful in general technical work.

Production work connected with the study of engineering

practice and electrical engineering not only extends the pupils' knowledge but also has an important educative function, since the habit of active thinking and a creative attitude to labour are inculcated in the process of applying acquired knowledge and solving practical production problems. Team work, whether at school or outside it, fosters such qualities as neatness and precision, a disciplined and organized approach, comradely behaviour, and team spirit in work. The effect of the entire system of relations characteristic of socialist production, and participation in the communal organization and planning of labour, lay the foundations in the pupils' minds for an economical, careful attitude towards all equipment, instruments, materials, electric current and other kinds of public property. Productive work develops initiative and resourcefulness and an active and creative attitude towards the tasks set.

In this way, properly organized studies in engineering practice and electrical engineering, closely linked with participation by the schoolchildren in socially useful work, are an important means of raising the general standard of education and polytechnical training and help the children in making a well-founded choice of a trade.

CHAPTER XVIII

TRAINING IN PRODUCTIVE WORK AND ITS PART IN POLYTECHNICAL EDUCATION IN SCHOOLS

by S. A. Shaporinsky and A. A. Shibanov

The main purpose of training in productive work is to prepare schoolchildren for productive and socially useful work and train them for this work while they are still at school. This is done in grades IX–XI. As a result, the pupils acquire the knowledge and practical skills that will enable them to work at the level of productivity attained by society.

The organized and planned occupational future of school-leavers is not the only concern that dictates the vocational trend of secondary education; a further reason is that the only way the schools can fulfil the task of educating their pupils in the spirit of communist morality is by making them work alongside workers and peasants and at the same level of productivity.

The Soviet Union possesses an extensive system of vocational training, with many branches, ranging from full-time vocational schools to factory courses. Every enterprise is a school for the training and further training of skilled workers. This system would still be adequate to cope with the vocational training of secondary-school leavers as well, as was the case before the education reform; but the task of educating people for the communist society of the future called for the organization of technical instruction in the secondary schools themselves, because that is the only place where the decisive process of habituating the pupils to work can be achieved.

The training of new workers, especially skilled workers, carried out by the enterprises themselves by means of individual and team instruction has serious drawbacks and does not always meet the demands the technical process makes upon the workers.

The aim of providing vocational training in the secondary school is to raise the level of such training among the young people. Experience has shown that three years' vocational training in the eleven-year secondary school is giving better results than individual or team instruction, or even the part-time courses followed by pupils who completed the former ten-year secondary school. It is not only the time factor—roughly the same amount of time devoted to vocational training, but spread over a longer period— that is important here; more important still is the close connexion between vocational training and general and polytechnical education. Until recently, the training of skilled workers for agriculture was carried out in different schools and at courses which were primarily in towns. These schools and courses were attended by young people who had received seven years' schooling.

The introduction of training in productive work in secondary schools is making it much easier for urban and rural young people to acquire a trade and to attract people with secondary education into production. This will have a great effect on the raising of work-standards in both industry and agriculture.

Another reason why vocational training has been introduced into secondary schools is that manual and technical training, productive and socially useful work cannot be achieved in the senior grades to the required extent without giving it a vocational trend, since work in production has such a trend.

The pronounced vocational trend of training in productive work in secondary schools not only moves in the same direction as polytechnical education but helps to make it more valuable. Lenin pointed out that polytechnical education should take place not only in schools of general education but in vocational schools also. Polytechnical education given in the process of teaching general subjects and the study of general technical subjects and poly-technical education in the process of vocational training are all closely linked.

TRAINING IN PRODUCTIVE WORK IN URBAN SCHOOLS AND ITS PART
IN POLYTECHNICAL EDUCATION

In the vocational-training and technical-education system, training in productive work means practical instruction, i.e., training in productive (vocational) knowledge and skills. Theoretical instruction in a specialized trade is treated separately and is not included in the concept of training in productive work.

In secondary schools, however, training in productive work means both theoretical instruction (the teaching of special technical subjects) and practical instruction, carried out on the basis and in the course of productive work.

Many thousands of skilled workers will be trained in the second-ary schools for non-productive branches of the economy and public services such as trade, public nutrition, municipal economy and so forth.

The term 'training in productive work' is therefore a purely conventional designation, indicating training for socially useful work in general, but mainly for productive work.

In all three senior grades in secondary schools (IX–XI) one-third of the teaching time is allotted to training in productive work and to actual productive work (two days a week or approximately a total of 1,350 periods in all), and approximately a quarter of this total to theoretical training in productive work. This is given, as a rule, over a period of two-and-a-half years: in grades IX and X and the first half of grade XI. In the second half of grade XI the whole time (two days a week) is devoted entirely to practical work.

Table 19 shows, by way of example, the timetable for general technical and specialized training in mechanical engineering and metalwork (fitters, turners, milling-machine operators, etc.).

TABLE 19

Type of training	Number of periods per week									Total for grades IX–XI
	Grade IX			Grade X			Grade XI			
	First half-year, per week	Second half-year, per week	Annual total	First half-year, per week	Second half-year, per week	Annual total	First half-year, per week	Second half-year, per week	Annual total	
General technical										
Machinery	2	2	78	—	—	—	—	—	—	78
Electrical engineering	—	—	—	—	2	44	2	—	34	78
Vocational										
Theoretical instruction	2	2	78	4	2	112	2	—	34	224
Practical instruction and productive work	8	8	312	8	8	312	8	12	352	976
TOTAL (periods)	12	12	468	12	12	468	12	12	420	1365

The aims and content of general technical instruction in mechanical and electrical engineering have been described in the previous chapter.

Theoretical training in productive work in an urban school is in most cases represented by one subject, which does, however, consist of several special, more or less independent sub-divisions or topics. As an example, Table 20 shows the break-down, by topics, of the special subject concerned in training a turner.

The theoretical instruction in training a turner shown below may be divided into two parts: (a) general instruction on machinery, largely of a general technical nature; (b) specialized instruction, of importance only to a turner. Topics 4, 5, 6, 7, 8 and 12 belong to the first category, and occupy approximately 45 per cent of the time allotted to theoretical instruction. Topics 4 (materials used) and 5 (interpretation of diagrams) are entirely of a general technical nature. Topics 6, 7 8 and, in part, 11 concern machinery in general. Topic 12 is of a general industrial nature and becomes particularly important in a socialist economy, where the economic and organizational structure of production is closely co-ordinated and the different branches of the national economy are all developed according to a single plan.

All curricula provide for familiarizing the pupils with the latest achievements of science and technology and with the automation of production. In some, for example in the training of weavers, spinners and others, automation is treated as a special topic; in the training of turners (see Table 20 overleaf) it is studied under Topic 10 (basic turning operations).

In training in productive work for other trades, for instance in chemistry or textiles, there is less general technical material in the corresponding special subjects than in the theoretical instruction course for training mechanical engineers. This is quite natural since mechanical engineering and metalworking are the most widespread branches of modern production. At present, training in productive work in urban secondary schools is concentrated primarily on these branches. In the future, as the education reform is carried further in the secondary schools, the training of skilled workers for other branches of industry and also for non-productive and auxiliary branches will be considerably expanded. Even after this, however, no less than 40 per cent of all secondary school pupils are expected to be taking engineering and metalworking.

Within the next few years it is planned to give training in the secondary schools for 1,150 out of 3,700 trades at present covered by vocational schools, courses and individual instruction, and for 86 out of 206 general industrial trades.

Table 20

Topic	Subject	Number of periods (approximate)
1.	General information on the branch of production and the trade concerned	4
2.	Safety measures. Industrial sanitation. Fire protection .	8
3.	General information on the turning lathe, cutting tool and cutting operations	20
4.	General information on the materials used in mechanical engineering	14
5.	Interpretation of diagrams	28
6.	Control and measuring instruments	12
7.	Permissible limits and settings	14
8.	Basic theory of cutting	16
9.	Basic turning operations	28
10.	New turning lathes and their automation	40
11.	Technological processes and technological documentation. General information on machine technology .	24
12.	Basic economics, organization and planning of production	16
	Total	224

The amount of theoretical instruction depends relatively little on the range of jobs in the trade concerned. As was noted above, the time allotted to theoretical instruction varies only within relatively narrow limits (200 to 250 periods). This means that secondary schools try to give all the pupils advanced theoretical training.

If the worker in any given trade is likely to perform a relatively small range of simple tasks (work at the machine in mass production or simple assembly work on a conveyor belt), the secondary schools try to give training in several alternative trades or to ensure that the pupils master a wide range of jobs covering as large a number of operations as possible. It is planned, for example, to train machine operators who would be able to operate several machines: turning lathe, drilling machine, grinder and so forth. The training of machine operators will be carried out side by side with the training of workers for general purpose jobs, such as turners, milling-machine operators and so forth.

In the theoretical part of training in productive work different methods are employed: lectures and discussions accompanied by demonstrations, the solution of problems of a quantitative and qualitative nature, practical laboratory work and excursions. The following examples will give an idea of the exercises and laboratory work used in theoretical instruction.

Problem. In preparing rings for a milling mandrel, it is required to drill a hole with a diameter of 20 mm. and a depth of 15 mm. The material is mark '30' steel, the drill an 'R–9'. Determine, using the handbook, at which cutting speed the drilling should be carried out and calculate the number of revolutions at which the turning lathe should be set.

Problem. Sketch the head of the cutting-off tool and state, using the handbook, what the length of the head and the width of the front cutting edge should be in cutting a 30 mm. diameter blank.

Problem. Explain how each of the following requirements of files is tested in practice: hardness, even height of teeth, absence of warping, absence of cracks.

Problem. A cylinder of diameter 32 mm. has to be turned twice (roughly and with a finish). The material: mark '45' steel, 40 mm. in diameter; cutting tool, 'R–9'. No cooling. Determine, for each process, the depth of cutting, the feed and the cutting speed.

Problem. Determine, according to the kinematic scheme of the gearbox of the '1 A 62' screw-cutting lathe, the minimum and maximum number of revolutions of its spindle.

Problem. Determine from the maximum error tables the permissible play for cylinders with rated diameters of 60 and 120 mm. when connected with apertures to two, three, four and five degrees of accuracy, with a sliding fit and with an aperture system.

Directions for pupils for laboratory work on 'Measurement by sliding calliper and micrometer'

1. Measure the specimen provided by means of sliding callipers, accurate to 0.05 mm. The measurement to be carried out at the points indicated by letters on the diagram. Record the figures obtained in the table:

Specimen \ Measurements	A	B	C	D

2. Measure the specimen provided to an accuracy of 0.02 mm. Proceed as in the first example.
3. Measure the specimen provided by means of a micrometer. Proceed as in the two preceding examples.

Directions for the teacher in setting laboratory work on 'Determining the method of cutting and the geometrical shape of the threading tools, and measuring the elements of the thread'

The laboratory work includes three tasks: (a) measuring the elements of a triangular thread; (b) determining the method of cutting and the geometric shape of the cutting tool in cutting triangular threads of a given diameter; (c) determining the method of cutting and the geometric shape of the cutting tool in cutting trapezoidal threads of a given diameter.

The study group is divided into three sections each of which carries out the three tasks in the course of the study (two periods, i.e., 90 minutes).

For the first task ten sets of specimens are prepared with threads of different diameters. Each set contains one specimen with a triangular thread (with the letter 'A' engraved in the end) and another specimen with a trapezoidal thread (with the letter 'B' engraved on the end). At the other end of the specimen the set number is engraved (1, 2, 3 . . . 10).

When the specimens are prepared the actual dimensions of the elements of their threads should be determined by the teacher and recorded in the table made out as indicated below, which he will use to check the pupils' work.

Number of set and specimen designation		Profile	Pitch	Outside diameter	Inside diameter	Mean diameter
1	A	triangular				
1	B	trapezoidal				
2	A	triangular				
2	B	trapezoidal				
...						
...						
10	A	triangular				
10	B	trapezoidal				

The teacher informs the pupils carrying out the second and third tasks about the material of the blanks, the shape and diameter of the thread (a different one for each) for which they have to determine the geometric shape of the cutting tool and the method of cutting.

Directions for pupils for laboratory work on 'Determining the method of cutting and the geometrical shape of the threading tools, and measuring the elements of the thread'

First task. Measure the elements of a triangular thread.
1. Sketch a table on the lines shown opposite.
2. Enter the numbers of the specimens provided in the table.
3. Measure the elements of the thread of each specimen and enter the results in the table.

358

Number of Set	Profile of thread	Pitch	Outside diameter	Inside diameter	Mean diameter

Second task. Determine the method of cutting the geometrical shape of the cutting tool in cutting a triangular thread.

1. Sketch a table on the following lines:

Material of the blank	Thread	Pitch	Height of profile	Sketch of head of threading tool						
				Method of cutting						
Angles of cutting tool				Width of the blunt end	Rough operations				Finishing-off operations				
ε	γ	α	α_1	α_2	a	Number of operations	t	s	v	n	Number of operations	t	s	v	n

2. Enter in the table the material of the blank and the diameter of the thread (as set by the teacher).
3. Determine the pitch and height of the profile of the thread, using the handbook, and enter in the table.
4. Sketch a diagram in the table (from two angles) of the head of the cutting tool for cutting triangular threads and mark the blunt angles with letters.
5. Determine the geometrical shape of the cutting tool, using the handbook, and enter it in the table.
6. Determine the method of cutting the thread, using the handbook, and enter it in the table.

Third task. Determine the method of cutting and the geometrical shapes of the cutting tool in cutting a trapezoidal thread.

Proceed in the same way as in the second task.

Below will be found a plan for the teacher, tasks for the pupils and diagrams (Figs. 32 and 33) of objects used in training in productive work in connexion with the training of workers assembling electrical instruments in the 315th school in Moscow (school base factory—the Fiselectropribor works).

Plan of practical laboratory work on 'Arrangement and technique of assembling a variable condenser'

Order of work	Time in min.	Objects used and visual aids	Equipment and instruments
Introductory instruction and setting of tasks	10	Set of condenser components and an assembly diagram for each pupil (Fig. 32). Electrical circuit stand for checking the condenser by switching on	Fixtures for assembling condenser. Box wrenches, screwdrivers and pliers
Study of the assembly diagram and selection of condenser components	10		
Assembly of condenser on the fixture	30		
Checking the assembled condenser by switching on . .	5		
Measuring the capacity of the condenser by laboratory methods and comparing these data with those obtained by calculation in the physics class	10		
Writing report	25		
TOTAL	90		

Task for pupils. Arrangement and assembly of a variable condenser.
1. Study the assembly diagram and select components and instruments for assembling the apparatus.
2. Using the assembly diagram assemble the variable condenser.
3. Make an operational and technological chart of the assembly of the condenser, along the following lines.

No.	List of operations carried out	List of components	Number of components	Material of components	Instrument used and appliances

4. Check the assembled condenser on the stand by switching it on.
5. Determine the capacity of the condenser by measurement (in the works laboratory).
6. Compare the calculated data of the condenser's capacity obtained in the physics class with the data obtained in laboratory conditions and explain the reasons for divergence.

Plan of practical laboratory study on 'Arrangement of electrical measuring instruments and the technique of their assembly'

Order of work	Time in min.	Objects used and visual aids	Equipment and instruments
Introductory instruction and setting of tasks	10	Ammeter and laboratory volt-meter	Conveyor
Completion of first part of task. Assembly of the instrument according to electrical plan	20	Additional resistances and shunts	Stands for adjusting instruments. Soldering irons, screw-drivers, etc.
Adjusting the instrument on the stand	10	Electrical circuit for plugging in	
Plugging in the instrument into the circuit and measuring the current or tension . .	10	Ammeter or volt meter. Electrical plan (description) of the instrument	
Calculation of the strength of the additional resistance or shunt and comparison with the actual data	15		
Writing report.	25		
TOTAL	90		

Task for pupils (for the ammeter). Arrangement of electrical measuring instruments and the technique of their assembly.

You are given an incompletely assembled electrical measuring instrument: an ammeter.

1. Study the plan of this instrument (plan attached). Using the plan, acquaint yourselves with the instrument and establish which component is missing. Find the missing component and, using the plan, insert it in the instrument (see Fig. 33).
2. By means of fitting a shunt and shunting the magnetic field of the permanent magnet, check the instrument on the stand according to the instructions (attached).
3. Close the lid of the instrument.
4. Using the assembled instrument, measure the power of the current in the electrical circuit (the circuit is assembled on the stand); to do this:
    (a) study the plan of the circuit;
    (b) determine the method of plugging the instrument into the circuit;
    (c) plug the instrument into the circuit (the switching-on of the

main current to the circuit is carried out by the teacher after checking the correct plugging of the instrument to the circuit).
5. Calculate the strength of resistance of the shunt or the additional resistance, if it is known that the instrument's resistance is 12 ohms and the current passing through the instrument is 0.008 amp.
6. Write an account of the work carried out.

Practical instruction and productive work starts in the vast majority of cases during the first days of instruction in grade IX, except in the case of training for those branches or sectors of industry in which practical instruction begins at the age of 16 or 17.

Practical instruction and work is carried out in training production workshops, in training works and in training sectors of enterprises, and also directly in the ordinary workshops of plants and factories. Such instruction is of two types. Where the instruction and work take place in training workshops, works or sectors, the group of pupils is led by a special instructor—a teaching skilled worker. This is group instruction. Where instruction takes place in ordinary workshops the pupils are attached to skilled workers, working and learning under their guidance. This is individual instruction. At present the individual type of instruction is prevalent but, as the school reforms are carried through and training works and workshops are built, the group type of instruction will be used more and more.

After the initial training, which lasts an average of ninety minutes, the pupils are transferred to work in ordinary workshops.

Below (Table 21), by way of example, is a list of the practical-instruction and productive-work subjects taught in training a general turner. From the list of subjects it can be seen that practical instruction and productive work in training a turner is based on the successive mastering of turning operations. Nevertheless, this is not a system of operations in general but a system of operations on specific objects, for the pupil is producing useful objects (manufactured articles) throughout almost the entire period of instruction. The articles are so chosen that a logical order can be adhered to in mastering the operations. This is achieved to a greater or lesser extent only in group training. It is more difficult when individual training is carried out directly, in ordinary production workshops, where the sequence in which different jobs are mastered depends mainly on the goods produced by the given sector of production.

While the pupil is mastering the basic operations of turning, he is at the same time acquiring general industrial, and in this sense, polytechnical knowledge and skills: how to interpret diagrams, mensuration techniques, how to organize the work and the

TABLE 21

Content of practical studies and work	Number of periods
Safety percautions and organization of the operator's position	8
Practice in operating and adjusting a turning lathe . . .	16
Filing outer cylindrical surfaces and cutting ends and projections	120
Cutting external grooves and excisions	32
Drilling, boring, counter-sinking and centring	32
Boring, counter-sinking and reaming roundholes	72
Filing outer and inner conical surfaces	36
Filing shaped surfaces	40
Cutting of thread with screw dies and taps	32
Cutting of thread with cutting tool	56
First- and second-grade turners' work	532
TOTAL	976

operator's position, how to recognize the properties and varieties of materials, how to handle machines, and so forth.

A constant check is kept on the pupil's progress in acquiring such knowledge and skills not only through the number and quality of the goods he produces, but also by directly testing the degree to which he has mastered a particular skill.

The following description of school exercises will give an idea of the methods used in practical training in productive work.

FILING CENTRED CYLINDRICAL SURFACES

Group instruction (45 minutes)

1. The teacher explains that the filing of cylindrical surfaces is one of the basic operations of turning. Few components leave the turning lathe without this type of work being done in the process of their production.

    Practice in filing cylindrical surfaces will be carried out in finishing the handles of a vice.
2. The teacher draws a diagram of the vice handles on the blackboard and asks the pupils to study it.
3. Bearing in mind that the subject 'Filing cylindrical surfaces' has been dealt with in the theoretical studies, the teacher examines the pupils' readiness for carrying out the exercise independently by posing the following questions:
    (a) What rules must be observed in centering?
    (b) Why is it essential to lubricate the back centre?
    (c) Why is a conical shape produced in centred filing?

(d) How do you check whether the tailstock is set correctly in preparing the lathe for filing cylindrical surfaces?

(e) How do you check the normal clamp pressure of the centres on the component to be processed?

(f) How do you remove the centre from the spindle of the headstock?

4. The teacher demonstrates and explains the sequence in filing when manufacturing a vice handle, the number of revolutions at which the lathe should be set and the depth of cutting with which the filing should be carried out.

Practical exercise (2 hours, 15 minutes)

Filing vice handles held in centres. For the lessons, two vice handles, with central apertures, are prepared for each pupil.

FILING CYLINDRICAL SURFACES IN CHUCKS

Group instruction (45 minutes)

1. The teacher explains that the exercise in filing cylindrical surfaces in chucks will be carried out in finishing off blanks for stud bolts.

2. The teacher draws a diagram of the blank for a stud bolt on the blackboard and shows the finished product.

3. During a discussion, the following questions are put to the pupils:

(a) How do you check the positioning of the material in the chuck?

(b) What rules must be observed in setting the cutting tool for filing cylindrical surfaces?

(c) By how much is the diameter of the component reduced if the cutting tool is shifted by 0.1 mm. transversely before use?

(d) What kind of defects can there be in filing cylindrical surfaces in a chuck?

(e) Why is it possible to produce an oval shape in filing cylindrical surfaces in a chuck?

(f) Why is it possible to produce a conical shape in filing cylindrical surfaces in a chuck?

4. The filing of the blank for a stud bolt in a chuck is demonstrated. The pupils are shown at which number of revolutions the lathe should be set and at what depth the cutting should be carried out.

Practical exercise (2 hours, 15 minutes)

The pupils file stud bolts (in a chuck), feeding the blanks by hand. During the exercise the teacher checks whether the pupils shift the support evenly.

FILING CYLINDRICAL SURFACES WITH PROJECTIONS

Group instruction (20 minutes)

1. The teacher informs the pupils that the exercise at that lesson will be filing blanks for keys for three-jawed self-centering chucks.

2. The key for the chuck is demonstrated and the key finished on the turning lathe.
3. The teacher draws a diagram of the key (as finished on the turning lathe) and asks the pupils (orally) to interpret the diagram.
4. The teacher explains and demonstrates the sequence of operations in finishing the key for the chuck.

Practical exercise

The pupils file the key for the chuck.

We have pointed out that the syllabus for theoretical training in productive work includes special subjects of a general technical nature and that, in training mechanical-engineering workers, up to 45 per cent of the time is allocated to these subjects. These may properly be regarded as a component of both polytechnical and vocational education: the former is an integral part of the latter.

If the main purposes of polytechnical education are to acquaint the pupil with the fundamentals of technology and the major branches of production, then training in productive work, though concerned primarily with fulfilling the first of these, is also partly concerned with the second. As a result of technical progress, industry and agriculture are becoming increasingly dependent on technology and the relative importance of the more universal forms of technology, or means of labour, is growing: electrical equipment, lifting and transport machinery, automation, and so forth.

Under modern conditions of production, mastery of one trade, through knowledge of one sector of production, is a great help in finding one's bearings in regard to the techniques used in others. Training in productive work goes some way towards fulfilling the second purpose of polytechnical education—familiarizing the pupil with different branches of production—in that it gives him a detailed and practical acquaintance with one branch. As can be seen from Table 20, for example, a turner's training includes, apart from the brief general introduction to mechanical engineering at the beginning of the course, a study of the fundamentals of machine technology (Topic 11).

In the training of weavers, the special-subject course includes the study of all the other processes in the textile industry (spinning, finishing, and so forth).

The syllabus for the training of workers in the chemical, metallurgical and other branches of industry using chemical technology includes less material of a general technological and industrial nature than that intended for the training of mechanical-engineering workers. Here, however, all the special-subject material, for instance, the technology of synthetic rubber or of nitric-acid production, is much more closely linked with chemistry than, say mechanical-engineering technology with physics.

Whereas the link between the special and general technical subjects is of paramount importance in training in productive work for the mechanical-engineering trades, the link between the special subjects and natural-science subjects—in this case primarily chemistry—matters most in training in productive work for the chemical, metallurgical and related trades.

In training workers for trades in the power industries (electrical engineers) both aspects of the connexion between vocational, polytechnical and general education have their place. In the syllabus for the theoretical training of electrical fitters or radio mechanics there is much material of a general technical nature (interpreting diagrams, study of materials, etc.), not to mention the fact that electrical engineering itself and all its numerous branches are general technical and general industrial subjects. Electrical engineering and radio engineering are very closely linked with and even overlap physics (with the 'electricity' section).

The educational link between the special subjects and natural-science subjects and, conversely, between the latter and the former, is the link between general, polytechnical and vocational education. Not every demonstrable application of the natural sciences in technology and in production, however, can be regarded as part of polytechnical education. Only in cases when such a demonstration is more than an illustration and aims not only at explaining and confirming some basic scientific principle but also at explaining the scientific basis of some technical or production object can one speak of polytechnical education.

The link between the natural sciences and production is achieved by means of the technical sciences. For this reason the connexion between scientific principles on the one hand and training in productive work and the labour of the pupils on the other—a connexion which goes beyond illustration—can be effected primarily in an indirect manner, through theoretical training in productive work and instruction in a special subject. It is therefore most important that vocational training be given on the basis of, and in close connexion with, scientific principles. There is a twofold connexion between general and polytechnical education and vocational training, established both in the process of teaching natural sciences and general technical subjects (in the direction of a link with vocational training) and in the process of vocational training (in the direction of a link with natural sciences and general technical subjects.)

Training in productive work therefore creates the most favourable conditions for this particular kind of application of the natural sciences in technology and production.

This does not exhaust the connexion between the content of vocational training and polytechnical education. The content of instruction in the fundamentals of science in a given school is influenced by the vocational trend of the school. Given an equal obligatory minimum of knowledge in general educational subjects, a certain degree of variety is achieved in the content of the material of instruction. Depending on the special character of vocational training, additional information is imparted on those general-education subjects which have the greatest importance for the training concerned.

The same applies also to the content of instruction in general technical subjects such as mechanical and electrical engineering. The regulations for secondary schools give the education committee of the school the right to introduce some alterations in the syllabuses. Changes connected with vocational training must not be such as to destroy the completeness and systematic character of instruction in the subjects, reduce the time devoted to any subject or lower the level of knowledge demanded of the pupils.

Of no less importance for the mutual connexion of general and polytechnical education and vocational training is the methodological aspect of the matter: the forms and methods of utilizing, in teaching natural sciences and general technical subjects, the material relating to training in production work, in order to open up and make real the material of these subjects on the basis of the branch or sector of production for which pupils are being trained.

TRAINING IN PRODUCTIVE WORK IN RURAL SCHOOLS AND ITS PART IN POLYTECHNICAL EDUCATION

Training in productive work in rural schools has for its purpose the training of a wide range of workers for industrialized socialist agriculture: crop-growing mechanics (with a bias towards field-cropping, horticulture or fruit and vegetable growing), animal-husbandry mechanics, electricians for work at maintenance and repair stations and inter-farm servicing workshops and so forth.

Training in productive work comprises two parts. The first part consists of studying the general bases of agricultural production, plant-growing, animal husbandry, agricultural machinery, electrical engineering, the economics and organization of agricultural production. A knowledge of the fundamentals of these agricultural sciences is obligatory for workers in all agricultural trades for which training is given in rural polytechnical labour schools providing training in productive work. The second part consists of special training (theoretical and practical) in one of the branches of agriculture.

The following is the timetable for training in productive work, adopted by the Lenin Memorial School (Moscow District).

TABLE 22. Timetable for the training of crop-growing mechanics at the Lenin Memorial School

Title of course	Number of periods per week			Total for grades IX–XI
	grade IX	grade X	grade XI	
Crop-growing and the agro-technics of vegetable and fruit crops. . .	3	3	—	180
The principles of animal husbandry .	2	—	—	60
Handling agricultural machinery . .	3	3	—	180
Electrical engineering	—	2	4	188
Fitting and repair work	—	—	3	96
Organization and economics of agriculture	—	—	1	32
TOTAL (periods)	8	8	8	736

Of the 736 periods (spread over 126 days) allotted to practical instruction and productive work, forty-eight days in grade IX are spent in working with agricultural machines for cultivating the school plot and six days in practical work at a livestock farm; in grade X, thirty-six days are spent in tractor work and eighteen in practical work in electrical engineering; in grade XI, eighteen days are spent in repair work on machinery and electrical equipment. Theoretical instruction takes place in the winter, practical training and productive work in the spring and summer.

Pupils in grade XI take an examination in their specialized subject at the end of the first half-year. A certificate is given after the pupil has passed his examinations in repair work, electrical engineering and the economics and organization of agriculture.

The timetable shown above is intended to train a worker capable of performing a wide range of jobs in connexion with the agro-technics of fruit-growing, the general mechanization of agricultural work and the utilization of electrical agricultural appliances.

In grade IX, under the headings of crop-growing and agricultural machinery, the pupils learn the fundamentals of agriculture and the agro-technics of the main crops and the structure and working principles of the main agricultural machines. This gives them a preparation for understanding the purpose of the spring and summer work on the farm. In the course of their theoretical studies the pupils also acquire certain abilities of a practical nature, which are of importance for production both from the standpoint of knowledge and practice. Under this heading come practical exercises in preparing seeds for sowing, selecting fertilizers, calculating the seeds and fertilizers required and drawing up agro-technical plans for the crops with which the pupils will be dealing. During the lessons problems of an organizational character are solved (study of norms, distribution of the labour force, assessment of work and so forth). The curriculum also includes class study of the fundamentals of animal husbandry.

Theoretical and practical training in grade X is of the same type but concentrates on the study of machines, particularly tractors, and their preparation for use. The pupils study the tractor, the techniques and technology of tractor work and prepare themselves for working in whichever branch of crop-growing or animal husbandry is to be their speciality. The work done by the pupils is a direct continuation of the instruction and is closely linked to it.

Finally, in grade XI the work of studying the special branch concerned is continued in conjunction with the labour which completes this special training. This includes, in regard to the mechanization of agriculture: repair of agricultural machinery, jobs in electrical engineering, and the study of the local agricultural economy; in regard to crop-raising and animal husbandry: the technology of storing and initial processing of products, jobs in electrical engineering and practical economics.

In the rural secondary schools two types of organization of training in productive work and productive labour have become established: (a) pupils' production brigades (Stavropol region) and (b) training and experimental farms in collective and State farms (Ryazan province).

From the educational point of view, the main value of the pupils' brigades and the training-and-experimental farms is that they preserve and strengthen the school community organizations through the live and interesting work of the pupils in agricultural production, with the result that the influence of teaching and training on the pupils is continuous and systematic. The pupils' work in these production brigades and on experimental farms under a well-organized system of self-government provides an opportunity for consolidating and developing team spirit, training the pupils to give and take orders, as well as inculcating other moral qualities. In natural, daily contact with working people, with the workers of the collective settlements, the pupils acquire from day to day a communal working experience which gives to boys and girls a more mature outlook on the life around them and on human relations in society. Experience has shown that these production brigades and training-and-experimental farms are the best basis for training in productive work in agriculture.

In the process of training in productive work, great attention is given to establishing the connexion between knowledge and labour. To this end there are lectures, discussions and excursions. Instruction is given before work, explaining not only the techniques of the work to be done but also its scientific and technical basis. The pupils are watched while they are at work and are asked questions in connexion with the job they are doing; questions which accustom them consciously to discover where they are succeeding and where they are failing.

In rural schools the connexion between instruction in the fundamentals of science and actual work is also established through learning the fundamentals of technology and, even more broadly, those of production. The scheme is as follows:

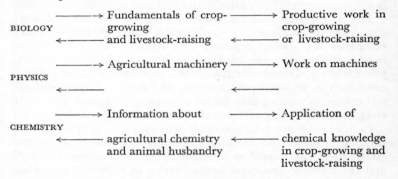

According to the same plan it is possible to establish a connexion between mathematics and draughtsmanship, geography and the practical economics of agricultural production. The two arrows show the way the component parts of the plan interact. Thus the first arrow (⟶) between biology and fundamentals of crop-growing or livestock-raising, placed above the other arrow, shows that a biological understanding of the scientific basis of crop-growing and livestock-raising or animal husbandry serves as a fulcrum for a scientific understanding of the production technology. This is not always achieved, however, and is not always feasible, since the requirements of production can, in practice, make demands and pose questions which cannot form part of a school course on the fundamentals of biology. In such cases the biology involved must be especially explained so that its content and form are accessible to the pupils' understanding. This requirement is designated by the arrow ($\longleftarrow$).

The second pair of arrows signifies that knowledge about the fundamentals of the branch of production concerned, in this instance crop-growing or animal husbandry, is the scientific basis of the pupils' individual work and of their experience in production. Scientific knowledge (biology and fundamentals of crop-growing, biology and animal husbandry) is the grounding for conscious, scientifically based performance of labour operations. In the plan this is shown by the arrow ($\longrightarrow$) between the fundamentals of crop-growing (or animal husbandry) and work in these branches of agriculture. In practice, however, questions frequently arise which cannot be foreseen in the studies on the fundamentals of production or technology. In such cases additional explanation is required. This is indicated by the arrow ($\longleftarrow$) between the fundamentals of crop-growing (or animal husbandry) and productive work in the corresponding branches of agriculture. The same kind of interrelation will be seen in the other plans mentioned. Direct links are also possible between knowledge of the fundamentals of the natural sciences and the pupils' labour, and these links can be revealed by setting special tasks and problems to be solved by the pupils when carrying out labour operations. In physics, chemistry and biology, however, the solution of such problems must be reached by utilizing knowledge and skills of a technological nature. Technological information is frequently included in the course on the fundamentals of the natural sciences.

To achieve the combination of instruction with productive labour it is particularly important that the pupils do experimental work in agriculture. This is common practice in the advanced rural schools, and applies to pupils in the senior grades. The very nature of the experimental work on collective and State farms is such that the pupils cannot possibly carry out their productive work without applying their knowledge of biology and crop-growing. In the process of experimental work the pupils learn the most up-to-date techniques for producing high crop yields and seek the most effective methods of tilling the soil and tending plants. This develops creative abilities essential to a future transformer of nature and innovator in collective farm production.

In the Lenin Memorial School, pupils who had studied the principles of crop-growing for three years carried out tests on different varieties of potato to determine relative yields and ripening times. This was a task of particularly topical importance for the farms in the Moscow area and was carried out on an experimental plot allocated by the Vladimir Lenin collective farm. In carrying out this experimental work on large areas the pupils were performing a serious production job which they approached with a great sense of responsibility. They helped the collective farm to find out which of the different varieties of potato were most suitable to grow, what amounts and which mixtures of organic and mineral fertilizers were most effective for this crop under local soil conditions, which of the various methods of vernalizing potato tubers were most economic and so forth. The pupils' work was very exhaustive and of great educational importance. Experimental work raises training in production work to a high level and enriches actual labour with experience which broadens the pupils' knowledge of the fundamentals of crop-growing.

If we take the theoretical and practical training of skilled agricultural workers as a single process based on combining instruction with labour, we can distinguish three aspects of this process: (a) the preliminary mastery of the theoretical knowledge required in order to perform productive work with understanding; (b) practical labour study, culminating in the mastery of all the elements of labour essential for the skilled worker; (c) mastery of organizational knowledge and skills in agriculture.

If the pupils do not rely on scientific knowledge in their production work the result is not only that mistakes in performance are made but also that the pupils get used to working mechanically, not thinking out their work; this leads to an artisan-type approach which hinders the polytechnical development of the pupils. The mastery of theoretical knowledge acquired in the course of studying natural sciences, combined with practice in applying this when examining the techniques and technology of production, sharpens the pupils' wits, makes them more attentive, develops their powers of observation and improves the quality of their practical training. In one of the experiments, for example, the pupils learnt to make a detailed analysis of the constructional and working principles of agricultural machines and their parts, using their engineering knowledge (the study of the mechanical principles of the construction and operation of a cutting apparatus, a combine reel, a conveyor and other units of a combine) and analysing the agro-biological and agro-chemical principles involved, based on their knowledge of biology and chemistry. They applied the theoretical training obtained in their practical lessons to their work on the machines. Results showed that they had received a sound training for productive labour.

In another experiment, similarly aimed at developing the pupils' polytechnical scope and their ability to apply scientific knowledge to productive work, the method of 'experimental defects' was introduced into instruction. The essence of this method is that an experienced instructor sets the machine in advance in a way which will produce a defect when it is working. Such a defect must, of course, be quite safe. When the defect appears the pupil has to find it and suggest ways of eliminating it, using his general and technical knowledge. The adoption of this method resulted in the pupils becoming accustomed to making more independent use of scientific knowledge in work and in their acquiring a surer mastery of machines.

The most important characteristic of a socialist agricultural worker is his orientation towards everything new, towards advanced methods of producing high yields, towards the experience of advanced workers and innovators in agriculture. Various methods recommended by Soviet didactics are employed in the process of training in productive work for the purpose of turning out workers of this kind. As training in productive work has its own special character these methods acquire certain peculiarities when they are used in that context.

In explaining the essentials of knowledge regarding production, for example, it is very important for the teacher to base himself on the previous practical working experience of the pupils. This rallies the pupils and stimulates them to ask questions and make comments which can be used to help them obtain a better grasp of the material they are learning.

The 'demonstration method' is an irreplaceable didactic means in teaching not only the theoretical principles of agricultural production but also the working knowledge and skills used in agricultural practice. Teachers have been found who ask the pupils to perform some practical task on the school experimental plot or on the collective farm but omit to demonstrate the correct method of work, wrongly believing that there was 'nothing difficult' in that particular task. In training pupils in working knowledge and skills the demonstration of correct working methods is of the greatest importance.

In explaining details about technology, production, work processes or operations, a diagram or plan is used, supplemented by specific examples during the exposition. Other visual aids, especially films, are also widely used. Both the complete film and the particular sequences and parts which fit into the general scheme of explanation are shown.

Excursions to farms are an important method of enabling the pupils to obtain clear ideas concerning agriculture. It is a mistake on the part of a teacher to imagine that once the pupils are at work on their own collective farm, they will see and understand everything without help from the teacher. In practice this does not happen. If the work of acquainting pupils with collective-farm production is not properly planned pedagogically, the pupils will never understand it and will miss a great deal even if they work on a particular farm for several years. Many examples could be cited to prove this, but one will suffice.

In the Lenin Memorial School collective-farm visits are arranged for pupils learning the fundamentals of agriculture. They meet the leading workers of a well-known collective farm and see the results of their work displayed graphically in the common room. There is no doubt that such visits leave much deeper and more lasting impressions than the best account by the teacher in the classroom.

Instruction in working skills is carried out on the basis of scientific knowledge, while during practical training and work theoretical knowledge is deepened and made more specific. Productive work must be instructive and educational. It is preceded and accompanied by instruction which includes not only details of the technique of carrying out the task but also the scientific basis of its productive character. Instruction is given either in the form of verbal explanations and demonstrations by the teacher or in the form of written notes. In all forms of instruction the aim is to induce the pupils to acquire correct working practices and to apply scientific knowledge in a creative way in work.

In the process of training in productive work the mastery of all elements of labour is ensured—machines, agricultural production processes, the working skills essential to a skilled worker in socialist agriculture, and also information about the economics and organization of agricultural production. Working on collective or State farms the pupils join in mass political and cultural-educational work among the rural population and acquire experience of communal work. With the active participation of the school *komsomol* organization the pupils' organizations assume and fulfil responsibly many organizing functions which are within their powers: planning, calculating, qualitative evaluation of work and its productivity, the organization of socialist competition, the distribution of work in a group and among its members, the distribution of the product for communal needs and among members of the group. All this contributes to the development of a proper fraternal relationship among the pupils and between them and the adults, educates the children in organizational practices and gives them the capacity to make independent decisions in the many problems of life and work,

LAW ON THE STRENGTHENING OF THE TIES OF THE SCHOOL WITH LIFE AND ON THE FURTHER DEVELOPMENT OF THE PUBLIC EDUCATION SYSTEM IN THE U.S.S.R.

The Supreme Soviet of the Union of Soviet Socialist Republics records that the question, introduced by the Central Committee of the Communist Party of the Soviet Union and the Council of Ministers of the U.S.S.R. for consideration by the Supreme Soviet of the U.S.S.R., relating to the strengthening of the ties of the school with life and the further development of the public education system in the country is of exceptional significance for the successful solution of the tasks of communist construction.

The national discussion of this question has demonstrated that the programme worked out by the Central Committee of the CPSU and the Council of Ministers of the U.S.S.R. for the further development of the public education system has met with the unanimous approval and support of the workers.

The Soviet people, united around the Communist Party, have achieved new and historic victories in the development of industry and agriculture, science and culture, and in the raising of the standard of the workers' well-being, and have accomplished such extensive transformations as afford our country the possibility of entering on a new, most important period of its development, the period of the establishment of a communist society on a large scale.

A genuine cultural revolution has taken place in the U.S.S.R. The Soviet school has played the decisive role in it and has contributed to raising the cultural level of the peoples of our multinational fatherland. As a result of the consistent application of Lenin's national policy, all the peoples in the U.S.S.R. have schools providing instruction in their native languages; wide opportunities for education and culture are available to all; universal seven-year instruction has been introduced; secondary, vocational and technical, and higher education have been widely developed; and science, literature and art are advancing at an unprecedented rate.

The gulf between physical and intellectual work was one of the chief defects of the old society. For centuries culture was for millions of ordinary people a forbidden fruit. The old society so organized schooling that it was, in fact, inaccessible to the workers in general.

Marxist–Leninist theory, borne out by all our experience in the building-up of communism in the U.S.S.R. and also by experience in the development of other socialist countries, has swept away the bourgeois legend that there would inevitably always be, on the one hand, unenlightened masses of people, destined to hard physical labour, and, on the other, a handful of people called, as though by nature, to reflection, government and the furtherance of science, technology, literature and art.

In socialist society, where the essential differences between the labour of hand and brain are gradually being eliminated, and the unity of intellectual and physical work is being established, the development of all sides, not only of material production but also of the spiritual activity of the workers on the broadest possible basis, is accelerated to an immense degree, and limitless scope is provided for all-round development of personality. Under socialism all the achievements of world culture become the property of the people.

As the building-up of communism proceeds, as productive forces expand further and as the wealth of society increases, the working day will be steadily shortened and the workers will have more and more free time which they can use for the broadening of their mental outlook and the satisfaction of their spiritual needs.

The accelerated development of the mechanization, automation and chemicalization of production, the wide application of electronics, computer devices, the universal development of electrification and other acievements of science and technology are radically changing the character of labour. The labour of workers and collective farmers is becoming ever closer in nature to the labour of engineers, technicians, agronomists and other specialists. Socialist production workers must now have the ability to handle modern machine tools and the most delicate measuring and control instruments and equipment, and a knowledge of complex technical calculations and drawings. The prospects of technical and economic development in the Soviet Union are making ever higher demands on all the workers in our society. All-round education is becoming for them an urgent need.

It would be a mistake to say that with the automation of production in communist society, physical labour will disappear. The stupendous progress of technology will immeasurably lighten physical labour; many occupations that exhaust man are vanishing and will disappear in the future. But physical labour will remain. The harmonious development of man is unthinkable without creative and joyful physical labour that strengthens the individual and heightens the body's vital functions.

The great founder of the Soviet State, V. I. Lenin, taught that it is essential for young people to combine their studies with work, with efforts for the reorganization of industry and agriculture and with the struggle for the culture and education of the people.

The communist transformation of society is indissolubly linked with the education of a new type of man, in whom must be harmoniously combined spiritual wealth, moral purity and physical perfection.

The socialist state is organizing its educational system to serve the people, give the workers knowledge, and contribute to the development of all the people's talents. The Soviet school brings up the rising generation in the spirit of the most progressive ideas, those of communism;

and inculcates in young people that materialist attitude which is the basis of a really scientific understanding of the world.

In Soviet society a remarkable generation of young people has been educated, devoting all their knowledge and energies, capabilities and talents to the building-up of communism. The high moral qualities of Soviet youth have been strikingly demonstrated on the labour fronts during the building-up of socialism in the years of the first five-year plans, in the second world war, in heroic efforts for the reclamation of virgin and waste lands, in the building of large electric power stations, mines and blast furnaces, in the construction of new industrial centres in the east and north of our country and in many other present-day labour exploits.

Soviet higher educational establishments and specialized secondary institutions have played an important part in bringing about the great victories of the Soviet people. At the present time about seven and a half million specialists who have had a higher and specialized secondary education are working in the national economy. The creation of numerous cadres of specialists is one of the biggest achievements of the Communist Party and the Soviet State.

The Soviet Union has become one of the leading countries in the world in the development of science and technology and has surpassed the most highly developed capitalist countries in the rate and the quality of its training of specialists. By their selfless labour in industry, construction, and transport, on state and collective farms, and in all branches of the economy and culture, Soviet specialists are successfully solving the tasks involved in building up communism.

The forthcoming seven-year period in the development of the Soviet Union will be characterized by a further rise of socialist culture, by the growth of Soviet society's spiritual wealth, and by the heightened consciousness of the workers, the active builders of communism. The problems of the communist education of the workers, especially the rising generation, are therefore, of exceptional importance and become the central question in the activities of State and public organizations.

Notwithstanding the notable achievements in the development of the Soviet school and in the training of cadres of specialists for all branches of the national economy and culture, our general-education, specialized secondary and higher educational establishments are lagging behind the requirements of communist construction and have serious defects. Chief among them is a certain divorce between schooling and life and the failure to prepare school graduates adequately for practical activity. At the present stage of communist construction, this defect in the public education system in particularly intolerable.

A reform of public education is needed to enable the Soviet secondary, vocational, technical and higher educational establishments to play a more active part in every aspect of the life of the Soviet people.

The Soviet secondary school is called upon to produce educated people with a good knowledge of the bases of science—men and women capable of systematic physical labour, anxious to be useful to society, and keen to take an active part in producing the goods it needs. The

377

scope of the secondary-education system must be substantially enlarged, first of all through the wide development of a network of schools for young people who are working in the national economy. The solution of this problem is an important prerequisite for the further improvement of the cultural and technical standards of the workers, the increase in the productivity of labour and the successful building-up of communism.

Further technical progress in all branches of the national economy is steadily raising the level of qualifications required of the main mass of workers. The inadequate standard of vocational and technical training among some of the workers is already, in certain cases, holding up the growth of production. For this reason, development of vocational and technical training for young people and improvement in the quality of training for skilled workers are of special importance.

The new tasks of communist construction call for the elimination of the defects that are also to be found in the organization of higher and specialized secondary education.

Soviet higher educational establishments are called upon to provide people with an all-round education and a thorough knowledge of the appropriate fields of science and technology. Special attention must be devoted to further improvement of the quality of training for specialists for industry, agriculture and construction. Modern production, being based on the latest achievements of science and technology, calls for a high standard of theoretical training in the graduates of higher and specialized secondary-education institutions and a thorough familiarity with practical problems.

In the new conditions, the training of specialists in the higher and specialized secondary-education institutions through correspondence and evening courses is becoming particularly important. The evening and correspondence systems of higher and specialized secondary education must be so organized that people who are engaged in useful work for society have an opportunity, if they so desire, to continue with higher or specialized secondary studies, or to improve their qualifications, in their spare time.

Decisive improvement of the work of higher and specialized secondary-education institutions is essential in the development of the Marxist-Leninist attitude among students, the enhancement of their communist consciousness and activity, and the education of young specialists in the spirit of collectivism and industriousness, awareness of public duty, socialist internationalism and patriotism, and in the observance of the high principles of communist morality.

Any work in a factory or on a collective farm, in an industrial enterprise, on a State farm, in a technical service station or in an office—honest, useful labour for society—is a sacred obligation for every man living in a socialist society and enjoying its benefits.

Every person living in a communist society must, by his labour, play his part in the building-up and further development of this society.

The progressive development of productive forces in the process of building-up a communist society, the perfecting of socialistic social relations, and the further development of Soviet democracy create favourable conditions for successfully solving the new tasks which confront the schools and which relate to the communist education and training of young people.

The Supreme Soviet of the Union of Soviet Socialist Republics *resolves:*

To approve the theses of the Central Committee of the Communist Party of the Soviet Union and the Council of Ministers of the U.S.S.R. 'On the Strengthening of the Ties of the School with Life and on the Further Development of the Public Education System in the U.S.S.R', which have received universal support in the course of national discussion.

To recognize that it is essential, even from the first years of instruction, to prepare children for their eventual participation in socially useful work. From the age of fifteen or sixteen, all young people should be engaged in socially useful work appropriate to their powers, and all their subsequent training should necessarily be linked with productive labour in the national economy.

I. ON THE SECONDARY SCHOOL

Article 1. The main task of the Soviet school is the preparation of pupils for life and for socially useful work, the further improvement of the level of general and polytechnical education, the training of educated people with a good basic knowledge of science, and the education of young people in the spirit of profound respect for the principles of socialist society and the ideas of communism.

One of the guiding principles of teaching and education in the secondary school must be the close connexion of instruction with work and with practical experience of communist construction.

Article 2. Universal compulsory eight-year education shall be introduced in the U.S.S.R. instead of universal compulsory seven-year education.

The eight-year school is an incomplete secondary general-education polytechnical industrial school, which should give pupils a sound foundation of general and polytechnical knowledge, foster a liking for work, inculcate a readiness for socially useful activity, and provide for the moral, physical and aesthetic training of children.

The schooling in the eight-year school should be built on a combination of instruction in the fundamentals of science, polytechnical education and work training and the wide enlistment of schoolchildren, according to age, in forms of socially useful work within their capacity.

Article 3. It shall be established that the complete secondary education of young people, beginning from ages fifteen or sixteen, is to be based on the combination of instruction with productive work, so that all young people of this age are drawn into socially useful work.

Article 4. The following basic types of educational institutions giving a complete secondary education shall be established:

1. Schools for young industrial and agricultural workers—evening (shift) secondary schools of general education in which persons who have completed their eight-year schooling and are working in one of the branches of the national economy, may obtain a secondary education and improve their occupational qualifications. The term of instruction in these schools shall be set at three years.

   In order to create the necessary conditions to enable students to attend evening (shift) secondary schools of general education, the Council of Ministers of the U.S.S.R. shall establish a shortened working day or shortened working week for those who study successfully without giving up work in industry.

2. Secondary, general, polytechnical schools with industrial training, in which persons who have graduated from the eight-year school may obtain a three-year course of secondary education and vocational training, for work in one of the branches of the national economy or culture.

   The proportion of theory and practice in the industrial training and the rotation of periods of instruction and work shall be established according to the type of special training and local conditions. In rural schools, the school year shall be arranged with due consideration for the seasonal nature of agricultural work.

   The industrial training and socially useful work may be conducted in the training and production shops of the nearest enterprises, in the apprentice brigades of collective farms and State farms, in experimental training farms, and in school and inter-school industrial training workshops.

3. *Tehnikums* and other specialized secondary educational institutions, in which persons who have completed their eight-year schooling may obtain a general secondary and specialized secondary education.

Article 5. In order to amplify the role of society and to assist the family in the education of children, the network of boarding-schools, and also of lengthened day schools and groups, shall be extended. It shall be established that boarding-schools are to be organized after the type of eight-year schools or secondary, general, polytechnical schools with industrial training.

Article 6. Real improvement is recognized to be necessary in the organization of educational work in school, to enable the school to implant in children love of knowledge and work, and respect for working people, to inculcate the communist outlook, and to bring children up in the spirit of selfless devotion to the fatherland and the people, in the spirit of proletarian internationalism. The most important task of teachers, parents and public organizations is the further improvement of work designed to instil in pupils habits of civilized behaviour at school, at home and in the street.

Article 7. It is recognized to be essential to reorganize the existing ten-year schools (their senior classes) into various types of urban and rural secondary schools of general education.

The reform of the public education system shall be brought about in a systematic and organized manner, with maximum consideration for local peculiarities and without premitting deterioration of any kind in the school service to the population. Attention shall be directed to the need for an increase in the enrolment of girls of indigenous nationalities in the senior classes of the schools of the Union and Autonomous Republics of the east.

The plan for the transition to the new system of school education shall be worked out in each Union Republic in the light of the special features of the Republic's economic and cultural development. The transition from seven-year to eight-year compulsory instruction, and the organization of various types of complete secondary schooling should, in this context, be begun from the 1959/60 school year and completed in three to five years. Pupils in the present grades VIII to X shall be given the possibility of completing their secondary schooling according to existing curricula and programmes, but with additional training for working life.

In working out the plans for the reorganization of secondary schools, provision must be made for the supply of a sufficient number of secondary-school graduates for the universities, since a break in the manning of the national economy with cadres of highly qualified young specialists would be inadmissible. For these purposes, a certain number of the existing secondary schools shall, where necessary, be maintained, in each Union Republic, during the transition period.

Article 8. The statutes on the compulsory eight-year school, the evening (shift) secondary school of general education and the secondary general, polytechnical school with industrial training shall be approved by the Councils of Ministers of the Union Republics.

Article 9. The beginning and ending of the school year and the period of vacations in the eight-year and the general secondary schools shall be fixed by the legislation of Union Republics.

Article 10. The Council of Ministers of the U.S.S.R. and the Councils of Ministers of the Union Republics shall take measures for consolidating the material basis of the schools, eliminating multiple-shift instruction, and organizing industrial training, and also for making school premises for vocational training and production practice available for the pupils of the senior classes in secondary schools.

Article 11. The Councils of Ministers of the Union Republics shall take measures for the retraining of teachers and the staffing of schools with teachers having the necessary qualifications for dealing with the new tasks of the general-education school, and also for the further improvement of teachers' working and living conditions and the raising of their theoretical and ideological level.

II. ON VOCATIONAL AND TECHNICAL EDUCATION

Article 12. The prospects of technological and economic development in the Soviet Union demand increasingly high standards of industrial qualification for the workers in all branches of the national economy. In these circumstances, the wide development of vocational and technical training for young people is of particular importance.

The main task of vocational and technical education for young people is the systematic and organized training of skilled workers with a background of general and technical education for all branches of the national economy, and of similarly prepared workers for agriculture, the communist education of pupils, their ideological tempering, and the inculcation in the young students of the communist attitude to labour.

Article 13. Urban and rural vocational and technical colleges shall be organized for the vocational and technical training of young people who go into industry after completing their eight-year schooling.

The vocational and technical colleges shall be specialized by branches of industry, and shall conduct their educational work on the basis of active and systematic participation by the young people in productive labour, and in close contact with industrial enterprises, construction projects, State and collective farms.

Article 14. The factory and workshop schools, the industrial, railway, mining, and building colleges and the agricultural-mechanization schools of the labour reserves, the vocational and technical schools, factory and workshop training schools and other vocational educational institutions of the councils of national economy and departments, shall be reorganized to form day and evening urban, vocational and technical colleges providing courses lasting one to three years, and rural vocational and technical colleges providing courses lasting one to two years.

The reorganization of existing vocational educational institutions into urban and rural, vocational and technical colleges shall be carried out in a period of three to five years, having regard to the characteristics of the economic administrative regions concerned.

Article 15. With the object of gradually converting the vocational and technical colleges into partially self-supporting institutions, the Council of Ministers of the U.S.S.R. and the Council of Ministers of the Union Republics shall work out and consistently implement measures to expand and increase the profits accruing to educational institutions from productive activities.

In connexion with the growth of the workers' material security, and in order to heighten the students' personal interest in the better mastery of the trades for which they are training, it is expedient that the existing conditions relating to students' material security be revised and that the payment of wages to students be introduced instead of the free provision of uniforms and food.

Full state security should be preserved for orphan pupils, inmates of children's homes, and children of parents with large families.

Collective farms shall be urged to consider the question of allotting appropriate funds for the training of collective-farm youth at vocational and technical colleges.

Article 16. The ministries, departments, councils of national economy, enterprises, offices and organizations shall provide vocational and technical colleges with production euipment for the school workshops and with salaried jobs at enterprises for the production practice of pupils, and shall also create the necessary conditions for the successful conduct of the educational process and for enabling the young people to master new techniques, advanced technology and highly productive working methods.

Article 17. The Council of Ministers of the U.S.S.R. and the Councils of Ministers of the Union Republics shall work out long-term and annual plans for the vocational training and placing in employment of young people who have completed courses at an eight-year general-education school, a vocational and technical college and a secondary school providing industrial training, bearing in mind the possibility of reserving vacancies at industrial undertakings for the initial employment of young people, and the need for strict observance of the regulations regarding labour protection and safety engineering.

Article 18. The reform of the system of vocational and technical education entails new and improved requirements regarding the standard of the technical, political and ideological, and actual teacher-training of industrial training instructors and teachers in vocational and technical colleges. The development of the network of these colleges will call for more instructors and teachers. It is therefore necessary to devote great attention to the training of such staff at *tehnikums* and higher educational institutions.

The quality of textbooks and visual aids must be improved and the output of them increased; the production of technical, educational and popular science films must be expanded; and wider use must be made of broadcasting and television in vocational and technical education.

Article 19. The statute on vocational and technical colleges shall be approved by the Council of Ministers of the U.S.S.R.

Article 20. The Council of Ministers of the U.S.S.R. and the Councils of Ministers of the Union Republics shall work out measures for achieving a fundamental improvement in the training of workers through individual brigade and course instruction and the raising of the standard of qualifications among skilled workers engaged in production.

III. ON SPECIALIZED SECONDARY EDUCATION

Article 21. In industrial and agricultural production, and also in cultural, educational and public-health services, technicians, as the immediate organizers of production, and other workers with a specialized secondary education, have an important place.

The interests of modern production, which is based on the latest achievements of science and technology, require that graduates of *tehnikums* shall have a high standard of theoretical training and a good knowledge of practice.

It is accordingly acknowledged that further perfecting of the system of specialized secondary education is necessary, as is improvement in the training of middle-grade specialists, on the basis of a close connexion between instruction and socially useful work and wide development of evening and correspondence instruction.

Article 22. The training of specialists in specialized secondary-education institutions shall be carried out on the basis of the eight-year school, and, for individual specialities, on the basis of a complete secondary education.

The length of the course as a whole and the duration of separate periods of instruction, both with and without stoppages of work in production, may vary, depending on the branch of the national economy for which specialists are being trained, and also on the working conditions in the enterprises, construction projects and other organizations concerned.

Article 23. It shall be laid down that instruction in specialized secondary-education institutions shall furnish pupils both with such general knowledge as is within the scope of the secondary school, and with the necessary theoretical and practical training in a special subject; in specialized technical and agricultural secondary-education institutions, pupils shall also be able to acquire a qualification together with a skill rating in one of the branches of work.

Article 24. The desirability of organizing, at industrial *tehnikums*, departments and workshops that put on the market industrial products made by the students, and at agricultural *tehnikums*, large farms in which all the basic work must be done by the pupils themselves, shall be recognized.

Article 25. The network of specialized secondary-education institutions shall be further developed in the direction of relating them more closely to production, with due regard to the requirements of the economic regions for skilled workers, and wide recourse to the co-operation of councils of national economy, ministries and departments in the training of specialists with a secondary education.

The expansion and improvement of correspondence and evening courses, as a basic means of training specialists with a specialized secondary education, shall be promoted through strengthening of the evening and correspondence *tehnikums*, and also by the organization of correspondence and evening departments attached to full-time educational institutions which have qualified teaching staff and an appropriate basis of school equipment.

Preference for enrolment in evening and correspondence courses shall be given to persons working in occupations allied to the chosen special subject.

Article 26. The statute on specialized secondary educational institutions shall be approved by the Council of Ministers of the U.S.S.R.

IV. ON HIGHER EDUCATION

Article 27. The tasks of communist construction necessitate bringing higher educational establishments into closer contact with life and with production, and raising the standard of the theoretical training of specialists, in conformity with the latest achievements of science and technology.

The further development and improvement of the higher education system in our country must provide for the better practical and theoretical training of specialists, considerable intensification of efforts to bring up the young on communist lines, and active participation by all teachers in the education of the students.

The chief tasks of higher educational establishments are:

The preparation of highly qualified specialists educated on the basis of Marxist-Leninist doctrine, who have mastered the latest achievements of Russian and foreign science and technology, are well acquainted with the practical side, and are capable not only of making full use of contemporary technology but also of creating the technology of the future.

The performance of scientific research work likely to contribute to solving the tasks of communist construction.

The training of educational research workers.

Improvement of the qualifications of specialists engaged in the various branches of the national economy, culture and education.

Dissemination of scientific and political knowledge among the workers.

Article 28. The training of specialists in higher educational institutions shall be conducted on the basis of a complete secondary education, founded upon the combination of study with socially useful labour. The ways in which instruction is actually combined with practice and with labour shall be determined in consideration of the characteristics of the higher educational establishment concerned, the composition of the students, and special national and local features.

Admission to higher educational institutions shall be on the basis of character references given by the Party, trade-union, Komsomol and other public organizations, by the directors of industrial undertakings and collective-farm managers, so that through competitive selection the most deserving, trained and capable people, who have proved themselves in production, may be enrolled in higher educational institutions. Preference for admission to higher educational institutions shall be given to persons who have experience of practical work.

Article 29. General improvement and expansion of evening and corres-

385

pondence courses is recognized to be necessary through the strengthening of the higher correspondence and evening schools, the development of a network of evening and correspondence courses on the basis of the full-time universities, and the organization of evening and correspondence training for specialists at large industrial and agricultural undertakings.

Article 30.   In the training of engineers the combination of teaching with labour shall be so organized that the productive labour of students helps them better to master their future special subject and enables them to study the technological process of production step by step. In the majority of the higher institutes of technology it is best to combine teaching with work on production by the system of evening or correspondence courses in the first two years of study.

For a number of special subjects in which students begin by studying a series of complicated theoretical subjects and at the same time do a large amount of practical laboratory work, it is desirable that the first two or three years should be spent in study, without working in industry. Thereafter, provision should be made for students to do practical work during the year in regular posts, on the production line, in laboratories or in design offices.

In perfecting the system of higher education, great attention should be devoted to the training of engineering staff for braches of new technology, and for the further development of scientific and designing work.

Article 31.   In the training of agricultural specialists, instruction shall be provided in institutes organized on the basis of large State farms and having big model educational farms where the agricultural work is done by the students. The training of specialists shall be adjusted to suit conditions in different zones of the country, and the combination of teaching with productive labour shall be organized with due regard to the seasonal nature of production.

Article 32.   The further development of university education is recognized to be essential; it is necessary, in particular, substantially to increase the output of specialists in the new departments of mathematical, biological, physical and chemical sciences, to intensify the theoretical and practical training of students, and to enlarge considerably the part played by the universities in solving the major problems of the natural sciences and the humanities. The staffing of universities and the combination of study with labour in them shall be so organized that, in the process of learning, the students gain working skills in a special subject, and specialists in the humanities (economists, philosophers, lawyers and others) also have definite experience of socially useful work.

Article 33.   It is recognized to be necessary to improve the training of teachers in institutes of education and in the universities; to expand the training of teachers for primary schools, with a view to staffing all schools, eventually, with teachers who had a higher education; to organize the training of teachers in agronomy, livestock-raising, technology and other special disciplines; to raise the scientific and theoretical standard of teaching in the institutes of education; and to give more importance to industrial and educational practice in the training of teachers.

Article 34. In the training of doctors at higher schools of medicine, account shall be taken of the specific requirements of the medical profession; in manning medical institutes, preference shall be given to young people who have had practical working experience as junior assistants at medical and therapeutic-prophylactic institutions; and the instruction of students shall be combined with continuous practice in clinics, dispensaries and health centres.

For persons who have had a secondary medical education and practical working experience in their special subject, instruction shall be organized at higher schools of medicine without their giving up work.

Article 35. In the training of specialists with a higher and secondary education in the fields of music, painting, drama, and other forms of art, the system of training without giving up work should be more widely developed, so as to give large numbers of workers the opportunity of taking this form of training, and to bring talent to light.

Article 36. It is considered essential to intensify the ideological and political education of students, to improve the teaching of Marxist–Leninist theory, to bring up young people in the spirit of the high principles of communist morality, of love for labour, and of implacable opposition to bourgeois ideology. In the training of specialists with a higher education, serious attention shall be directed to the formation in students of a scientific method of acquiring knowledge, a creative approach toward the mastering of sciences, and a responsible attitude toward learning and independence in work. The graduates of Soviet higher educational establishments should be exemplary in performance of State and social duty.

Article 37. It is considered desirable to enlist on a wider scale, for teaching in higher educational establishments, the services of the most highly qualified engineers and technicians of enterprises, construction projects, design offices and scientific research institutes, agronomists, doctors and other practical workers who are capable of teaching, and making use in their teaching of the latest methods of production and contemporary achievements of science and technology.

Article 38. On the principle that scientific work should be an integral part of the activities of every higher educational institution, it is essential to extend the role of higher educational institutions in the conduct of scientific research of a high theoretical standard and of real importance for the development of the national economy, and science and culture.

It is considered desirable to organize scientific research institutes and laboratories at higher educational establishments, and to unite certain scientific research institutions with the higher schools.

The councils of national economy, ministries, departments and agencies responsible for agricultural management shall assist higher educational institutions in applying the results of scientific research and in organizing production experiments.

Article 39. The councils of national economy, enterprises, institutions and organizations shall put at the disposal of specialized higher and secondary educational institutions regular paid posts and technical appointments for filling by their students, and shall provide the necessary living accommodation and overalls for the production training of students.

Article 40. The statute on higher educational institutions shall be approved by the Council of Ministers of the U.S.S.R.

Article 41. The Council of Ministers of the U.S.S.R. and the Councils of Ministers of the Union Republics shall work out and implement measures for the development of higher education in the country in accordance with the terms of the present law, at the same time providing for:

1. Regularization of the network of higher educational institutions in the country, with a view to increasing the number of higher educational establishments in the new industrial regions, bringing higher schools into closer contact with production, and uniting higher schools of one type.
2. Broadening and improvement of the basic technical equipment of higher educational establishments, and the equipment of the laboratories of universities and higher institutes of technology with electronic machines, accelerators and other modern apparatuses.
3. Organization of technical-college factories and also of industrial plants and workshops at higher educational institutions, and production of goods made by the students.
4. Institution of specialized publishing houses and printing plants to supply all the textbook requirements of students at specialized higher and secondary educational institutions, particularly those who are studying without breaking off their work in production.
5. Granting of additional privileges for students in the senior classes of higher educational establishments and *tehnikums*, who are studying without leaving their jobs.
6. Improvement of the basic technical equipment for evening and correspondence courses in specialized higher and secondary education, providing for the wide use of films, broadcasting, television and other modern scientific and technical media.

Article 42. The reorganization of specialized higher and secondary education shall be carried out in a period of three to five years, beginning from the 1959/60 school year, with due regard to national and local conditions, and in such a manner that the number of specialists graduating each year for service in the national economy, science and culture steadily increases as the demand for them grows.

The Councils of Ministers of the Union Republics shall submit, for the consideration of the Supreme Soviets of the Union Republics, proposals deriving from the present law providing for the strengthening of the ties of the school with life, the introduction of universal compulsory eight-year education and the further development of general secondary, vocational and technical, specialized secondary, and higher education in the republics.

The Supreme Soviet of the Union of Soviet Socialist Republics considers that the bringing of the school into closer contact with life will create the necessary conditions for the better education of the rising generation, who will live and work under communism. The reorganization of the system of public education will be of immense importance for the further material and spiritual development of Soviet society, will enhance the role of the Soviet school in the education and training of young people, will secure better training of highly qualified staff for all branches of the national economy, science and culture, and will in a still greater degree contribute to the growth of the might of the Soviet Union.

K. VOROSHILOV
President of the Presidium of the
Supreme Soviet of the U.S.S.R.

M. GEORGADZE
Secretary of the Presidium of the
Supreme Soviet of the U.S.S.R.

Moscow, Kremlin, 24 December 1958

THE STATUTE ON THE EIGHT-YEAR SCHOOL

(Approved by Decision No. 2027 of the Council of Ministers of the
R.S.F.S.R., dated 29 December 1959)

I. AIMS AND PURPOSES

Article 1. The eight-year school is an incomplete secondary general-education labour polytechnical school providing compulsory co-education for all children (of both sexes) from the age of seven to fifteen or sixteen inclusive.

In carrying out the tasks of communist education, the eight-year school provides a sound grounding in general and polytechnical subjects, fosters in the pupils a liking for work, prepares them for socially useful activities, and provides for their moral, physical and aesthetic education.

By closely associating study and life, the eight-year school prepares its pupils for various kinds of productive activities and for continuing their secondary education by combining the latter with socially useful production work.

Those who have completed the course at an eight-year school may continue their studies at evening (shift) secondary schools of general education while working in an industrial undertaking, on a collective or State farm or in an office, may enter a secondary general-education labour polytechnical school with industrial training, an urban or rural vocational and technical college, a *tehnikum* or other specialized secondary-education institution, or may enrol in the correspondence department of a secondary general-education labour polytechnical school with industrial training or evening (shift) general-education school.

II. ORGANIZATION AND STRUCTURE

Article 2. Eight-year schools shall be opened by decision of the Executive Committees of the district (municipal) soviets of workers' deputies in agreement with the appropriate Ministries of Education of Autonomous Republics and Territorial and Regional Departments of Public Education. Eight-year schools shall be under the authority of the District (Municipal) Departments of Public Education.

Article 3. The eight-year school shall comprise grades I to VIII inclusive.

If there are enough pupils, parallel classes may also be set up.

The number of pupils in each class should not exceed forty.

Elementary schools comprising grades I to IV shall remain in sparsely populated areas. Those who have completed the course at such schools shall be transferred to the fifth grade of the nearest eight-year or secondary school.

Article 4. In accordance with the law 'On the Strengthening of the Ties of the School with Life and on the Further Development of the Public Education System in the U.S.S.R.', responsibility for the provision of universal compulsory eight-year education for children rests with the Councils of Ministers of Autonomous Republics and the Executive Committees of territorial, regional, area, municipal, district, settlement and rural soviets of workers' deputies.

Article 5. With a view to providing universal compulsory eight-year education and creating conditions for the successful education of children:
1. A definite area of jurisdiction shall be allocated by the District (Municipal) Department of Public Education to each eight-year school and secondary general-education labour polytechnical school with vocational training, comprising grades I to VIII, and the school shall take measures to enrol all children residing in this area and subject to compulsory education.
2. The local soviets of workers' deputies shall make regular arrangements for taking pupils to and from schools if they live more than three kilometres from the school, or shall set up a boarding-school functioning in accordance with the relevant statute approved by the Ministry of Education of the R.S.F.S.R.
3. Hot meals shall be provided for children at schools by the public catering trusts in cities and by consumer co-operative societies in country districts, with the participation of parents' committees and the assistance of trade unions, collective farms and other public organizations.
4. At the request of parents, after-school groups shall be set up at schools, principally for children whose parents are working. An extended day-school may be set up in case of need. The number of such groups and schools and the number of pupils in them shall be determined by the enrolment plan for the district (or city).
5. In order to provide material assistance for needy pupils (free meals, shoes, clothing, textbooks and other forms of material aid) at eight-year schools or secondary schools providing industrial training, comprising grades I to VIII, a Universal Education Fund shall be set up in accordance with the provisions contained in the relevant statute.

Article 6. Parents or legal guardians shall be responsible for enrolling children in school at the proper time and seeing that they attend throughout the term. Those who fail to ensure the children's attendance shall be administratively answerable in accordance with the terms of decisions of the Councils of Ministers of Autonomous Republics and the resolutions of the Executive Committees of territorial and regional soviets of workers' deputies.

Article 7. Industrial enterprises, collective farms, State farms and offices which are in charge of schools shall assist them with equipment, and with the organization of educational work and vocational-training activities.

III. INSTRUCTIONAL AND EDUCATIONAL WORK

Article 8. Instruction and education in the eight-year school shall be provided in accordance with the syllabuses and curricula approved by the Ministry of Education of the R.S.F.S.R. The Ministries of Education of Autonomous Republics and the territorial and regional departments of public education shall be authorized, with the agreement of the Ministry of Education of the R.S.F.S.R., to make any necessary changes in the syllabus and curriculum of the eight-year school in the light of local conditions, subject to observance of the specified number of hours laid down in the curriculum for each grade. (*Note.* The syllabuses for instruction in the native language and literature in the case of national schools shall be approved by the Ministries of Education of the Autonomous Republics.)

Article 9. Studies in eight-year schools shall begin on 1 September and end, for grades I to IV, on 31 May, for grades V to VII, on 19 June, and for grade VIII on 25 June (including examinations).

The autumn holiday for schools shall run from 5 to 9 November inclusive, the winter holiday from 30 December to 10 January inclusive, and the spring holiday from 24 to 31 March inclusive. The dates of the spring holiday may be changed, provided its duration remains the same, by decision of the Executive Committees of the district (municipal) soviets of workers' deputies, in consideration of local conditions.

The school year shall be divided into terms: the first term from 1 September to 4 November, the second from 10 November to 29 December, the third from 11 January to 23 March and the fourth from 1 April to the end of the school year.

Article 10. The length of a lesson in grades I to VIII shall be forty-five minutes; in certain circumstances, the length of the lesson for grade I may be reduced, by decision of the school's Educational Council, to thirty-five minutes.

There shall be a break of ten minutes between lessons and a longer break after the second or third lesson, which should be not less than thirty minutes in length. Depending on local conditions, there may be two breaks instead of one long break, each lasting twenty minutes, the first after the second lesson and the other after the third.

Article 11. Instruction in schools shall be given in the pupils' mother tongue. In Autonomous Republics, autonomous regions and national areas where teaching is conducted in different languages, parents shall be entitled to choose a school employing the language they prefer.

In schools in which instruction is given in the language of the Autonomous Republic, autonomous region or national area, pupils may study the Russian language if they so desire, just as, in Russian schools, pupils may, if they wish, study the language of the Autonomous Republic, autonomous region or national area.

Article 12. Instruction in the fundamentals of science, and polytechnical and vocational training in the eight-year school shall be conducted on the basis of close ties with life, the practice of communist construction, and participation by the children in various kinds of socially useful work within their powers.

Article 13. The basic form for the organization of educational work in school shall be the lesson conducted by a teacher for a given class with a fixed number of pupils in it. Besides lessons in class, excursions shall be arranged and work done in the workshops and on the school's experimental plot. Such forms of organization as team work, group projects and individual work with the pupil may also be used for carrying out particular functions in the process of education.

Various methods of education should be creatively employed in the educational work of schools to ensure an intelligent and sound assimilation of knowledge, to encourage an active approach in the pupils and to assist the development of habits of independent work and the ability to apply knowledge in practice.

The pupils' progress shall be evaluated by the numerical 5-mark scale: 5 (excellent), 4 (good), 3 (satisfactory), 2 (poor), 1 (very poor).

Article 14. The pupils' education shall be brought by the teachers and class teachers through instruction, practical work and extra-curricular activities, and also through Pioneer and pupils' organizations. A liking for knowledge and work, and respect for working people, shall be fostered in pupils; the communist attitude shall be inculcated in them; they shall be brought up in the spirit of straightforwardness and honesty, desiring and ready to help their comrades, children, the disabled or the aged, and in the spirit of collectivism, communist morality, selfless devotion to their country and the people, in the spirit of proletarian internationalism.

The aesthetic education of the children shall be conducted through lessons in literature, singing, drawing and other subjects, and also through various extra-curricular activities, differing in content and form, such as choirs, clubs, talks, visits to museums and theatres, exhibitions, film shows, etc.; it should be designed to develop in the children good artistic taste, a sense of the beautiful, and civilized behaviour.

The physical education of the pupils shall be conducted through physical training, lessons and extra-curricular sports and physical exercises, and through proper organization of their work and recreation.

Article 15. In the course of its work of instruction and education, the school shall acquaint the children with various kinds of work in our society, and shall help them to bring to light their abilities and to choose their future occupations intelligently.

Article 16. Pupils shall be promoted from grade to grade on their annual marks; for pupils who have failed in one or two subjects, additional studies lasting two weeks may be organized, by decision of the school's Educational Council, at the end of the school year, after which it shall be decided whether the pupils in question can be promoted to the next higher grade; or these pupils may be given work to do during the summer and the question of their promotion to the next grade decided before the beginning of the new school year in the light of the results of what they have done on this summer work.

Examinations shall be held and certificates awarded to pupils who have completed grade VIII in accordance with the instructions of the Ministry of Education of the R.S.F.S.R.

At the end of the school year, each pupil in grade VIII shall submit the set work he has done in the workshops on the teacher's instructions.

Article 17. Pupils who have completed the course at an eight-year school shall be awarded a certificate in the prescribed form.

IV. TEACHING STAFF AND OTHER SCHOOL WORKERS

Article 18. The staff of the eight-year school (supervisors, teachers, educational assistants and other ancillary personnel) shall be determined in accordance with the provisions of the staffing schedule.

Article 19. The eight-year school shall be headed by a director, who shall be responsible for the school's general conditions and work.

The director of an eight-year school shall be appointed by the District (Municipal) Department of Public Education from among those outstanding teachers with organizational abilities who are graduates of a senior teacher-training institution and have had not less than three years' experience of teaching.

The elementary school shall be headed by a manager appointed by the District (Municipal) Department of Public Education from among people who have had a teacher training of at least secondary standard. The manager of an elementary school shall be responsible for the general conditions and work of his school.

The director of the school shall provide for a proper distribution of the teaching staff and take measures for establishing the necessary material conditions for the school's work; he shall guide the teaching staff and help them to improve their qualifications; shall enrol pupils and direct the activities of the student body and pupils' organizations, contributing to the development of their initiative and creative ability by every means in his power; he shall be responsible for the provision of universal compulsory eight-year education for children in the area assigned to his school, for observance of the syllabuses and curricula, the educational work of the school and the vocational training of the pupils, and for compliance with health regulations, labour protection and industrial safety requirements; he shall take measures to influence any persons violating labour discipline; and, in co-operation with the school's social organizations, he shall recommend employees for awards and commendations.

The director shall guide the school on the basis of a combination of individual and collective management, founded upon the Educational Council and the Party, Komsomol, and trade union organizations, and enlistment of the aid of parents and the sponsoring enterprises and institutions.

Article 20. The head of the school's curriculum department shall be appointed by the District (Municipal) Department of Public Education from among persons who are graduates of a senior teacher-training institution and have shown themselves to be able organizers and methodologists.

The head of the curriculum department shall be responsible for the organization and arrangement of the school's instructional and educational work and methodology, and of the work of teachers and class teachers.

Article 21. The foreman of school workshops (the manager of inter-school training workshops) shall be appointed by the District (Municipal) Department of Public Education from among persons who have had a specialized training. He shall take measures to equip workshops and supply them with materials, see that their work is properly organized, and be responsible for observance of labour-protection regulations and safety measures and for the care and maintenance of the equipment and materials in his charge.

Article 22. The biology teacher assigned by the director of the school to take charge of the school's experimental garden plot shall draw up a plan for practical work on the plot for all grades in accordance with the curriculum, and shall see that this plan is carried out, devoting special attention to the conduct of experiments and seeking to ensure that the experimental plot provides an example of how agricultural work should be conducted for the people living in the area.

Article 23. The assistant director for economic affairs (or economic manager) shall be appointed by the director of the school and be responsible for the economic state of the school, the provision of equipment and educational facilities, the care and maintenance of the school's property, the ordinary use and maintenance of the premises and observance of proper sanitary and fire prevention requirements.

Article 24. The teachers of eight-year schools shall be appointed by the District (Municipal) Department of Public Education.

395

Teachers for grades I to IV of the eight-year school shall be appointed from among people who have had a teacher training of at least secondary standard, and for grades V to VIII from among those who have had a higher education.

Teachers shall be responsible for carrying out syllabuses and curricula, for the proper use of the most effective methods of teaching, having regard to the age of the children, for the standard of the pupils' knowledge and skills and their correct evaluation, for the promotion of pupils to higher grades and their graduation, and for bringing them up in accordance with the requirements of the Soviet school. Teachers shall be required to combine respect for and attention to the children with reasonable demands upon them, paying due regard to child psychology and special features characteristic of their age.

Teachers should constantly improve their ideological and political standards and their theoretical and professional qualifications.

Article 25. Vocational training in workshops shall be conducted by teachers of vocational subjects appointed by the District (Municipal) Department of Public Education from among people who have had a specialized vocational training.

The vocational-training teachers shall be required to see that the work programme is carried out and that safety and industrial-health rules are observed, and shall be responsible for the protection of the pupils' safety and health during instruction in the workshops, excursions to industrial undertakings and industrial training practice.

Article 26. Class teachers shall be appointed by the director of the school from among the teachers working with a particular grade. The class teacher shall be in charge of the day-to-day educational work for the pupils in his class, supervise their conduct and progress and take steps to ensure the strict observance of the Regulations for Pupils; in co-operation with the other teachers working with the class, he shall strive to unite all his pupils into a close-knit, well-disciplined, industrous group of students; he shall give assistance to the Pioneer detachment of his class and organize extra-curricular activities with the children; he shall keep in constant touch with the parents and enlist their co-operation in measures for the children's education; he shall give educational guidance to the pupils to foster socialist competition in self-help, socially useful activities and sport.

Article 27. The post of special tutor shall be established for the organization of work with children after school hours in the extended day groups and schools. The special tutor shall be appointed by the District (Municipal) Department of Public Education and shall organize the children's extra-curricular work, recreation, and the preparation of their homework.

Article 28. Senior Pioneer leaders shall be appointed by the District (Municipal) Department of Public Education in agreement with the

District (Municipal) Komsomol Committee from among Komsomol or Communist Party members who are not less than eighteen years of age and have a secondary or higher education and an aptitude for work with children.

The senior Pioneer leader shall base his work on the statute on senior Pioneer leaders of detachments of the All-Union Lenin Pioneer Organization, approved by the Central Committee of the Komsomol.

Article 29. The director of the school shall place the study rooms and laboratories under the charge of the teachers of the subject concerned.

Having regard to the budgetary appropriations available, those in charge of study rooms and laboratories shall provide them with the equipment necessary for carrying out the laboratory and practical work specified in the curricula and shall be responsible for the care and maintenance of the equipment in their charge.

Article 30. The school librarian shall be appointed by the director of the school from among persons having the requisite qualifications.

The librarian shall organize the regular work of the library and, in co-operation with the teachers, help pupils in choosing books for outside reading, teach them to make good use of books, and conduct a programme on the books they read; he shall also provide for stocking the library and be responsible for the keeping of the book stocks.

Article 31. The school medical service is the responsibility of the District (Municipal) Department of Public Health.

Medical workers serving in the schools shall carry out public health and therapeutic and prophylactic measures conducive to the protection of pupils' health, their physical development and their successful instruction and education. They shall base their work on the instructions of the Ministry of Public Health of the R.S.F.S.R. and the Ministry of Education of the R.S.F.S.R.

Article 32. The teaching staff of the school shall systematically propagate educational knowledge and take part in the work of spreading scientific and political information among the population.

V. EDUCATIONAL COUNCIL

Article 33. An Educational Council shall be established in the school for discussion and settlement of the main problems arising in connexion with the instruction and education of the pupils.

The Educational Council shall consist of the director of the school (chairman), the head of the curriculum department, the teachers of general and vocational subjects, the librarian, the senior Pioneer leader, the school doctor, the chairman of the Parents' Committee and a representative of the sponsoring undertaking or instituion.

The Educational Council shall discuss problems relating to the linking of school work with practical life, improvement of the standards of general and polytechnical education and vocational training, the perfecting of methods of teaching and education, and the experience of the best teachers and other schools; it shall approve the school's programme of work, the progress reports by the director and the head of the curriculum department on the results of teaching and educational work; settle problems connected with the promotion of pupils from one grade to another and their final certification; and receive progress reports from teachers, class teachers, Pioneer leaders, the school doctor and other school workers.

The Educational Council shall base its work on the statute approved by the Ministry of Education of the R.S.F.S.R.

VI. PARENTS' COMMITTEE

Article 34. For the purpose of ensuring constant and close ties between the school and the parents, a Parents' Committee shall be elected at a general meeting of parents. The Parents' Committee shall elect one of its members as chairman.

The Parents' Committee shall enlist the active assistance of parents in school activities and shall help in instructional and educational work, in the enforcement of universal compulsory education, in organizing self-help among the pupils and their socially useful and extra-curricular activities, in the conduct of health work among the children, in the spreading of educational knowledge among the population, and in carrying out measures to improve the economic position and educational facilities of the school.

Participation by the parents in the school's work shall be based on the statute on the work of Parents' Committees approved by the Ministry of Education of the R.S.F.S.R.

VII. THE PUPILS

Article 35. Children living in the area served by the school shall be admitted to the first grade of the eight-year school if they are seven years of age on the entrance day, 1 September.

Article 36. Children may be enrolled by the director of the school between 1 June and 25 August.

For the admission of children to the first grade of the school, parents or legal guardians shall be required to submit an application, a document certifying the child's age, and a health certificate in the prescribed form; for admission to other grades, a certificate from the school where the child has previously been studying must be submitted in addition to the above documents.

Pupils shall be admitted to all grades of the school without examinations.

Article 37. Pupils are required to comply with the regulations laid down, observe discipline and conform strictly to the standards of conduct in school, at home, in the street and in public places.

Rewards and punishments shall be applied in the school in accordance with the provisions of the appropriate regulations and instructions of the Ministry of Education of the R.S.F.S.R.

For particularly grave misdemeanours (cases of hooliganism, insulting teachers, persistent defiance of teachers' instructions and the school rules), a pupil may be expelled from school by decision of the Education Council.

Decisions of the Educational Council on the expulsion of a pupil shall be subject to confirmation by the District (Municipal), Department of Public Education, which, in co-operation with the pupil's parents, shall make arrangements for continuing the child's education or finding employment for him.

Article 38.   All the pupils of an eight-year school shall form a united group actively taking part in the life of the school.

A Pupils' Committee (Council of Monitors) may be set up in the eight-year school to assist the director, teaching staff, and the council of the Pioneer detachment in fostering a conscientious attitude to their duties in pupils, inculcating habits of civilized behaviour, improving school discipline, developing the pupils' initiative and self-reliance, and organizing socialist competition in socially useful activities and sport.

The Pupils' Committee (Council of Monitors) shall base its work on the statute approved by the Ministry of Education of the R.S.F.S.R.

Article 39.   A Pioneer organization and, if there are Komsomol members among the pupils, a primary Komsomol organization, shall be set up in the eight-year school.

One of the most important tasks of the teaching staff shall be to render all possible forms of assistance to the school's Pioneer and Komsomol organizations in order to develop the self-reliance and initiative of Pioneers and Komsomol members.

Article 40.   The pupils of the eight-year school as a whole shall take part in various forms of socially useful, cultural, sports and organised activities and also in nation-wide social and political campaigns.

One of the most important types of socially useful work within the pupils' capacity is self-help designed to foster the most common habits of work necessary to life in the children. Self-help activities shall be conducted under the guidance of the teachers and with the co-operation of the Parents' Committee, having regard to public-health requirements and the necessary safety measures, without detriment to the pupils' studies and health and without placing too heavy a burden upon them.

VIII.   EDUCATIONAL FACILITIES

Article 41.   For the organization of its instructional and educational work and the pupils' labour activities, each eight-year school should have, in

399

addition to the appropriate premises for academic studies, physics, chemistry and biology laboratories, woodwork and metalwork workshops, premises and equipment for domestic-science instruction, an experimental plot, a gymnasium and sports ground, a library, a Pioneers' room, a dining-room or buffet and other premises, together with educational equipment in conformity with the specifications duly approved.

Inter-school workshops and experimental plots may be set up by decision of the executive committees of the district (municipal) soviets of workers' deputies. The industrial-training activities of pupils in grades V to VIII may be carried out at the nearest industrial undertakings, repair stations and State and collective farms.

IX. FINANCE AND ACCOUNTING

Article 42.   Eight-year schools shall be financed out of the resources of the district (municipal) and rural (settlement) budgets, in accordance with the approved estimates.

Article 43.   Eight-year schools shall perform such clerical work as is prescribed, keep records, financial and statistical accounts, and report on the progress of their work to the District (Municipal) Department of Public Education.

Article 44.   The eight-year school shall have the legal status of a body corporate and shall have a stamp of the pattern prescribed by the Ministry of Education of the R.S.F.S.R.

Article 45.   The operation of the elementary school shall be based on the relevant articles of this statute.

THE STATUTE ON THE SECONDARY GENERAL-EDUCATION LABOUR POLYTECHNICAL SCHOOL WITH VOCATIONAL TRAINING

I. AIMS AND PURPOSES

Article 1. The aim of the secondary general-education labour poly-technical school with vocational training is to provide for the all-round development of pupils' capacities and to produce people brought up in the spirit of communism with a good basic knowledge of science and capable at the same time of systematic physical work.

The secondary general-education labour polytechnical school with vocational training shall provide a full secondary, general and poly-technical education and vocational training for work in some branch of the national economy or culture, on the basis of a combination of study with socially useful productive labour.

Completion of the course at a secondary general-education labour polytechnical school with vocational training shall qualify young men and women for work in their chosen field and for admission to higher educational establishments.

II. ORGANIZATION AND STRUCTURE

Article 2. Secondary general-education labour polytechnical schools with vocational training shall be opened by decision of the Councils of Ministers of Autonomous Republics and of the Executive Committees of territorial, regional, municipal (Moscow and Leningrad) soviets of workers' deputies in accordance with the enrolment plans of the Autonomous Republic, territory, region or municipality.

Secondary general-education labour polytechnical schools with vocational training may be opened only if there are appropriate school premises, facilities for vocational training and production work, the necessary educational and ancillary equipment, and possibilities of staffing the newly opened schools with teachers and administrative officers who have had a higher education.

These schools shall be under the authority of the District (Municipal) Departments of Public Education.

Article 3. A secondary general-education labour polytechnical school with vocational training may be set up either separately from an eight-year school, comprising grades IX to XI, or together with an eight-year school. A secondary school with vocational training organized separately from an eight-year school should have not less than nine grades. The period of study in the senior grades of a secondary school with vocational training shall be three years.

Article 4. When there are not less than a hundred correspondence students, the Councils of Ministers of Autonomous Republics, or territorial and regional Executive Committees may open correspondence departments attached to secondary general-education labour polytechnical schools with vocational training, so that young workers may complete their secondary education.

Correspondence departments attached to such secondary schools with vocational training shall function in accordance with article 6 of the Statute on Evening (Shift) Secondary Schools of General Education.[1]

Article 5. The trades and professions for which students are to be trained at secondary general-education labour polytechnical schools with vocational training shall be determined by the Councils of Ministers of Autonomous Republics and the Executive Committees of territorial, regional, area, district and municipal soviets of workers' deputies in the light of the industrial facilities available and the staff requirements of the national economy.

In determining the trades and professions for which training is to be provided, account shall be taken of the special features of urban and rural schools and of girls' employment.

Article 6. The number of students in each grade of a secondary general-education labour polytechnical school with vocational training (grades IX to XI) shall not exceed thirty-five.

Article 7. Arrangements shall, if necessary, be made at such secondary schools with vocational training for regularly taking to and from school pupils in grades I to VIII who live at a distance from the school, or alternatively, a boarding-school shall be set up in accordance with the statute approved by the Ministry of Education of the R.S.F.S.R. Boarding accommodation attached to the school may also be provided for pupils in grades IX to XI.

III. SCHOOLS AND PRODUCTION

Article 8. For the vocational training and production work of pupils attending secondary general-education labour polytechnical schools with vocational training, each school shall be assigned, by decision of the Councils of Ministers of Autonomous Republics, or of the Executive

---

1. See p. 414.

Committees of territorial, regional, municipal (Moscow and Leningrad) soviets of workers' deputies, to one or more of the neighbouring industrial undertakings, construction projects, public-service undertakings, State farms, repair stations, collective farms, etc.

The managers of undertakings, construction projects, State farms and repair stations shall be responsible for establishing suitable conditions for the pupils' vocational training and production work and shall be obliged to:

Set up training workshops in their factories for the pupils' vocational training, or set aside permanent work places in the ordinary workshops.

Work out, in co-operation with the director of the school, syllabuses and curricula for the pupils' vocational training.

Designate engineering or agricultural staff and skilled workers to see to the pupils' vocational training, and make available the necessary tools and materials.

Provide opportunities for the pupils to work at the undertaking and improve their qualifications once they have had an initial vocational grounding and acquired the appropriate skills.

Provide for the observance of labour-protection and industrial-health regulations.

On collective farms, the production training of the pupils shall be conducted in training teams, on experimental sections and in collective-farm teams. It is recommended that collective farms establish proper conditions for the pupils' vocational training and assign agricultural and technical staff for this purpose.

The engineering, agricultural and other staff of industrial undertakings, construction projects, State farms, repair stations and collective farms shall co-operate in ensuring the wide dissemination of industrial and technical knowledge in the school and in acquainting the students with the achievements of persons who have introduced innovations in production.

The schools shall assist undertakings, construction projects and State and collective farms in work for the propagation of scientific and political knowledge among manual and clerical workers and collective farmers.

IV. INSTRUCTIONAL AND EDUCATIONAL WORK

Article 9. Instruction and education in secondary general-education labour polytechnical schools with vocational training shall be provided in accordance with the syllabuses and curricula approved by the Ministry of Education of the R.S.F.S.R. The Ministries of Education of Autonomous Republics and the Territorial and Regional Departments of Public Education shall be authorized, with the agreement of the Ministry of Education of the R.S.F.S.R., to make any necessary changes in the syllabuses and curricula in the light of local conditions, subject to observance of the specified number of hours laid down in the curriculum for each grade. (*Note.* The syllabuses for instruction in the native language and literature in the case of national schools shall be approved by the Ministries of Education of the Autonomous Republics.)

Article 10. Studies in these schools shall begin on 1 September and end on 25 June (including examinations in the final grade). The Councils of Ministers of Autonomous Republics and the executive committees of territorial and regional soviets of workers' deputies may change the dates of the beginning and end of studies in such schools in rural districts, in consideration of the seasonal character of agricultural work, without, however, curtailing the total length of the school year.

The school year in these schools (for grades IX to XI) shall be divided into two terms: the first from 1 September to 29 December and the second from 11 January to the end of the school year.

Provision shall be made for the following holidays for pupils during the year: the autumn holiday from 5 to 9 November inclusive; the winter holiday from 30 December to 10 January inclusive; and the spring holiday from 24 to 31 March inclusive. The dates of the spring holiday may be changed, provided its duration remains the same, by decision of the executive committees of the district (municipal) soviets of workers' deputies, in consideration of local conditions.

The length of a lesson in grades IX, X and XI shall be forty-five minutes. There shall be a break of ten minutes between lessons and a longer break after the second or third lesson, which should be thirty minutes in length.

Article 11. In order to prepare the pupils for independent life and socially useful production work, two-thirds of the time spent in study during the year in grades IX, X and XI shall be devoted to general and polytechnical subjects, and one-third to vocational training and production work; as a rule, pupils in grade IX should be given a preliminary vocational grounding in most special subjects so that, in grades X and XI, they may be able to engage in socially useful production work and to continue and perfect their vocational training.

Article 12. Instruction in general and polytechnical subjects in secondary general-education labour polytechnical schools with vocational training shall be conducted on the basis of close ties with practical life, and the practice of communist construction, and shall give the students a sound knowledge of the fundamentals of science, a broad background of general and polytechnical knowledge, a scientific understanding of the law of the development of nature and society, and the ability to apply knowledge in practice.

The teaching of physics, chemistry, biology, mathematics and technical drawing should be so organized as to help the pupils to understand the scientific bases of production engineering and technology, including the field in which they are working.

The Educational Council of the school may, with the consent of the Ministries of Education of Autonomous Republics or of the Territorial or Regional Departments of Public Education, make changes in the

404

syllabuses for subjects which are necessary to give pupils an understanding of a particular field of production, provided that the general standard of knowledge specified in the secondary-school curriculum is maintained.

Article 13. The vocational training of pupils in secondary schools of this type shall be carried on by means of theoretical and practical production training designed to enable pupils to acquire a sound knowledge of, and skills in, the special field they have chosen.

On completing their preliminary vocational training, pupils shall, with the school's co-operation, according to established procedure, be given a trade rating, with a corresponding wage rate or class, after which they may be allowed to do independent work according to their classification. The wages or working-day units for such pupils shall be calculated according to the established rates and quotas, having regard to their output. Later on, as their skill improves and the productivity of their work rises, these gradings or classifications shall be reviewed by the qualifying commissions and finally determined when the students leave school.

In the course of their vocational training and production work, the qualities necessary in contemporary socialist production shall be cultivated in the students: high standards of work and civic labour discipline, a creative approach, readiness to work for a steady increase in quantitative and qualitative results, ability to work as part of a team, and perseverance.

Article 14. The educational methods employed in these schools should be conducive to the sound and intelligent assimilation of the fundamentals of science and the development of the pupils' self-reliance and initiative; they should accustom pupils to solving independently various types of theoretical and practical problems, to systematic observation, and to conducting experiments in laboratories, in the field and in production, besides enabling them to handle computing and measuring apparatus, reference books, dictionaries, tables and catalogues.

Special attention should be paid to the use of visual aids in teaching and extensive recourse should be made to films and television.

The basic form of organization for teaching the fundamentals of science shall be the class lesson. In addition, wide recourse shall be had to excursions, and activities in workshops and laboratories, for the fostering of technical invention, the designing of new apparatus, models and technical sevices, and agricultural experiments. Group and individual methods of education shall be used for vocational training.

The pupils' knowledge, skills and working habits shall be systematically appraised by oral and written tests and laboratory assignments, and by individual tests on the various sections and subjects in the syllabus; the 5-mark system of assessment shall be used.

Article 15. The education of pupils in secondary general-education labour polytechnic schools with vocational training shall be brought about by the study of the fundamentals of science, productive and socially useful labour, and extra-curricular activities, and also by the work of Komsomol

405

and pupils' organizations. A liking for knowledge and work, and respect for working people, shall be fostered in pupils; the communist attitude shall be inculcated in them; and they shall be brought up in the spirit of collectivism, communist morality, selfless devotion to their country and the people, in the spirit of proletarian internationalism.

The aesthetic education of pupils in grades IX to XI shall be conducted through lessons in literature and other subjects and also through the organization of optional courses in various forms of art, and through extra-curricular activities; it shall be designed to develop good artistic taste, a sense of the beautiful, and civilized behaviour.

Physical education shall be conducted through physical-training lessons and extra-curricular sports and physical exercises, and through proper organization of the pupils' work and recreation.

Such activities as excursions to places of general or special local interest shall also be organized in schools. Pupils shall be encouraged to take part in community projects and the activities of sports clubs.

Article 16. Pupils shall be promoted from grade to grade in these schools on the basis of their annual marks in all subjects and the assessment of their practical production work. On completion of the course for grade XI, final examinations shall be held in accordance with the instructions of the Ministry of Education of the R.S.F.S.R. Those who pass these examinations and complete a qualifying test assignment shall be awarded an appropriate certificate of secondary education in the prescribed form and an attestation of their trade rating in the occupation they have chosen.

Article 17. The Councils of Ministers of Autonomous Republics and the Executive Committees of territorial, regional, municipal and district soviets of workers' deputies shall provide for the employment of graduates of secondary general-education labour polytechnical schools with vocational training in some branch of the national economy or culture appropriate to their qualifications.

V. TEACHING STAFF AND OTHER SCHOOL WORKERS

Article 18. The staff of the secondary general-education labour polytechnical school with vocational training (supervisors, teachers, educational assistants and other ancillary personnel) shall be determined in accordance with the provisions of the staffing schedule.

Article 19. A school of this type shall be headed by a director, who shall be responsible for the school's general conditions and work.

The director shall be appointed by the Ministry of Education of the Autonomous Republic or the Territorial or Regional Department of Public Education from among the best teachers with organizational abilities who are graduates of a senior teacher-training institution and have had not less than three years' teaching experience.

The director shall guide the work of the school. He shall provide for a proper distribution of the teaching staff and the enrolment of pupils; he shall make arrangements to create the necessary material conditions for the school's work and shall be responsible for the organization of its educational activities and the pupils' general, polytechnical and vocational training, for observance of the syllabuses and curricula, and compliance with labour-protection and industrial-safety rules; he shall guide the teaching staff and help them to improve their qualifications, direct the activities of the student body and the work of pupils' organizations, contributing in every possible way to the development of their initiative and creative ability; he shall take measures to influence any persons violating labour discipline and, in co-operation with the schools' social organizations, shall recommend workers for awards and commendations.

The director shall guide the school's work on the basis of a combination of individual and collective management, founded upon the Educational Council and the Party, Komsomol and trade-union organizations of the school; he shall organize the pupils' parents to assist the school and enlist the aid, in its instructional and educational work, of the employees of the industrial undertakings, collective and State farms and repair stations at which the pupils are engaged in production work.

Article 20. The head of the school's curriculum department shall be appointed by the District (Municipal) Department of Public Education from among teachers who are graduates of a senior teacher-training institution and have shown themselves to be able organizers and methodologists.

The head of the curriculum department shall be responsible for the organization and arrangement of the school's instructional and educational work and methodology and of the work of subject and class teachers.

Article 21. The head of the curriculum department for vocational training shall be appointed by the District (Municipal) Department of Public Education from among persons who have had a specialized higher education and experience of work in industry. He shall be responsible for the proper organization and conduct of the pupils' vocational training and production work.

Article 22. The head of the training workshops and the head of the experimental training farm shall be appointed by the District (Municipal) Department of Public Education from among persons who have had a higher or specialized secondary education and practical experience. They shall take steps to ensure the proper organization of work in the training workshops and on the experimental training farm, and to enforce compliance with labour-protection and industrial-safety rules, and shall be responsible for the care and maintenance of the equipment and materials in their charge.

Article 23. The school's assistant director for economic affairs (or economic manager) shall be appointed by the director of the school and shall be responsible for its economic operation, the provision of its ordinary running and educational facilities, the care and maintenance of its property, the ordinary use and maintenance of the premises, and proper sanitary and fire-prevention conditions.

Article 24. Teachers for grades IX to XI shall be appointed by the District (Municipal) Department of Public Education from among persons who have had a higher education.

Teachers shall be responsible for the instruction and education of the pupils in accordance with the requirements of the Societ school, for carrying out syllabuses and curricula, for the proper use of the most effective methods of teaching, for the standard of the pupils' knowledge and skills and their correct evaluation, and for the promotion of pupils to higher grades and their graduation. Teachers shall be required to combine respect for and attention to the pupils with reasonable demands upon them, having due regard to the special characteristics of their age.

Teachers should constantly improve their ideological and political standards and their theoretical and professional qualifications.

Article 25. Vocational-training instructors in the training workshops shall be appointed by the District (Municipal) Department of Public Education from among people who have had the necessary specialized training and practical experience.

The instructor shall be responsible for the vocational training and the organization of the production work of his pupils, and for compliance with the labour-protection and industrial-safety regulations.

Article 26. Class teachers shall be appointed by the director of the school from among the teachers working with a particular grade. Their duties shall include giving general educational guidance to the class, uniting the pupils into a close-knit, industrious and well-disciplined group, studying their individual peculiarities and fostering their activity, self-reliance, a responsible attitude to their studies, industry, individual abilities and interests, and assisting in the rational organization of the pupils' educational and socially useful work.

The class teacher shall carry out his duties on the basis of help from the school's Komsomol organization and constant contact with other teachers, parents, public organizations and the undertakings at which the parents are employed, and with the enterprise at which the pupils' socially useful work is performed.

Article 27. The school librarian shall be appointed by the director of the school from among persons having at least a secondary education.

The librarian, in co-operation with the teachers, shall guide the pupils' extra-curricular reading, provide for the stocking of the library, and be responsible for the keeping of the book stocks entrusted to him.

Article 28. The director of the school shall place the study rooms and laboratories under the charge of the teachers of the appropriate subjects. Having regard to the budgetary appropriations available, those in charge of study rooms and laboratories shall provide them with the equipment necessary for carrying out the laboratory and practical work specified in the curricula and shall be responsible for the care and maintenance of the equipment in their charge.

Laboratory assistants for study rooms and laboratories shall be appointed by the director of the school and work under the guidance of the heads of the appropriate study rooms and laboratories.

Article 29. The school medical service is the responsibility of the District (Municipal) Department of Public Health.

Medical workers serving in the schools shall carry out public-health and therapeutic and prophylactic measures conducive to the protection of the pupils' health, their physical development and their successful instruction and education. They shall base their work on the instructions issued by the Ministry of Public Health of the R.S.F.S.R. and the Ministry of Education of the R.S.F.S.R.

VI. EDUCATIONAL COUNCIL

Article 30. An Educational Council shall be established in the school for discussion and settlement of the main problems arising in connexion with the instruction and education of the pupils.

The Educational Council shall consist of the director of the school (chairman), the head of the curriculum department, the head of the curriculum department for vocational training, the head of the training workshops, the head of the experimental training farm, the teachers of the school, the senior Pioneer leader, the vocational-training instructors, the librarian, the school doctor, a representative of the enterprise or collective farm, and the chairman of the Parents' Committee.

As a rule, the secretary of the Komsomol Committee of the school and the chairman of the Pupils' Committee shall be invited to meetings of the Educational Council.

The Educational Council shall discuss problems relating to the linking of school work with practical life and production, the improvement of the standards of general and polytechnical education and vocational training, the perfecting of methods of teaching and education, and the experience of the best teachers in other schools; it shall approve the school's programme of work, the progress reports by the director and the head of the curriculum department on the results of teaching and educational work; shall settle problems connected with the promotion of pupils from one grade to another and their final certification, and receive reports from the teachers on the carrying-out of the curricula, from class teachers on the progress of instructional and educational work and discipline among the pupils, and from the school doctor on the state of the pupils' health and measures for its improvement, and other questions.

The Educational Council shall base its work on the statute approved by the Ministry of Education of the R.S.F.S.R.

VII. PARENTS' COMMITTEE

Article 31. For the purpose of ensuring constant and close ties with the pupils' parents, a Parents' Committee shall be elected at a general meeting of the parents. The Parents' Committee shall elect one of its members as chairman.

The Parents' Committee shall enlist the active assistance of parents in the life of the school and shall help in instructional and educational work, in the organization of vocational training and the pupils' production and socially useful work and extra-curricular activities, in the carrying-out of measures to improve the economic position and educational facilities of the school, in the organization of the pupils' self-help activities, and in the conduct of health work among them.

Participation by the parents in the school's work shall be based on the statute on the work of Parents' Committees approved by the Ministry of Education of the R.S.F.S.R.

VIII. THE PUPILS

Article 32. Those who have completed the course at an eight-year school and desire, besides continuing their secondary education, to learn a trade in which the school in question provides training, may be admitted, without examination, to the ninth grade of a secondary general-education labour polytechnical school with vocational training.

Article 33. Those wishing to be admitted to the ninth grade of such a school may submit their applications and be enrolled between 1 July and 25 August. Applicants shall submit their applications, a certificate stating that they have completed the course at an eight-year school, and a medical certificate attesting their fitness for work in the special branch selected.

Article 34. Pupils shall be required to comply with the disciplinary regulations, to observe the school's rules and industrial-safety regulations in the factory, and conform to the standards of civilized conduct in school, at the industrial undertaking, at home, in the street and in public places.

Rewards and punishments shall be applied in the school in accordance with the appropriate regulations approved by the Ministry of Education of the R.S.F.S.R.

For particularly grave misdemeanours (cases of hooliganism, insulting teachers, persistent defiance of teachers' instructions and the rules of the school and the enterprise) a pupil may be expelled from school by decision of the Educational Council. This decision shall be subject to confirmation by the District (Municipal) Department of Public Education which, in co-operation with the pupil's parents, shall take steps to find employment for him.

Article 35. A Pupils' Committee (Council of Monitors) shall be elected

410

by a general meeting of pupils for the purpose of uniting the pupils into a close-knit and industrious group, assisting the management and teachers in carrying out the tasks of communist education. The Pupils' Committee (Council of Monitors) shall conduct its work in accordance with the statute on pupils' organizations approved by the Ministry of Education of the R.S.F.S.R.

Article 36. A Komsomol organization shall be set up in the secondary general-education labour polytechnical school with vocational training.

Article 37. The pupils of the school as a whole shall take part in various forms of socially useful, cultural and recreational and sports activities organized in the school and at the enterprise, and also in nation-wide social and political campaigns, under the guidance of the school's director and teachers, with the object of developing the pupils' creative initiative and self-reliance and the wide application of the method of socialist competition.

One of the most important types of socially useful activity for bringing up young people with a respect for labour and developing the working habits necessary to life is self-help. This shall be organized by the school without detriment to the pupils' studies, with due regard to educational and public-health requirements and to the observance of the necessary safety measures, and without placing too heavy a burden upon the pupils.

IX. EDUCATIONAL FACILITIES

Article 38. The following study rooms and laboratories shall be set up in secondary general-education labour polytechnical schools with vocational training: physics and electrical engineering, chemistry, biology, technical drawing, principles of industrial production (in urban schools) and principles of agricultural production (in rural schools) and, if necessary, training workshops appropriate to the type of school. In addition, special premises shall be set aside for domestic-science instruction.

All the study rooms and laboratories shall be equipped in accordance with the specifications approved in the prescribed form.

The school shall have an assembly hall and gymnasium, sports grounds, a library with a reading room, a dining room and other premises.

Article 39. School and inter-school training workshops shall be set up by decision of the Councils of Ministers of Autonomous Republics and the Executive Committees of territorial and regional soviets of workers' deputies in cases when the school is unable to arrange for vocational training and production work at industrial undertakings for pupils in grades IX to XI. These workshops shall be financed out of special funds or shall be run on a self-supporting basis, and shall be provided with the necessary equipment for organizing production work.

411

X. FINANCE AND ACCOUNTING

Article 40. Secondary general-education labour polytechnical schools with vocational training shall be financed out of district, municipal and settlement budgets, in accordance with approved estimates.

Article 41. These schools shall perform such clerical work as is prescribed, shall keep records, financial and statistical accounts, and shall report on the progress of their work to the District (Municipal) Department of Public Education.

Article 42. These schools shall have the legal status of a body corporate and shall have stamps of the pattern prescribed by the Ministry of Education of the R.S.F.S.R.

Article 43. The operation of grades I to VIII in a secondary general-education labour polytechnical school with vocational training shall be based on the Statute on the Eight-Year School.[1]

---

1. See p. 390.

THE STATUTE ON THE EVENING (SHIFT) SECONDARY SCHOOL OF GENERAL EDUCATION
(Approved by Decision No. 2027 of the Council of Ministers of the R.S.F.S.R., dated 29 December 1959)

I. AIMS AND PURPOSES

Article 1. The evening (shift) secondary school of general education is intended to provide a full secondary education for persons who have completed the course at an eight-year school and are working in various branches of the national economy and culture, and wish to improve their vocational qualifications.

Those studying at evening (shift) secondary schools of general education do not discontinue their work in industry. Depending on the actual conditions in which the pupils are working (shift work, seasonal work, etc.), the courses at such schools may be held in the evening or in the daytime (shift school) or may be concentrated in periods when the pupils are free from work (seasonal schools in rural districts, and when feasible in river fleet enterprises and other such branches of the economy).

The teaching of general, polytechnical and specialized subjects in evening (shift) secondary schools of general education should take account of the pupils' practical experience and promote their cultural development and the improvement of their qualifications and skills and social and political activities.

II. ORGANIZATION AND STRUCTURE

Article 2. Evening (shift) secondary schools of general education shall be opened in towns, working settlements and rural districts by decision of the Councils of Ministers of Autonomous Republics or of the Executive Committees of territorial, regional or municipal (Moscow and Leningrad) soviets of workers' deputies in accordance with the enrolment plans drawn up by the Autonomous Republic, territory, region or municipality.

Such evening (shift) schools shall be under the authority of the District (Municipal) Department of Public Education.

Article 3. If there are a sufficient number of pupils, such evening (shift) schools may be set up at industrial and transport undertakings, building sites, State farms, repair stations and collective farms. They may also be set up to provide education for young people from a number of

413

industrial undertakings, institutions, collective and State farms. In such circumstances the area to be served by each such evening (shift) secondary school shall be determined by the District (Municipal) Department of Public Education.

Article 4. Evening (shift) secondary schools of general education shall comprise grades IX, X and XI, and the course of study shall last three years.

For young workers who have not had an eight-year education, these schools may include all grades from the third upwards.

Grades III to VIII may also be set up in eight-year schools.

Classes for grades III to V shall be opened if there are twenty-five pupils for each grade, and for grade IX if there are twenty pupils for this grade.

In certain exceptional cases, grade nine classes may be opened in country districts if there are fifteen pupils.

Article 5. Evening (shift) secondary schools of general education shall be opened if there are not less than three grades.

If there are not enough pupils for enrolment to warrant the opening of a separate independent evening (shift) secondary school of general education, individual classes may be set up in secondary general-education labour polytechnical schools with vocational training for the education of young workers without their discontinuing work.

Article 6. If necessary, correspondence departments may be attached to these evening (shift) secondary schools in order to enable persons who cannot attend the school to obtain a secondary education.

Correspondence departments attached to such schools shall be opened by decision of the Councils of Ministers of Autonomous Republics or the Executive Committees of territorial, regional, municipal (Moscow and Leningrad) soviets of workers' deputies, if there are not less than a hundred correspondence students.

Evening (shift) secondary schools of general education which have correspondence departments shall set up tutorial centres for pupils in their area if there are not less than sixty correspondence students. If there are fewer correspondence students, they shall be enrolled at the nearest evening (shift) secondary school or secondary general-education labour polytechnical school with vocational training for obtaining advice and sitting tests.

Tutorial centres shall operate in accordance with the statute on such centres approved by the Ministry of Education of the R.S.F.S.R.

III. ENTERPRISES AND SCHOOLS

Article 7. The managers of factories, building sites, State farms, repair stations and institutions shall be obliged to provide the necessary conditions

414

for the successful work of evening (shift) secondary schools and their pupils:

1. To provide, whenever necessary, premises suitable for educational purposes, equipment and heating, to carry out ordinary maintenance and capital repairs to the buildings and to make available engineers and technicians and agricultural specialists for teaching special subjects which will help to improve the pupils' qualifications.

2. In consultation with the public education authorities, to draw up long-term plans for the education of young people needing to complete their secondary education, to organize explanatory work among such young people to get them to enrol at evening (shift) secondary schools of general education, and to establish conditions enabling them to attend regularly.

It is also recommended that collective farms make the necessary arrangements to enable their young people to study at such evening (shift) school without discontinuing their work.

Article 8. In order to provide systematic help to the teaching staffs of evening (shift) schools in the organization of studies for young people attending school without discontinuing their work, a permanent Promotion Committee shall be set up by the District (Municipal) Department of Public Education. The membership of this committee shall include the directors of schools and representatives of the management and the Party, trade-union and Komsomol organizations of factories, offices, State farms, repair stations and collective farms. The Promotion Committee shall work under the guidance of the head of the District (Municipal) Department of Public Education.

In cases where the students of an evening (shift) school are manual and clerical workers belonging to one enterprise, a Promotion Committee may be set up at the enterprise in question. The committee shall then work under the guidance of the director of the enterprise or a person appointed by him.

Article 9. A shortened working week or a shortened working day, with payment of 50 per cent of the average wages at the principal place work of (but not less than the minimum wage) during the pupils' absence from work, shall be introduced for successful students in grades IX to XI of evening (shift, seasonal) and correspondence secondary schools of general education during the school year.

The pupils of evening (shift, seasonal) and correspondence secondary schools of general education shall be allowed a shortened working week or a shortened working day, and twenty working days' additional leave during the final examination period in grade XI, with payment of wages at the principal place of work calculated on the basis of the pay rates or fixed wages, in accordance with the terms of Decision No. 1233 of the Council of Ministers of the R.S.F.S.R., dated 5 November 1959.

Article 10. The Educational Councils of evening (shift) secondary schools of general education shall be entitled, if there are any good reasons, to change the dates of examinations for individual pupils.

415

Article 11. The directors and teachers of evening (shift) schools shall maintain constant contact with the factories, institutions and State and collective farms at which their pupils are working, shall familiarize themselves with the conditions of the young people's work, and shall take an active part in general education and other cultural activities among the manual and clerical workers and collective farmers.

IV. INSTRUCTIONAL AND EDUCATIONAL WORK

Article 12. Courses of study at evening (shift) secondary schools of general education shall be provided in accordance with the syllabuses and curricula approved by the Ministry of Education of the R.S.F.S.R. The Ministries of Education of Autonomous Republics and the Territorial and Regional Departments of Public Education shall be authorized, with the agreement of the Ministry of Education of the R.S.F.S.R., to make any necessary changes in the syllabuses and curricula of these evening (shift) schools in the light of local conditions, subject to observance of the specified number of hours laid down in the curriculum for each grade and without detriment to the standards of knowledge imparted. (*Note.* The syllabuses for instruction in the native language and literature in the case of national schools shall be approved by the Ministries of Education of the Autonomous Republics.)

Article 13. The length of the school year in evening (shift) secondary schools of general education shall be thirty-six weeks.

The school year for such schools shall begin on 1 September and end on 25 May, for grades III to VII, IX and X; on 10 June, for grade VIII; and on 20 June, for grade XI.

To allow for the special conditions of the pupils' work, the dates for the beginning and ending of the school year in seasonal secondary schools of general education shall be determined by the Ministries of Education of Autonomous Republics and the Territorial or Regional Departments of Public Education, subject to observance of the prescribed length of the school year.

The school year in evening (shift) schools shall be divided into two terms, with ten days' winter holiday between them.

The length of a lesson in all grades shall be forty-five minutes. There shall be a break of ten minutes between lessons and a longer break after the second or third lesson, lasting not less than twenty minutes.

Article 14. The pupils of evening (shift) secondary schools of general education are persons working in various branches of the national economy and culture. The instructional and educational work in such schools should therefore be so organized as to take account of the students' practical experience and to promote improvement of their skills and qualifications, social and political activities and cultural standards.

The teaching of such subjects as physics, mathematics, chemistry, biology and technical drawing in such evening (shift) secondary schools should help the pupil to a deeper understanding of the scientific bases of engineering and technology, especially in their own sphere of production, and should assist them in applying the knowledge they acquire in practice.

Article 15. For the purpose of improving the pupils' vocational qualifications, the curricula of evening (shift) secondary schools of general education shall provide for optional courses on general engineering and technological problems or problems of agricultural production of special interest to the particular factory, State farm, collective farm or group of enterprises served by the school.

Article 16. Evening (shift) secondary schools of general education should foster in their pupils the communist attitude to life and bring them up in the spirit of collectivism, communist morality and selfless devotion to their country and the people, in the spirit of proletarian internationalism, and should inculcate the communist attitude towards labour and its obligations.

The schools should encourage pupils to take an active part in social and political, cultural and sports activities conducted at enterprises, collective farms and institutions and should also organize for their pupils, lectures and reports on various questions relating to science, engineering, culture and art, and encourage them to make use of libraries.

Article 17. Various educational methods shall be used in evening (shift) secondary schools of general education, with due regard for the pupils' experience of life and work, so as to promote an intelligent and sound assimilation of knowledge, the devlopment of the pupils' ability to learn and work actively, habits of self-education, and the ability to apply knowledge in practice. In this connexion, substantial provision should be made for introductory and general talks and for practical work in study rooms and laboratories. In addition to class lessons, systematic use should be made of group and individual tutorials and of such forms of educational activities as excursions and conferences.

The pupils' knowledge, abilities and skills should be systematically tested at evening (shift) secondary schools by oral questioning, written class work and laboratory assignments, and by individual tests on the sections of the curriculum covered; the 5-mark system of evaluation should be used.

Article 18. The promotion of pupils from one grade to another and the examinations in grades VIII and XI of evening (shift) secondary schools of general education shall be arranged in accordance with instructions approved by the Ministry of Education of the R.S.F.S.R.

Article 19. Those who have completed, by correspondence or otherwise, the course for the eighth grade of an evening (shift) secondary school of general education, shall receive certificates entitling them to admission to a specialized secondary-education institution or enabling them to continue their education at a secondary school of general education.

417

Those who have completed the course for grade XI shall receive a certificate of secondary education qualifying them for admission to higher educational institutions.

V. TEACHING STAFF AND OTHER SCHOOL WORKERS

Article 20.   The staff of evening (shift) secondary schools of general education (supervisors, teachers, educational assistants and other ancillary personnel) shall be determined in accordance with the provisions of the staffing schedule.

Article 21.   The evening (shift) secondary school of general education shall be headed by a director, appointed by the Ministry of Education of the Autonomous Republic or the Territorial or Regional Department of Public Education from among persons with organizational abilities who are graduates of a senior teacher-training institution and have had not less than three years' experience of teaching.

The director shall guide the work of the school. He shall be responsible for the carrying-out of the enrolment plan, the syllabuses and curricula, and the conduct of the school's instructional and educational work; he shall see that the normal material conditions for the school's work are provided, shall take measures for the recruitment of suitable teaching staff, provide guidance for the teachers and promote the development of their creative initiative and the improvement of their teaching qualifications; he shall direct the activities of the student body.

The director shall guide the school's work on the basis of a combination of individual and collective management and shall carry on his work in close contact with the managements and the Party, trade-union and Komsomol organizations of the enterprises, institutions and State and collective farms served by the school.

Article 22.   The head of the curriculum department of an evening (shift) secondary school of general education and the head of the correspondence department thereof shall be appointed by the District (Municipal) Department of Public Education from among persons who are graduates of a senior teacher-training institution and have shown themselves to be able organizers and methodologists.

The head of the curriculum department shall be responsible for the progress of the school's instructional and educational work and methodology, and shall control and supervise the teachers' work.

Article 23.   The head of the correspondence department shall be responsible for the organization and progress of all the instructional and educational work of the correspondence department and its tutorial centres, shall be in direct charge of the carrying-out of syllabuses and curricula, supervise the work of teachers and test the quality of the pupils' knowledge, shall study and introduce the results of constructive experience in correspondence education, and shall draw up the programme of studies.

Article 24. The methodologist of the correspondence department attached to an evening (shift) school shall be appointed by the District (Municipal) Department of Public Education from among teachers who are graduates of a senior teacher-training institution.

The methodologist shall organize and supervise the instructional and educational and methodological work at tutorial centres and the work with pupils enrolled at eight-year and secondary schools for the purpose of obtaining advice and sitting tests individually. He shall furnish methodological aid to the heads of tutorial centres and individual teachers.

Article 25. Teachers at evening (shift) secondary schools of general education shall be appointed by the District (Municipal) Department of Public Education from among persons who have had a teacher training of secondary standard, for grades III and IV, and a higher teacher training for grades V to XI.

The teacher shall be responsible for the quality of the pupils' instruction and education and for the carrying-out of the curriculum and syllabuses in his subject.

Having regard to the special features of evening (shift) secondary schools of general education, the teacher shall employ the most effective methods for the instruction and education of the pupils in close contact with the social organizations of the enterprises, State and collective farms and offices at which they are employed.

In order to carry out their duties successfully, teachers shall systematically improve their ideological and political standards and familiarize themselves with the industrial situation in the school's vicinity.

Article 26. For each class in an evening (shift) secondary school of general education from grade V upwards, the director of the school shall appoint a class teacher from among the teaching staff. The duties of the class teacher shall be determined by the statute on class teachers in evening (shift) secondary schools of general education, approved by the Ministry of Education of the R.S.F.S.R.

Article 27. The assistant director for economic affairs (or economic manager) shall be appointed by the director of the school and shall be responsible for the state of the school's facilities, the material provision for its educational activities, the care and maintenance of its property and the normal use and maintenance of the school's premises and observance of proper sanitary and fire-prevention requirements.

Article 28. The director of the school shall place study rooms and laboratories under the charge of the teachers of the appropriate subjects.

Those in charge of study rooms and laboratories shall provide them with the necessary equipment for carrying out the laboratory and practical work specified in the curricula and shall be responsible for the care and maintenance of the equipment in their charge.

Article 29. The school librarian shall be appointed by the director of the

419

school. In collaboration with the teachers, he shall organize the pupils' extra-curricular reading, see to the stocking of the library with new books and be responsible for the keeping of the book stocks entrusted to him.

Article 30. The director of an evening (shift) secondary school of general education which has a correspondence department shall appoint heads of tutorial centres in accordance with the provisions of the staffing schedule.

VI. EDUCATIONAL COUNCIL

Article 31. An Educational Council shall be established at evening (shift) secondary schools of general education for the discussion and settlement of the main questions arising in connexion with its instructional and educational work.

The Educational Council shall consist of the director of the school (chairman), the head of the curriculum department, the teachers, the librarian, a representative of the Council of Monitors and representatives of the social organizations of the undertakings, collective and State farms and institutions served by the school.

In schools having correspondence departments, the Educational Council shall also include the head of the correspondence department, methodologists and the heads of tutorial centres.

The Educational Council shall discuss problems relating to the linking of school work with practical life and production, measures for improving the standard of instruction and education and of the pupils' vocational qualifications, and the general introduction of the results of the best educational experience; it shall discuss and approve the plans for the school's work, progress reports by the director or the head of the curriculum department on the results of the instructional and educational work, and reports by the teachers on the carrying-out of the syllabuses and the pupils' progress and discipline, and shall settle problems relating to the promotion of pupils from one grade to another and their final certification.

The Educational Council shall base its work on the statute approved by the Ministry of Education of the R.S.F.S.R.

VII. THE PUPILS

Article 32. Persons who are working at an industrial enterprise or in an office and who have completed the course at an eight-year school shall be admitted to the ninth grade in an evening (shift) secondary school of general education, and those who have completed the courses for grades IX and X at a secondary school shall be admitted respectively to grades X and XI.

Persons who can produce evidence of the appropriate educational qualifications and are working in a factory or institution shall be admitted to grades III, IV, V, VI, VII and VIII, as appropriate.

An applicant seeking enrolment at an evening (shift) school shall submit documentary evidence of his educational attainments and an attestation from his place of work.

If an applicant has no documentary evidence of educational attainments, he may be enrolled in the appropriate grade after a preliminary test of his knowledge of Russian (mother tongue) and mathematics.

Article 33. Applicants for admission to an evening (shift) school may submit their applications and be enrolled between 15 May and 25 August.

Article 34. The pupils of evening (shift) secondary schools of general education are required to attend classes regularly, be diligent and persistent in their studies, comply with the requirements of the administration and teaching staff of the school, observe strictly the rules of socialist conduct and be exemplary in their work at the enterprise.

Pupils who systematically absent themselves without adequate excuse or who neglect their studies may be expelled by decision of the school's Educational Council, notification of this action being transmitted to the management and social organizations of the factories, institutions, State farms and collective farms at which the pupils are employed.

Article 35. Since the pupils of evening (shift) schools are members of the Party, trade-union and Komsomol organizations of the factories, institutions, State farms and collective farms at which they are employed, these organizations shall not be set up in the schools.

Article 36. A Council of Monitors including pupils representing each grade shall be set up in the evening (shift) school with a view to uniting the pupils in a close-knit, industrious group and directing their activities to the improvement of the school's work.

VIII. EDUCATIONAL FACILITIES

Article 37. Evening (shift) secondary schools of general education shall be accommodated in school buildings appropriate to the requirements of these educational institutions.

If no special school buildings are available, such schools shall be housed in premises set aside by the Executive Committees of the district (municipal) or rural (settlement) soviets of workers' deputies, enterprises or State and collective farms, if such premises are suitable for educational purposes. Evening (shift) schools may also be housed in the premises of eight-year or secondary general-education labour polytechnical schools with vocational training.

Article 38. If an evening (shift) secondary school is housed in a separate building, physics, chemistry and technical-drawing laboratories shall be set up for the conduct of theoretical studies and practical work, besides a study room for the principles of industrial production in urban schools and one for the principles of agricultural production in rural schools.

Evening (shift) secondary schools of general education shall be furnished with the necessary equipment and materials for all subjects in the curriculum, in accordance with the specifications approved in the prescribed form.

IX. FINANCE AND ACCOUNTING

Article 39.   Evening (shift) secondary schools of general education and their correspondence departments shall be financed out of municipal, district and settlement budgets in accordance with approved estimates.

Article 40.   These schools shall perform such clerical work as is prescribed, shall keep records and financial and statistical accounts, and shall report periodically on the progress of their work to the District (Municipal), Territorial or Regional Department of Public Education or the Ministry of Education of the Autonomous Republic, as appropriate.

Article 41.   Evening (shift) secondary schools of general education shall have the legal status of a body corporate and shall have stamps of the pattern prescribed by the Ministry of Education of the R.S.F.S.R.

BIBLIOGRAPHY[1]

BASIC MATERIAL RELATING TO POLYTECHNICAL EDUCATION

Rezoljucii XX s″ezda Kommunističeskoj partii Sovetskogo Sojuza [Resolutions of the XXth Congress of the Communist Party of the Soviet Union]. Gospolitizdat, 1956.

Rezoljucija XXI s″ezda Kommunističeskoj partii Sovetskogo Sojuza po dokladu tovarišča N. S. Hrusceva 'O kontrol'nyh cifrah razvitija narodnego hozjajstva SSSR na 1959–1965 gody' [Resolution of the XXIst Congress of the Communist Party of the Soviet Union concerning N. S. Khrushchev's report on the control figures of the development of the U.S.S.R. national economy for the years 1959–65]. Moskva, Gospolitizdat, 1959.

Materialy ijun'skogo plenuma CK KPSS [Documents of the June plenum of the Central Committee of the Communist Party of the Soviet Union]. Moskva, Gospolitizdat, 1959.

'O hode vypolnenija rešenij XXI s″ezda KPSS 'O razvitii promyšlennosti, transporta i vnedrenii v proizvodstvo novejših dostizenij nauki i tehniki'. Postanovlenie ijul'skogo plenuma CK KPSS' [The effect given to the decisions of the XXIst Congress of the Communist Party of the Soviet Union concerning the development of industry, transport and the introduction into the field of production of the latest scientific and technical achievements. Decisions of the July plenum of the Central Committee of the Communist Party of the Soviet Union]. *Pravda*, 17 July 1960.

Ob ukreplenii svjazi školy s zizn'ju i o dal'nejšem razvitii sistemy narodnogo obrazovanija v strane. Tezisy CK KPSS i Soveta Ministrov SSSR [Strengthening of the links between the school and the life, and the further development of the public education system in the U.S.S.R. Theses of the Central Committee of the Communist Party of the Soviet Union and of the U.S.S.R. Council of Ministers]. Gospolitizdat, 1958.

'Zakon ob ukreplenii svjazi školy s žizn'ju i o dal'nejšem razvitii sistemy narodnogo obrazovanija v SSSR' [Law on the strengthening of the links between the school and the life and on the further development of the public education system in the U.S.S.R.]. Moskva, *Izvestija Sovetov deputatov trudjaščihsja SSSR*, 1958.

---

1. The order of the entries in this bibliography follows that of the original Russian text.

MARX, K. *Kapital*, Vol. I. Moskva, Gospolitizdat, 1955.

————. 'Instrukcija delegatam vremennogo central′nogo soveta po otdel′nym voprosam' [Instructions to the delegates of the Provisional Central Council concerning various questions]. In: K. Marx and F. Engels, *Sočinenija* [Works], Vol. XIII, Part I, 1936, p. 198–9.

ENGELS, F. *Anti-Djuring. Perevorot v nauke, proizvedennyj gospodinom Evgeniem Djuringom* [Anti-Dühring. A revolution in science brought about by Mr. Eugen Dühring], Section III, 'Socialism'. Moskva, Gospolitzdat, 1957.

————. *Dialektika prirody* [Dialectics of nature]. Moskva, Gospolitizdat, 1955.

LENIN, V. I. 'Perly narodničeskogo prožekterstva' [Priceless examples of hare-brained narodniks' plans]. In: *Sočinenija* [Works], 4th ed., Vol. II, ch. IV.

————. 'Proekt programmy RKP (b), prazdel 9, punkt programmy v oblasti narodnogo prosveščenija' [Draft programme of the Russian Communist Party (Bolsheviks), section 9, item of the programme relating to public education]. In: *Sočinenija* [Works], 4th ed., Vol. XXIX.

————. 'Zadači sojuzov molodeži' [Tasks of youth organizations]. In: *Sočinenija* [Works], 4th ed., Vol. XXXI.

————. 'Direktivy CK kommunistam, rabotnitkam NKP' [Directives of the Central Committee to the communists, workers of the People's Commissariat for Education]. In: *Sočinenija* [Works], 4th ed., Vol. XXXII.

————. 'O politehničeskom obrazovanii. Zametki na tezisy Nadeždy Konstantinovny' [On polytechnical education. Comments on the theses of Nadezhda Konstantinovna]. In: *Sočinenija* [Works], 3rd ed., Vol. XXX.

HRUŠČEV, N. S. *O kontrol′nyh cifrah razvitija narodnogo hozjajstva SSSR na 1959–1965 gody* [On the control figures of the U.S.S.R. national economy for the years 1959–65]. Gospolitizdat, 1959.

————. *Za dal′nejšij pod″em proizvoditel′nyh sil strany, za tehničeskij progress vo vseh otrasljah narodnogo hozjajstva* [For a further increase in the productive focus of the country, for technical progress in all branches of the national economy]. Gospolitizdat, 1959.

————. 'Vospityvat′ aktivnyh i soznatel′nyh stroitelej kommunističekogo obščestva. Reč′ na XIII s″ezde VLKSM 18 aprelja 1958 goda' [For the education of active and conscious builders of a communist society. Address to the XIIIth Congress of the All-Union Leninist Organization of Communist Youth on 18 April 1958]. *Molodaja gvardija*, Izd-vo CK VLKSM, 1958.

————. *Za pročnyj mir vo imja sčast′ja i svetlogo buduščego narodov* [For a lasting peace with a view to the happiness and bright future of the peoples]. Moskva, 1960.

Položenija o vos′miletnej škole RSFSR, o srednej obščeobrazovatel′noj trudovoj politehničeskoj škole s proizvodstvennym obučeniem RSFSR, o večernej (smennoj) srednej obščeobrazovatel′noj škole RSFSR [Regulations governing the following schools in the Russian Soviet Federated Socialist Republic:

the eight-year school, the general secondary polytechnical and labour school with productive training, the evening (shift) general secondary school]. Moskva, 1960.

Učebnye plany vos'miletnej i srednej školy RSFSR [Curricula of the eight-year and secondary schools in the Russian Soviet Federated Socialist Republic]. Moskva, 1960.

Programmy vos'miletnej vecernej (smennoj, sezonnoj, zaočnoj) obščeobrazovatel'noj srednej školy i srednej trudovoj politehničeskoj školy s proizvodstvennym obučeniem [Syllabuses of the eight-year evening (shift, seasonal, correspondence) general secondary school, and of the secondary polytechnical and labour school with productive training]. Moskva, 1960.

GENERAL QUESTIONS RELATING TO POLYTECHNICAL EDUCATION

KRUPSKAJA, N. K. 'O kommunističeskom vospitanii' [On communist education]. Moskva, *Molodaja gvardija*, 1956.
————. *Trudovoe i politeniceskoe obučenie. Izbrannye pedagogičeskie proizveenija* [Labour and polytechnical training. Selected educational works]. Moskva, Izd-vo APN R.S.F.S.R., 1957.

MAKARENKO, A. S., 'Trudovoe vospitanie, otnošenija, stil', ton v kollektive (lekčija 4)' [Labour training, relations, style and tone in group life. (Lecture 4)]. In: *Sočinenija* [Works], Vol. V, Moskva, Izd-vo APN R.S.F.S.R., 1951.

Materialy Krasnodarskoj sessii Akademii pedagogičeskih nauk RSFSR po voprosam politehničeskogo obučenija v sel'skoj škole. 2–3 dekabrja 1956 g. [Documents of the Krasnodar session of the R.S.F.S.R. Academy of Pedagogical Sciences on polytechnical education in rural schools. 2–3 December 1956]. Moskva, Izd-vo APN R.S.F.S.R., 1958.

Materialy Novosibirskoj naučnoj konferencii Akademii pedagogičeskih nauk po voprosam politehničeskogo obučenija. 13–16 maja 1957 [Documents of the Novosibirsk scientific congress of the Academy of Pedagogical Sciences on polytechnical education. 13–16 May 1957]. Moskva, Izd-vo APN R.S.F.S.R., 1958.

Novaja sistema narodnogo obrazovanija v SSSR [New system of public education in the U.S.S.R.]. Edited by N. K. Gončarov and F. F. Korolev. Moskva, Izd-vo APN R.S.F.S.R., 1960.

SKATKIN, M. N., *O didaktičeskih osnovah svjazi obučenija s trudom učaščihsja* [The didactic principles governing the link between study and work by the pupil]. Moskva, Učpedgiz, 1960.

Soedinenie obučenija s proizvoditel'nym trudom učaščihsja [Combining study with productive work by the pupils]. Edited by S. G. Šapovalenko. Moskva, Izd-vo APN R.S.F.S.R., 1958.

Soedinenie obučenija s proizvoditel'nym trudom učaščihsja v promišlennosti. Iz opyta škol s proizvodstvennym obučeniem [Combining study with work by the pupils in industry. Examples from the experience of schools with productive teaching]. Edited by M. N. Skatkin and P. R. Atutov. Moskva, Izd-vo APN R.S.F.S.R., 1960.

SUHOMLINSKIJ, V. A. *Vospitanie kommunističeskogo otnosenija k trudy. Opyt vospitatel'noj raboty v sel'škole* [Inculcation of a communist attitude to labour. Examples from the experience of educational work in rural school]. Edited by N. I. Boldyrev. Moskva, Izd-vo APN R.S.F.S.R., 1959.

'Učebno-opytnye hozjajstava škol Rjazanskoj oblasti. Sb. statej.' [Experiments at training forms of schools in the Ryazan region]. Collection of articles compiled by M. F. Truevcev. Moskva, Učpedgiz, 1959.

ŠABALOV, S. M. *Politehničeskoe obučenie* [Polytechnical education]. Moskva, Izd-vo APN R.S.F.S.R., 1956.

ŠAPOVALENKO, S. G. *Politehničeskoe obučenie v sovetskoj škole na sovremennom ètape* [Polytechnical education in Soviet schools during the present stage]. Moskva, Izd-vo APN R.S.F.S.R., 1958.

ŠIBANOV, A. A. *Politehniceskoe obučenie v sel'skoj škole* [Polytechnical education in rural schools]. 3rd ed., revised and enlarged. Moskva, Izd-vo APN R.S.F.S.R., 1958.

Škola, trud, kommunizm [School, work, communism]. Stavropol', Kraevoe knižnoe izd-vo, 1958.

Školy Stavropol'ja na novom ètape [Stavropol schools during the new stage]. Stavropol', Kraevoe knižnoe izd-vo, 1958.

ŠČUKIN, S. V. *Obščestvenno poleznyj trud učaščihsja v sel'skom hozjajstve* [Socially useful work by pupils in agriculture]. Edited by V. Z. Smirnov. Moskva, Izd-vo, APN R.S.F.S.R., 1957.

III. POLYTECHNICAL TRAINING IN PRIMARY GRADES

ZAVITAEV, P. A. *Trud učaščihsja I–IV klassov na učebno-opytnom učastke* [Work of the pupils in grades I to IV on school experimental plots]. Učpedgiz, 1957.

PČELKO, A. S.; ZAVITAEV, P. A. *Èlementy politehničeskogo obučenija v načal'noj škole. Metodičeskoe posobie* [Elementary polytechnical training in primary schools. Methodological guide]. 3rd ed. Moskva, Izd-vo APN R.S.F.S.R., 1956.

ROZANOV, I. G. *et al. Uroki ručnogo truda v pervom klasse* [Manual work in grade I]. Edited by M. N. Skatkin. 3rd ed., revised. Moskva, Učpedgiz, 1958.

———; ZAVITAEV, P. A. *Uroki ručnogo truda vo vtorom klasse* [Manual work in grade II]. Edited by M. N. Skatkin. 3rd ed., revised and enlarged. Moskva, Učpedgiz, 1958.

———; ———. *Uroki ručnogo truda v tret'em klasse* [Manual work in grade III]. Edited by M. N. Skatkin. 3rd ed., enlarged. Moskva, Učpedgiz, 1958.

———; ———. *Uroki ručnogo truda v četvertom klasse* [Manual work in grade IV]. Edited by M. N. Skatkin. 3rd ed., revised and enlarged. Moskva, Učpedgiz, 1959.

IV. POLYTECHNICAL TRAINING IN THE TEACHING OF THE FUNDAMENTALS
OF SCIENCE

Mathematics and technical drawing

ABRIKOSOV, A. A. *Čerčenie. Rukovodstvo dlja učaščihsja srednej školy* [Drawing. Guide for secondary school pupils], Part. I. Moskva, 1958.

BANASEK, S. I.; KOLESNIKOVA, V. P.; SLONIMSKAJA, L. G.; TRISELEV, A. V.; ČEKOVA, M. D. *Tipovye plany urokov čerčenija v srednoj škole* [Typical plans for technical-drawing lessons at secondary schools]. Moskva, 1959.

BOTVINNIKOV, A. D. *Nekotorye voprosy politehniceskogo obučenija v prepodavanii čerčenija. Posobie dlja učitelej* [Questions relating to polytechnical training in the teaching of technical drawing. Guide for teachers]. Učpedgiz, 1956.

———. *Spravočnik dlja učitelej čerčenija* [Handbook for teachers of technical drawing]. Učpedgiz, 1956.

VLADIMIROV, JA. V. *Kabinet čerčenija srednej školy. Posobie dlja učitelej* [Secondary school classroom for technical drawing. Guide for teachers]. Moskva, Izd-vo APN R.S.F.S.R., 1956.

———; KALIŠEVSKAJA, V. A. *Prepodavanie čerčenija v škole* [The teaching of technical drawing in schools]. Moskva, 1956.

VOROB'EV, G. V. *Voprosy prepodavanija geometrii v VI–VIII klassah v svjazi s rabotoj v škol'nyh masterskih* [Questions concerning geometry teaching in grades VI–VIII in connexion with work in the school workshops]. Moskva, Učpedgiz, 1960.

GOSUDARSKIJ, L. M.; ZELENIN, E. V.; KALIŠEVSKAJA, V. A.; ĖJDEL'S, A. M. *Pouročnye razrabotki po čerčeniju* [Preparation of technical-drawing lessons]. Moskva, 1956.

DORF, P. JA.; RUMER, A. O. *Izmerenija na mestnosti* [Field surveying]. Moskva, Izd-vo APN R.S.F.S.R., 1957.

ZELENIN, E. V. *Čerčenie v srednej skole* [Technical drawing at secondary schools]. Moskva, 1957.

LOMOV, B. F. *et al. Svjaz' čepčenija s mašinovedeniem v srednej škole* [Technical drawing in relation to machine operations at secondary schools]. Edited by Professor P. A. Znamenskij. Moskva, Izd-vo APN R.S.F.S.R., 1958.

NAČAPKIN, F. L. *Škol'nyj teodolit i izmeritel'nye raboty s nim na mestnosti* [School theodolite and its use in field surveying]. Moskva, Izd-vo APN R.S.F.S.R., 1957.

NIKITIN, N. D. *Glazomernaja s'emka* [Visual surveying]. Moskva, Učpedgiz, 1960.

Politehničeskoe obučenie v prepodavanii matematiki. Sobornik statej [Polytechnical training in the teaching of mathematics]. Collection of articles edited by A. D. Semušin. Moskva, Izd-vo APN R.S.F.S.R., 1956.

Politehniceskoe obučenie v škole. Sbornik statej [Polytechnical training in schools]. Collection of articles edited by A. I. Fetisov. Moskva, Izd-vo APN R.S.F.S.R., 1957.

Pročuhaev, V. G. *Svjaz' teorii s praktikoj v prepodavanii matematiki* [Relationship between theory and practice in the teaching of mathematics]. Moskva, Učpedgiz, 1958.

Physics

Pokrovskij, A. A. *Praktikum po fizike v starših klassah srednej školy* [Practical work in physics in the senior grades at secondary schools]. 3rd ed. Moskva, Učpedgiz, 1956.

———; Zvorykin, B. S. *Frontal'nye laboratornye zanjatija po fizike v srednej škole* [Groups laboratory experiments in physics at secondary schools]. 5th ed. Moskva, Učpedgiz, 1956.

Reznikov, L. I.; Évenčik, É. E. *et al. Proizvodstvennye ékskursii po fizike* [Visits to production plants in connexion with the teaching of physics]. Moskva, Izd-vo APN R.S.F.S.R., 1954.

Jus'kovič, V. F.; Reznikov, L. I.; Enohovič, A. S. *Politehničeskoe obučenie v prepodavanii fiziki* [Polytechnical training in the teaching of physics]. 3rd ed. Moskva, Izd-vo APN R.S.F.S.R., 1957.

Chemistry

Gloriozov, P. A.; Drizovskaja, T. M. *et al. Voprosy politehničekogo obučenija v prepodavanii himii* [Questions concerning polytechnical training in chemistry teaching]. Edited by S. G. Šapovalenko. Moskva, Izd-vo APN R.S.F.S.R., 1957.

———; Smorgonskij, L. M. *Praktišeskie zanjatija po himii v srednej škole* [Practical work in chemistry at secondary schools]. Moskva, Izd-vo APN R.S.F.S.R., 1955.

———. *Formirovanie umenij i navykov v processe obučenija himii* [Development of proficiency and skill in the process of studying chemistry]. Moskva, Izd-vo APN R.S.F.S.R., 1959.

Grabeckij, A. A. *Opyty po himii v svjazi s oznakomleniem učaščihsja s naučnymi osnovami himiceskih proizvodstv* [Chemistry experiments designed to familiarize pupils with the scientific bases of chemical industries]. Moskva, Izd-vo APN R.S.F.S.R., 1956.

Drizovskaja, T. M. *Opyt postanovki fakul'tativnogo kursa himičeskogo analiza v škole* [Experiment in the organization of an optional school course in chemical analysis]. Moskva, Izd-vo APN R.S.F.S.R., 1960.

Kleščeva, E. P.; Épštejn, D. A. *Opyt proizvodstvennogo obučenija učaščihsja srednej školy na himičeskih zavodah* [Experience of production training for secondary-school pupils at chemical plants]. Moskva, Izd-vo APN R.S.F.S.R., 1959.

Prepodavanie himii v škole [Chemistry teaching in schools]. Collection edited by L. A. Cvetkov. Moskva, Izd-vo APN R.S.F.S.R., 1959.

Proizvodstvennye ékskursii po himii v škole [Visits to production plants in connexion with chemistry teaching in schools]. Collection edited by L. A. Cvetkov. Učpedgiz, 1953.

Šapovalenko, S. G. *Prepodavanie himii v škole i podgotovka učaščihsja k praktičeskoj rabote* [Chemistry teaching in schools and the preparation

of pupils for practical work]. Moskva, Izd-vo APN R.S.F.S.R., 1953.
Êpštejn, D. A. *Nagljadnye posobija po himičeskim proizvodstvam dlja srednej školy* [Visual aids for secondary schools in respect of the chemical industries]. Moskva, Izd-vo APN R.S.F.S.R., 1958.

Biology

O prepodavanii biologii v vos'miletnej škole [Biology teaching in the eight-year school]. Edited by M. I. Mel'nikov. Moskva, Izd-vo APN R.S.F.S.R., 1959.

Padalko, N. V. *Svjaz' v prepodavanii biologii s praktikoj sel'skogo hozjajstva* [Link with agricultural practice in the teaching of biology]. Moskva, Izd-vo APN R.S.F.S.R., 1955.

Proizvoditel'nyj trud učaščihsja v svjazi s izučeniem biologii. Iz opyta škol RSFSR [Pupils' productive work in connexion with the study of biology. Based on the experience of schools in the R.S.F.S.R.]. Edited by N. A. Rykov. Moskva, Učpedgiz, 1958.

Šalaev, V. F.; Padalko, N. V. *et al. Politehničeskoe obučenie v svjazi s kursom biologii* [Polytechnical training in connexion with the biology course]. Edited by V. F. Šalaev. Moskva, Izd-vo APN R.S.F.S.R., 1956.

————. *Svjaz' teorii s praktikoj v kurse zoologii* [Coupling of theory and practice in the zoology course]. Moskva, Izd-vo APN R.S.F.S.R., 1959.

Ščukin, S. V., *Učebno-opytnyj učastok srednej školy* [Experimental plots at secondary schools]. Moskva, Učpedgiz, 1957.

Jahontov, A. A. *Ėkskursii v životnovodčeskoe hozjajstvo* [Visits to stock farms]. Moskva, Izd-vo APN R.S.F.S.R., 1957.

Geography

Bibik, A. E.; Samojlov, I. I., *Prepodavanie geografii v svete zadač politehničeskogo obučenija* [Geography teaching in the light of the aims of polytechnical training]. Moskva, Izd-vo APN R.S.F.S.R., 1953.

Voprosy politehničeskogo obučenija v prepodavanii geografii [Questions of polytechnical training in geography teaching]. Collection edited by I. I. Samojlov. Moskva, Izd-vo APN R.S.F.S.R., 1954.

Kirin, F. Ja. *Kraevedenie kak sredstvo politehničeskogo obučenija v prepodavanii geografii* [Regional studies as a means of polytechnical training in geography teaching]. Čeljabinskoe knižnoe izd-vo, 1957.

Ščerbakov, A. I., *Kraevedčeskaja rabota po geografii* [Regional studies in connexion with geography]. Učpedgiz, 1959.

V. MANUAL AND TECHNICAL INSTRUCTION

Verzilin, N. M.; Zavitaev, P. A. *et al. Metodika raboty s učaščimisja na škol'nom učebno-opytnom učastke* [Methods of work with pupils on the school experimental plot]. Edited by N. M. Verzilin. Moskva, Izd-vo APN R.S.F.S.R., 1956.

Dubov, A. G. *Praktičeskie zanjatija v učebnyh masterskih. Metodičeskoe posobie*

429

dlja prepodavatelej truda V–VII klassov [Practical work in school workshops. Methodological guide for labour instruction in grades V and VI]. Moskva, Izd-vo APN R.S.F.S.R., 1957.

Kivotov, S. A. *Praktičeskie zanjatija na škol'nom učebno-opytnom učastke. Posobie dlja učeščihsja V–VI klassov srednej školy* [Practical work on school experimental plots. Handbook for pupils in grades V and VI at secondary schools]. 4th ed. Moskva, Učpedgiz, 1959.

———. *Praktičeskie zanjatija na škol'nom učebno-opytnom učastke i v kolhoze. Posobie dlja učaščihsja VII klassov srednej školy* [Practical work in the school experimental plot and on collective farms. Handbook for pupils in grade VII at secondary school]. 2nd ed. Moskva, Učpedgiz, 1959.

Markin, V. I.; Kutilovskij, M. P. *Praktičeskie zanjatija v škol'nyh učebnyh masterskih. Učebno-tehničeskoe posobie dlja prepodavatel'ej V–VII klassov sred. školy* [Practical work in the school workshops. Technical teaching guide for teachers of grade VII at secondary schools]. Moskva, Učpedgiz, 1958.

Peškov, E. O.; Fadeev, N. I. *Tehničeskij slovar' škol'nika* [Schoolchild's technical dictionary]. Moskva, Učpedgiz.

Padalko, N. V. *Praktičeskie zanjatija na učebno-opytnom učastke. V–VI klassy* [Practical work on the school experimental plot. Grades V and VI]. 2nd ed. Učpedgiz, 1957.

Unkovskij, A. M. *Formirovanie umenij i navykov u učaščihsja V–VI klassov na učebno-opytnom učastke. Posobie dlja učitelej sel'skih škol* [Development of proficiency and skill in pupils in grades V and VI during work on the school experimental plot. Guide for rural school teachers]. Moskva, Učpedgiz, 1959.

Cenciper, M. B. *Trudovaja dejatel'nost škol'nogo učeničeskogo kollektiva. Iz opyta raboty školy No. 437 g. Moskvy* [Practical work by school groups. Based on the working of experience of School No. 437, Moscow]. Moskva, Učpedgiz, 1956.

Ščukin, S. V. *Učebno-opytnyj učastok srednej školy* [Experimental plots at secondary schools]. Učpedgiz, 1954.

VI. GENERAL TECHNICAL SUBJECTS AND PRODUCTION TRAINING

Andrievskij, S. K.; Bartnovskij, A. L. *Praktikum po êlektrotehnike. Učebnoe posobie dlja X klassa srednej školy* [Practical work in electrical engineering. Textbook for grade X at secondary schools]. 2nd ed. Moskva, Učpedgiz, 1959.

Bespal'ko, V. P.; Židelev, M. A.; Nikitin, B. P. *Mašinovedenie, č I* [Machine operation. Part I]. Učpedgiz, 1957.

———; ———; ———. *Mašinovedenie, č II* [Machine operation, Part II]. Učpedgiz, 1957.

Bulatov, N. P. *Proizvodstvennaja praktika učaščihsja* [Production practice by pupils]. Moskva, Izd-vo APN R.S.F.S.R., 1956.

Demina, A. G. *Skola i zavod (iz opyta školy No. 96 g. Moskvy)* [School and factory (based on the experience of School No. 96, Moscow)]. Moskva, Učpedgiz, 1958.

ŽIDELEV, M. A. *Proizvodstvennoe obučenie i proizvoditel'nyj trud v srednej škole* [Production training and production labour at secondary schools]. Edited by S. G. Šapovalenko. Moskva, 1959.

ZVORYKIN, B. S. *Praktikum po ĕlektrotehnike v srednej škole. Iz opyta raboty školy No. 315 Moskvy* [Practical work in electrical engineering at secondary schools. Based on the working experience of School No. 315, Moscow)]. Moskva, Izd-vo APN R.S.F.S.R., 1957.

ZNAMENSKIJ, P. A.; NIKEROVA, L. I. *Mehanika i mašinovedenie v srednej škole* [Mechanics and machine operation at secondary schools]. Edited by P. A. Znamenskij. Moskva, Izd-vo APN R.S.F.S.R., 1959.

ŽIDELEV, M. A. *Praktikum po mašinovedeniju v VIII–X klassah gorodskoj srednej školy* [Practical work in machine operation in grades V–X at urban secondary schools]. Učpedgiz, 1956.

————. *Mašinovedenie v VIII–X klassah gorodskoj srednej školy. Metodicskie ukazanija dlja prepodavatelej* [Machine operation in grades V–X at urban secondary schools. Methodological instructions for teachers]. Moskva, Izd-vo APN R.S.F.S.R., 1956.

Obščestvenno poleznyj trud učaščihsja škol g. Omska [Socially useful labour by schoolchildren in Omsk]. Collection of articles compiled by V. E. Zjabkin. Moskva, Učpedgiz, 1959.

Opyt politehniceskogo obucenija v sel'skoj škole [Experience of rural schools]. Collection of articles edited by S. V. Ščukin. Moskva, Izd-vo APN R.S.F.S.R., 1956.

Praktika učaščihsja v promyšlennom i sel'skohozjajstvennom proizvodstve [Practical work by pupils in industrial and agricultural production]. Collection edited by M. N. Skatkin and N. P. Bulatov. Moskva, Izd-vo APN R.S.F.S.R., 1957.

Proizvodstvennaja praktika učaščihsja na zavode [Pupils' production training in factories]. Edited by O. F. Fedorova. Moskva, Izd-vo APN R.S.F.S.R., 1959.

SMETANIN, B. M. *Ělektrotehnika v X klasse* [Electrical engineering in grade X]. Moskva, Izd-vo APN R.S.F.S.R., 1956.

Uroki po mašinovedeniju v VIII klasse srednej školy (metodičeskoe posobie dlja prepodavatelej) [Machine operation lessons in grade VIII at secondary school (methodological guide for teachers)]. Moskva, Učpedgiz, 1958.

ČISTJAKOV, N. N. *Proizvoditel'nyj trud škol'nikove Kuzbassa na stroitel'stve učebnyh pomeščenij* [Productive labour by Kuzbass schoolchildren in the construction of school buildings]. Kemerovo, 1960.

ŠIBANOV, A. A.; STAVROVSKIJ, A. E. *et al. Izučenie sel'skohozjajstvennogo proizvodstva sel'skoj škole* [Study of agriculture in rural schools]. Moskva, Izd-vo APN R.S.F.S.R., 1956.

VII. OUT-OF-CLASS WORK, TECHNICAL AND MANUAL

AŠKENAZI, E.; ROGOVA, O.; SMIRNOVA, L.; ČERNYŠEVA, A. *Junym rukodel'nicam* [For young girl needleworkers]. Leningrad, Detgiz, 1957.

BELJAKOV, N. D.; POKROVSKAJA, A. I.; CEJTLIN, N. E. *Kružok 'Umelye ruki' v škole* ['Nimble fingers' clubs in schools]. 2nd ed. Moskva, Moskva, Učpedgiz, 1957.

BOGATKOV, V.; GAL'PERŠTEJN, L.; HLENBIKOV, P. *Elektročestvo dvižet modeli* [Models worked by electricity]. Moskva, Detgiz, 1958.

BUBENINA, G.; GOSLAVSKAJA, T. 'Samodelki iz prirognogo materiala' [Making things from natural materials]. Moskva, *Molodaja gvardija*, 1960.

BULATOV, N. P. *Vneklassnye zanjatija po ělektrotehnike v srednej škole* [Out-of-class electrical-engineering work at secondary schools]. Učpedgiz, 1951.

———; SMETANIN, B. M. *et al.* 'Tehničeskoe tvorčestvo' [Technical creation]. Moskva, *Molodaja gvardija*, 1956.

Vneklassnaja rabota po fizike i tehnike [Out-of-class work relating to physics and technique]. Collection edited by P. N. Bulatov. Moskva, Izd-vo APN R.S.F.S.R., 1955.

VERHALO, JU. *Samodel'nye pribory po ělektrotehnike* [Electrical equipment made by the pupils themselves]. Leningrad, Detgiz, 1956.

Domovodstvo (dlja starših škol'nikov) [Home economics (for pupils in the senior grades)]. Moskva, Učpedgiz, 1959.

'Kalendar' junogo naturalista' [Young naturalist's calendar]. Moskva, *Molodaja Gvardija*, 1960.

LEONT'EV, P. *Raboty po metallu* [Metalwork]. Leningrad, Detgiz, 1956.

PAVLOVIČ, S. *Pribory i modeli po neživoj prirode* [Apparatus and models relating to inanimate nature]. Moskva-Leningrad, Detgiz, 1953.

PETROVA, V. I. *Domašnij trud mladšego škol'nika* [Young pupils' homework]. Moskva, Učpedgiz, 1959.

'Pionerskaja družina letom' [Pioneer activities in summer]. Moskva, *Molodaja gvardija*, 1960.

POMERANCEV, L. *Junyj tehnik-konstruktor* [The young technical constructor]. Gor'kij, Gor'kovskoe knižnoe izd-vo, 1959.

'Tehničeskoe tvorčestvo. Posobie dlja rukovoditelej tehničeskih kružkov' [Technical creation. Handbook for leaders of technical clubs]. Moskva, *Molodaja gvardija*, 1956.

'Umelye ruki' [Nimble fingers]. 2nd ed. Moskva, *Molodaja gvardija*, 1954.

ŠEPELEV, A. 'Sdelaj sam! V pomošč' tem, kto šagaet po stupenjam' [Do it yourself! Guide for those who advance step by step]. Moskva, *Molodaja gvardija*, 1959.

Junyj modelist. (Modeli promyslovyh sudov, buera aěrosanej, katera. Samodel'naja bajdarka) [The young model-maker. (Models of seal-catchers' vessels, an ice-yacht, an aerosleigh, a cutter, a home-made kayak)]. Leningrad, Detgiz, 1956.

VIII. MATERIAL BASIS OF TEACHING

Školovedenie [School administration]. Edited by A. N. Volkovskij and M. P. Malyšev. 2nd ed. Moskva, Učpedgiz, 1955.

Mebel' dlja škol'nyh kabinetov. Al'bom čertežej [Furniture for school study rooms. Album of sketches]. Edited by K. Ja. Parmenov. 2nd ed. Moskva, Učpedgiz, 1955.

KONOBEEVSKIJ, N. P. *Nagljadnye posobija kak sredstvo obučenija v načal'noj škole* [Visual aids in primary-school teaching]. Moskva, Izd-vo APN R.S.F.S.R., 1958.

POKROSKIJ, A. A. *Oborudovanie fizičeskogo kabineta* [Equipment of physics study rooms]. Moskva, Učpedgiz, 1959.

Novye škol'nye pribory po fizike i astronomii [New school apparatus for physics and astronomy]. Edited by A. A. Pokrovskij. Moskva, Izd-vo APN R.S.F.S.R., 1959.

DORF, P. JA. *Nagljadnye posobija po matematike i metodika ih primenenija* [Visual aids for the teaching of mathematics and methods of utilizing them]. Moskva, Učpedgiz, 1955.

DUBININ, L. A. *Himičeskij kabinet srednej školy* (Secondary-school chemistry room). Moskva, Izd-vo APN R.S.F.S.R., 1955.

EPŠTEJN, D. A. *Nagljadnye posobija po himičeskim proizvodstvam v srednej škole* [Secondary-school visual aids relating to chemical industries]. Moskva, Izd-vo APN R.S.F.S.R., 1958.

KOZYR', I. V. *Kabinet biologii srednej školy* [Secondary-school biology room]. Moskva, Izd-vo APN R.S.F.S.R., 1956.

GERASIMOV, T. A. *Kabinet istorii v škole* [School history room]. Moskva, Učpedgiz, 1959.

ANDRIANOV, P. N. *Ručnoj instrument i prisposoblenija dlja obrabotki drevesiny v škol'nyh masterskih* [Hand instruments and for woodwork apparatus in school workshops]. Moskva, Izd-vo APN R.S.F.S.R., 1959.

KORŽEV, I. D. *Oborudovanie učebnyh masterskih v škole* [Equipment of school workshops]. Moskva, Učpedgiz, 1959.

FIGANOV, I. S. *Učebnoe oborudovanie po mašinovedeniju* [School equipment for machinery operation]. Moskva, Izd-vo APN R.S.F.S.R., 1959.

KOZYR', I. V.; ŠUHRIN, S. A. *Ručnoj sel'skohozjajstvennyj inventar' dlja škol* [Agricultural hand implements for schools]. Moskva, Izd-vo APN R.S.F.S.R., 1950.

Učebnoe oborudovanie načal'noj školy. Katalog-spravočnik [Primary-school teaching equipment. Catalogue/handbook]. Moskva, Učpedgiz, 1959.

Učebnoe oborudovanie po fizike dlja srednej školy. Katalog-spravočnik [Secondary-school teaching equipment for physics. Catalogue/handbook]. Moskva, Učpedgiz, 1958.

Učebnoe oborudovanie po himii dlja srednej školy. Katalog-spravočnik [Secondary-school equipment for chemistry. Catalogue/handbook]. Moskva, Učpedgiz, 1958.

Učebnoe oborudovanie po biologii dlja srednej školy. Katalog-spravočnik [Secondary-school equipment for biology. Catalogue/handbook]. Moskva, Učpedgiz, 1958.

Učebnoe kinofilmy dlja škol. Annotirovannyj katalog-spravočnik [Educational films for schools. Annotated catalogue/handbook]. Moskva, Učpedgiz, 1958.